Contemporary Enterprise and Entrepreneurship in Context

Contemporary Enterprise and Entrepreneurship in Context is the core debut for the Routledge Applied Enterprise and Entrepreneurship Series (AEES). This book introduces contemporary sectoral discussions and the theories, considerations and contexts relating to them from a wide range of contemporary academics, thinkers and entrepreneurs.

This book brings together many of today's discourse in the area of enterprise and entrepreneurship alongside relevant and experienced practitioners to launch the AEES series' foundational book. The book's structure will distinguish, yet pull together theoretical underpinning and practitioner accounts of enterprise and entrepreneurship in context.

This book is suitable for both undergraduate and postgraduate students in the area of business studies, innovation, entrepreneurship and enterprise. The book will also be of interest to a range of roles in the enterprise and entrepreneurship community, including academics and practitioners.

Russ Hepworth-Sawyer is an associate professor at York St John University. Russ also acts as a consultant and author alongside running several businesses when not at the university. Russ's experience is in the music industry and as an academic in music production practice, creative business and entrepreneurship. Russ leads the Executive MBA Programme at York Business School and is a seasoned author with Routledge, including the Innovation in Music series of books linked to the conference of the same name.

Mark Marrington is an associate professor (Music Production) at York St John University, among whose primary research interests are the history of record production and classical music recording. His recently published book *Recording the Classical Guitar* (2021) won the 2022 ARSC Award for Excellence in Historical Recorded Sound Research.

Jenny Hall is a senior lecturer at York St John University, UK. As a cultural geographer, she specialises in the geographies of tourism, leisure, sport and heritage. Her work is interdisciplinary and draws from across the social sciences. Issues of sustainability and social and ecological justice are central to her work, and she has focused on the intersectional experiences of inequality in adventure. Working with public agencies, her research has influenced policy in mountaineering organisations in the UK.

Emily Beaumont is an academic and business owner, residing in Plymouth, Devon, UK. As an academic, Emily has studied at some of the leading higher education institutions in the UK, including the UCL, the University of Exeter and Loughborough University. She has dedicated her teaching and research to the disciplines of enterprise, entrepreneurship and employability, and the quality of her work in this area led her to be voted for President for Enterprise Educators UK (2021–2023). She was awarded with Senior Fellowship of the Higher Education Academy, Fellow of the Chartered Management Institute and Fellow of the Royal Society for the Encouragement of Arts, Manufactures and Commerce.

Routledge Research in Applied Enterprise and Entrepreneurship

Edited by Emily Beaumont, Jenny Hall, Mark Marrington and Russ Hepworth-Sawyer

The Routledge Research in Applied Enterprise and Entrepreneurship series (RRAEE) offers a collection of books that apply contemporary enterprise and entrepreneurship theory and practice to a series of disciplines, interests, and industries. The series provides a space for researchers to write where enterprise and entrepreneurship intersects with context.

Books within RRAEE apply accepted research and principles within the lexicon of enterprise and entrepreneurship to disciplines, where the peculiarities and distinct features of the context require special consideration. Considerations such as employment traditions, traditional skills, behaviours and competencies, typical venture creation experience, legal requirements within the sector, planning, marketing, and economic issues within a sector. The books feature primary research and practitioner guidance alongside case studies from established entrepreneurs and business owners in each sector.

Contemporary Enterprise and Entrepreneurship in Context
Edited by Russ Hepworth-Sawyer, Mark Marrington, Jenny Hall and Emily Beaumont

Contemporary Enterprise and Entrepreneurship in Context

Edited by Russ Hepworth-Sawyer,
Mark Marrington, Jenny Hall
and Emily Beaumont

Routledge
Taylor & Francis Group
NEW YORK AND LONDON

First published 2025
by Routledge
605 Third Avenue, New York, NY 10158

and by Routledge
4 Park Square, Milton Park, Abingdon, Oxon, OX14 4RN

Routledge is an imprint of the Taylor & Francis Group, an informa business

ISBN: 978-1-032-34978-7 (hbk)
ISBN: 978-1-032-34979-4 (pbk)
ISBN: 978-1-003-32473-7 (ebk)

DOI: 10.4324/9781003324737

Typeset in Times New Roman
by Apex CoVantage, LLC

Contents

Editor biographies

Russ Hepworth-Sawyer is Associate Professor at York St John University. Russ also acts as a consultant and author alongside running several businesses when not at university. Russ' experience is in the music industry and as an academic in music production practice, creative business, and entrepreneurship. Russ leads the Executive MBA programme at York Business School and is a seasoned author with Routledge, including the *Innovation In Music* series of books linked to the conference of the same name.

Mark Marrington is Associate Professor (Music Production) at York St John University, among whose primary research interests are the history of record production and classical music recording. His recently published book, *Recording the Classical Guitar* (2021), won the 2022 ARSC Award for Excellence in Historical Recorded Sound Research.

Jenny Hall is Senior Lecturer at York St John University, United Kingdom. As a cultural geographer, she specialises in the geographies of tourism, leisure, sport, and heritage. Her work is interdisciplinary and draws from across the social sciences. Issues of sustainability, social and ecological justice are central to her work, and she has focused on the intersectional experiences of inequality in adventure. Working with public agencies, her research has influenced policy in mountaineering organisations in the United Kingdom. This is reflected in her recently published books Gender, Politics and Change in Mountaineering: Moving Mountains and The Mountain and the Politics of Representation.

Emily Beaumont is an academic and business owner, residing in Plymouth, Devon, UK. She has dedicated her teaching and research to the disciplines of enterprise, entrepreneurship and employability, and the quality of her work in this area saw her voted to be President for Enterprise Educators UK (2021–2023) and awarded with Senior Fellowship of the Higher Education Academy, Fellow of the Chartered Management Institute, and Fellow of the Royal Society for the encouragement of Arts, Manufactures and Commerce. As Associate Professor and Associate Head of School at the University of Gloucestershire, Emily combines excellence in teaching with a strong research ethos, creating a business school which is dynamic in its offer, and flexible and reactive to the rapidly changing and evolving world of business.

Contributors by chapter

Afsaneh Bagheri is a Lecturer of Entrepreneurship at the University of Lincoln. She has been engaged in research on entrepreneurship since 2009. Her papers have been published by top-tier journals such as the *Journal of Business Ethics*, *Journal of Small Business Management*, *Technological Forecasting & Social Change*, and *International Journal of Hospitality Management,* among others. She has also presented her research findings at several national and international conferences. Her paper titled "Not for Me: Parents' Entrepreneurial Struggles and Children's Family Business Succession. In Academy of Management, accepted for the 84th Annual Meeting of the Academy of Management, August 2024, Chicago, Illinois" Selected as one of the best accepted papers.

Simon Bridge took degrees in engineering and business and worked in the field of aero engines and shipbuilding before joining Northern Ireland's small business agency in 1984 as the Enterprise Development Director. Nine years later Simon started his own consultancy/facilitation business helping government departments, enterprise agencies, educational establishments, private businesses and voluntary and community bodies – plus a number of overseas assignments. Simon has written or co-written various papers and books on the subject of enterprise, including, with Ken O'Neill, Understanding Enterprise, Entrepreneurs and Small Business (Palgrave, 5th edition 2018) and is a visiting professor at Ulster University.

Dr Simon Brown is a dynamic program developer and educator with extensive experience supporting early career researchers through tailored training and development initiatives. Currently leading both ICURe Engage and Explore programmes, equipping researchers with essential skills for commercializing their research and intellectual property. Known for crafting curriculum content that builds commercial insight, entrepreneurial acumen, and professional competencies. A collaborative facilitator, leveraging industry connections and academic partnerships through P2T Consulting to drive impactful learning experiences. Skilled in developing comprehensive guidance materials—including financial checklists and needs assessments—to maximize participant readiness and ensure program effectiveness.

Dr Andrew Clarke has over 30 years' experience in engineering, science and academia and joined the University of Central Lancashire's Business School in 2020. His expertise lies in exploring the interface between entrepreneurship principles and theories and their application in humanities, arts, health, science and engineering. Andrew has a PhD from UMIST and an MBA from Sheffield Hallam University, and has written books, book chapters and peer reviewed publications on entrepreneurship theories and principles, and how these relate to recognising value.

James Cunningham is Associate Professor in Entrepreneurship at Robert Gordon University, Aberdeen. He has published widely in the fields of entrepreneurship and small family business. Further, he has a particular interest in creative and artisan work, including studies on artists in urban locations, rural literary festivals, and the evolving craft beer sector. His research appears in journals such as: Entrepreneurship & Regional Development, Family Business Review, and the International Journal of Entrepreneurial Behavior & Research.

Ashley Evenson is a lecturer in creative enterprise and retail management, sustainability and technology at Goldsmiths college. She began her career in local theatre communities and then moved to producing international tours. She started her own production company, Oval Productions and leads organizationally based community storytelling workshops. She also mentors and coaches creative industry-based businesses to expand their audience. Her research interests include mental health in solo-founders and solo-entrepreneurs.

Beki Gowing is a senior lecturer in fashion enterprise and pathway lead for the Fashion Business School and Communications Programme Enterprise Pathways. She began working in John Lewis & Partners' fashion and homeware buying teams, before launching the textile design studio Print & Press London where she worked with brands including Jigsaw, The White Company and the V&A. Beki has a Masters degree in Creative & Cultural Entrepreneurship and a PG Cert in Acceptance and Commitment Therapy (ACT) informed coaching, both from Goldsmiths College, University of London. Her research interests include peer coaching, enterprise communities, empathy and collaboration. Beki works as a coach supporting creative founders to launch and develop their businesses.

Amy Gresock obtained her Ph.D. in Business Administration from the University of Central Florida with a major area of management and specializations in Entrepreneurship and Strategy. She currently serves as the Director of the Business Management Program at the University of Pittsburgh at Bradford.

Basel Hammoda, PhD, is a lecturer in Entrepreneurship in the Department of Business Administration at Tallinn University of Technology (TalTech) in

Estonia. His research centers on innovative approaches to entrepreneurial learning and its intersections with broader fields of entrepreneurship and management. He has several publications in the areas of entrepreneurship, digital technology, and education, and is the editor of the Routledge book *Contemporary Entrepreneurship: Global Perspectives and Cases.*

Masoud Karami is a Lecturer in the Department of Marketing at Otago University in New Zealand. Masoud's research area is Entrepreneurial marketing, Co-creation, Effectuation theory, and International Entrepreneurship. He has published in journals such as the *Journal of Business Venturing, Journal of International Marketing, Technovation, Journal of Business Research, and Small Business Economics,* among others.

Dr Paulina MacKrell has been part of the University of Central Lancashire's Business School since 2019. She currently leads postgraduate programmes and develops and delivers a range of subjects across different courses, with a particular focus and expertise in research methods, entrepreneurship and sustainability. Paulina's research encompasses interdisciplinary studies, mainly concentrating on SMEs and sustainability, globalisation and migration. Currently, Paulina supervises postgraduate projects and dissertations in the areas of business, leadership, management and sustainability.

Dr Claire Mercer joined the University of Salford in 2015 and is currently the Head of Radiography at the University of Salford. A radiographer by background, specialising in mammography advanced practice, Claire additionally has 10 years' experience in NHS management and a PhD by published works in mammography. Claire is passionate about educating and supporting the developing AHP workforce and has numerous peer reviewed publications. Her research interests lie in workforce development, wellbeing and education through digital health. Claire currently mentors others through leadership and academia.

Victoria Mountford-Brown is an assistant professor in Entrepreneurship at Northumbria University, UK. Vicky's research interests include identities, social class and neurodiversity, entrepreneurship as practice, researcher entrepreneurial development and enterprise education pedagogy.

Robert Newbery is a Professor of Entrepreneurship and Head of the Entrepreneurship, Innovation and Strategy department at Newcastle Business School, Northumbria University. He has worked extensively in Asia, Africa, Europe and North America and has founded and run a number of entrepreneurial businesses. He is a co-editor of the International Journal of Entrepreneurial Behaviour and Research and a member of the board of directors for the Institute of Small Business and Enterprise. His research interests are focused on entrepreneurship in developing contexts.

Philip T. Roundy is the Mary Harris Distinguished Professor of Entrepreneurship at the University of Tennessee at Chattanooga. His research focuses on the role of entrepreneurship in economic and community revitalization. He is particularly interested in how entrepreneurs assist in the renewal of struggling regions, "dying" industries, and displaced technologies. He is associate editor at the Journal of Business Venturing Insights and serves on the editorial boards of Strategic Entrepreneurship Journal, Small Business Economics, Strategic Organization, and Entrepreneurship Research Journal. He earned his PhD in strategic management and organization theory from the University of Texas at Austin.

Meike Siefkes is currently a Ph.D. candidate at the Department of Industrial Economics and Technology Management at the Norwegian University of Science and Technology. She holds a dual Master of Science in Innovation Management, Entrepreneurship, and Sustainability from the Technical University of Berlin and the Norwegian University of Science and Technology. Her research interests include green entrepreneurial finance, angel investors, and sustainable entrepreneurship. Her research is supported by research supported by NTRANS Norwegian Centre for Energy Transition Strategies. She has contributed articles to international refereed journals such as Journal of Small Business Management and Business Strategy and the Environment.

Gero Stocksmeier holds a dual Master of Science in Innovation Management, Entrepreneurship, and Sustainability from the Technical University of Berlin and the Norwegian University of Science and Technology. With a background as a founder in sustainable entrepreneurship and a career in product management, he now works as an innovation manager in the renewable energy industry. Gero's practitioner-focused perspective enriches his research on sustainable business incubation. He also shares his passion for holistic wellbeing as a yoga teacher, bringing a blend of sustainability, innovation, and mindfulness to his professional and personal pursuits.

Mike Wilson is a lecturer at York St John University in Entrepreneurship, Innovation and Strategic Human Resource Management. He also teaches Operational and Departmental Management and Leadership. Mike has 33 years' experience as a Business Consultant and has supported over 4,000 businesses across the NorthWest providing a tailored solutions-based approach focused on the development of new Entrepreneurs and Business Start-ups, and advising mature companies to ensure effective growth and exit strategies. He is the Chair of Simply Doughnuts and works as a freelance Mentor, Coach, Trainer and Employee Engagement specialist.

Figures

Tables

1 Introduction

Emily Beaumont, Jenny Hall,
Russ Hepworth-Sawyer and Mark Marrington

Enterprise and entrepreneurship activity is heavily influenced by the unique context in which it occurs. Therefore, identifying and understanding the specific context in which enterprise and entrepreneurship operate are crucial for fostering innovation, economic growth, and social development. However, this can occur only if entrepreneurs and their organisations recognise the political, economic, social and cultural, and technological contexts they operate within, as well as the discipline and/or industry in which they are situated. Context-specific knowledge enables entrepreneurs not only to identify unmet needs, market gaps, and emerging trends within their industries, but also to tailor their strategies and anticipate and navigate challenges effectively.

Different contexts present unique challenges and opportunities for entrepreneurs. Political factors, such as the formulation of policies, regulatory frameworks, political stability, and the broader governance environment, can significantly shape the business environment in which entrepreneurs operate. The economic context, including factors such as market demand, access to capital, and regulatory frameworks, can impact entrepreneurial opportunities and outcomes (Shane & Venkataraman, 2000). In economies characterised by high levels of innovation and investment, entrepreneurship may flourish due to favourable conditions for business creation and growth (Audretsch, 2007). Conversely, in economies with limited access to financing, bureaucratic barriers, and weak institutional support, entrepreneurship may be constrained, leading to lower rates of business formation and innovation (Acs & Amorós, 2008). The social and cultural context shapes attitudes towards entrepreneurship, risk-taking, and failure, influencing individuals' propensity to engage in entrepreneurial activities (GEM Global Report, 2020). In cultures that value entrepreneurship and celebrate success, individuals may be more inclined to pursue entrepreneurial ventures and experiment with innovative ideas (Liñán & Fayolle, 2015). Conversely, in cultures that stigmatise failure or prioritise stable employment, individuals may be more risk-averse and less likely to pursue entrepreneurial opportunities (Aldrich & Cliff, 2003). The technological context, including advancements in information technology, digitalisation, and automation, creates new opportunities and challenges for entrepreneurship

DOI: 10.4324/9781003324737-1

(Sussan & Acs, 2017). Entrepreneurs must adapt to technological changes and leverage emerging technologies to create competitive advantages and drive innovation (Venkataraman, 1997). Technological disruptions, such as the rise of artificial intelligence and blockchain, can create new market opportunities while rendering existing business models obsolete, necessitating entrepreneurial adaptation and agility (Zott & Amit, 2010). Finally, different industries and discipline areas present varying opportunities and challenges for entrepreneurship. On the one hand, emerging industries, such as renewable energy and biotechnology, may offer abundant opportunities for entrepreneurial ventures due to growing demand and rapid technological advancements (Gruber et al., 2013). Established industries, on the other hand, may present barriers to entry and entrenched competitors, requiring entrepreneurs to identify niche markets or develop disruptive innovations to succeed (Christensen, 1997).

Academics with an interest in enterprise and entrepreneurship operating in a specific context are very familiar with the conditions in which they exist. Many devote their research practice to a specific setting or subject and contribute greatly to furthering knowledge and understanding of enterprise and entrepreneurship in this locale. Yet few collections do this with acknowledgement of the distinctive features of the operating context and how this influences the experience and outcomes of the entrepreneurial journey. To that end, the Applied Enterprise and Entrepreneurship Series (AEES) has been created to offer a series of books that apply contemporary enterprise and entrepreneurship theory and practice to draw out the significance of context. The series provides a space for researchers to write where enterprise and entrepreneurship intersect with context, exploring the push and pull of each unique situation. The series begins with a book that encompasses a compilation of chapters that situate enterprise and entrepreneurship across an array of contexts including political, economic, social, and cultural, and technological contexts they operate within, as well as the discipline and/or industry in which they are situated. The Applied Enterprise and Entrepreneurship Series will then move to present volumes which focus on a specific context, taking a deeper dive to fully appreciate the opportunities and challenges presented.

References

Acs, Z. J., & Amorós, J. E. (2008). Entrepreneurship and competitiveness dynamics in Latin America. *Small Business Economics*, 31(3), 305–322.

Aldrich, H. E., & Cliff, J. E. (2003). The pervasive effects of family on entrepreneurship: Toward a family embeddedness perspective. *Journal of Business Venturing*, 18(5), 573–596.

Audretsch, D. B. (2007). *Entrepreneurship capital and economic growth*. Oxford University Press.

Christensen, C. M. (1997). *The innovator's dilemma: When new technologies cause great firms to fail*. Harvard Business Review Press.

GEM Global Report (2020). *Global entrepreneurship monitor 2019/2020 global report*. Global Entrepreneurship Research Association.

Gruber, M., MacMillan, I. C., & Thompson, J. D. (2013). Escaping the prior knowledge corridor: What shapes the number and variety of market opportunities identified before market entry of technology start-ups? *Organization Science*, 24(1), 280–300.

Liñán, F., & Fayolle, A. (2015). A systematic literature review on entrepreneurial intentions: Citation, thematic analyses, and research agenda. *International Entrepreneurship and Management Journal*, 11(4), 907–933.

Shane, S., & Venkataraman, S. (2000). The promise of entrepreneurship as a field of research. *Academy of Management Review*, 25(1), 217–226.

Sussan, F., & Acs, Z. J. (2017). The digital entrepreneurial ecosystem. *Small Business Economics*, 49(1), 55–73.

Venkataraman, S. (1997). The distinctive domain of entrepreneurship research: An editor's perspective. In *Advances in entrepreneurship, firm emergence and growth* (Vol. 3, pp. 119–138). JAI Press.

Zott, C., & Amit, R. (2010). Business model design: An activity system perspective. *Long Range Planning*, 43(2–3), 216–226.

2 Modelling contextualised entrepreneurial development

Victoria Mountford-Brown, Robert Newbery and Simon Brown

Introduction

Whereas universities more traditionally were considered as scholarly communities immersed in a disinterested pursuit of truth (Jaspers, 1960), neoliberalism became the dominant force in education in the UK from 1979, transforming the landscape and creating a form of governance infused with market principles (Jones, 2003). Such repositioning of UK higher education (HE) as industry is encapsulated in the now well-established term 'marketisation of education', whereby the increasingly competitive nature of institutions and scarce resources is constructed as liberating individual entrepreneurial freedoms and skills within a free market institutional framework (Harvey, 2005: 2). The concept of the 'Entrepreneurial University' involves the incorporation of economic and social development in its mission and purpose (Etzkowitz, 1998). However, this 'second revolution' of academia, otherwise termed as the 'capitalisation of knowledge', represents the growth of commercial ethos within academia and affects 'normative changes in science' (Etzkowitz, 1998: 824) – the controversy of which continues to reverberate in certain university spaces. This is because the 'knowledge economy', for many, 'replaces an epistemological with an economic definition of knowledge' and as a result, universities are increasingly seen as agents of economic growth (Usher, 2002: 144), taking them away somewhat from the 'academic heartland' (Clark, 1998). However, whilst this continues to trouble many academics, the magnitude of the triple, quadruple and now, quintuple helix (Carayannis et al., 2012) and the significance of universities engaging with industry, government and publics very much structure the landscape of contemporary British academia and its assessments of research quality. One of the most prominent measures used in UK HE is the Research Excellence Framework (REF) and in 2021, 25% of each institution's submission to this review process was focused entirely on research impact cases, serving to cement the importance of research impacting in ways beyond academic readership.

The UK's governmental mission to address future innovation skills needs (BEIS, 2017) is not new – technology transfer and the commercialisation of

DOI: 10.4324/9781003324737-2

intellectual property have long been the practice of universities globally (Goldfarb & Henrekson, 2003); however, significant investment and development of researchers have increased dramatically in the last 10 years arguably more so in the last 5+ years in the UK. Sir Gareth Roberts (Roberts, 2002) elevated the focus on researchers as central to future social and economic prosperity and set in motion a policy initiative to support the (transferable) skills development of research students and postdoctoral research staff, paving the way for major cultural change in UK HE for career support (Hodge et al., 2011). In preparing researchers and developing their abilities to cope with the demands of the mission (and conditions) of the entrepreneurial university, Vitae introduced the Researcher Development Framework (RDF) in 2010 as an innovative approach to establishing and enhancing the opportunity for the UK to develop world-leading researchers and increase successful research outputs. The framework focuses on researcher professional development, supporting both the researcher and the research by exploring, articulating and demonstrating the vital capabilities of researchers in order to support a stable economy whilst providing solutions to societal challenges.

The RDF is a key element of a wider network of initiatives and resources to establish researcher development as an embedded methodology. Of particular interest is the 'enterprise lens' on researcher development (Vitae, 2012), which highlights a broad range of knowledge, behaviours and attributes across the vast majority of the RDF 'wheel' of researcher competencies. Vitae has embedded enterprise and entrepreneurship as key to employability, with industry guidance such as QAA (2018) demonstrating the effectiveness of developing entrepreneurial capabilities, and researcher-specific guidance such the Concordati Strategy Group (CSG) that explicitly recommends all researcher development activity should include supporting researchers so they are equipped to be adaptable and flexible in an increasingly diverse, mobile, global research environment (Researcher Development Concordat, 2019). Importantly, the development of the individual via enterprise and entrepreneurship education (EEE) interventions is proposed to add 'economic, social and cultural value to the UK' (QAA, 2018: 2). These emphases on the academic researcher as an 'agent of change' and the substantial investment in the development of researchers in the UK indicate a need to evaluate the impact of interventions designed to boost skills and commercial impact outputs.

Several innovative, collaborative approaches are being used to harness the capabilities of early-career academic researchers, and we have developed a model of 'Commercialisation Intent' (CI) to assist others who are developing their own programmes. To explore this in detail, we will present an examination of pertinent literature in the field of EEE in HE and unpack some of the theoretical underpinning of evaluation modelling linked to 'Entrepreneurial Intention' (EI) and go on to explore how this has been used to develop and refine the modelling of 'CI' model, which is designed and built-for-purpose within these specific contexts. The methodology section will outline the specific approaches utilised in the development and refinement of the model and highlight and unpack interesting observations in the model variables, particularly in Personal Attitudes (PA). To understand this, we further explore the challenges of using 'entrepreneurship' terminology in the academia, exploring arguments that problematise the use of different language in HE and the disjuncture perceived in the fundamental premise of the university that we argue may (at least in part) structure and reinforce disjuncture in PA to commercialisation and entrepreneurship more broadly. Finally, we will focus on the developmental potential for understanding behavioural intentions across the broad spectrum of research impact, and advanced 'entrepreneurial' researcher development programmes.

Measuring and understanding impact of EEE

EEE is certainly not new to UK universities; as Kuratko (2005: 582) notes, entrepreneurship education emerged in the 1980s; and EEE has now been embedded across UK HE institutions (2018a, 2018b) and continues to grow worldwide (Kuratko, 2005). A variety of approaches for differing contexts exist, as do numerous interventions that are typically focused on the development of enterprise and entrepreneurship capabilities and skills as well as more focused venture creation programmes. The Quality Assurance Agency (QAA) is commonly regarded as defining the industry standards for HE in the UK and has championed the benefits of EEE for some time now (QAA, 2011, 2018), with UK HE supporting the importance of both enterprise education and entrepreneurship education and defining differences in the two terms. Enterprise is defined as 'the generation and application of ideas, which are set within practical situations during a project or undertaking' (QAA, 2018: 7). Entrepreneurship is defined as applying to 'both individuals and groups (teams or organisations), and the value creation in private, public and third sectors, and in any hybrid combination of the three' (QAA, 2018: 7). Entrepreneurship education is defined as 'the application of enterprise behaviours, attributes and competencies into the creation of cultural, social or economic value. This can, but does not exclusively, lead to venture creation' (QAA, 2018: 7). Therefore, enterprise is about developing individual capabilities as well as ideas, whereas entrepreneurship is more about using the capabilities to make ideas a reality. Observing Vitae's definition of enterprise as 'a set of capabilities and attitudes that can enable a culture of innovation, creativity, risk taking and opportunism that underpins employability, enables entrepreneurship and intrapreneurship and facilitates knowledge transfer' (Goodman et al., 2014: 3), the significance of EEE for researchers is clear, in policy terms at least.

As the Quality Assurance Agency for Higher Education (QAA, 2018) documents, EEE can be used across disciplinary boundaries and can play a central role in boosting the employability of students and graduates. Routinely, the focus is on the outcomes of taught programmes, which tend to exclude researchers. One of the most prolific measurements of graduate outcomes in the UK, for example, collects data on whether students have started their own business or entered professional-level work 6 months after graduation, and these results are often influential in university league tables. The scale of this data collection is vast and carried out by the Higher Education Statistics Agency on behalf of the UK funding and regulatory bodies. The positive impact of graduate start-ups in the UK economy (UUK, 2023) and strong connections with employability (QAA, 2018) are such that increasing emphasis on EEE intervention efficacy measures is likely to continue. However, there remains the need to ensure that interventions themselves are going to generate the kinds of developmental competencies and behaviours required for graduate success. In the research context, whilst the number of cases of technology transfer or spin-out companies created may be useful for institutions, understanding what catalyses such action is needed.

To understand the impact of HE EEE interventions on the likelihood to start a new venture or engage in an entrepreneurial career pathway, a model of EI has been used extensively in the UK and in other international contexts (Liñán & Fayolle, 2015; Krueger et al., 2000; Zhang et al., 2015; Turulja, 2020; Israr & Saleem, 2018; Su et al., 2021; Prajapati, 2019 inter alia). There exist arange of EEE interventions that are evaluated to understand the efficacy of entrepreneurial education (extra-) curricula/programmes and large-scale business competitions on start-up and entrepreneurial career pathways upon graduation (Liñán, 2004; Liñán et al., 2011; McKenzie, 2017; Nabi et al., 2017; Newbery et al., 2016). However, owing to the different stages in career decisions from the typical undergraduate or postgraduate taught student, the early career researcher (ECR) has arguably made the career pathway decisions and, therefore, propensity to start a business upon graduation is not a feasible measure of success of EEE interventions. An alternative measurement tool is likely to be needed to contextualise the outcomes/outputs of EEE interventions. Nevertheless, the theoretical bases on which this model rests will be unpacked here in a little more detail to aid understanding of the ways in which EEE impact is commonly measured and the ways in which we have selectively adapted an evaluation tool to test 'Commercialisation Intent' rather than 'Entrepreneurial Intent'.

The development of the model of 'Entrepreneurial Intent' is based on the Theory of Planned Behaviour (TPB; Ajzen, 1985, 1991), which is 'part of the larger family of intentional models that have been used to try and explain the emergence of entrepreneurial behaviour' (Fayolle et al., 2006: 705). The TPB, broadly speaking, is premised in social psychology and rests on the idea that action is reasoned and planned and as such was a reformulation of the Theory of Reasoned Action (TRA) (Ajzen & Fishbein, 1980; Ajzen, 1985, 1991; Fishbein & Ajzen, 1975). TPB and the bases of it are considered superior to 'situational and personality' measures alone in predicting entrepreneurial activity (Kreuger et al., 2000: 413). The broad application and testing of TPB modelling provide a rich source of understanding of the ways in which the theoretical components relate to different contexts. The substantial critical engagement with these social psychology theories (see Manstead, 2011) is also useful in developing an understanding of the ways in which contextual factors are interwoven.

According to TRA, behaviour is informed by intention, which is shaped by the direct *personal* beliefs and evaluation of the behaviour in question and the motivation to comply with this behaviour along with *normative* beliefs, thereby placing the context of the sense of normativity as important in any use of this theory. TRA positions Attitudes and Social Norms as separate constructs and criticism has been levelled on the assumptions that these exist as unidimensional constructs rather than influencing each other (Hankins et al., 2000: 152). For example, whilst Attitude is 'hypothesized to be formed taking into account all salient beliefs, it is still one psychological construct' (Hankins et al., 2000: 152). Likewise, the construct of 'Subjective Norms' (SN), whilst many studies demonstrate this as a multidimensional construct, the TRA restricts this as a unidimensional construct; TPB reformulates this point, with multidimensionality of these constructs and with the addition of a third construct of 'Perceived Behavioural Control' (PBC).

As Kreuger et al.'s (2000: 413) exploration of competing models of EI states, '[w]e best predict, rather than explain, any planned behaviour by observing intentions towards that behaviour – not by attitudes, beliefs, personality, or mere demographics. Intentions are the best predictor of planned behaviour' (Begozzi et al., 1989). However, the theory also recognises that intentions themselves are formed and forged through attitudinal antecedents of intention, namely, PBC, SN and PA towards the Behaviour (e.g., venture creation, entrepreneurial career pathway). The latter two of these three include influences such as normative beliefs/perceived social norms, and expectations for value of the behaviour. PBC relates more to a sense of personal control or situational competency in the behaviour, otherwise known as self-efficacy (Bandura & National Institute of Mental Health, 1986). As TRA and TPB have underpinned extensive application in studies interested in EI, this was used for the basis of development of a tool to measure intention to commercialise ideas after taking part in the programme (See Figure 2.1). To share the development of this approach, in the next section we first outline the context of the sample programme, the development of the questionnaire tool and finally, validation of the CI model.

Methodology

Context

For this research, we selected an anonymised programme that invites application from ECRs and principal investigators (PIs), who supervise the ECRs. Entry to this programme is predicated on the development of 'an idea' for commercialisation from research findings; however, this can be in very early stages of development. The development of the measurement tool for this programme was carried out in collaboration with the course architects and trainers.

The selected programme aims to help early career academics explore opportunities for their research and involves several stages: first when the applicant is successful, they are invited to attend a 'Bootcamp' training event, which is typically in the form of an intensive 3-day residential programme. This element of the programme consists of a series of activities focused on the development of an entrepreneurial mindset, and enterprising behaviours to produce change-provoking-action (Kirketerp, 2011), and involves the use of several experiential learning exercises and opportunities for 'serious games' (Clark, 1980; Newbery et al., 2016) resulting in an action plan and budget that will enable the participant to engage in a large number of meaningful conversations around the world with industry and thought leaders in their field. The length of the programme spans several weeks or months, with participants invited to attend events around the globe as well as additional support to let the team focuses on the key learning and insights from the conversations. The end of the journey is an opportunity for participants to share their learning with a panel of 'experts' and propose their next best step for their research. This might be to commercially exploit the IP, to license the IP, to conduct further research (sponsored or UKRI funded) or to follow some other path based on the external feedback. The 'expert' panel gives their feedback, and for some of the teams involved, an opportunity is provided to support for further work to progress towards the spinning out of the IP from the institution. To measure the changes in the participants over the course of the programme, three data capture points were used: pre-start of the training, post-final day of training and post-'the final pitch'.

The development of an evaluation tool needed to be able to measure efficacy to the extent that it would provoke entrepreneurial action in some way; the approach needed to measure the impact of the programme on the individuals/cohorts on an ongoing basis, to allow for data to help refine the programme. The survey tool was refined across a number of these programmes spanning over 12 years. The approach used was to measure the impact of the programme on the intentions of participants. This was intended to measure change at the point of training and to track change over time. Following results and feedback during the initial cohorts, the tool was adjusted to measure CI for subsequent cohorts, as this was seen as a more appropriate measure of impact for the intended academic researcher audience. We also developed and agreed a list of skills thought most relevant to research commercialisation for researchers (based on academic literature and on agreement with the programme architects) – this was later used to create an overall measure of commercialisation skills.

A measure of CI was tracked through a quasi-experimental methodology, with pre- and post-intervention measurement. The research shows a robust and replicable increase in research commercialisation capacity and that the structure of the programme appears stable across cohorts. Overall, this provides evidence

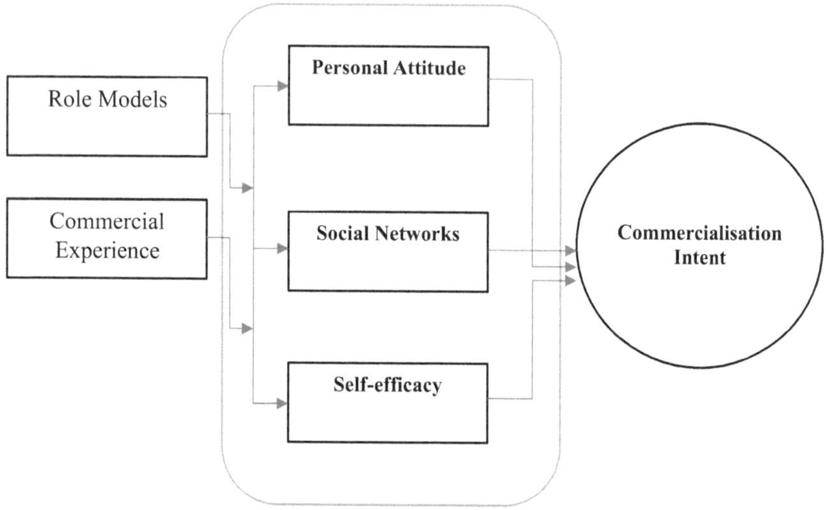

Figure 2.1 A model of Commercialisation Intent.

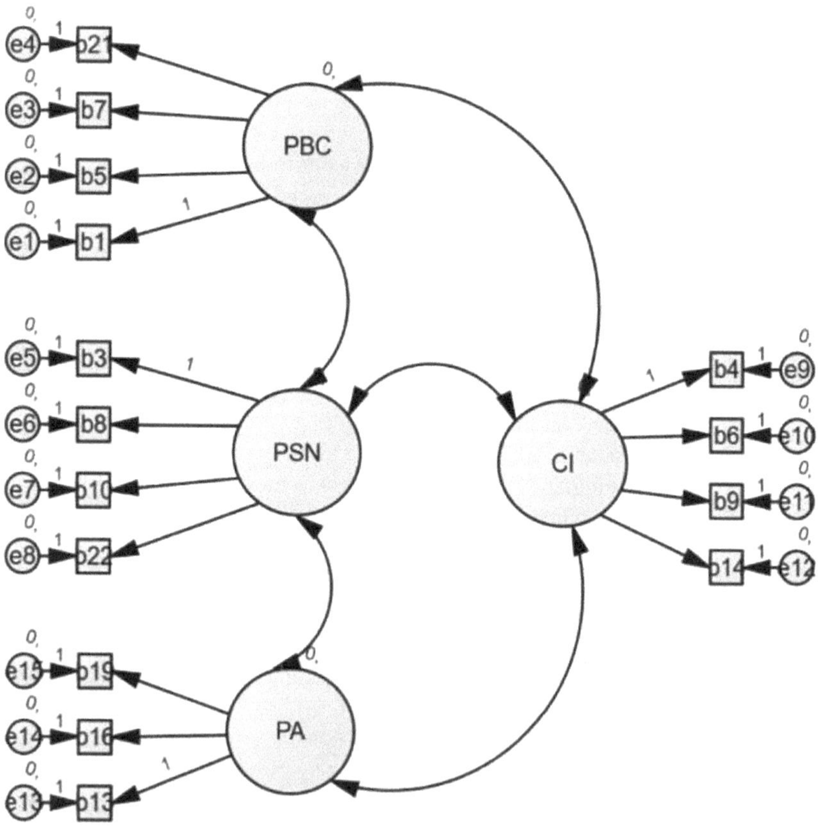

Figure 2.2 Measurement model of Commercialisation Intent.

that such programmes provide a robust and replicable series of interventions that provide a significant and measurable change in research CI and skills. Whilst being able to demonstrate efficacy for the measurement of programme interventions, the ways in which the different components of the TPB structure behind the model of CI (see Figures 2.2 and 2.3) were particularly interesting in terms of the HE context. Before analysing these findings, we demonstrate the development of the questionnaire tool (see Table 2.1) in the next section.

Questionnaire development

We used the Liñán et al. (2005) EI questionnaire as the basis for a revised CI questionnaire. We maintained the 7-point Likert scale approach but changed the language to better represent the target population of academics undertaking research that may have commercial value. The language was changed in consultation with the architects of the programme, resulting in the questionnaire instrument shown in Table 2.1.

We then embedded these questions in a survey of academics participating in the programme. For each item, the respondents were given a statement and asked to indicate level of agreement on a scale of 1–7. The questionnaire was completed by participants: before initial training, immediately after training activity

Table 2.1 Questionnaire instrument

Item	*Question*
1	Developing an idea to commercial viability would be easy for me
2	*A commercial career is totally unattractive to me*
3	My friends would approve of me commercialising the idea
4	I am ready to dedicate myself to exploiting the idea
5	*I believe I would be completely unable to create a working business model*
6	I will make every effort to take this idea to the market
7	I am able to manage the market development process for a new idea
8	Immediate family would approve of me commercially exploiting the idea
9	*I do not want this idea to make any money*
10	My superiors would approve of me commercially exploiting the idea
11	If I had the opportunity and resources, I would love to commercialise this
12	Other academics would approve of me commercially exploiting the idea
13	*Amongst various options, I would rather be anything but an entrepreneur*
14	I am determined to commercialise this idea in the future
15	If I want to make a profit from an idea, I will do so successfully
16	Making money from the idea would give me great satisfaction
17	*It would be very difficult for me to develop an idea for a business*
18	A key professional goal for me is to be commercially aware
19	I see more advantages than disadvantages in being an entrepreneur
20	*I have a very low intention of ever making a profit from this idea*
21	I know all about the practical details needed to exploit an idea
22	Peers on this programme would approve of me commercialising the idea

Note: Italics indicates a negative question that is reversed for analysis.

and then typically between 3 and 6 months (varied to attempt an increase in return rate which tended to deplete in the final collection) after the programme. Each instance aimed to capture the changing CI picture of participants. For the purposes of model validation, we were interested in the underlying relationship and not the progression experienced by participants *per se*; thus, we drew from the results of each survey as independent. With many cohorts and 3 measurement points, this provided a sample of 1,110 discrete observations.

Model validation

We took a two-step approach to validate the model, using an initial Exploratory Factor Analysis (EFA) followed by Confirmatory Factor Analysis (CFA) to test empirical validity. The Kaiser-Meyer-Olkin Measure of Sampling Adequacy of .831 and significant Bartlett's Test of Sphericity demonstrated that the data were suitable for EFA. We used a maximum likelihood approach for factor extraction and varimax rotation. Using the full 22 measures from the questionnaire, we found that some items had saturations on more than one factor. We removed the cross-loaded factors (items: 2, 11, 12, 15, 17, 18 and 20) and found a solution using 15 factors that exhibited high loadings (being above 0.4 as per convention) within factors and no major cross-loadings between factors (indicated in bold in Table 2.2). The reliability of the scales for each construct all exceeded the usual threshold of .70 alpha value presented in the literature (Hair et al., 2010). The model supported the expected four-factor solution found in the TPB theoretical framework. Table 2.2 shows the final component matrix, loadings and reliability for the CI constructs.

Table 2.2 Final component matrix, loadings and reliability

Measure	*Item*	*PSN*	*CI*	*PBC*	*PA*
PBC	b1	0.118	0.119	**0.842**	0.021
PSN	b3	**0.797**	0.175	0.091	0.004
CI	b4	0.232	**0.776**	0.179	0.009
PBC	b5	0.066	0.323	**0.514**	0.005
CI	b6	0.183	**0.837**	0.173	−0.038
PBC	b7	0.119	0.218	**0.824**	0.026
PSN	b8	**0.799**	0.276	0.038	−0.033
CI	b9	0.051	**0.598**	0.087	0.025
PSN	b10	**0.796**	0.111	0.042	−0.004
PA	b13	−0.059	0.064	0.031	**0.901**
CI	b14	0.174	**0.791**	0.208	0.012
PA	b16	−0.003	−0.028	0.037	**0.918**
PA	b19	0.011	−0.019	0.031	**0.916**
PBC	b21	0.102	0.085	**0.825**	0.058
PSN	b22	**0.732**	0.057	0.257	−0.027
Cronbach	alpha	0.817	0.800	0.795	0.898

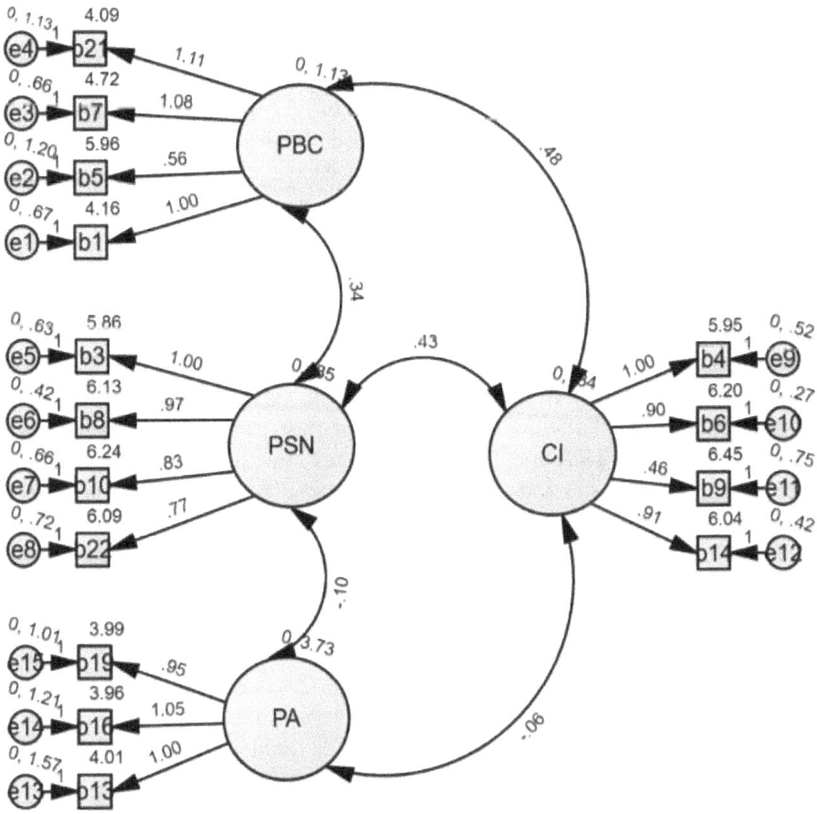

Figure 2.3 Predicted relationships in the model of Commercialisation Intent.

We then used CFA to explore the relationships between constructs. Figure 2.2 shows the expected relationships in the measurement model. Following TPB and EI, we expected that CI would be predicted by PBC, PSN and PA. The actual measurement model (see Figure 2.3) demonstrates an adequate model fit, with a TLI and CFI above .900 (at .974 and .973, respectively) and RMSEA below .050 at .039. PBC and PSN demonstrated a significant positive relationship with CI; however, PA had no significant relationship with CI. Context is an important criterion of understanding these findings, particularly with regard to PA. The next section will focus on the context of academia in order to critically analyse the finding of this departure from the significance of this variable, in this context.

Discussion

In the development of the CI model, we noticed an irregularity in the application of TPB to intention to commercialise, namely that PAs were not significant to the prediction of CI. The model of EI has been adapted in this endeavour and reworded to relate more strongly to terminology that is more contextually relevant to the target group of ECRs, that is, commercialisation, rather than entrepreneurship. However, in finding the disjuncture of PAs with commercialisation in our testing of the model, we suggest this is worthy of further scrutiny, particularly with the specific context of academia. Whilst we have outlined the differentiation between terms such as 'enterprise' and 'entrepreneurship' earlier, we acknowledged that the latter term is routinely understood as indelibly linked to venture creation and therefore aligned to commercial activity. This is an important starting place for considering the role of PAs towards such endeavours. Whilst the wording was changed from questioning around whether the individual would 'start a business', to a more contextual 'commercialise the idea', the role of PAs regarding such activities in the context of academia is interesting.

Manstead's (2011) review of a number of past papers adopting a critical stance in relation to TRA and TPB demonstrates how this allows us to develop and extend these theories and a number of these studies showcased in this article are helpful to think through the context of our findings. Some of the other ways we might consider this further is through the role of self-identity (and the social in identity), of moral norms and habits, of perceived sense of control and the role of affect in attitude and behaviours. Godin et al.'s (2005: 497) exploration of the role of 'moral norms' suggests that the TPB should more clearly 'acknowledge the importance of internalised norms and self-expectations in the development of one's motivation to adopt a given behaviour'. As Manstead (2011: 367) points out, Ajzen and Fishbein (1980) highlight that the kind of social behaviour that often serves as a dependent variable in studies of attitudes and behaviour is one that is shaped by social forces, not only private preferences. Our social behaviour is not always a perfect reflection of our attitudes because we are also subject to social influence.

We might link the insignificance of PA to CI with identity, specifically academic identities. Terry et al. (1999: 226) considered the role of social identities in TPB and, using role theory, they maintained that '[c]entral to identity theory is the view that to understand action – or in more psychological terms, to understand and predict behaviour – it is necessary to conceive of the self and the wider social structure as being inextricably linked'. Their exploration of self-identity as performative and an important component of a person's self-concept may be useful to consider *in this context.*

Despite the significance placed on development of enterprising behaviours and capabilities in policy, an underlying antagonism between policy makers and researchers exists that positions a (restrictive) view of entrepreneurialism as 'opposing the traditional functioning of universities' (Walsh et al., 2015: 786–787). Whilst entrepreneurship has become the 'mainstay across educational institutions' (Turner & Gianiodis: 131), an air of resistance is often palpable, relating chiefly to epistemological premises of the purpose of (higher) education.

The focus on income generation in universities is the subject of much disagreement in academia – wherein the term 'academic capitalism' (Slaughter & Leslie, 1997) has been used to describe and politicise the ongoing nature of change in academic labour and the impact of the embeddedness of the knowledge economy. What 'entrepreneurship' or 'academic capitalism' means and how researchers respond to such opportunities and demands can differ significantly depending upon 'how close or distant the field is from the market' (Ylijoki, 2003: 307). The distinctions between disciplinary and institutional cultures, motivations and expected outputs create much difference in the way academics respond and adapt to the demands of academic capitalism (Ylijoki, 2003). However, it is the perceived distance between the ideals of the 'academic heartland' (Clark, 1998) and the notion of 'entrepreneurship' as it is discursively and socially constructed (Swail et al., 2014) that creates a distinction so powerfully felt because of its association with conflicting values. Entrepreneurship is often seen by researchers as a selfish activity – a 'dirty word' couched in self-motivated, profit-hungry ideals; standing in opposition to the disinterested pursuit of truth of 'pure' academic research (Walsh et al., 2015). In a similar vein, the wording of 'commercialisation' arguably has a more direct interpretation of this sort of activity.

The 'image problem' may also stem from a widespread misconception of entrepreneurship that is not necessarily exclusive to HE. For example, Swail et al.'s (2014: 860) examination of 'entre-tainment' looks at the impact cultural media has in influencing attitudes, citing popular TV shows and well-known figures such as 'Richard Branson, Alan Sugar and Donald Trump [that] have come to stand for the 'entrepreneur' (ibid., 860), and, therefore, in restricting perspectives. However, likewise, the discursive and social construction of 'academic capitalism' in HE is also worthy of note as cultural/environmental/social discourses integrate with the economic (Steyart & Katz, 2004); it is often senior academics that transfer limiting and negative foci on what is meant by 'entrepreneurship' to junior academics (Walsh et al., 2012, 2015). The preoccupation with gaining funding and focusing on money of academic 'reluctant entrepreneurs' (Morales-Gualdron et al., 2009), rather than value creation more broadly, is considerable in understanding the 'image problem' and how it is socially constructed in HE. Researchers tend to be more motivated to engage with industry to pursue opportunities to further their research rather than simply commercialisation (D'Este & Perkmann, 2011), and, therefore, researcher development efforts should acknowledge this.

Clearly, the social constructions of entrepreneurship in academia are complex. Mars and Rios-Aguilar (2010) used content analysis of five leading HE journals examining a multitude of the different uses, understandings and definitions of entrepreneurship. They conceive of 'academic entrepreneurs' to be those who 'innovatively leverage internal and external opportunities to not only generate economic resources for their own profit or in support of their academic units and institutions, but also to create within the academy social and political change platforms' (ibid., 444). This broader understanding of academic entrepreneurship, as innovations within and beyond academia, widens the scope for a range of values and ideals, rather than conflictual values solely premised on the pursuit of profits. As Walsh et al. (2015: 787) acknowledge:

> If this reluctance was replaced by informed and proactive engagement, researchers' attitudes and behaviour regarding entrepreneurship might change. Instead of associating entrepreneurship with commerce and a 'dirty word', more researchers might use entrepreneurial means to 'improve the future'.

The focus on values is of great importance in every sense. Research suggests that the perception of two very different sets of values between the 'academic heartland' and 'profit-hungry' entrepreneurship (understood as commercial activity) creates tensions at the site of the individual – in their identity (Ylijoki, 2003; Walsh et al., 2015; Hakala, 2009; Jain et al., 2009). It also reminds us that PA towards commercialisation and behaviour associated with entrepreneurship, for many, imply a disjuncture from the real sense of purpose of their chosen career pathway – from their own (self/role) identity. Furthermore, notions of 'academic capitalism' and/or the 'academic heartland' as well as discourses about entrepreneurship and commercialisation are likewise couched in personal and moral associations of value, and therefore suggest the potential for fracturing of the sense of self and/or role identity. Bourdieu and Wacquant's (1992) identification of the 'academic habitus' as a construct of identity that internalises structural conditions of the field may be a useful way to understand and explore the ways in which academic practice both structures and is structured by different relationships to the 'rules of the game', that is, the implicit ways of being and doing that are institutionalised in academia.

Conclusion

In this chapter, we have outlined the context of academic researcher development in the UK and highlighted the importance placed on researchers as agents of change and the increased importance on research impact as exemplified in the 'Quintuple Helix' (Carayannis et al., 2012). The emergence and growth of researcher development programs in the UK suggest a need to understand the impact of such funding. The questionnaire tool was developed to understand the impact of the training programme on developing entrepreneurial abilities and likelihood to generate commercial impact with their research. It was developed closely with the course architects, and language used in other EI questionnaires was adapted to better suit the context of research commercialisation.

Whilst the development of this evaluation tool and model of CI has been established as fit for purpose and has been effective in demonstrating the positive impact of participation in raising intentions to commercialise, our analyses highlight the importance of context. The influence of the sociocultural context of academia in which these measures are taken may be impacted by fundamental epistemological positions on the purposes of higher education – and themselves as academic researchers. In many cases, a deeply embedded sense of disjuncture with entrepreneurship and commercialisation is likely to impact PA, but we have argued here that this does not necessarily separate them from the likelihood to commercialise a research idea they have.

The data examined in this chapter refers only to the first 15 cohorts of the programme, and at the time of writing, there have been an additional 10 cohorts, which have also included a conversion from the intensive, residential setting and approach used in the first 15 programmes. The circumstances of the Covid-19 pandemic resulted in the creation of a programme adapted to run entirely online, and subsequent approaches have adopted a hybrid model, with all of the last 10 iterations developed and delivered by a different consortium. The programme has also been renamed and expanded to include non-HEI research centres, which further reinforces the premise of knowledge-*exchange* and breadth of research activity in our societies. These incremental changes perhaps offer new scope for further analyses of the ways in which attitudes towards commercialisation and research impact may be affected. In addition, there is scope to investigate the potential impact of the online/hybrid methods of delivery and how this can shape educator/researcher-developer/policy-maker's preparedness for the challenges researchers face currently, and in the future in their roles as agents of change.

Research impact is a firm part of the UK Research landscape and only one aspect of this is commercialisation; researchers may be motivated to create impact with their research but perhaps not have as positive an attitude towards commercialisation *per se*. The challenges to the perceptions and uses of different terminology in academic contexts gain prominence when attempting to understand the ways in which researcher development training can engage researchers sufficiently to develop entrepreneurial behaviours and competencies, which they would use to create value from their research. Therefore, we propose that attitudes may be more significant and positive if the EEE intervention is focused towards creating research impact of all kinds – not just commercialisation. Such a reframing may assist in differentiating the notion of 'academic capitalism' and, therefore, some of the politicising of the commercialisation of research. In the quest to extend the reach and impact of the important research taking place across academia and to reaffirm the importance of academic research, we need to demonstrate the valuing of this; perhaps most clearly, this would be observed through funding programmes with a broad focus on the value of research impact, rather than a tendency to prioritise income-generating activities. Suggestions for future research, therefore, may be to focus on and develop a more nuanced evaluation of intentions to create impact with research, rather than a narrower investigation of commercialisation. If we value other forms of impact as much as commercialisation, perhaps researcher development programmes should focus on broadening the opportunity for exploration and development of entrepreneurial behaviours and competencies for research impact more generally, rather than solely on commercialisation and the creation of spin-out companies. The latter emphases are likely to provoke a particular perspective which may, to some extent, limit the potential of generating impactful outputs.

References

Ajzen, I. (1985) 'From intentions to actions: A theory of planned behavior.' In J. Kuhl & J. Beckmann (Eds.), *Action-control: From cognition to behavior* (pp. 11–39). Heidelberg: Springer.
Ajzen, I. (1991) 'The theory of planned behavior.' *Organizational Behavior and Human Decision Processes*, 50: 179–211.
Ajzen, I., & Fishbein, M. (1980) *Understanding attitudes and predicting social behavior*. Englewood Cliffs, NJ: Prentice-Hall.
Ajzen, I., & Fishbein, M. (2005) 'The influence of attitudes on behavior.' In D. Albarracín, B. T. Johnson, & M. P. Zanna (Eds.), *The handbook of attitudes* (pp. 173–221). Mahwah, NJ: Lawrence Erlbaum Associates Publishers.
Bandura, A., & National Institute of Mental Health. (1986) *Social foundations of thought and action: A social cognitive theory*. Prentice-Hall, Inc.
BEIS (2017) *Industrial strategy: Building a Britain fit for the future*. London: Department for Business, Energy & Industrial Strategy.
Begozzi, R. P., Baumgartner, J., & Yi, Y. (1989) 'An investigation into the role of intentions as mediators of the attitude-behavior relationship.' *Journal of Economic Policy*, 10 (1): 35–62.
Bourdieu, P., & Wacquant, L. (1992) *An invitation to reflexive sociology*. Polity Press.
Carayannis, E. G., Barth, T. D., & Campell, D. F. J. (2012) 'The Quintuple Helix Innovation model: Global warming as a challenge and driver for innovation.' *Journal of Innovation and Entrepreneurship*, 1 (2): 1–12.
Clark, C. (1980) *Serious games*. New York: Viking.
Clark, B. R. (1998) 'The entrepreneurial university: Demand and response.' *Tertiary Education and Management*, 4: 5–16.
D'Este, P., & Perkmann, M. (2011) 'Why do academics engage with industry? The entrepreneurial university and individual motivations.' *Journal of Technology Transfer*, 36: 316–339.
Etzkowitz, H. (1998) 'The norms of entrepreneurial science: Cognitive effects of the new university-industry linkages.' *Research Policy*, 27: 823–834.
Fayolle, A., Gailly, B., & Lassas-Clerc, N. (2006) 'Assessing the impact of entrepreneurship education programmes: A new methodology.' *Journal of European Industrial Training*, 30: 701–720.
Fishbein, M., & Ajzen, I. (1975) *Belief, attitude, intention and behavior: An introduction to theory and research*. Reading, MA: Addison-Wesley.
Godin, G., Connor, M., & Sheeren, P. (2005) 'Bridging the intention-behaviour "gap": The role of moral norm.' *The British Journal of Social Psychology*, 44: 497–512.
Goldfarb, B., & Henrekson, M. (2003) 'Bottom-up versus top-down policies towards the commercialization of university intellectual property.' *Research Policy*, 12 (4): 639–658.

Goodman, A., Mitchell, A., Pateman, H., Shinton, S., Videler, T., & Wilkinson, J. (2014) *The enterprising researcher*. Cambridge: VITAE.

Hankins, M., French, D., & Horne, R. (2000) 'Statistical guidelines for studies of the theory of reasoned action and the theory of planned behaviour.' *Psychology and Health*, 15: 151–161.

Hair, J. F., Black, W. C., Babin, B. J., Anderson, R. E., & Tatham, R. L. (2010) *Multivariate data analysis* (7th ed.). Upper Saddle River, NJ: Prentice Hall.

Hakala, J. (2009) 'The future of the academic calling? Junior researchers in the entrepreneurial university.' *Higher Education*, 57: 173–190.

Harvey, D. (2005) *A brief history of neoliberalism*. Oxford: Oxford Academic.

Hodge, A., Bownes, M., Burgess, R., Chambaz, J., Dodson, E., Johnes, G., Loving, C., Mcvitty, D., O'Carroll, C., & Ritchie, E. (2011). *Review of progress in implementing the recommendations of Sir Gareth Roberts, regarding employability and career development of PhD students and research staff: A report for research councils UK by an independent review panel, October 2010*. London: RCUK.

Israr, M., & Saleem, M. (2018) 'Entrepreneurial intentions among university students in Italy.' *Journal of Global Entrepreneurship Research*, 8 (20): 1–14.

Jain, S., George, G., & Maltarich, M. (2009) 'Academics or entrepreneurs? Investigating the role of university scientists involved in commercialization activity.' *Research Policy*, 38: 922–935.

Jaspers, K. (1960) *The idea of the university*. London: Peter Owen.

Jones, K. (2003) *Education in Britain: 1944 to the present*. Cambridge: Polity Press.

Kirketerp, A. (2011) *Entrepreneurship didactics – the push method*. ETC Toolkit: https://www.etctoolkit.org.uk/media/28484/kirketerp-entrepreneurship-didactics-the-push-method.pdf

Krueger, N. F., Reilly, M. D., & Carsrud, A. L. (2000) 'Competing models of entrepreneurial intentions.' *Journal of Business Venturing*, 15 (5–6): 411–432.

Kuratko, D. F. (2005) 'The emergence of entrepreneurship education: Development, trends, challenges.' *Entrepreneurship, Theory & Practice*, 29: 577–598.

Liñán, F. (2004) Intention-based models of entrepreneurship education. *Piccolla Impressa/Small Business*, 3: 11–35.

Liñán, F., & Fayolle, A. (2015) 'A systematic literature review on entrepreneurial intentions: Citation, thematic analyses, and research agenda.' *International Entrepreneurship & Management Journal*, 11: 907–933.

Liñán, F., Rodriguez-Cohard, J. C., & Reuda-Cantuche, J. M. (2005) 'Factors affecting entrepreneurial intention levels.' In *45th Congress of the European Regional Science Association: "Land Use and Water Management in a Sustainable Network Society,"* 23–27 August 2005, Amsterdam, The Netherlands, European Regional Science Association (ERSA), Louvainla-Neuve.

Liñán, F., Rodriguez-Cohard, J. C., & Reuda-Cantuche, J. M. (2011) 'Factors affecting entrepreneurial intention levels: A role for education.' *International Entrepreneurship Management Journal*, 7: 195–218.

Manstead, A. S. (2011) 'The benefits of a critical stance: A reflection on past papers on the theories of reasoned action and planned behaviour.' *British Journal of Social Psychology*, 50 (3):366–373.

Mars, M. M., & Rios-Aguilar, C. (2010) 'Academic entrepreneurship (re)defined: Significance and implications for the scholarship of higher education.' *Higher Education*, 59 (4): 441–460.

McKenzie, D. (2017) 'Identifying and spurring high-growth entrepreneurship: Experimental evidence from a business plan competition.' *American Economic Review*, 107 (8): 2278–2307.

Morales-Gualdron, S. T., Gutierrez-Gracia, A., & Roig Dobon, S. (2009) 'The entrepreneurial motivation in academia: A multidimensional construct.' *International Entrepreneurship and Management Journal*, 5 (3): 301–317.

Nabi, G., Linan, F., Fayolle, A., & Walmsley, A. (2017) 'The impact of entrepreneurship education in higher education: A systematic review and research agenda.' *Academy of Management Learning & Education*, 16 (2): 277–299.

Newbery, R., Lean, J., & Moizer, J. (2016) 'Evaluating the impact of serious games: The effect of gaming on entrepreneurial intent.' *Information Technology and People*, 29 (4).

Prajapati, B. (2019) 'Entrepreneurial intention among business students: The effect of entrepreneurship education.' *Westcliff International Journal of Applied Research*, 3(1): 54–67.

QAA (2018) *Enterprise and entrepreneurship education: Guidance for UK higher education providers*. Gloucester, UK: The Quality Assurance Agency for Higher Education.

Researcher Development Concordat (2019) *The concordat to support the career development of researchers*. https://researcherdevelopmentconcordat.ac.uk/wp-content/uploads/2022/01/Researcher-Development-Concordat_Sept2019-1.pdf (accessed 10th October 2024).

Roberts, G. (2002) *Set for success*. London: HM Treasury.

Slaughter, S., & Leslie, L. L. (1997) *Academic capitalism: Politics, policies, and the entrepreneurial university.* Baltimore: John Hopkins University Press.

Steyart, C., & Katz, J. (2004) 'Reclaiming the space of entrepreneurship in society: Geographical, discursive and social dimensions.' *Entrepreneurship and Regional Development*, 16 (3): 179–196.

Su, Y., Zhu, Z., Chen, Z., Jin, Y., Wang, T., Lin, C. T., & Xu, D. (2021) 'Factors influencing entrepreneurial intention of University students in China: Integrating the perceived University support and theory of planned behavior.' *Sustainability*, 13 (8): 4519.

Swail, J., Down, S., & Kautonen, T. (2014) 'Examining the effect of "entre-tainment" as a cultural influence on entrepreneurial intentions.' *International Small Business Journal*, 32 (8): 859–875.

Terry D. J., Hogg M. A., & White K. M. (1999) The theory of planned behaviour: self-identity, social identity and group norms. *British Journal of Social Psychology*. 38 (Pt 3): 225–244.

Turulja, L. (2020) 'Entrepreneurial intention of students in Bosnia and Herzegovina: What type of support matters?' *Economic Research*, 33 (1): 2713–2732.

Usher, R. (2002) 'A diversity of doctorates: Fitness for the knowledge economy?' *Research and Development*, 21: 143–153.

UUK [Universities UK] (2023) 'How do universities support the creation of new businesses': https://www.universitiesuk.ac.uk/latest/insights-and-analysis/how-do-universities-support-creation-new Last accessed 4/11/24

VITAE (2012) *Enterprise lens on the vitae researcher development framework*. Cambridge: Careers Research and Advisory Centre (CRAC) Limited. See: https://www.vitae.ac.uk/vitae-publications/rdf-related/enterprise-lens-on-the-vitae-researcher-development-framework-rdf-apr-2012.pdf/@@download/file/Enterprise-Lens-on-the-Vitae-Researcher-Development-Framework-RDF-Apr-2012.pdf

Walsh, E., Anders, K., & Hancock, S. (2012) 'Understanding attitude and environment: The essentials for developing creativity in STEM researchers.' *International Journal for Researcher Development*, 4 (1): 19–38.

Walsh, E., Hargreaves, C., Hilleman-Delaney, U., & Li, J. (2015) 'Doctoral researchers' views on entrepreneurship: Ranging from "a responsibility to improve the future" to "a dirty word".' *Studies in Higher Education*, 40 (5): 775–790.
Ylijoki, O. H. (2003) 'Entangled in academic capitalism? A case-study on changing ideals and practices of university research.' *Higher Education*, 45: 307–335.
Zhang, P., Wang, D., & Owen, C. (2015) 'A study of entrepreneurial intention of University students.' *Entrepreneurship Research Journal*, 5 (1): 61–82.

3 Reasons for a reassessment

Simon Bridge

Introduction

It is not uncommon for the knowledge supposedly gained about a subject to become accepted over time, passed on and treated as established fact – and Galbraith referred to such understanding as the conventional wisdom:

> Economic and social behavior are complex, and to comprehend their character is mentally tiring. Therefore we adhere, as though to a raft, to those ideas which represent our understanding. . . . It will be convenient to have a name for the ideas which are esteemed at any time for their acceptability, and it should be a term that emphasizes this predictability. I shall refer to these ideas henceforth as the conventional wisdom.
>
> (Galbraith, 1958)

The aim of this chapter is to present the case for reassessing the 'conventional wisdom' that seems to have evolved about the area of human endeavour variously referred to as enterprise, entrepreneurship and/or small business. It does this first by explaining why it is reasonable to expect that such established 'knowledge' might be questionable; then, by examining what appears to be the conventional wisdom, suggesting what might be its basis and why it would seem to be misguided; and finally by presenting different perspectives which would appear to be justified and which might form the basis for a new paradigm of understanding.

Enterprise as a subject of official interest is relatively new. While there appears to have been some academic exploration as early as the 1930s and a few early small business support initiatives were launched from the 1960s onwards, significant interest only began to develop in the 1980s. In many countries unemployment had started to rise alarmingly in the 1970s – so Birch's finding, released in 1979, that it was small businesses which created net new jobs attracted attention, especially in government circles. That interest was supported by budgets, which in turn stimulated an enterprise industry manifest, for instance, in enterprise policies and agencies which then sought guidance about the enterprise and

DOI: 10.4324/9781003324737-3

small businesses they wanted to encourage. This stimulated a search for relevant knowledge and consequently, as Gibb put it:

> Since the 1980s and particularly into the 1990s there has been an explosion of research into entrepreneurship and the small and medium enterprise. This is reflected in a substantial growth in both the academic literature and in the grey literature of the press, journals and consultant reports . . . [and] the growth in "knowledge" has been exponential.
>
> (Gibb, 2000)

This chapter suggests that this 'knowledge' has now become the 'conventional wisdom' informing areas of application such as promotional programmes and enterprise education – but that does not mean that it is correct. Already a number of commentators have pointed out aspects of observed behaviour which appear not to conform to the accepted thinking and those policies apparently influenced by it appear not to have worked (as described, for example, in Chapter 16 of Bridge and O'Neil, 2018). Indeed, in the same paragraph as the quote above, Gibb added:

> Despite the increase in academic knowledge, indeed perhaps because of it, there has been a growth of ignorance . . . and . . . a major manifestation of this growth of ignorance is the emergence of a number of outstanding "mythical concepts" and "myths" which are considerably influencing the establishment of policy priorities.
>
> (Gibb, 2000)

Why suspect knowledge might be expected

If the conventional wisdom about enterprise is suspect, it is not unique in thus being found wanting. It has been suggested that in (almost) every subject area, knowledge has a half-life: the period of time after which half of the current 'knowledge' will no longer be recognised as correct or useful. Perfect knowledge does not exist and, as the history of human understanding shows, improvement is always possible because, over time, problems are found stimulating new theories which prove to be better than the earlier thinking even though that may have been widely accepted and used.

This process of replacing old theories can be observed in the history of medicine – and an example is the once widespread and officially promoted practice of bleeding patients to cure a variety of ailments. This had been encouraged by the long-established 'humours' theory which held that disease was caused by an imbalance in the humours present in every body. Blood was one of those humours and so, as it was supposed to make you hot and wet, someone with a fever must have too much blood. Eventually discoveries such as that of the circulation of blood led to the end of bleeding as a cure, but still a legacy of the humours theory was that, because it had no room in it for things like germs, evidence that cleanliness in surgery led to better patient survival rates was discounted as having no rational explanation. Indeed medical understanding continues to develop and, even today, it is suggested that the half-life of knowledge in some branches of medicine is less than ten years.

As Popper explained in his exposition of the growth of scientific knowledge:

> The way in which knowledge progresses, and especially our scientific knowledge, is by unjustified (and unjustifiable) anticipations, by guesses, by tentative solutions to our problems, by conjectures. . . . But, once accepted, knowledge does not change easily not least because, as Descartes declared, we are clearly persuaded more by custom and example than by any certain knowledge.
>
> (Popper, 1989)

Indeed, as Popper added, if not checked: "erroneous beliefs may have an astonishing power to survive." Could that be the case with current 'enterprise' thinking?

Examining the enterprise case

If it is a science, enterprise (and/or entrepreneurship) is an applied one, like medicine. Also, as explained earlier, its understanding has only been developed relatively recently, not as the result of a long, slow and rigorous process but, as is often the case, relatively hastily assembled to satisfy a sudden demand. Therefore it must be expected that, if not checked and verified as Popper recommended, it too could be subject to error.

In support of this suggestion, there do appear to be examples of observed enterprise behaviour which do not fit the current paradigm – but are these just isolated 'exceptions which prove the rule' or are they instead frequent enough to disprove it? Here it is suggested that they do indeed justify questioning the conventional wisdom about enterprise – but what is that 'wisdom'? Unfortunately, but possibly not surprisingly, it is not recorded as such and the current enterprise understanding does not seem to be clearly stated – and therefore needs to be extracted and/or deduced by other means. The hypothesis explored in this chapter is that it is based on, or at least consistent with and/or explained by, a set of assumptions which, it can be shown, could have been made, do indeed appear to have been made, but yet which would also seem to be misconceived – such as the following:

- *Enterprise is a sub-set of business*: It is assumed that enterprise is a part of that aspect of activity often labelled 'business.'
- *Big-business-based thinking is applied*: Consequently, on the assumption that all businesses are essentially homogeneous, what is essentially big-business-based thinking is applied to enterprise.

- Therefore, for example, following supposed business thinking, the following are assumed:
  - *Profit maximisation*: It is assumed that the aim of any 'business' is to maximise its profits – and therefore it must want to grow.
  - *Deterministic thinking*: It is also assumed that a 'business' should prepare for the future by researching, forecasting and then planning based on those forecasts.
  - *Logical action*: It is further assumed that 'business' decisions will be based on logic not on social influence.

Assumption – enterprise is a sub-set of business

To support that hypothesis, the following section examines these assumptions to see both why they might have been made and whether there is evidence that they were made – and it also asks if they are correct. As indicated earlier, enterprise (and the term 'entrepreneurship' is sometimes substituted) was of particular interest because of its apparent connection to small businesses and their job-creation potential. So it would have seemed reasonable to look at it from a business perspective and see it as relating primarily to business – and there is evidence that this was done as teaching, that researching it has usually been assigned to business schools and that it has been promoted to business agencies. However, even in the 1980s, there were two main views on what enterprise was – as expounded in an education context, for instance, in an OECD monograph:

> There are, in effect, two definitions of, or approaches to, the word "enterprise" and the practice of it. One, which can be termed a "narrow" one, regards enterprise as business entrepreneurialism, and sees its promotion and development within education and training systems as an issue of curriculum development which enables young people to learn, usually on an experiential basis, about business start-up and management. The second approach, which can be termed the "broad" one, regards enterprise as a group of qualities and competencies that enable individuals, organisations, communities, societies and cultures to be flexible, creative, and adaptable in the face of, and as contributors to, rapid social and economic change.
>
> (OECD, 1989)

Assumption – big-business-based thinking

Although two perspectives of enterprise might thus have been acknowledged, it does seem that, at least in some quarters, it was the narrow business view which prevailed in official thinking and enterprise was viewed as a sub-set of business. Thus, business thinking was applied to it, but much received 'business' understanding is based essentially on the supposed practice of big business and so, as it is assumed that businesses are relatively homogeneous, big business thinking is applied subconsciously to new and small businesses. Thus, they are often treated as if they were small big businesses despite observations such as those of Penrose who had explained in 1959 that:

> The differences in the administrative structure of the very small and the very large firms are so great that in many ways it is hard to see that the two species are of the same genus. . . . We cannot define a caterpillar and then use the same definition for a butterfly.
>
> (Penrose, 1959)

Assumption – profit maximisation

Nevertheless, despite such comments and being in line with big-business-based thinking, it would have seemed reasonable to assume that businesses, including small ones, seek to maximise their profits, and this would have been reinforced by pronouncements like that of Friedman, who declared in 1970 that "the social responsibility of business is to increase its profits." Consequently it would have seemed reasonable to think that, in order to maximise profits, all businesses would have a growth imperative, and evidence of this view is reflected in comments such as this introduction to an article in a small business advice booklet: "One of the things that most, if not all, businesses have in common is a desire to grow and expand" (Gundy, 2008).

However, this is despite the findings of those who have actually looked at smaller businesses and their aims. For instance:

> Reijonen and Komppula reported in 2007 on research which found that the entrepreneurs studied: "measured their success primarily through customer satisfaction and respect. Other criteria related to job satisfaction, quality of products and making a reasonable living."
>
> Kay (2010) reported that: "The most profitable businesses are not the most profit-oriented" and paradoxically . . . "visionary companies make more money than . . . purely profit driven companies."
>
> Hurst and Pugsley (2011) used data from entrepreneurs sampled just before they started their businesses and found that: "Most small businesses have little desire to grow big" and, "at the time of formation, most small business owners do not want or expect their businesses to grow." If anything, "those who reported nonpecuniary benefits as a primary motivation had a higher probability of survival."
>
> In a survey of micro-businesses in Ireland, Bourke and Roper (2019) found that: "Over 80 per cent of the micro-business owners reported freedom to adapt my own approach to work" and "greater flexibility for personal and family life" as key personal motivators.

Assumption – deterministic thinking

Also, again possibly following big business practice, it seems to be assumed that in business the best way to reduce future uncertainty is by forecasting and planning. Humans, it has been pointed out, have a clear desire for forecasts and "the more unpredictable the world becomes, the more we seek out and rely on forecasts and predictions to determine what we should do" (Gimpl and Dakin, 1984). Also, possibly influenced by the example of Newton, a belief has arisen that with enough effort we should be able to discover the mechanism behind things and from that establish what will happen. As Voltaire is reported to have said: "no problem can withstand the assault of sustained thinking."

This seems to have led to a belief in determinism, and consequently businesses are expected to research, forecast and plan for the future and business plans are often advocated as if they were the essential tool for start-ups – despite many contrary views. For instance, Sarasvathy (2008), in her questioning of successful entrepreneurs, found that they generally distrusted market research and preferred an approach, not of planning and then trying to make that plan happen, but of evolving their enterprises depending on how things developed and what opportunities and/or partners were found – an approach which she labelled 'effectuation.' Indeed, as Bjerke put it:

> I am more than ever convinced that entrepreneurship cannot be planned to any major extent in advance and that planning even goes against the entrepreneurial idea.
>
> (Bjerke, 2007)

Assumption – logical actions

Conventional enterprise thinking seems to have followed traditional economic theory in assuming that people in their business activities act logically to maximise their benefit (which is often thought primarily to be financial gain). Consequently, despite the alternative views advocated by behavioural economics, the nature and use of social capital is rarely taught in business schools, and neither is its application included in business plans. Nevertheless, despite this, it is clear, at least to psychologists, that human beings are not as rational as sometimes supposed:

> My first exposure to the psychological assumptions of economics was in a report . . . in the early 1970s. Its first or second sentence stated that the agent of economic theory is rational and selfish, and that his tastes do not change. I found this list quite startling, because I had been professionally trained as a psychologist not to believe a word of it.
>
> (Kahneman, 2003)

Others also have pointed out that, despite presumptions of rational individual decision-making, human beings are instead very socially influenced, and this can often override or preclude rational analysis:

> The refusal to acknowledge human nature is like the Victorians' embarrassment about sex, only worse: it distorts our science and scholarship, our public discourse and our day-to-day lives.
>
> (Pinker, 2003)

> We do what we do because of other people and what they seem to be doing.
>
> (Earls, 2009)

> The notion that we are rational individuals who respond to information by making decisions consciously, consistently and independently is, at best, a very partial account of who we are. A wide body of scientific knowledge is now telling us what many have long intuitively sensed – humans are a fundamentally social species, formed through and for social interaction.
>
> (Rowson and McGilchrist, 2013)

Back to the hypothesis

The previous paragraphs have summarised not only why the suggested assumptions might have been made, but also the reasons for thinking that they were made. They may not have been consciously made and/or deliberately recorded as such, but it is suggested that together the suggested assumptions do provide a basis for, and/or an explanation of, received thinking. However, the analysis also indicates reasons for thinking that each of those assumptions is wrong or at least misconceived. Nevertheless, if it is credible to think that such assumptions, although misguided, do explain the conventional wisdom, or are at least consistent with it, then it too must be suspect.

Towards a new paradigm?

That raises the question of if, as indicated, the conventional wisdom is questionable, how it might be improved? Finding a problem with established understanding is not new, and Ferguson (1987) has suggested that, when problems are found with an aspect of our thinking, there are four ways by which it might be addressed:

By exception – assuming that the problem is an exception to the rule (not an exception which disproves the rule).

Incremental – changing so slowly as to be hardly noticeable.

Like a *pendulum* – abandoning all current thinking and going to the other extreme (but there might be some good parts of current thinking and any new thinking is unlikely to be complete and without its own faults).

Paradigm change – consciously developing a new way of thinking.

She also adds that "[c]hange by exception, incremental change, and pendulum change stop short of transformation. The brain cannot deal with conflicting information unless it can integrate it . . . [and] harmonize the ideas into a powerful synthesis. That is paradigm change."

It might be tempting to recognise that parts of the current thinking are wrong and to try to change those individual misconceptions piecemeal – but that will not be helpful if the foundations for that thinking are at fault and they remain unaltered. Here it is suggested that the many exceptions to established enterprise thinking do disprove the rule and that incremental change would take a long time during which the conventional wisdom would continue to mislead. However, not all the current thinking is wrong and there is no contrary foundation worked out and ready to down-load. So, that indicates that a pendulum change would not be appropriate and instead paradigm transformation is needed.

However, knowing that a new paradigm is needed does not immediately indicate everything which it might include, but it does indicate the need to look for better insights – and that search might be assisted by seeing the subject from different perspectives. Just as in medicine, ending the practice of bleeding to cure fevers was not on its own enough to end the legacy of the humours theory and a new perspective on how illnesses might be transmitted was necessary for the practices advocated by people like Semmelweis, Pasteur and Lister to become the accepted way to reduce infections. Therefore, the following thoughts are offered to suggest possible aspects of an alternative perspective which might come from questioning the assumptions indicated. Of course there are many examples that might be raised, but these are offered as some of the possible implications of the current thinking and/or the changes that might therefore be considered.

Confusing language. One of the problems encountered when studying enterprise thinking is the language used. Often the dialogue can include words which can have more than one meaning and do not help to improve understanding when it is not clear which meaning is intended or understood. An example is the two different interpretations of the word 'enterprise' which are highlighted earlier in this chapter but other words which may be misunderstood include:

Entrepreneurship. There is no single, widely accepted definition of 'entrepreneurship': for instance, Gartner in 1988 was able to present a summary of 29 views on entrepreneurs, 21 of which included some sort of a definition. In some circles, possibly with an element of wishful thinking, 'entrepreneurship' appears to refer to the activity of starting or growing a business (or even just a high-growth one), whereas others interpret it more widely as being enterprising/entrepreneurial. Because of the potential confusion, Bridge (2017) has even suggested that the use of the word should be dropped.

Business. Possibly because it is a convenient way to interpret the available data, anyone who is self-employed is sometimes said to have a business although such an occupational endeavour has very little in common with a large, shareholder-driven corporation. But, because nevertheless they are both often described as businesses, it can lead to a false assumption that they are very similar.

What is enterprise?

If the assumption that enterprise is a sub-set of business is not helpful, then what is enterprise? This question is especially relevant for enterprise (or 'entrepreneurship') education where observers (such as Hytti and Kuopusjärvi, 2004; Hannon, 2005) have reported different aims. This might be encompassed in Mitra's (2016) categorisation of courses as being about, for, through or with entrepreneurship which might be summarised as:

About: awareness of the significant and nature of enterprise and entrepreneurship and a focus on knowledge specific to new firm formation or innovation.
For: encouraging the development of new business ventures.
Through: student-centred experimental and action learning.
With: added-value entrepreneurship supplementing a wide range of disciplines.

There are many other observations about this which could also be added but, nevertheless, is the key issue here the distinction that has been made between what is labelled as 'for' and 'through': between learning how to be an entrepreneur and start a business and learning how to be entrepreneurial and/or enterprising in any field of endeavour? Unfortunately it would appear to have been convenient often to conflate those two things as if they were different aspects of the same activity. Consequently, even when it is claimed that a course is about being enterprising/entrepreneurial, often it is still linked to business applications – as, for example, in this description apparently appealing across disciplines but still stressing prototyping and business modelling as key components:

> At its core, entrepreneurship education is boundary spanning. The tools of an entrepreneurship education (eg prototyping, business modelling, ideation, effectuation, etc.) are interdisciplinary and designed to engage learners from across the college campus and beyond. The lessons of entrepreneurship education are acquired in a problem-centric environment where learners from diverse disciplines combine resources to tackle specific problems and derive unique solutions that alone they may struggle to accomplish.
>
> (USASBE, 2022)

Linking different interpretations of enterprise in this way has the benefit of implying both that, being business linked, all forms of enterprise education have a direct economic benefit and so can deliver economic policy aims, and that they can be taught using the same syllabus. But is that correct? Instead, if they were clearly separated, what could and/or should be taught for each of them?

There is of course sometimes a link between them in that some people who are enterprising want to start businesses, but many people apply their enterprise in other ways – for instance, as enterprising explorers, artists, theatre directors or care workers – and they don't need to learn the mechanics of starting a business to do that. It is also the case that some businesses are started by not very enterprising people – for instance, when it is the usual way to practice the trade they happen to have learnt. Acknowledging that being enterprising and starting a business are different things would allow a fresh perspective to be taken: considering, for instance, how being enterprising for any aspect of life should be taught if it is not essentially conflated with the process of starting a business.

The motivation to start a business

That does not mean that starting a business should be ignored. It is still a relevant activity for many people and policy makers still want to encourage it. But it is relevant for this to consider why someone would be inclined to start a business. Traditional policy thinking appears to assume that, if support is provided to assist business start-up, people will do it. This would explain the approach of the UK's Small Business Service (SBS, 2003) which, in order to increase the number of entrepreneurs, adopted the aim of "making the UK the best place in the world to start or grow a business." However, as the proverb puts it: "you can lead a horse to water but you cannot make it drink" and providing start-up assistance does not appear to have led to an increase in start-up rates (Bridge and O'Neill, 2018, p. 336). It is therefore interesting that, early in 2022, a press release from the UK's Enterprise Research Centre reported a finding that "more than 70% of Britons believe it is easy to start a business in the UK," but, despite this, "less [sic] than one in ten has any intention of doing so" (ERC, 2022).

What does influence people's intentions? What, for instance, might people perceive to be the pros and cons of attempting business start-up – and therefore the triggers to their intentions which policy might seek to influence? The book *The Rainforest* (Hwang and Horowitt, 2012) with its analysis of Silicon Valley suggests an interesting comparison:

The traditional perspective is likely to be:

Pros: You might make more money. (But, while some people do make money this way, the evidence suggests that on average self-employed people earn less than their comparable employed peers.)

Cons: It requires a considerable investment of time, effort and stress. It is also likely to mean sacrificing, not only any existing career investment and future prospects, but also the social standing and respect that comes being seen to be in a recognised profession.

Whereas the Silicon Valley perception is more likely to be:

Pros: It can earn you money but it might also satisfy a sense of adventure, opportunity, discovery, independence and/or passion. It has social approval and often the joy of sharing/successful teamwork. And it can leave a legacy for others.

Cons: It does require time and effort and it involves exposing yourself and your ideas to new contacts (but this can be compensated by making new friends). It might lead to 'failure' (but you could regret not trying and set back is often mitigated by social support.

This suggests that recognising that human intentions are often more influenced by social pressures than by the supposed economic logic of a situation might provide a better perspective from which to develop an appropriate policy for encouraging and/or supporting small business start-ups.

The aims of those with a business – and consequent business behaviour

What about those people who already have a business – what are their aims? Often programmes designed to help businesses are labelled 'growth' programmes as if growth is what most business owners want. A focus on growth clearly conforms to an assumption that businesses aim primarily to make money and therefore want to grow – but what if for many businesses success is something different? What implications does that have for understanding business behaviour?

Businesses themselves don't have aims – but their owners do. It is the people who own and/or run them who have aims and try to achieve them through their businesses. Thus, the enterprise is not the aim but, as has been observed: "an enterprise is a goal-achievement device" (Hunter, 2007). So why do people operate businesses and what are their aims/goals? Is personal wealth (and therefore business growth) actually only a minority or subordinate aim, as some research suggests, and does significant growth tend to shorten the life of a business – as West indicates in his book *Scale* (2017)? In reality, are people's aims often plural and actually very heterogeneous – for example, to sustain a living and/or a lifestyle, to enjoy it and or gain fulfilment, to use/practice/develop a skill/trade/ability, to explore an idea, to follow a family tradition, to fulfil a community need or to make a contribution?

Policy seeks growth and businesses are often assumed to want growth – but is that like the medical establishment preaching bleeding as a cure and doctors believing it was the correct treatment. Suppose, however, the aim was to foster business success. What would that mean for those seeking to help businesses, and their owners? This perspective could also lead to a better understanding of business behaviour and a recognition that business owners who do not take apparent opportunities to grow their businesses are not necessarily managing them badly.

Determinism or an uncertain future

Conventional business wisdom may emphasise the need to research and forecast and to plan on that basis, but history shows us that often the future does not conform to predictions. Therefore, instead of thinking that, with the right application, the business future can reliably be determined, how can and/or should people with businesses prepare instead for uncertainty? Planning is not without its uses, and it should be one of the tools in the business toolkit, but there should be others. Instead of recommending that future uncertainty can be reduced by careful research, forecasting and planning, would a perspective based on accepting uncertainty indicate the applicability of approaches such as effectuation (Sarasvathy, 2008 – mentioned earlier) and also:

Trial and error. The process commonly known as 'trial and error' (although if correctly applied it is not 'error') is acknowledged to be a good way to proceed when the only practical way to assesses the efficacy of an idea (eg for a product or service) is to try it in a real setting and observe the results. Then, if it does not work as hoped, that can be investigated and ways sought to improve the offering before testing it again. As Harford observes:

Whether we like it or not, trial and error is a tremendously powerful process for solving problems in a complex world, while expert leadership is not.

(Harford, 2011)

In the context of trial and error the word 'failure' can be misunderstood. Suppose someone does something which does not work – but with reasonable prior reconnaissance and/or thought they should have foreseen that outcome, that is failure. However, another sort of failure occurs when trying something is the only, or at least the most practical, way to see if it does work. If it does not, that can be labelled 'failure,' but it is actually a successful experiment. Does a belief in determinism lead to the stigmatization of 'failure' because all failure is assumed to be the first sort – whereas, sometimes, risking the second sort is the best way to make progress? Thus, while the first sort of failure is bad, the second may often be the result of good practice.

Lean start-up. Lean start-up is a version of trial and error which advocates market testing a product as early as possible, as customer reactions are often not predictable and so the sooner corrections can be made the less resource will be wasted on things that will later need to be corrected. As the saying goes: "fail early, fail cheap."

Exploration. Bridge and Hegarty (2013) suggest that new ventures have more in common with explorers than with established big businesses – and suggest 10 exploration principles to guide them.

Ready-fire-aim. Most people will have heard the expression 'ready-aim-fire' which is applicable for rifle shooting when, once the trigger is squeezed, the shooter has no further control over the bullet. However, life is much more like a guided missile which, after preparation, once under way can be steered in flight. Therefore ready-fire-aim is often the better course to follow.

Antifragility. Taleb (2013) invented the word 'antifragile' for the opposite of fragile. This is not, he suggests, 'robust' because if something fragile is handled roughly it is liable to be damaged and something robust is liable to be unchanged – and what he wanted was a label for something which, when handled roughly, becomes better and/or stronger as a result. However, that will only happen from exposure to adverse conditions, rather than trying to hide from them, and the wherewithal to learn from their effects and apply that learning.

Using social capital

It is suggested earlier that people's intentions may be influenced more by social encouragement than institutional support. The concept of social capital recognises this and other benefits that can be obtained from social connections – but has the tendency to ignore social influence on business led to this being neglected? As Schuller *et al.* (2000) have commented, social capital is relatively immature as a concept and it "has several adolescent characteristics: it is neither tidy nor mature; it can be abused, analytically and politically; its future is unpredictable" but, they add, "it offers much promise."

The word 'social' implies that it comes from social connections, but the word 'capital' suggests that, like financial capital, social capital needs to be accumulated for it to be available for use. In considering its nature and use, might Coleman's (1990) observations be a helpful starting point as he suggested that social capital 'is not a single entity, but a variety of different entities having two characteristics in common: They all consist of some aspect of social structure, and they facilitate certain actions of individuals who are within the structure.' He also suggested (1988) that its different applications or effects include accessing relevant information channels, developing trust and mutual obligations and establishing norms of behaviour and sanctions for transgressing them.

Conclusion

This chapter suggests that there are good reasons to reassess our thinking about enterprise. The analysis explores and supports the hypothesis that there is a conventional wisdom about enterprise which can be explained by a set of assumptions which do seem to have been made but which appear to be misguided. If the supposed knowledge upon which we are accustomed to rely is indeed based on such problematic foundations, this indicates that, if enterprise is to be better understood and polices to promote it are to be effective, a new paradigm is needed – but not precisely what that could be. However, a start might be made by exploring some of the different perspectives revealed by questioning the suggested assumptions. If they provide a better understanding of enterprise and could assist efforts to encourage, to help and/or to teach it, should they be examined further? (For more analysis of this, see Bridge, 2022.)

References

Birch D. L. (1979), *The Job Generation Process*, unpublished report prepared for the Economic Development Administration (Cambridge, MA: MIT Program on Neighborhood and Regional Change)

Bjerke B. (2007), *Understanding Entrepreneurship* (Cheltenham: Edward Elgar) p. xiii

Bourke J. and Roper S. (2019), *Micro-Businesses in Ireland: From Ambition to Innovation* (Cork: Cork University Business School, University College, Cork)

Bridge S. (2017), *The Search for Entrepreneurship: Finding More Questions Than Answers* (Abingdon: Routledge)

Bridge S. (2022), *The Persistence of Entrepreneurship Myths: Reclaiming Enterprise* (Abingdon: Routledge)

Bridge S. and Hegarty C. (2013), *Beyond the Business Plan – 10 Principles for New Venture Explorers* (Basingstoke: Palgrave Macmillan)

Bridge S. and O'NeillK. (2018), *Understanding Enterprise, Entrepreneurs and Small Business* (London: Palgrave)

Coleman J. S. (1988), 'Social Capital in the Creation of Human Capital', *American Journal of Sociology*, Vol. 94 Supplement, pp. S102–S104.

Coleman J. S. (1990), *Foundations of Social Theory* (Cambridge, MA: Belknap Press of Harvard University Press) p. 302

Earls M. (2009), *Herd: How to Change Mass Behaviour by Harnessing Our True Nature* (Chichester, UK: John Wiley & Sons Ltd)

ERC (2022), Enterprise Research Centre, Press release, 10 February 2022.

Ferguson M. (1987), *The Aquarian Conspiracy* (Los Angeles: J P Tarcher Inc)

Friedman M. (1970), 'The Social Responsibility of a Business is to Increase Its Profits', *The New York Times Magazine*, 13 September

Galbraith J. K. (1958), *The Affluent Society*, first published in USA 1958 (4th edition, London: Penguin, 1991)

Gartner W. B. (1988), '"Who Is an Entrepreneur?" Is the Wrong Question', *American Journal of Small Business*, Vol. 12, Issue 4, pp. 11–32

Gibb A. A. (2000), 'SME Policy, Academic Research and the Growth of Ignorance, Mythical Concepts, Myths, Assumptions, Rituals and Confusions', *International Small Business Journal*, Vol. 18, Issue 3, pp. 13–35

Gimpl M. L. and Dakin S.R. (1984), 'Management and Magic', *California Management Review*, Vol. XXVII, No. 1, Fall, pp. 125–136

Gundy A. (2008), *Business Bite* (Belfast: Ulster Bank)

Hannon P. (2005), 'Philosophies of Enterprise and Entrepreneurship Education and the Challenges for Higher Education in the UK', *International Journal of Entrepreneurship and Innovation*, Vol. 6, No. 2, pp. 105–114

Harford T. (2011), *Adapt: Why Success Always Starts with Failure* (London: Little, Brown)

Hunter L. (2007), 'Speaking at University of Ulster Seminar on 'Developing a Strategy and vision for Social Entrepreneurship', 10 September

Hurst E. and Pugsley B.W. (2011), 'What Do Small Businesses Do', Brookings Papers on Economic Activity, Fall

Hwang V. and Horowitt G. (2012), *The Rainforest: The Secret to Building the Next Silicon Valley* (Los Altos Hills, CA: Regenwald)

Hytti U. and Kuopusjärvi P. (2004), 'Three Perspectives to Evaluating Entrepreneurship Education: Evaluators, Programme Promoters and Policy Makers', paper presented at the efmd 34th EISB Conference, Turku

Kahneman D. (2003), 'A Psychological Perspective on Economics', *American Economic Review*, Vol. 93, No. 2, May, pp. 162–168

Kay J. (2010), *Obliquity* (London: Profile Books)

Mitra J. (2016), 'Holistic Experimentation for Emergence: A Creative Approach to Post-graduate Entrepreneurship Education and Training', *Industry and Higher Education*, Vol. 31, No. 1, pp. 34–50

OECD (1989), 'Towards an "Enterprising" Culture – A Challenge for Education and Training', *OECD/CERI Educational Monograph,* No. 4, pp. 6–7

Penrose E.T. (1959), *The Theory of the Growth of the Firm* (Oxford: Basil Blackwell)

Pinker S. (2003), *The Blank Slate: The Modern Denial of Human Nature* (London: Penguin)

Popper, SirKarl (1989), *Conjectures and Refutations* (5th edition, London: Routledge)

Reijonen H. and Komppula R. (2007), 'Perception of Success and Its Effect on Small Firm Performance', *Journal of Small Business and Enterprise Development*, Vol. 14, No. 4, pp. 689–701

Rowson J. and McGilchrist I. (2013), *Divided Brain, Divided World* (London: RSA, February)

Sarasvathy S.D. (2008), *Effectuation: Elements of Entrepreneurial Experience* (Cheltenham: Edward Elgar)

SBS (2003), *Small Business Service, a Government Action Plan for Small Business, Making the UK the Best Place in the World to Start and Grow a Business* (London: Department of Trade and Industry)

Schuller T., Baron S. and Field J. (2000), 'Social Capital: A Review and Critique', in S. Baron, J. Field and T. Schuller (editors) *Social Capital: Critical Perspectives* (Oxford: Oxford University Press) p. 24 and p. 35

Taleb N. N. (2013), *Antifragile, Things that Gain from Disorder* (London: Penguin)

USASBE (2022), 'Letter from the Chair', in *The Liaison* (Newsletter, 24 September)

West G. (2017), *Scale* (London: Wiedenfield & Nicholson)

4 Context-enhanced social entrepreneurship

How social entrepreneurs leverage entrepreneurial ecosystems to address societal problems

Philip T. Roundy

Introduction

Social entrepreneurship is the pursuit of business opportunities that alleviate societal problems (Austin et al., 2006; Kickul and Lyons, 2020; Saebi et al., 2019). To address problems such as poverty, lack of access to healthcare, and animal abuse, social entrepreneurs create hybrid ventures that combine revenue-generating business models with innovative social impact models (Battilana and Lee, 2014; Lortie et al., 2022). The hybridity of their ventures means that social entrepreneurs must successfully balance the demands of a consumer-oriented market logic with a beneficiary-focused social mission (Doherty et al., 2014; Roundy and Bonnal, 2017). However, designing a financially viable business that generates value for consumers while simultaneously addressing societal issues is challenging, particularly for early-stage entrepreneurs (Sparviero, 2019).

A growing body of research examines social entrepreneurship as a contextual, place-based phenomenon (de Bruin et al., 2023; Lyons and Roundy, 2023; Ricket et al., 2023). Like all entrepreneurs, social entrepreneurs depend, in part, on their local entrepreneurial ecosystem (EE) – the "set of interdependent actors and factors that are governed in such a way that they enable productive entrepreneurship within a particular territory" (Stam, 2015: 1765). Social entrepreneurs are influenced by the availability of local resources and often address problems in their immediate communities (Bosma et al., 2016). Even if social entrepreneurs target problems that are not confined to their local communities, they often become aware of the problems through local exposure (Corner and Kearins, 2021). But despite the strong connections between social entrepreneurship and local contexts, it is unclear how EEs enable social entrepreneurs to develop solutions to social problems.

This theoretical and practical void in the understanding of social entrepreneurship and entrepreneurial ecosystems led to the overarching question guiding this chapter: *how do entrepreneurs leverage their EEs to engage in social*

DOI: 10.4324/9781003324737-4

entrepreneurship? I addressed this question through an inductive, qualitative case study of social entrepreneurs in Austin, Texas (USA). Austin is one of the most vibrant EEs in the United States (Stephens et al., 2019). Austin's "social entrepreneurship ecosystem" (i.e., the sub-EE focused on supporting social entrepreneurs) is particularly fertile, and the city has even aspired to be the "social innovation capital of the world" (Loeb, 2018). Thus, the Austin EE represents an especially rich context to examine the interface of social entrepreneurship and entrepreneurial ecosystems.

The findings from the case study revealed how entrepreneurs leveraged their local startup community to acquire resources. By interacting with other EE participants, social entrepreneurs learned from their ecosystem how to create and operate their ventures. Specifically, social entrepreneurs gained knowledge about how to create an effective social impact model, how to incorporate their ventures and navigate financial issues, and how to communicate with diverse stakeholders. Insights from the study produced a framework of context-enhanced social entrepreneurship.

The study presented in this chapter contributes to research at the intersection of social entrepreneurship and entrepreneurial contexts. The purpose of the study was to open the "black box" of social entrepreneurs' interactions with their EEs (Guéneau et al., 2023) by identifying precisely how social entrepreneurs' local contexts influence and interact with specific aspects of the social entrepreneurship process. The findings respond to recent calls to tease apart the mechanisms through which the structural characteristics of EEs influence entrepreneurs (Wurth et al., 2022) and, particularly, entrepreneurs focused on sustainable development and social problems (Volkmann et al., 2021). Second, by drawing attention to the role of local contexts in social entrepreneurship, the findings identify one potential source of the resources that entrepreneurs need to create effective solutions to social problems: entrepreneurial ecosystems. The findings also contribute by exploring a previously unexamined pathway through which the micro-level activities of social entrepreneurs (i.e., entrepreneurs' processes, behaviors, and decisions) interact with the contextual, macro-level factors in their external environments. Finally, the study contributes to the burgeoning stream of research focused on social entrepreneurs and their unique EE dynamics (cf. de Bruin et al., 2023; Guerrero and Lira, 2023; Lyons and Roundy, 2023) by revealing the points of connection between social entrepreneurs' distinct activities (e.g., learning from beneficiaries, designing social impact models) and their local communities.

The remainder of the chapter proceeds as follows. In the next section, I describe the study's context and case study methodology. I then present the main findings about how social entrepreneurs leverage their local EEs. Finally, I conclude the chapter with a discussion of the theoretical and practical contributions to research at the intersection of social entrepreneurship and entrepreneurial contexts.

Research methodology

To investigate how social entrepreneurs interact with their EEs and induce an empirically grounded framework that explains how the phenomenon unfolds, this study analyzed social entrepreneurs in a specific context: the Austin, Texas EE in the southwestern United States. Austin was selected for the case study because the city is home to a large number of social entrepreneurs and has an especially vibrant general EE focused on conventional (non-social) entrepreneurship as well as a thriving social entrepreneurship sub-ecosystem. Thus, the city represented an ideal setting that was likely to produce highly "revelatory" insights about the focal phenomenon (Ozcan et al., 2017).

An inductive design that focused on process dynamics (Langley, 1999) guided the methodology because the lack of research on how social entrepreneurs leverage their EEs suggested that theory-building, rather than theory-testing, was appropriate (Eisenhardt et al., 2016). An inductive design was also appropriate for studying EE dynamics, which involve social interactions, complex causal chains, feedback loops, temporal and discursive forces, and multiple levels of analysis (Roundy et al., 2018). A qualitative approach was selected because the richness, granularity, and flexibility of qualitative data make it well-suited for teasing apart how multifaceted contextual forces influence entrepreneurship (Graebner et al., 2012).

Data collection followed a two-pronged approach, primarily focused on in-depth, semi-structured interviews with EE participants and also utilizing archival data. To increase the breadth of insights, informants were selected from a range of EE roles including social entrepreneurs (n = 20), investors (traditional and impact-focused; n = 6), and ancillary EE participants (n = 4) (e.g., attorneys, university staff, support organization members focused on social entrepreneurship). Entrepreneurs were considered "social entrepreneurs" if they were creating or operating hybrid ventures (i.e., ventures that pursued business revenue and had an explicit social mission; Battilana and Lee, 2014). Informants were identified through snowball and purposive sampling and, when possible, were selected to gain multiple perspectives from the same venture (e.g., entrepreneurs, employees, investors), which enabled triangulating claims across individuals. In total, 31 interviews with 30 informants formed the primary empirical base. To supplement the interviews, archival data was gathered from sources including news outlets, magazines, and venture websites.

The study began as an open-ended exploration of how social entrepreneurs pursue resources. Although it was not identified as an important meta-theme at the outset, how social entrepreneurs leveraged their EEs and, specifically, how (and what) they learn from their EEs emerged as a central theme in the data. The analytic approach was partly emergent and partly planned and involved iterating between the raw data, emerging patterns, and extant theory on social entrepreneurship and EEs. To guide the initial coding, a sensitizing concept was used:

"EE interactions" – instances of social entrepreneurs interacting with the EE. To increase analytical rigor, data were coded and analyzed using the "Gioia" method for grounded theorizing (Gehman et al., 2018). During the initial pass through the data, first-order concepts (codes) were identified. Specifically, data was coded for "learning events": EE interactions through which social entrepreneurs described to have changed their thinking. After coding, second-order concepts (themes) were formed by abstracting from the first-order concepts. As common themes emerged, data were re-coded and the consistency of themes was assessed within and across informants using the "constant comparison and contrast" approach (Miles and Huberman, 1994). The goal was to identify "commonalities, key themes, and patterns" and to account for "contrasts and irregularities" (Andresen et al., 2014: 716). Finally, based on their similarity, themes were grouped into aggregate dimensions. The findings, described next, emerged from an iterative process of analyzing the data, returning to the literature, and revising the explanations for the observed patterns.

Findings

Social entrepreneurs described leveraging the Austin entrepreneurial ecosystem (hereafter "the EE") for resources commonly needed during the entrepreneurship process and that are also needed by conventional (non-social) entrepreneurs. For instance, social entrepreneurs used the EE to identify co-founders (SE1, SE4), early employees (SE2), board members (SE4), initial customers (SE3), and business partners (SE4, SE6). However, social entrepreneurs also leveraged the EE to acquire specialized resources unique to the social entrepreneurship process. In particular, social entrepreneurs frequently described leveraging the EE for specific knowledge (described next), which they gained by learning during ecosystem interactions.

Entrepreneurial ecosystems as learning contexts for social entrepreneurs

A unique challenge in social entrepreneurship, representing a key issue that entrepreneurs must navigate, is balancing business and social missions – that is, creating financially viable businesses while pursuing social impact (Muñoz and Kimmitt, 2019). In many social ventures, tension exists between a business (or financial) logic, focused on profit-maximization, efficiency, cost-minimization, competition, and value capture, and a social impact logic, focused on community, value creation, and cooperation (Roundy and Bonnal, 2017). Social entrepreneurs often struggle to strike a balance between the activities associated with these two logics, which involve developing products that create economic value for customers while creating social value for beneficiaries.

Social entrepreneurs explained that they leveraged their ecosystems to learn how to navigate this tension. For instance, an entrepreneur described how an experience at a social entrepreneurship pitch competition reinforced his belief in the ability of social entrepreneurship to combine business and social missions.

> [I]t doesn't have to be a choice now. You don't have to choose between making money . . . or having a great mission. You can do both. You can make money and have a mission. And that's really where I put [the social venture].
>
> (SE9)

Social entrepreneurs learn from interacting with their EE in different ways. Some social entrepreneurs took advantage of opportunities to learn from sub-contexts within the EE that are designed to bring together social entrepreneurs, such as the pitch competition highlighted in the previous quotation. Another entrepreneur emphasized her participation in a social entrepreneurship co-working space. She described the co-working space as:

> a physical space for likeminded individuals that are involved in non-profits and social ventures to work [together] and think and imagine and communicate . . . there's no reason for us not to all talk to each other and I guess learn from each other . . . that's the goal of the space.
>
> (SE4)

In addition to co-locating in physical proximity to other social entrepreneurs, entrepreneurs pursued less formal pathways to learning. For example, an entrepreneur described joining an informal consortium that operated like an industry association for social entrepreneurs in the EE.

> In our case, we've taken it a little bit further, and we've cofounded a group called ["Change Our City"]. And we are a coalition of for-benefit businesses. There are currently eight of us in Austin.
>
> (SE9)

Through formal organizational structures, like the social entrepreneurship co-working space, and through less formal arrangements, like the social entrepreneurship industry association, it was common for social entrepreneurs to describe being aware of and learning from other social entrepreneurs in the EE. For instance, a social entrepreneur who worked to find employment for international refugees who had relocated to the city described communicating with several similar social ventures in the EE.

> We talked with [other social ventures] quite a bit about how they [honed their mission] . . . And we've kind of made decisions based on what other groups are doing here in town.
>
> (SE14)

Yet, effectively balancing business and social missions is challenging. SEs reported having to learn from fellow ecosystem participants how to resolve three key issues related to (1) creating a social impact model, (2) incorporating their ventures and pursuing early-stage financing, and (3) communicating with diverse stakeholders. In the sections that follow, I describe the knowledge associated with each of these aspects of social entrepreneurship and how entrepreneurs acquired this knowledge by learning from their ecosystems.

Learning to create an effective social impact model

Social entrepreneurship involves recognizing social problems and identifying innovative potential solutions. Social entrepreneurs reported that they often discover social problems by interacting with local community members. By observing the activities in their ecosystem, entrepreneurs realized that there is not an organization already targeting the social problem they sought to address (e.g., SE4). For example, an entrepreneur explained how interacting with a group in the EE led to the realization that no one was addressing a particular problem: women not having access to construction skills.

> [I]t was sort of existential, I was like "what am I doing, what do I want to do, what do I love?" And so, I started volunteering for local organizations and looking at organizations that were doing design and building projects. And so I went to [a local nonprofit association], their meeting. . . . and I just was there to volunteer and learning about different building projects that were happening. And [I asked] the co-director, which was [co-founder] at the time, I just kind of asked the group, is there a women in construction group here?
>
> (SE4)

After learning that such a group did not exist in the city, the entrepreneur created her venture targeting this problem. Another social entrepreneur, who created a venture focused on environmental sustainability, described joining and ultimately becoming the president of a local professional association that focused on the same cause as his venture.

> I myself wanted to learn more about what other people were doing in that space [resource conservation] to be more efficient, leave a smaller footprint, the whole deal. So I joined that organization, [the] professional chapter when it formed . . . and have been active on the board until very recently.
>
> (SE1)

Another social entrepreneur, who created a venture that provided English-language skills to immigrants so they could more easily find employment, described how local interactions made her aware of this issue.

> I was working as a waitress at [local restaurant], after having come back from teaching in Guatemala. . . . I also saw the serious problems that having non-English speaking or limited English-speaking employees presented for employers. So I was sympathetic to both sides. At the same time, I was at the [local university]. . . . So one day I was wandering around the restaurant thinking to myself, how could I help these coworkers of mine, who are the hardest workers I know, my immigrant coworkers? Who are the hardest workers I know, who want to learn English more than anything else, but cannot access traditional providers [of language skills]. They can't get there on the bus, because it takes too long, or they're balancing three jobs, or for the women, they're balancing a job, plus they're taking care of their grandmother, plus they're taking care of their kids.
>
> (SE17)

Interactions with EE participants provided general knowledge about the issues addressed by the social entrepreneurs (SE1, S9) and were opportunities to learn specific strategies for addressing social problems, such as design thinking (Elsbach and Stigliani, 2018). An entrepreneur described how she learned the design thinking process, which she later applied to her social venture, from a local organization in the ecosystem.

> [T]he design process that we learned at [local educational institution], but really any design process, should be based on solving a problem, and focused on solving not your own problem, but the problem of whoever you're serving. And so, in our case, as a social enterprise, it's the problem of our customers. . . . And so, we – anything that we do – we approach from . . . the perspective of how does that person need this to be? How do they want this to be? And so, all the decisions that we make, whether it's the design, whether it's a business decision, we always have that as a focus, and as a foundation [for our decisions].
>
> (SE6)

Social entrepreneurs also leveraged EE interactions to get feedback on their proposed solutions to social problems so that they could iterate and improve their initial ideas and develop better solutions to customers and beneficiaries. Social entrepreneurs described getting feedback on the early stages of impact models and early versions of products from EE participants, such as local customers (e.g., SE2) by piloting their ideas (e.g., SE5). For instance, one SE explains, "we had a big open house event where we just kind of presented the idea to the community and got their feedback and . . . developed a program with them" (SE4). A social entrepreneur who created a venture that addressed the issue of modern slavery described developing a more refined understanding of this problem through EE interactions.

> [W]e learned in our campaign . . . the "What's your response?" coaster campaign, that as many times as we kept saying it [that slavery is still a problem that] people still, [were] like, "Here? In Austin? Really?" But for me, doing this campaign led me to more and more research, more and more trying to understand like, "What does slavery look like today, now that it's illegal, as opposed to what it looked like when it wasn't . . . and very quickly, and very obviously it came that like the products that we buy, since production for most everything for our iPhone, for our tech, for our clothing, for food – coffee, tea, sugar, chocolate, olive oil – the hands of slaves touch all of it. And people who have been oppressed or treated unfairly, subjugated somehow, are paid minimal [wages] – not even minimal, but like pennies.
>
> (SE16)

Finally, social entrepreneurs described leveraging the EE to identify and learn about specific beneficiaries their social ventures could serve. For instance, a social entrepreneur whose business model involved generating funds for children in need described relying on local nonprofits to identify specific beneficiaries.

> I'm asking [local nonprofit] to find kids for us because they already have resources of kids that need help.
>
> (SE3)

Learning how to incorporate their social ventures and navigate financial issues

A second topic that entrepreneurs described leveraging the EE to learn about was the incorporation of their social ventures, which is a unique challenge because social entrepreneurs have a range of incorporation options: for-profit, nonprofit, and hybrid. Some entrepreneurs received direct guidance from local legal professionals. For instance, a tax attorney who has worked with numerous social entrepreneurs in the EE explained how he helps entrepreneurs who are unsure if they should incorporate as a for-profit, nonprofit, or hybrid.

> [T]he first time someone comes to me, I always try to get, before anything, I want to understand what they're trying to do. I want to see what their motivations are. . . . usually, they're able to tell me the purpose, but then I try to get an idea within that purpose what are their specific activities going to be. What is going to be their primary source of revenue? Are they going to be offering something [a product]? Are they trying to create a service or a good or something to be offered to the public? You just try to get, overall, what they're trying to do. . . . Sometimes, I can see they really are a for-profit, but they have a socially conscious awareness aspect of them. What we've found is . . . that

> socially conscious aspect of it is sometimes almost a marketing tool to differentiate them from other for-profits, but that doesn't make them a non-profit themselves. It makes them a for-profit with maybe a slightly lower profit line.
>
> (Support1)

Entrepreneurs often assume that because they are planning to operate a social venture, and because their ventures will have a strong social mission, they will be best served by a nonprofit legal structure. However, the tax attorney reported explaining to entrepreneurs that a nonprofit distinction has limitations.

> Most of the time when people come in to visit with me . . ., I spend some time advising them on how transparent non-profits are expected to be. Sometimes that causes them to rethink the whole issue.
>
> (Support1)

Social entrepreneurs described that other entrepreneurs and support organization managers also helped them work through the for-profit/not-for-profit issue. For instance, one entrepreneur described how conversations with other EE participants reinforced her decision to incorporate as a for-profit entity and refined her understanding of what it meant to be a business with a social mission.

> [We were asked] "Why aren't you a non-profit?" . . . And we kept having to push back on that and make a case for being a [for-profit] social enterprise. . . . we wanted to build something that can sustain itself, and that doesn't mean that we're spending our time applying for grants or putting out fundraising calls and all of that. . . . We wanted something that can keep itself going, and hopefully keep itself growing, while maintaining the focus on the social issues. Whenever we explain it to people who are familiar with all these terms [like "social enterprise"], we try to explain we are a business. We are for profit, but our profit goes into sustaining the business and sustaining the social mission.
>
> (SE6)

Another entrepreneur described leveraging her EE by utilizing a local community foundation and "borrowing" its 501(c)(3) nonprofit status while the entrepreneur figured out if she wanted to incorporate as a for-profit or nonprofit venture.

> And a lot of time people start a [social] venture and they don't know if it's going to be a nonprofit or for-profit, or what the mission of it's going to be, so [working with the community foundation] allows you to determine your identity on the fiscal end of things before you just put all that money into [getting 501(c)(3) status].
>
> (SE4)

Relatedly, another entrepreneur described how she learned from a team of volunteers associated with a local university about how to get her venture's 501(c)(3) status.

> I knew I wanted to do nonprofit. But they came along and like took me on as a project and worked with me for years to get my nonprofit status. Because it turned out the IRS didn't give us our 501c3 right away. It took us a year and a half to get it, because I already had a business involved. We just had [. . .] a team of attorneys, volunteer attorneys that helped us.
>
> (SE7)

Learning the advantages and disadvantages of pursuing professional investment. The decision to pursue professional investment is an issue related to how social entrepreneurs incorporate their ventures. Social entrepreneurs described learning the pros and cons of pursuing outside investment from their experiences in the EE and interactions with EE participants. Sometimes social entrepreneurs' ties to participants in the local ecosystem connected them to local investors.

> I have two advisors on board that are both very wealthy business[people] here in Austin. They've got a lot of connections to angels.
>
> (SE3)

Despite these connections, in some cases, entrepreneurs described learning that professional investment was not a good fit for their social ventures.

> [T]hat was one of the things I learned from the Internet company [prior venture] is I didn't really want to bring in outside funding if that took away our ability to run the shop the way we wanted to.
>
> (SE18)

> And so, that's where having the community . . . was really helpful, because I think we came to that conclusion from talking to – I don't know if you've talked to [another Austin social venture]? . . . They came out the year before us. And so, they have a bit more experience than we do. . . . and it was only [while] talking to them we realized their approach and their experience. At that point we realized, "Oh. It's okay not to have $1 million [in funding] just yet." [But] we were feeling that pressure. Sort of like, "Well, you've got a business. Now you've got to get funded." And we were feeling a little bit panicked about it, in the sense that we didn't really know how to pitch it. We didn't know how to put together the deck for it, because we didn't have the business model worked out, and there was a lot of stress around trying to force it into – or trying to come up with projections, plus fit the mold that it really wasn't ready to fit yet.
>
> (SE6)

Sometimes EE interactions do not result in social entrepreneurs acquiring investment but instead allow entrepreneurs to realize that they are not ready for outside investment.

> [EE participant/mentor] got them [investors] in touch with us. And so, we had a brief conversation with them, but both sides concluded that we have to be ready to take investment, and we're not really interested in that right now. We'd rather figure out our business model, figure out that we can make it work. And if we [didn't have] the influence from our communities here, we might have tried to be pushing [getting investment] without ever realizing that we didn't need to.
>
> (SE6)

A social entrepreneur explained that by interacting with investors he realized that most traditional angel investors in Austin were not a good fit for his venture.

> And unfortunately I'm not pitching a tech company so I can't be like, "we'll be like Google and it will be a 10X return" . . . . So it's interesting and particularly in Austin I find that challenging. [Investors say] "I love your story, I love why you founded the company, the market looks great, but I just don't get it and it's not enough of a return, like I can get in tech."
>
> (SE1)

Learning how to communicate with diverse stakeholders

A final type of knowledge that social entrepreneurs described learning from the EE involved how to communicate with their diverse stakeholders. The tension between the business and social sides of ventures often made it difficult for entrepreneurs to know how to effectively communicate with different groups, including customers, investors, and the media. However, entrepreneurs learned how to improve their communication through EE initiatives. For instance, one social entrepreneur explained learning how to strike the balance between emphasizing the business and social mission "sides" of the venture with customers, in part, by serving as a judge in a local sustainable business plan competition. Through these experiences, the entrepreneur learned that, for many customers, "at the end of the day it comes down to [communicating] how great the products are, why they work as well as they do, why we build [them]" (SE1).

Entrepreneurs explained that they often have difficulty knowing what aspect of their ventures – the social mission or business mission – to emphasize when pitching to investors. For instance, one social entrepreneur explained that in the early stages of her business when she pitched the venture she naturally focused on the social mission and communicated:

> "we're going to do something good but we're also going to do well [i.e., create social and business value] . . ." but what would come out of our mouth

> was [just] the "doing good" part. We weren't able to convince people that we would "do well" even though we had the financials.
>
> (SE2)

However, social entrepreneurs' interactions with both traditional investors (e.g., angels, VCs) and impact investors (i.e., investors who target ventures that generate both financial and social returns; cf. Agrawal and Hockerts, 2021) served as opportunities for them to learn how to operate, and communicate about, a socially responsible venture – or, in the words of one impact investor, to "successfully navigate that line between for-profit and a deep sense of stakeholder concern" (Impact Investor1). For example, a social entrepreneur described learning how to pitch a social venture to different groups by interacting with local investors.

> [The social mission] is a small part of the story but there again it's kind of audience dependent – depending on the investment community that I'm talking to. So if I'm pitching investors, a lot of those guys, particularly angel investors (and I'm not dealing with any institutional so VC or private equity), but angel investors, they want to know that the market is stable, that our product is what it is . . . that we have a management team that's able to pull this off, and that there is a big enough market to make whatever X return.
>
> (SE1)

An impact investor in the EE described another social entrepreneur who had a similar progression in how she learned to pitch her social venture.

> It was originally framed as a social venture . . . I don't think she [the founder] had any idea how it could be monetized but just had faith in the concept. [The evolution of her message is] something that has been a natural response to other investors, to clients, basically to the market. The market provides feedback to her vision, to her pitch. So she's responding to all of the questions people are asking.
>
> (Impact Investor1)

An investor provided his advice for social entrepreneurs in the EE who are trying to learn how to successfully navigate the business/social tension when communicating with traditional investors.

> [M]y advice to social entrepreneurs would be, try to figure out a way to make this an actual interesting business case that can be beneficial socially, but that can also make money [for investors], because that's the way – that's the easiest way you're going to get investors.
>
> (Traditional funder4_angel)

Beyond communicating with investors, social entrepreneurs also learned important lessons from other ecosystem members about how to communicate their social problems in ways that are not exploitative. For instance, the founder of an employment-based social venture described learning from another EE participant how to talk about her beneficiaries in an empowering way.

> She's a photographer. She works with Charity Water and Tom's Shoes . . . . She's here in Austin. . . . We've talked a lot about issues of representation and then we've had – you know, a lot of her pictures are very empowering and . . . trying to not show kids in Africa with flies on them but families that are doing a great job of providing for their families.
>
> (SE14)

Ultimately, interactions with EE participants helped social entrepreneurs understand their ventures (i.e., sensemaking) and how best to communicate their ventures and their missions to others (i.e., sensegiving). This dynamic is encapsulated in the following description of this learning process by a social entrepreneur.

> But still, it's hard, when it's your baby, to figure out what exactly [to emphasize] – so, for me, the learning was learning how fundraising works, learning, "What are they interested in seeing? What numbers do they need to see? How does it need to be positioned?" And then continually getting feedback and feedback and feedback, and practicing and fine-tuning and switching slides out and, "Which slide is more important? And gosh, I pitched to this group, and how did it work?"
>
> (SE20)

The main findings about how social entrepreneurs learn from their local contexts are summarized in the framework of "context-enhanced social entrepreneurship" (Figure 4.1).

Discussion

To explore how local contexts influence how entrepreneurs address social problems, this chapter described a study of social entrepreneurs and their local community. The framework of context-enhanced social entrepreneurship illustrates how social entrepreneurs, a unique entrepreneurial market actor, can address their resource limitations by leveraging their local communities for support. The findings emphasize a common strategy: acquiring resources from a local entrepreneurial ecosystem. The findings underscored a specific type of resource – knowledge about the social entrepreneurship process – that entrepreneurs gained from ecosystem participants. Through social entrepreneurs' interactions with their local contexts, they learned how to create an effective social

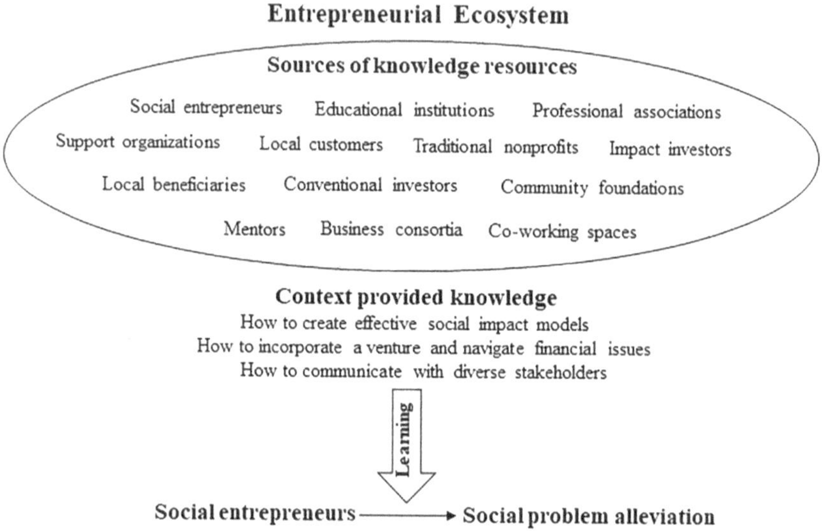

Figure 4.1 Context-enhanced social entrepreneurship.

impact model, incorporate their social ventures, navigate early-stage financial issues, and communicate with diverse stakeholders. The sections that follow unpack how these findings inform research and represent practical insights for social entrepreneurs and ecosystem builders.

Contributions to research

Social entrepreneurs' pursuit of dual (business and social) missions and their concomitant desire to produce value for consumers and beneficiaries require different resources than conventional entrepreneurship. The findings identify one source of these resources: EEs. The study provides support for the contention that EEs can be "knowledge repositories" for entrepreneurs (e.g., Roundy, 2020). Social entrepreneurs use their local contexts as sources of general knowledge about entrepreneurship and specific knowledge about social entrepreneurship.

This study illustrates that EEs represent rich learning contexts. In addition to the city's general EE, a distinct sub-ecosystem, a "social entrepreneurship ecosystem" (SEE), helped to provide resources. The Austin SEE consisted of a network of support organizations, investors, and professionals that targeted social entrepreneurs. From SEE participants, entrepreneurs learned specialized knowledge about the social entrepreneurship process.

Social entrepreneurs did not, however, receive knowledge exclusively from the SEE. They also interacted with participants in the general EE who were focused on conventional (i.e., non-social) entrepreneurship. Social entrepreneurs benefited from going "outside" of the SEE and getting knowledge and feedback from non-social entrepreneur participants. For instance, from the conventional EE participants, such as angel investors, social entrepreneurs often learned that their businesses were not suited for traditional equity investment and that they needed to develop a stronger, more financially viable business model. In some cases, interactions with non-social entrepreneurship participants were seemingly negative (e.g., when social entrepreneurs were denied funding). However, these interactions served the purpose of making entrepreneurs rethink their assumptions and encouraged them to go beyond a, sometimes myopic, focus on their social missions. Thus, the findings help to tease apart the relationship between social entrepreneurs, their EE, and their SEE (cf. Warnecke and Balzac-Arroyo, 2023). In Austin, the EE and SEE were overlapping, but not perfectly so; the ecosystems shared some participants and organizations, but other elements were distinct.

Implications for entrepreneurs and ecosystem builders

The findings indicate that social entrepreneurs are deliberate about learning from their EEs. This suggests that, like conventional entrepreneurs, social entrepreneurs benefit from having an EE mindset, which is an orientation towards a local context that consists of three characteristics: entitativity (i.e., acknowledging that a local EE exists), humility (i.e., acknowledging that the entrepreneur needs assistance and that the EE has resources that could help), and prosociality (i.e., a desire to help others and contribute resources) (Roundy, 2023). An EE mindset gives social entrepreneurs an external orientation that acknowledges their dependence on their local contexts. It is the opposite of a "go-it-alone" or "do-everything-yourself" mindset.

Insights from the case study suggest that social entrepreneurs are also deliberate about teaching others and passing on their knowledge to their local communities. For instance, one social entrepreneur described transitioning from entrepreneurship to working at a local university, primarily to share the insights she had gained about being a social entrepreneur with others.

> "[H]ow do you start a social enterprise?", "what does a double bottom line really mean?"[,] "what is the effect of capital?", "what are different types of capital?" . . . my interest is in kind of disseminating these learnings so that's how I came to cross over to the [university]. The sense that what I was learning and observing needed to be codified and disseminated to the rest of the world.
>
> (SE19)

Thus, social entrepreneurs should look for opportunities not just to take knowledge from their EE but also to contribute knowledge to their local community.

The findings from the case study also suggest that if a local community desires to increase the number of social entrepreneurs, and/or improve social entrepreneurs' impact, community leaders should take steps to increase the effectiveness of the EE (i.e., the EE's ability to enable entrepreneurship) (Roundy & Evans, 2024). Improving EEs is the focus of EE leaders, the individuals in a local community who make deliberate attempts to improve EE effectiveness (Stam and Van de Ven, 2021). EE leaders work to strengthen the health and vitality of EEs by improving an ecosystem's social, cultural, and material attributes, for example, by strengthening an EE's networks or culture (Spigel, 2017). EE leaders' actions make the ecosystem a more fertile environment for entrepreneurs.

The findings suggest that EE leaders may need to pursue distinct activities to make their local ecosystems beneficial to social entrepreneurs, not just conventional entrepreneurs. For instance, initiatives solely aimed at attracting traditional, for-profit-minded investors might not result in sufficient capital to support the unique financial profile of social entrepreneurs. In addition, EE leaders seeking to improve their local ecosystem should consider how they can make it a better learning environment. For instance, leaders should promote events and programs that increase the number of EE interactions and create opportunities for "collisions" (Nylund and Cohen, 2017): informal and unplanned interactions between EE participants during which knowledge can be shared. EE participants who are in the position to train and provide advice to social entrepreneurs (e.g., university members) should encourage entrepreneurs to leverage their local context for resources and be good EE "citizens" by contributing knowledge and other resources to their local communities.

Limitations and directions for future research

Despite the study's contributions, it is not without limitations, which suggest directions for future research. First, the case study focused on social entrepreneurs in a single EE. Thus, research is needed to understand the findings' boundary conditions, the range of contexts in which the insights have explanatory power, and the constraints on the findings' generalizability. For instance, the Austin EE is unique in its "munificence" (Spigel and Harrison, 2018); it has ample social entrepreneurs, abundant resources, and the full complement of social, cultural, and material EE attributes. However, EEs may also be resource-constrained (cf. Roundy, 2019), which may attenuate or alter the enhancing-effects of an EE (and SEE) on social entrepreneurs. Social entrepreneurs in unmunificent ecosystems may need to leverage their EEs differently or look beyond them for knowledge-based resources.

The study emphasized social entrepreneurs rather than other EE participants. However, non-entrepreneur EE actors might also benefit from leveraging their local contexts for knowledge. For instance, scholars could examine if there are meaningful differences in the leaders of support organizations or university entrepreneurship centers in their willingness to learn from their contexts and the performance implications of these differences.

Concluding remarks

Social entrepreneurship is difficult. It "takes a village" to create and scale a social venture. However, social entrepreneurs can respond to these challenges by leveraging the contextual dynamics of their entrepreneurial ecosystems. This chapter highlights a unique set of mechanisms that explains how social entrepreneurs overcome intra-organizational resource constraints and the challenges of addressing social problems by using their extra-organizational ties to local communities to enable and enhance their impact. The findings from the study of social entrepreneurs in the Austin entrepreneurial ecosystem reveal the points of connection between entrepreneurs' activities (e.g., learning from beneficiaries, designing impact models) and their ecosystem. I hope this chapter lays the groundwork for a rich stream of research exploring the intersection between social entrepreneurs and their local contexts.

References

Agrawal, A., & Hockerts, K. (2021) "Impact investing: Review and research agenda", *Journal of Small Business & Entrepreneurship*, *33*(2), 153–181.

Andresen, E., Lundberg, H., & Wincent, J. (2014) "Processes in collaborative entrepreneurship: A longitudinal case study of how multiple actors exploit a radically new opportunity", *International Entrepreneurship and Management Journal*, *10*, 713–726.

Austin, J., Stevenson, H., & Wei-Skillern, J. (2006) "Social and commercial entrepreneurship: Same, different, or both?" *Entrepreneurship Theory & Practice*, *30*, 1–22.

Battilana, J., & Lee, M. (2014) "Advancing research on hybrid organizing–Insights from the study of social enterprises", *Academy of Management Annals*, *8*(1), 397–441.

Bosma, N. S., Schutjens, V. A. J. M., & Volker, B. (2016) "Local social entrepreneurship and social capital", in *Handbook on Social Capital and Regional Development*, eds. H. Westlund & J. P. Larsson. Cheltenham: Edward Elgar, 55–81.

Corner, P. D., & Kearins, K. (2021) "Scaling-up social enterprises: The effects of geographic context", *Journal of Management & Organization*, *27*(1), 87–105.

de Bruin, A., Roy, M. J., Grant, S., & Lewis, K. V. (2023) "Advancing a contextualized, community-centric understanding of social entrepreneurial ecosystems", *Business & Society*, *62*(5), 1069–1102.

Doherty, B., Haugh, H., & Lyon, F. (2014) "Social enterprises as hybrid organizations: A review and research agenda", *International Journal of Management Reviews*, *16*(4), 417–436.

Eisenhardt, K. M., Graebner, M. E., & Sonenshein, S. (2016) "Grand challenges and inductive methods: Rigor without rigor mortis", *Academy of Management Journal*, *59*(4), 1113–1123.

Elsbach, K. D., & Stigliani, I. (2018) "Design thinking and organizational culture: A review and framework for future research", *Journal of Management*, *44*(6), 2274–2306.

Gehman, J., Glaser, V. L., Eisenhardt, K. M., Gioia, D., Langley, A., & Corley, K. G. (2018) "Finding theory–method fit: A comparison of three qualitative approaches to theory building", *Journal of Management Inquiry*, *27*(3), 284–300.

Graebner, M. E., Martin, J. A., & Roundy, P. T. (2012) "Qualitative data: Cooking without a recipe", *Strategic Organization*, *10*(3), 276–284.

Guéneau, G., Chabaud, D., & Sauvannet, M. C. C. (2023) "Sticky ties: Quest for structural inter-organizational configurations in entrepreneurial ecosystems", *Technological Forecasting and Social Change*, *190*, 122416.

Guerrero, M., & Lira, M. (2023) "Entrepreneurial university ecosystem's engagement with SDGs: Looking into a Latin-American University", *Community Development*, *54*(3), 337–352.

Kickul, J., & Lyons, T. S. (2020) *Understanding social entrepreneurship: The relentless pursuit of mission in an ever changing world.* New York: Routledge.

Langley, A. (1999) "Strategies for theorizing from process data", *Academy of Management Review*, *24*(4), 691–710.

Loeb, B. (2018) "Building the social innovation capital of the world", Available at: https://foundingaustin.com/2018/10/building-the-social-innovation-capital-of-the-world/ (Accessed: 19 August 2023).

Lortie, J., Cox, K. C., & Roundy, P. T. (2022) "Social impact models, legitimacy perceptions, and consumer responses to social ventures", *Journal of Business Research*, *144*, 312–321.

Lyons, T. S., & Roundy, P. T. (2023) "Building our understanding of social entrepreneurship ecosystems", *Community Development*, *54*(3), 353–358.

Miles, M. B., & Huberman, A. M. (1994) *Qualitative Data Analysis: An Expanded Sourcebook* (2nd ed.).Thousand Oaks: Sage.

Muñoz, P., & Kimmitt, J. (2019) "Social mission as competitive advantage: A configurational analysis of the strategic conditions of social entrepreneurship", *Journal of Business Research*, *101*, 854–861.

Nylund, P. A., & Cohen, B. (2017) "Collision density: Driving growth in urban entrepreneurial ecosystems", *International Entrepreneurship and Management Journal*, *13*, 757–776.

Ozcan, P., Han, S. and Graebner, M.E. (2017) "Single cases: The what, why, and how", in *The Routledge Companion to Qualitative Research in Organization Studies*, eds. R. Mir & J. Sanjay. Abingdon, Oxfordshire, UK: Routledge, 92–112.

Ricket, A. L., Knutsen, F. B., Jolley, G. J., & Davis, S. C. (2023) "Appalachian social entrepreneurship ecosystem: A framework for rural development", *Community Development*, *54*(3), 315–336.

Roundy, P. T. (2019) "Back from the brink: The revitalization of inactive entrepreneurial ecosystems", *Journal of Business Venturing Insights*, *12*, e00140.

Roundy, P. T. (2020) "The wisdom of ecosystems: A transactive memory theory of knowledge management in entrepreneurial ecosystems", *Knowledge and Process Management*, *27*(3), 234–247.

Roundy, P. T. (2023) "Embracing the 'village' or going-it-alone? Understanding the entrepreneurial ecosystem mindset", in *Research Handbook on Entrepreneurial Ecosystems*, eds. J. A. Cunningham, M. Menter, C. O'Kane, & M. Romano. Cheltenham: Edward Elgar.

Roundy, P. T., & Bonnal, M. (2017) "The singularity of social entrepreneurship: Untangling its uniqueness and market function", *The Journal of Entrepreneurship*, *26*(2), 137–162.

Roundy, P. T., Bradshaw, M., & Brockman, B. K. (2018) "The emergence of entrepreneurial ecosystems: A complex adaptive systems approach", *Journal of Business Research*, *86*, 1–10.

Roundy, P. T., & Evans, W. R. (2024) "Entrepreneurial ecosystems as multiteam systems: Navigating independence and interdependence in the leadership of startup communities", *Journal of Business Venturing Insights*, *21*, e00445.

Saebi, T., Foss, N. J., and Linder, S. (2019) "Social entrepreneurship research: Past achievements and future promises", *Journal of Management*, *45*(1), 70–95.
Sparviero, S. (2019) "The case for a socially oriented business model canvas: The social enterprise model canvas", *Journal of Social Entrepreneurship*, *10*(2), 232–251.
Spigel, B. (2017) "The relational organization of entrepreneurial ecosystems", *Entrepreneurship Theory and Practice*, *41*(1), 49–72.
Spigel, B., & Harrison, R. (2018) "Toward a process theory of entrepreneurial ecosystems", *Strategic Entrepreneurship Journal*, *12*(1), 151–168.
Stam, E. (2015) "Entrepreneurial ecosystems and regional policy: A sympathetic critique", *European Planning Studies*, *23*(9), 1759–1769.
Stam, E., & Van de Ven, A. (2021) "Entrepreneurial ecosystem elements", *Small Business Economics*, *56*, 809–832.
Stephens, B., Butler, J. S., Garg, R., and Gibson, D. V. (2019) "Austin, Boston, Silicon valley, and New York: Case studies in the location choices of entrepreneurs in maintaining the Technopolis", *Technological Forecasting and Social Change*, *146*, 267–280.
Volkmann, C., Fichter, K., Klofsten, M., & Audretsch, D. B. (2021) "Sustainable entrepreneurial ecosystems: An emerging field of research", *Small Business Economics*, *56*(3), 1047–1055.
Warnecke, T., & Balzac-Arroyo, J. (2023) "Community, capabilities, and the social entrepreneurship ecosystem", *Community Development*, *54*(3), 359–381.
Wurth, B., Stam, E., & Spigel, B. (2022) "Toward an entrepreneurial ecosystem research program", *Entrepreneurship Theory and Practice*, *46*(3), 729–778.

5 Supporting sustainable start-ups

Different approaches applied by business incubators

Meike Siefkes and Gero Stocksmeier

Introduction

Our global society is facing challenges resulting from rapidly expanding environmental and social crises that require action from various stakeholders. Entrepreneurship scholars argue that understanding how, why, and when entrepreneurs solve social and environmental problems is central to the field (Shepherd *et al.*, 2019; Wiklund, Wright and Zahra, 2019). Given the hybridity of sustainable entrepreneurs' objectives – to promote environmental and social welfare while being financially sustainable – sustainable entrepreneurship (SE) requires specific knowledge and skills: both entrepreneurial and sustainability-related competences and the capabilities to nurture the attitudes for both are required (Parrish, 2010; Bocken, 2015). Developing a sustainable venture is a complex process that requires specific support and sustainability-related knowledge (Neumeyer and Santos, 2018). To support the creation and development of sustainable solutions, intermediaries that provide specific support services have emerged (Klofsten *et al.*, 2020; Bergman and McMullen, 2022).

One group of intermediaries in the sustainable entrepreneurial ecosystem are business incubators (BIs) (Lamine *et al.*, 2018; Theodoraki, Messeghem and Rice, 2018; Volkmann *et al.*, 2021). BIs are increasingly expected to contribute to a sustainable development by facilitating sustainability-driven innovation in new ventures (Klofsten, Bank and Bienkowska, 2016; Lamine *et al.*, 2018; Millette, Eiríkur Hull and Williams, 2020; Klofsten and Bienkowska, 2021; Sohail, Belitski and Castro Christiansen, 2023). Traditional BIs provide services such as financing, legal support, physical facilities, goals, and structure (Barbero *et al.*, 2014). They support start-ups in their initiation and development while providing access to resources, knowledge, and important stakeholders. Additionally, BIs have been observed to implement sustainability elements (e.g. Nicolopoulou *et al.*, 2017; Surana, Singh and Sagar, 2020). Sustainability-oriented business incubators (SBIs) support "the establishment and growth of new businesses and business models that create future goods and services that sustain the natural and/or communal environment and contribute to the Sustainable Development

DOI: 10.4324/9781003324737-5

Goals" (Fichter and Hurrelmann, 2021, p. 480). SBIs can increase the likelihood of their incubatees to realize sustainable entrepreneurial opportunities by offering value-adding services such as funding, business support, and network access (Bergmann and Utikal, 2021; Yi, 2021; Karahan, Rashid and Kratzer, 2022). Scholars have described the application of specific tools in individual phases, for example, sustainable business model development (Fichter and Hurrelmann, 2021). Many incubators consider sustainability an important concern for their start-ups' business development; however, only a minority offer specific support for sustainability within their program (Klofsten and Bienkowska, 2021).

Previous research has highlighted the need to identify tools and methods that support a sustainability orientation during the incubation program (Klofsten, Bank and Bienkowska, 2016). Existing literature has not investigated how such sustainability-oriented tools are integrated into the overall incubation process, and a lack of a deeper understanding of the services offered by SBIs persists. Thus, this study aims to identify the tools that are employed to support a sustainability orientation during business incubation programs. Hence, we ask: *how do business incubators modify their programs for sustainable entrepreneurship?*

To answer this, a multiple case study with 11 BIs from major European entrepreneurial ecosystems was conducted. Given the current state of the literature, studying the facilitation of SE in BIs requires qualitative approaches to explore the facets of the phenomenon. Based on interview data and secondary data such as workshop documents, we present six activity fields for SE in incubation programs. We highlight tools that the sampled incubators apply, differentiating between low-hanging fruit tools and more advanced tools. We show that there is potential to implement measures throughout the program, starting with the overall strategy and traversing through pre-incubation to post-incubation.

This way, we contribute to the current literature stream on SBIs (Bank and Kanda, 2016; Bergmann and Utikal, 2021; Fichter and Hurrelmann, 2021; Klofsten and Bienkowska, 2021; Volkmann *et al.*, 2021; Cirule and Uvarova, 2022; Karahan, Rashid and Kratzer, 2022; Lamperti, Sammut and Courrent, 2023). We extend the concepts by Bergek and Norrman (2008) and Mian (2014) that are purely aimed at conventional business incubation, and add an SE perspective to them, also integrating Fichter and Hurrelmann's (2021) institutional framework for sustainability. Our study contributes novel perspectives on how SE is facilitated in BIs in practice. By building on existing research and incorporating practitioners' experience, we contextualize the phenomenon of SBIs and expand the emergent existing literature on SBI support services.

In this chapter, we first present the literature on BIs and the support services they offer, developing a conceptual framework to identify the different elements of the incubation process. We introduce the context of SE and its specificity and then take stock of the current state of research on SBIs, introducing relevant terms and concepts. We then present the methods used and the data sampled during our study. Subsequently, the data is analyzed and discussed, bringing together existing literature and our empirical insights. The final section draws conclusions regarding practical and theoretical implications, limitations of the study, and avenues for future research.

Background and related work

Business incubators and their support services

BIs hold a central position in entrepreneurial ecosystems, supporting the creation and development of new ventures based on a broad variety of measures (Lamine *et al.*, 2018). Traditionally, business incubation was based on the physical col-location of the ventures involved in the program. Recently there has been an increasing focus on value-adding support activities, also in digital incubation programs. Thus, the business incubation process can be described as "the way in which an incubation entity provides support to start-ups to improve the probability of survival of the portfolio companies and accelerate their development" (Pauwels *et al.*, 2016, p. 14). An output of the management and technological support offered by incubators is the expansion of the entrepreneurs' human capital, for example, knowledge and skills (Sarasvathy, 2004; Rashid, Alzafari and Kratzer, 2020).

The planned outcomes of the incubation program depend on the incubators' types of organization and goals (Aaboen, 2009). Zedtwitz (2003) distinguishes five archetypes of incubators: regional, university, independent commercial, company-internal, and virtual. While the latter three types typically have a for-profit objective, the first two fulfill a public mission, for example, employment or regional innovation capacity (Carayannis and von Zedtwitz, 2005). This influences the institutional framework, that is, the vision, mission, goals strategy, culture, and structures within the incubator (Fichter and Hurrelmann, 2021).

BIs are active in three phases throughout the incubation process (Mian, 2014): first, pre-incubation activities where business ideas are initiated and aspiring entrepreneurs are supported during the very early stages of idea germination. Second, the main phase of incubation where the business plan is implemented and the firms' operations have already begun, so that the incubator can assist with support services. And finally, post-incubation support where BIs support the consolidation and growth of the start-ups.

The incubation phase itself also has three components (Bergek and Norrman, 2008). It begins with the selection of suitable ventures. The focus of the selection process can lie on the business idea or the team/entrepreneur. Batch-size-wise, either a large number of start-ups are invited to the batch and the market will decide at a later point which idea or team turns out to be successful ("survival-of-the-fittest"), or only a few curated start-ups will be allowed to enter the batch ("picking-the-winners"). The next components are business support activities, that is, coaching or training activities undertaken to develop the incubatees. Their intensity depends on the intervention philosophy: strong intervention, where the incubator staff guide the entrepreneurs through the incubation process, sometimes even supplying entire management teams, versus a laissez-faire approach, where incubatees are independent, receiving minimum assistance unless requested. Finally, the incubation phase ends with mediation, connecting the incubatees with each other and to the external environment. There are two forms of mediation: network mediation resembles networking activities undertaken by the incubator to match start-ups with other actors, for example, new customers, partners, workforce, researchers, or investors. Institutional mediation is a form of anticipatory action by the incubator to prepare start-ups for external demands such as institutional regulations, laws, or even values and cultural factors (ibid.).

Zooming in on the business support services, it becomes clear that incubators offer a variety of value-adding services. These activities can be generic or individually customized, including tangible and intangible resources (Fichter and Hurrelmann, 2021). There are three central business incubation support services (Bergek and Norrman, 2008; Bruneel *et al.*, 2012; Pauwels *et al.*, 2016; Woolley and MacGregor, 2022): the provision of shared resources and infrastructure, the facilitation of business support services, and access to network and financial funding. These support services are outlined in the following paragraphs.

First-generation incubators offer mostly infrastructure and shared resources (Bruneel *et al.*, 2012). This includes but is not limited to office space (Bergek and Norrman, 2008). Additionally, the incubator typically installs shared resources and facilities, such as reception, meeting rooms, office kitchens, and parking (Grimaldi and Grandi, 2005). Some technology-focused incubators even offer prototyping platforms or makerspaces for piloting and testing value propositions (Kanda *et al.*, 2018), or laboratories or scientific equipment (Mian, 1996; Grimaldi and Grandi, 2005). This way, start-ups can reduce costs, leverage economies of scale, and get easier access to resources (Bruneel *et al.*, 2012).

Business support services aim at enhancing incubatees' knowledge and skills on entrepreneurial topics such as business development, strategic planning, accounting, marketing, legal, and finance (Bergek and Norrman, 2008). Such services comprise enabling entrepreneurs to develop, test, and enhance their start-ups' business model (Klofsten, Bank and Bienkowska, 2016). They typically include individual coaching and team-building support (Rice, 2002).

Finally, it becomes increasingly central for start-ups to leverage and mobilize external network support and funding early on to overcome resource scarcity. Therefore, incubators provide links between various of their start-ups' stakeholders (Bergek and Norrman, 2008), for example, to first customers or strategic partners (Kanda *et al.*, 2018). Incubators also initiate connections with investors and offer guidance for public funding and grant applications (Bruneel *et al.*, 2012).

As demonstrated, incubators have shifted from mere office spaces toward an environment that accentuates the process of founding, including business

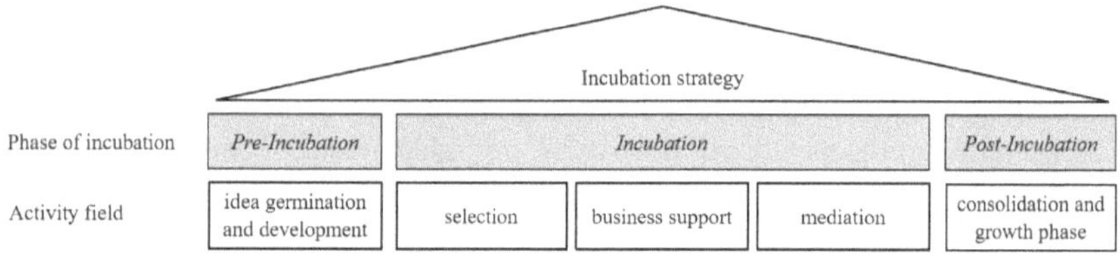

Figure 5.1 The elements of the business incubation process.

Source: own creation based on Bergek and Norrman (2008); Mian (2014); Fichter and Hurrelmann (2021)

development, access to networks, capital, professional services, or learning opportunities (Hackett and Dilts, 2004; Bergek and Norrman, 2008; Nicolopoulou *et al.*, 2017; Hausberg and Korreck, 2020). To emphasize elements of the business incubation process, we conjoin previous findings into one comprehensive framework (Figure 5.1). This framework comprises pre-incubation and post-incubation (Mian, 2014), and the components of selection, business support, and mediation during the incubation (Bergek and Norrman, 2008) as a decisive part of the overall incubation strategy (Fichter and Hurrelmann, 2021). To highlight the active role of the incubator, we call these components within the subsequent incubation phases "activity fields".

As the concept of sustainability has gained traction among entrepreneurs, supporting them in creating such ventures is an opportunity for BIs. Insights from the SE literature are required.

The context of sustainable entrepreneurship

SE can be defined as "an innovative, market-oriented and personality driven form of creating economic and societal value by means of break-through environmentally or socially beneficial market or institutional innovations" (Schaltegger and Wagner, 2011, p. 226). Even though it has grown exponentially in the last years (Bank, Fichter and Klofsten, 2017), SE research is still maturing and there are a plethora of SE definitions applied, both in theory and in practice. The most referenced scholarly works in the field apply differing definitions of SE (Cohen and Winn, 2007; Dean and McMullen, 2007; Hockerts and Wüstenhagen, 2010; Schaltegger and Wagner, 2011; Shepherd and Patzelt, 2011 in Terán-Yépez *et al.*, 2020). They still find common ground, basing their understanding on Elkington's (1998) "triple bottom line", uniting economic, social, and environmental value. Muñoz and Cohen (2018) identify a hybridity objective as another common ground of the various definitions for SE, as sustainable entrepreneurs go beyond the rent-seeking behavior that traditional entrepreneurial scholars have attributed to entrepreneurs.

SE differs significantly from traditional entrepreneurship regarding its intended and realized impact to initiate social and environmental change in society through a pronounced value-based approach (Hockerts and Wüstenhagen, 2010; Volkmann *et al.*, 2021). Its context is characterized by prosocial motives, the traits and identities of entrepreneurs (Parrish, 2010), more challenging resource mobilization, as well as institutional voids and associated market failures (Vedula *et al.*, 2022), and also a unique level of uncertainty and complexity during commercialization (Randjelovic, O'Rourke and Orsato, 2003; Gaddy *et al.*, 2017; Mrkajic, Murtinu and Scalera, 2019).

Thus, challenges in addition to the already difficult process of creating and developing new ventures emerge. Research on SE suggests that the recognition and implementation of business opportunities linked to sustainability goals are more complex for the entrepreneur than traditional business development, that is, through business model development, networks, and other counselling (Patzelt and Shepherd, 2011). Traditional actors often perceive their hybrid business cases as risky and difficult to understand (de Lange, 2017). This can create information asymmetries complicating investor and entrepreneur relations, but also other relations within the ecosystem (Carpenter and Petersen, 2002; Hall and Lerner, 2010). Because of these additional complexities and challenges, other individuals and organizations that can assist start-ups on their journey of creating, recognizing, and exploiting sustainable opportunities are needed (Kanda *et al.,* 2018).

Business incubators as facilitators of sustainable entrepreneurship

SBIs support entrepreneurs in developing the necessary resources and capabilities to create sustainable businesses (Kanda *et al.*, 2018; Fichter and Hurrelmann, 2021). They do so by providing the entrepreneur with value-adding resources during the incubation processes.

The support services lined out earlier are especially relevant for sustainability. This has been aggregated by Karahan, Rashid and Kratzer (2022): by reducing infrastructure and resource costs, sustainable incubators can allow entrepreneurs to focus on developing sustainable business activities. They relieve the psychological load, making space for the founders' cognitive freedom and capacity to pursue the prosocial and environmentally motivated actions that would otherwise have been weakened by bureaucratic tasks and external stressors (Rashid, 2022). Furthermore, it can reduce the danger of moral disengagement from values and increasing socially and environmentally harmful behaviors (Shepherd, Patzelt and Baron, 2013). Similarly, business support services support the entrepreneurs in building human capital, that is, improving relevant capabilities and competencies (Bruneel *et al.*, 2012; Ploum *et al.*, 2018), such as opportunity recognition, critical thinking, and interpersonal skills (Lans, Blok and Wesselink, 2014). Business support services also promote the entrepreneurs' technological knowledge regarding social and environmental sustainability, enabling the development of sustainable products and services (Ploum *et al.*, 2018). Social impact assessments and ethics training are perceived as especially valuable for business development by the incubatees (Sansone *et al.*, 2020). By offering business support services, incubators catalyze the translation of sustainability intention into action (Yi, 2021). The success of sustainable start-ups is especially reliant on leveraging and mobilizing external networks (Freudenreich, Lüdeke-Freund and Schaltegger, 2020). External networks can help start-ups overcome the technological, financial, and regulatory barriers mentioned earlier (Polzin, von Flotow and Klerkx, 2016). Thus, using funding and network support services enables start-ups to exploit external knowledge and expertise for sustainable innovation (Kanda *et al.*, 2018). Sustainable incubators encourage collaboration and co-creation among the incubatees to create and scale sustainable impacts (Nicolopoulou *et al.*, 2017). Yet, research has shown that while many incubators consider sustainability an important concern for their start-ups' business development, only a minority offer specific support for sustainability within their program (Klofsten and Bienkowska, 2021).

The importance of incorporating the demand side perspective into the design of sustainability incubators becomes particularly striking when measuring, assessing, or forecasting the effectiveness of incubator activities (Lamine *et al.*, 2018). Incubators across all industries can profit from gaining SE competences but lack specific services to enhance them (Lamine *et al.*, 2018), which is also an issue with other intermediaries such as investors (Siefkes, Bjørgum and Sørheim, 2023; Siefkes *et al.*, 2024). It is central to understand the relationship between activities and sustainable outcomes; otherwise, start-up support programs risk being vague and arbitrary (Åstebro and Hoos, 2021; Diekel, Bach and Finkbeiner, 2023), and might even endanger the legitimacy for public spending on such incubators (Lamine *et al.*, 2018; Klofsten *et al.*, 2020). Fichter and Hurrelmann (2021) highlight the importance of not just implementing plenty service offers, but also anchoring sustainability in the incubators' organizational framework.

While researchers make explicit recommendations for furthering SE in higher education contexts (e.g. Nave and Franco, 2019), the sustainability-enabling management processes of sustainability-specific incubators are under-researched (Lamine *et al.*, 2018). The literature on sustainable incubation is emergent and often case-study based. Research mostly focuses on region-specific case studies (Potts, 2010; Nicolopoulou *et al.*, 2017; Gonsalves and Rogerson, 2019; Oliveira, Cahen and Borini, 2019; Lamperti, Sammut and Courrent, 2023) or individual case-studies that exemplify sustainable incubation elements (Bank, Fichter and Klofsten, 2017; Bergmann and Utikal, 2021). Some research focuses on the operational aspects and assess the "greening" stages of incubators (Fonseca and Jabbour, 2012). Few scholars take a process perspective and look at the practical aspects of introducing SE in incubation programs. The majority of research investigates specific focal points of the incubation program, for example, institutional framework and selection criteria (Hirschmann, Moritz and Block, 2022), generation of tenants also considering the influence of the external environment (Bank and Kanda, 2016; Bank, Fichter and Klofsten, 2017), the applied tools for sustainable business model development (Bergmann and Utikal, 2021; Fichter and Hurrelmann, 2021), and the sustainability impacts of the support services (Karahan, Rashid and Kratzer, 2022). Very few studies have looked at the overall incubation strategy for sustainability, encouraging incubators activities to focus on explicit sustainability activities throughout the program (Klofsten, Bank and Bienkowska, 2016; Bank, Fichter and Klofsten, 2017; Dias Brito, Brunstein and Amaro, 2018; Ballering and Masurel, 2020).

Modifying traditional incubation programs for sustainable entrepreneurship

Method and data

To investigate how BIs modify their programs for SE, a multiple case study was conducted (Eisenhardt, 1989, 1991). For this, we interviewed 11 BIs located in major entrepreneurial ecosystems in Europe. Studying these multiple cases allowed us to add to the existing literature and frameworks with empirical evidence on the phenomenon, also considering its real-life, social, and organizational context (Eisenhardt, 1989, 1991; Yin, 2009). By enriching real-time and retrospective data collection with secondary data, informant biases can be mitigated (Eisenhardt and Graebner, 2007).

For the case selection, we followed Patton's (1990) purposeful sampling. Cases were identified as relevant for this study based on the following criteria:

- Situated in Europe.
- At least one cohort has finished the program.
- Cohort contains sustainable start-ups.
- The incubator positioned itself toward sustainability topics, say, as business opportunities; the strategy included SE, for example, in form of an SE vision; the incubator had a claim, for example, "sustainability is the next big thing"; the incubator had a name that hinted at sustainability; the program was designed to combat sustainability challenges.

The case selection had its starting point in the ENHANCE University Alliance (for more information, see https://enhanceuniversity.eu/de/). The ENHANCE University Alliance is an excellent environment to study sustainability-profiled BIs because as innovation and sustainability are important contemporary topics, their university incubators have great incentives to invest in the topic. The further connections building up on the ENHANCE network provided the opportunity to find additional cases following Patton's (1990) snowballing critical cases, resulting in 11 BIs from 9 different European countries (Table 5.1). The interviewees occupied a middle or top management position, accentuating the strategic importance of the topic.

Table 5.1 Cases characteristics

Case	*Country*	*Type*
1	Estonia	Independent Commercial Incubator
2	France	University Business Incubator
3	Germany	University Business Incubator
4	Germany	Regional Business Incubator
5	Italy	University Business Incubator
6	The Netherlands	Independent Commercial Incubator
7	Norway	Independent Commercial Incubator
8	Scandinavia	Virtual Accelerator
9	Spain	University Business Incubator
10	Sweden	University Business Incubator
11	Sweden	Regional Business Incubator

Source: Own creation

The data collection included an initial screening – where we gathered data on the size, scope, and history of the incubator which was included in the fact sheet sent out to the participating start-ups of each incubator – empirical data from the interviews, and additional information material that was either provided by the BIs or retrieved online.

Our main data source was semi-structured interviews conducted in February and March 2021. The interviews resulted in over 600 minutes of audio material which was then transcribed. Detailed case data was anonymized to ensure confidentiality and build trust. The interviews were conducted online, using a conference tool. For guidance during the data collection and analysis, we used the preliminary framework presented in Figure 5.1 to guide the interview questions. Thus, open-ended questions addressed selection, business support and mediation, but also the institutional framework, as well as pre- and post-incubation offers.

The interview data was analyzed with a thematic analysis approach as an analytical framework, offering a rich, detailed, yet complex account of our data (Braun and Clark, 2006). It enabled us to identify, analyze, and interpret patterns of meaning (themes) within the collected data. For this, the author team generated initial codes in NVIVO together, followed by searching for themes, reviewing themes, defining and naming themes, and producing the report. In addition, we included information provided in the interviews with the information accessible on the incubators' websites and additional information material provided by the interviewees themselves. This helped validate the participants' answers and complete the information given in the interviews (Jick, 1979).

Then, we conducted a cross-case analysis to recognize patterns, looking for similar constructs and themes in the cases (Eisenhardt and Graebner, 2007). We began this cross-case analysis after all data had been collected to apply the same logic across cases (Eisenhardt, 1989; Yin, 2009). We compared the measures and concepts by using tables to keep an overview over the various constructs (Miles and Huberman, 1994).

To achieve a result that brings together empirical data with existing literature, we iterated between literature, interview data, and secondary data to find an underlying logic of the emergent relationships among constructs (Eisenhardt, 1989; Eisenhardt and Graebner, 2007). This iteration between theory and data helped sharpen constructs and measures (Eisenhardt, 1989). As the development of the framework took shape, we consulted the literature to also find theoretical similarities and differences, strengthen the internal validity of findings, sharpen construct definitions and measures, and increase the generalizability of the emergent framework. In addition, we used tools as described by the incubators to illustrate the activity fields and make them more applicable. The result of repeated iterations among the available data and literature is a framework for business incubation modified for SE, which follows in the upcoming section.

Results and analysis

In the following section, we will introduce and illustrate the six activity fields for SBIs with tools that the sampled incubators apply. We extend existing concepts on conventional business incubation, by adding an SE perspective that integrates Fichter and Hurrelmann's (2021) institutional framework as an overarching incubation strategy for sustainability (Figure 5.2). Depending on the incubators' maturity of SE facilitation, these tools range from

- *low-hanging fruit tools*, which are tools that are easy to implement for incubators in the beginning of their SE journey (i.e., low maturity level) who are

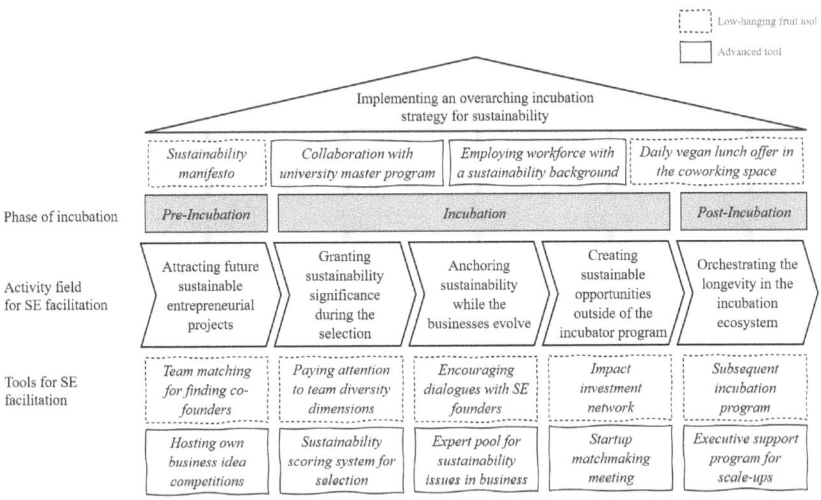

Figure 5.2 Supporting SE in Business Incubation: Insights and Tools for Activity Fields in Each Phase of Incubation.

Source: own creation

now provided with a starting point, for example, the offer of a team-matching service to find co-founders with a sustainability mindset, to

- more *advanced tools* which build up on prior SE facilitation and encourage more mature incubators that have a more profound sustainability understanding (i.e., higher maturity level) to take their activities to the next level, for example, the application of a sustainability scoring system for the selection process.

The empirical data offered insights into the anchoring of sustainability in the institutional framework of the overall incubation strategy. Overall, the interview data shows that SE is a trend topic that BIs are very interested to contribute to (Klofsten, Bank and Bienkowska, 2016), due to the business opportunities it holds for the incubators. They incorporate sustainability through fully dedicated sustainability programs, mixed batches, or specialized sustainable verticals. Karahan, Rashid and Kratzer (2022) have highlighted the benefits of targeted SBIs rather than general ones. Part of anchoring sustainability on a deeper level is the employment of managers with a sustainability background, the formation of strategic collaborations within the ecosystem, or even to act as an impact investor from within the incubator. Sustainability is often part of the sampled incubators' vision, yet often implemented through seemingly arbitrary tools, for example, creating a visible "sustainability manifesto". The BIs aim to exhibit a position as a role model and try to establish a sustainability mindset throughout all business activities. However, the data does not always reflect a systematic approach underlying this implementation, supporting recent studies (Fichter and Hurrelmann, 2021; Klofsten and Bienkowska, 2021). What stands out: a vague definition of SE and open interpretations of impact can reduce the overall value added. The incubators that tend to have a less substantial understanding of SE also employ less tangible sustainability strategies or less profound approaches to further SE. The resulting incubation program is therefore less thorough and less focused on concrete SE facilitation. Thus, the underlying SE definition influences the whole subsequent design of the incubation program, necessitating a knowledgeable and intentional program design (Lamine *et al.*, 2018). Also, the incubators want to show the societal impact of their incubation activities, yet struggle to quantify the added value. When done correctly, goal setting and tracking can legitimize the incubators' activities among its own stakeholders, as proposed by Klofsten *et al.* (2020) and Surana, Singh and Sagar (2020).

The facilitation of SE begins before the actual business support of incubatees. A well-planned recruitment strategy is critical for the success of SBIs (Mian, 2014; Bank, Fichter and Klofsten, 2017). Incubators can create excitement and buzz for the topic, as attitude is a key driver for SE (Schaltegger and Wagner, 2011). Hence, the attraction of future sustainable projects is at the center of pre-incubation activities. Surprisingly, only a few of the interviewed incubators build a pipeline of potential new incubatees. Instead, they rely on isolated approaches such as business idea competitions. Being visible through pre-incubation activities and communicating the strength of their sustainability-focused programs to attract the most promising future sustainable entrepreneurial ventures holds great potential to increase the incubators' visibility (Bank and Kanda, 2016; Klofsten *et al.*, 2020). About half of the sampled incubators follow this idea by hosting incubation-like "preview-programs" such as digital pre-accelerators. Specific tools that incubators apply are a start-up bootcamp to gather teams, open consulting for potential incubatees with sustainable business ideas, or team-matching services for researchers and innovators who are looking for entrepreneurs and idea partners.

For many of the sampled incubators, sustainability was either at the center or at least one criterion of the selection of new start-ups. Most of the incubators follow a "picking-the-winners" selection strategy, while the "survival of the fittest" approach was less popular in the sample (Bergek and Norrman, 2008). There is no dominating selection focus, that is, team focus, idea focus, or both are equal. The criteria in place for selecting sustainable start-ups are less advanced than expected considering existing studies (Bank, Fichter and Klofsten, 2017; Hirschmann, Moritz and Block, 2022). While many incubators state that sustainability plays a role in the selection process and in their own vision, the criteria applied in the selection process are surprisingly immature and not necessarily connected to the incubators' strategic goals. This mirrors what the SE investment literature observes (Diekel, Bach and Finkbeiner, 2023; Harrer and Owen, 2022; Siefkes, Bjørgum and Sørheim, 2023; Siefkes *et al.*, 2024). Some BIs consider factors like team diversity arguing that this can facilitate SE at later stages (Parrish, 2010; Lans, Blok and Wesselink, 2014; Haldar, 2019; Terán-Yépez *et al.*, 2020). Others simply assess the start-ups' contribution to the United Nation's sustainable development goals. A more advanced tool is a sustainability scoring system which includes factors such as potential CO_2e reduction. Such a quantifiable approach can raise awareness for sustainability and nudge start-ups to consider their sustainability impact from the initiation. It also equips them with a measurement logic for after the incubation program, as this becomes more and more relevant for follow-on financing (Bocken, 2015).

With business support at the center of the incubation process, the interviewed incubators aim to anchor the topic of sustainability in the start-ups while their businesses evolve (Bergmann and Utikal, 2021). The interfering approach, the "steady hand of the incubator" (Bergek and Norrman, 2008), dominates the involvement of the interviewed incubators, for example, by scheduling regular meetings or compulsory training programs to nudge start-ups toward sustainability during the business development stage. Our findings illustrate a variety of ways to ensure a profound sustainability implementation: most incubators offer dedicated trainings for sustainability, for example, through applying the "theory of change" framework, or reporting on sustainability performance and/or impact. By quantifying this impact, sustainable start-ups and their incubators can monitor progress and compete with conventional start-ups, using their social and environmental added value as a unique selling proposition that differentiates them from others (Karahan, Rashid and Kratzer, 2022). As shown by Fichter and Hurrelmann (2021), most incubators impart knowledge on integrating sustainability along the business development, for example, with the Triple Layered Business Model Canvas (Joyce and Paquin, 2016). Additionally, the incubators strengthen entrepreneurial attitudes, for example, by hosting inspirational talks with successful sustainable founders, and by ensuring a long-term orientation toward SE (Tiba, van Rijnsoever and Hekkert, 2020; Lamperti, Sammut and Courrent, 2023). Both the literature (Parrish, 2010; Cirule and Uvarova, 2022) and practitioners recognize the importance of the incubator, sharing an SE vision with the incubatees as well as furthering collaboration and co-development across start-ups. While scholars focus on strengthening the SE spirit, teaching sustainability-oriented problem-solving, and creating arenas (e.g., social events, alumni networks, role model exposure), practitioners focus on attitude: many incubators offer trainings to develop competences, attitudes, and team culture to nurture sustainability. Personal mentorship programs within the cohort enhance team culture for social sustainability and well-being. Lastly, BIs assist start-ups indirectly in their business development. Mentorship or access to an expert pool offers the possibility to discuss sustainability-oriented business questions in a highly individualized way. Potential reasons for this high level of involvement are that SE is still a topic in rapid development (Biggs, Westley and Carpenter, 2010; Terán-Yépez *et al.*, 2020). Also, sustainability can add more complexity to entrepreneurship and thus make the incubation process longer and riskier, and require more advanced tools (Klofsten *et al.*, 2020).

Mediation is about creating sustainable opportunities outside of the incubator program. Mediation activities can reduce uncertainty and increase the chance of finding new sustainable business opportunities (Bergek and Norrman, 2008), as incubators are highly connected to their regional ecosystems, that is, industrial clusters, academic institutions, research labs, or investors (Lamine *et al.*, 2018). This is crucial for sustainable start-ups since new ventures generally lack information, know-how, and partnerships within the ecosystem (Meyskens and Carsrud, 2013). A simple, yet powerful example to create suitable funding opportunities is to build a network of impact investors around the incubator or host a specific impact investment day. The incubators support follow-on funding for the start-ups, by encouraging impact measurement approaches as described earlier. However, based on the interviewed practitioners' experience, tailored connections are even more valuable for sustainable entrepreneurs. Here, advanced SBIs host start-up matchmaking meetings to forge meaningful and targeted alliances for the incubatees. Also, incubators introduce industry partners or first customers, by matching incubatees and specialized partners or communities, creating first business opportunities. Most of the incubators try to prepare the start-ups for external demands and help to build knowledge in institutional surroundings. The latter is done by giving guidance in legal matters, for example, on laws regarding sustainability or partnering up with lawyers. Considering the ongoing regulatory developments in the EU, for example, on circular economy, carbon reduction, and the Green New Deal investment scheme, mediation services provided by the incubator must go beyond networking opportunities and prepare the start-ups for the market reality after the incubation program (Theodoraki, Messeghem and Rice, 2018).

Finally, during the post-incubation phase, the longevity of the start-ups' and the incubators' relationship is orchestrated and can be sustained in a lasting way (Mian, 2014). Several of the interviewed incubators aspire to take patronage of the start-ups even after the incubation has ended. Surprisingly, the incubators hardly organize evident measures such as alumni events, and post-incubation networking events with the ecosystem. No interviewee directly addressed the option of connecting the start-ups with sophisticated R&D networks or technology-based firms (Nave and Franco, 2019). They rather employ accessible post-incubation activities, such as channeling start-ups into subsequent programs or arranging fundraising opportunities. A more advanced tool is the development of a subsequent sustainability-aimed support program for scale-ups. The sample shows differences between university incubators and commercial incubators, suggesting that different incubator types can collaborate along the stages of the entrepreneurial journey to facilitate SE as their shared mission (Volkmann *et al.*, 2021). Carefully considering the post-incubation offer can complement the incubation program and function as a final steppingstone to support the sustainable start-ups' experience in the ecosystem (Theodoraki, Messeghem and Rice, 2018).

Conclusion

In this study, we investigated how BIs modify their programs for SE. Practitioners' experience on which activities exist throughout the entire sustainability-oriented incubation process helps us exemplify which tools are employed to support a sustainability orientation during business incubation programs. By conducting a multiple case study based on eleven incubators in major European entrepreneurship ecosystems, the findings incorporate existing research and practitioners' experience to contextualize the phenomenon of SBIs. This way, we were able to identify a variety of tools that incubators employ to support a sustainability orientation during business incubation programs in six activity fields: implementing an overarching incubation strategy for sustainability, attracting future sustainable projects, granting sustainability significance during the selection, anchoring sustainability while the businesses evolve, creating sustainable opportunities outside of the program, and finally, orchestrating the longevity in the incubation ecosystem. Our findings suggest that not only the individual elements of the incubation program are relevant for an incubator's approach to facilitate SE. The incubators' sustainability understanding plays a vital role for the whole subsequent design of the incubation program. Depending on the maturity of SE facilitation in the incubator, they apply the presented low-hanging fruit tools or advanced tools for the different incubation elements. The more mature an incubator's understanding of SE, the more sophisticated are the tools applied. Incubators have the opportunity to use the early stage of business development to anchor sustainability within all stages of value creation and not use the label "sustainability" purely as a marketing add-on (Bank and Kanda, 2016). Also, the different incubator archetypes can be complementary agents to boost SE. Lamine *et al.* (2018) argue that incubation mechanisms might even be the main environment to grow sustainable enterprises, as they play a major role accompanying start-ups from pre-seed ideas toward realizing the market entry. In line with existing literature, our findings highlight that the interplay of the entire ecosystem is central to facilitate SE and a successful initiation, development, and commercialization of sustainable innovation.

With these results, we extend the concepts by Bergek and Norrman (2008) and Mian (2014) that are based on conventional business incubation and add an SE perspective to them, also integrating Fichter and Hurrelmann's (2021) institutional framework as an overarching incubation strategy for sustainability. Thereby, we contribute to the currently emerging literature stream on SBIs (Bank and Kanda, 2016; Bergmann and Utikal, 2021; Fichter and Hurrelmann, 2021; Klofsten and Bienkowska, 2021; Volkmann *et al.*, 2021; Karahan, Rashid and Kratzer, 2022; Lamperti, Sammut and Courrent, 2023).

Our results offer avenues for future research to investigate. Future research can advance the usage of these tools as an analytical lens and combine them with other theoretical lenses. We see that not all knowledge on SE facilitation is applied in practice and that accessible hands-on tools beyond sustainable business model development are missing. Scholars could develop a concrete toolbox for SE facilitation based on the foundation of the six activity fields. Here, the effectiveness and efficiency of the tools could be assessed as well. Furthermore, the research could be linked to the sustainability maturity by making finer distinctions. Collaboration among entrepreneurs within the incubation program is a promising future research avenue in the realm of entrepreneurial learning theory (Bergman and McMullen, 2022). We suggest that scholars and practitioners can learn from each other's knowledge and collaborate to create new and applicable tools for SE facilitation, as seen in Fichter and Hurrelmann (2021).

Practitioners could put more emphasis on individualized services because it can thereby counter the challenge that no one-size-fits-all approach during business support is possible (Lamine *et al.*, 2018). These business support activities do not stand alone; they must be considered in the context of the overall incubation strategy. To successfully leverage SE as an incubator's competitive advantage, it is not necessary to offer a large range of tools but rather to focus on a carefully orchestrated SE incubation strategy with targeted and effective tools. Sustainability needs to be incorporated in all elements of the sustainability business incubation process, including the milestone planning and subsequent measurements. Previous research has highlighted the need for carefully designed sustainability-oriented incubation programs (e.g. Karahan, Rashid and Kratzer, 2022) with sustainability anchored in the incubators' organizational framework (Fichter and Hurrelmann, 2021) to avoid vague and arbitrary start-up support programs (Åstebro and Hoos, 2021; Diekel, Bach and Finkbeiner, 2023), as this can in turn put the legitimacy for public spending on such incubators at risk (Lamine *et al.*, 2018). In conclusion, we advise both policymakers and incubator managers to recognize and consider the distinct support needs of sustainable entrepreneurs and tailor incubation programs toward specific sustainability challenges instead of generalized missions.

Like any empirical research, our study has some limitations. Evidently, the generalization of our findings requires caution, given the limited sample size and the exploratory nature of the analysis. With only 11 cases, we limited generalizability concerns by following the principle of purposeful sampling and taking a broad picture from nine different countries in the sample. Since the data is self-reported through the conducted interviews, there may be a tendency for biased results. The validity and robustness of the findings were complemented by secondary data from information material provided by the participants and retrieved from the incubators' websites. Also, the participants were assured anonymity to address potential key informant bias. The multiple case study approach supported the mitigation of the negative effects of observer bias. For this study, we did not assess the effectiveness or performance of the incubators but focused on what the business incubation process for SE looks like.

References

Aaboen, L. (2009) 'Explaining incubators using firm analogy', *Technovation*, 29(10), pp. 657–670. Available at: https://doi.org/10.1016/j.technovation.2009.04.007.

Åstebro, T. and Hoos, F. (2021) 'Impact measurement based on repeated randomized control trials: The case of a training program to encourage social entrepreneurship', *Strategic Entrepreneurship Journal*, 15(2), pp. 254–278.

Ballering, T. and Masurel, E. (2020) 'Business incubators and their engagement in sustainable development activities: Empirical Evidence from Europe', *International Review of Entrepreneurship*, 18(2).

Bank, N., Fichter, K. and Klofsten, M. (2017) 'Sustainability-profiled incubators and securing the inflow of tenants – The case of Green Garage Berlin', *Journal of Cleaner Production*, 157, pp. 76–83. Available at: https://doi.org/10.1016/j.jclepro.2017.04.123.

Bank, N. and Kanda, W. (2016) 'Tenant recruitment and support processes in sustainability-profiled business incubators', *Industry and Higher Education*, 30(4), pp. 267–277.

Barbero, J.L. et al. (2014) 'Do different types of incubators produce different types of innovations?', *The Journal of Technology Transfer*, 39(2), pp. 151–168. Available at: https://doi.org/10.1007/s10961-013-9308-9.

Bergek, A. and Norrman, C. (2008) 'Incubator best practice: A framework', *Technovation*, 28(1–2), pp. 20–28. Available at: https://doi.org/10.1016/j.technovation.2007.07.008.

Bergman, B.J. and McMullen, J.S. (2022) 'Helping entrepreneurs help themselves: A review and relational research agenda on entrepreneurial support organizations', *Entrepreneurship Theory and Practice*, 46(3), pp. 688–728. Available at: https://doi.org/10.1177/10422587211028736.

Bergmann, T. and Utikal, H. (2021) 'How to support start-ups in developing a sustainable business model: The case of an European social impact accelerator', *Sustainability*, 13(6), p. 3337. Available at: https://doi.org/10.3390/su13063337.

Biggs, R., Westley, F.R. and Carpenter, S.R. (2010) 'Navigating the back loop: Fostering social innovation and transformation in ecosystem management', *Ecology and Society*, 15(2), p. art9. Available at: https://doi.org/10.5751/ES-03411-150209.

Bocken, N.M.P. (2015) 'Sustainable venture capital – catalyst for sustainable start-up success?', *Journal of Cleaner Production*, 108, pp. 647–658. Available at: https://doi.org/10.1016/j.jclepro.2015.05.079.

Braun, V. and Clarke, V. (2006) 'Using thematic analysis in psychology', *Qualitative Research in Psychology*, 3(2), pp. 77–101.

Bruneel, J. et al. (2012) 'The evolution of business incubators: Comparing demand and supply of business incubation services across different incubator generations', *Technovation*, 32(2), pp. 110–121. Available at: https://doi.org/10.1016/j.technovation.2011.11.003.

Carayannis, E.G. and von Zedtwitz, M. (2005) 'Architecting gloCal (global–local), real-virtual incubator networks (G-RVINs) as catalysts and accelerators of entrepreneurship in transitioning and developing economies: Lessons learned and best practices from current development and business incubation practices', *Technovation*, 25(2), pp. 95–110. Available at: https://doi.org/10.1016/S0166-4972(03)00072-5.

Carpenter, R.E. and Petersen, B.C. (2002) 'Capital market imperfections, high-tech investment, and new equity financing', *The Economic Journal*, 112(477), pp. F54–F72. Available at: https://doi.org/10.1111/1468-0297.00683.

Cirule, I. and Uvarova, I. (2022) 'Open innovation and determinants of technology-driven sustainable value creation in incubated start-ups', *Journal of Open Innovation: Technology, Market, and Complexity*, 8(3), p. 162. Available at: https://doi.org/10.3390/joitmc8030162.

Cohen, B. and Winn, M.I. (2007) 'Market imperfections, opportunity and sustainable entrepreneurship', *Journal of Business Venturing*, 22(1), pp. 29–49. Available at: https://doi.org/10.1016/j.jbusvent.2004.12.001.

Dean, T.J. and McMullen, J.S. (2007) 'Toward a theory of sustainable entrepreneurship: Reducing environmental degradation through entrepreneurial action', *Journal of Business Venturing*, 22(1), pp. 50–76. Available at: https://doi.org/10.1016/j.jbusvent.2005.09.003.

Dias Brito, M.D., Brunstein, J. and Amaro, R.A. (2018) 'Education for sustainability beyond the classroom: Companies born in university incubators', *REGEPE – Revista de Empreendedorismo e Gestão de Pequenas Empresas*, 7(2), pp. 01–30. Available at: https://doi.org/10.14211/regepe.v7i2.676.

Diekel, F., Bach, V. and Finkbeiner, M. (2023) 'Assessing the climate performance potential of start-ups: Insights and guidance on environmental sustainability assessment of young ventures', *Highlights of Sustainability*, 2(4), pp. 207–223. Available at: https://doi.org/10.54175/hsustain2040015.

Eisenhardt, K.M. (1989) 'Building theories from case study research', *Academy of Management Review*, 14(4), pp. 532–550.

Eisenhardt, K.M. (1991) 'Better stories and better constructs: The case for rigor and comparative logic', *Academy of Management Review*, 16(3), pp. 620–627.

Eisenhardt, K.M. and Graebner, M.E. (2007) 'Theory building from cases: Opportunities and challenges', *Academy of Management Journal*, 50(1), pp. 25–32.

Elkington, J. (1998) 'Partnerships from cannibals with forks: The triple bottom line of 21st-century business', *Environmental Quality Management*, 8(1), pp. 37–51. Available at: https://doi.org/10.1002/tqem.3310080106.

Fichter, K. and Hurrelmann, K. (2021) 'Sustainability-oriented business incubation: Framing and supporting sustainable entrepreneurship', in S. Mian, M. Klofsten, and W. Laminc (cds.) *Handbook of Research on Business and Technology Incubation and Acceleration*. Edward Elgar Publishing, pp. 478–495. Available at: https://doi.org/10.4337/9781788974783.00038.

Fonseca, S.A. and Jabbour, C.J.C. (2012) 'Assessment of business incubators' green performance: A framework and its application to Brazilian cases', *Technovation*, 32(2), pp. 122–132.

Freudenreich, B., Lüdeke-Freund, F. and Schaltegger, S. (2020) 'A stakeholder theory perspective on business models: Value creation for sustainability', *Journal of Business Ethics*, 166, pp. 3–18.

Gaddy, B.E. et al. (2017) 'Venture capital and cleantech: The wrong model for energy innovation', *Energy Policy*, 102, pp. 385–395. Available at: https://doi.org/10.1016/j.enpol.2016.12.035.

Gonsalves, M. and Rogerson, J.M. (2019) 'Business incubators and green technology: The Gauteng Climate Innovation Centre, South Africa', *Urbani izziv, Supplement*, (30), pp. 212–228. Available at: https://doi.org/10.5379/urbani-izziv-en-2019-30-supplement-014.

Grimaldi, R. and Grandi, A. (2005) 'Business incubators and new venture creation: An assessment of incubating models', *Technovation*, 25(2), pp. 111–121. Available at: https://doi.org/10.1016/S0166-4972(03)00076-2.

Hackett, S.M. and Dilts, D.M. (2004) 'A systematic review of business incubation research', *The Journal of Technology Transfer*, 29(1), pp. 55–82. Available at: https://doi.org/10.1023/B:JOTT.0000011181.11952.0f.

Haldar, S. (2019) 'Towards a conceptual understanding of sustainability-driven entrepreneurship', *Corporate Social Responsibility and Environmental Management*, 26(6), pp. 1157–1170.

Hall, B.H. and Lerner, J. (2010) 'Chapter 14 – The financing of R&D and innovation', in B.H. Hall and N. Rosenberg (eds.) *Handbook of the Economics of Innovation*. North-Holland Handbook of the Economics of Innovation, Vol. 1, pp. 609–639. Available at: https://doi.org/10.1016/S0169-7218(10)01014-2.

Harrer, T. and Owen, R. (2022) 'Reducing early-stage Cleantech funding gaps: An exploration of the role of environmental performance indicators', *International Journal of Entrepreneurial Behavior & Research*, 28(9), pp. 268–288. https://doi.org/10.1108/IJEBR-10-2021-0849

Hausberg, J.P. and Korreck, S. (2020) 'Business incubators and accelerators: A co-citation analysis-based, systematic literature review', *The Journal of Technology Transfer*, 45(1), pp. 151–176. Available at: https://doi.org/10.1007/s10961-018-9651-y.

Hirschmann, M., Moritz, A. and Block, J.H. (2022) 'Motives, supporting activities, and selection criteria of social impact incubators: An experimental conjoint study', *Nonprofit and Voluntary Sector Quarterly*, 51(5), pp. 1095–1133. Available at: https://doi.org/10.1177/08997640211057402.

Hockerts, K. and Wüstenhagen, R. (2010) 'Greening Goliaths versus emerging Davids – Theorizing about the role of incumbents and new entrants in sustainable entrepreneurship', *Journal of Business Venturing*, 25(5), pp. 481–492. Available at: https://doi.org/10.1016/j.jbusvent.2009.07.005.

Jick, T.D. (1979) 'Mixing qualitative and quantitative methods: Triangulation in action', *Administrative Science Quarterly*, 24(4), pp. 602–611.

Joyce, A. and Paquin, R.L. (2016) 'The triple layered business model canvas: A tool to design more sustainable business models', *Journal of Cleaner Production*, 135, pp. 1474–1486. Available at: https://doi.org/10.1016/j.jclepro.2016.06.067.

Kanda, W. et al. (2018) 'Roles of intermediaries in supporting eco-innovation', *Journal of Cleaner Production*, 205, pp. 1006–1016. Available at: https://doi.org/10.1016/j.jclepro.2018.09.132.

Karahan, M., Rashid, L. and Kratzer, J. (2022) 'Gearing-up for purpose: The relationship between entrepreneurs' usage of incubation support services and sustainable impacts', *Journal of Cleaner Production*, 377, p. 134315. Available at: https://doi.org/10.1016/j.jclepro.2022.134315.

Klofsten, M. et al. (2020) 'Incubator specialization and size: Divergent paths towards operational scale', *Technological Forecasting and Social Change*, 151, p. 119821. Available at: https://doi.org/10.1016/j.techfore.2019.119821.

Klofsten, M., Bank, N. and Bienkowska, D. (2016) *The Role of Incubators in Supporting Sustainable Entrepreneurship*. Berlin, Germany: SHIFT [Preprint].

Klofsten, M. and Bienkowska, D. (2021) 'Business incubators within entrepreneurial ecosystems: Sustainability aspects of new venture support and development', in *Handbook of Research on Business and Technology Incubation and Acceleration*. Cheltenham: Edward Elgar Publishing.

Lamine, W. et al. (2018) 'Technology business incubation mechanisms and sustainable regional development', *The Journal of Technology Transfer*, 43(5), pp. 1121–1141. Available at: https://doi.org/10.1007/s10961-016-9537-9.

Lamperti, S., Sammut, S. and Courrent, J.-M. (2023) 'From incubator's knowledge transfer to sustainability start-ups' impact: A case study in a French support program', *Journal of Knowledge Management*, ahead-of-print(ahead-of-print). Available at: https://doi.org/10.1108/JKM-09-2022-0690.

de Lange, D.E. (2017) 'Start-up sustainability: An insurmountable cost or a life-giving investment?', *Journal of Cleaner Production*, 156, pp. 838–854. Available at: https://doi.org/10.1016/j.jclepro.2017.04.108.

Lans, T., Blok, V. and Wesselink, R. (2014) 'Learning apart and together: Towards an integrated competence framework for sustainable entrepreneurship in higher education', *Journal of Cleaner Production*, 62, pp. 37–47. Available at: https://doi.org/10.1016/j.jclepro.2013.03.036.

Meyskens, M. and Carsrud, A.L. (2013) 'Nascent green-technology ventures: A study assessing the role of partnership diversity in firm success', *Small Business Economics*, 40(3), pp. 739–759. Available at: https://doi.org/10.1007/s11187-011-9400-1.

Mian, S.A. (1996) 'The university business incubator: A strategy for developing new research/technology-based firms', *The Journal of High Technology Management Research*, 7(2), pp. 191–208. Available at: https://doi.org/10.1016/S1047-8310(96)90004-8.

Mian, S.A. (2014) 'Business incubation and incubator mechanisms', in *Handbook of Research on Entrepreneurship*, pp. 335–366. Cheltenham, UK and Northampton, MA, USA: Edward Elgar Publishing.

Miles, M.B. and Huberman, A.M. (1994) *Qualitative Data Analysis: An Expanded Sourcebook*. Thousand Oaks: Sage Publications.

Millette, S., Eiríkur Hull, C. and Williams, E. (2020) 'Business incubators as effective tools for driving circular economy', *Journal of Cleaner Production*, 266, p. 121999. Available at: https://doi.org/10.1016/j.jclepro.2020.121999.

Mrkajic, B., Murtinu, S. and Scalera, V.G. (2019) 'Is green the new gold? Venture capital and green entrepreneurship', *Small Business Economics*, 52(4), pp. 929–950. Available at: https://doi.org/10.1007/s11187-017-9943-x.

Muñoz, P. and Cohen, B. (2018) 'Sustainable entrepreneurship research: Taking stock and looking ahead: Sustainable entrepreneurship research', *Business Strategy and the Environment*, 27(3), pp. 300–322. Available at: https://doi.org/10.1002/bse.2000.

Nave, A. and Franco, M. (2019) 'University-Firm cooperation as a way to promote sustainability practices: A sustainable entrepreneurship perspective', *Journal of Cleaner Production*, 230, pp. 1188–1196. Available at: https://doi.org/10.1016/j.jclepro.2019.05.195.

Neumeyer, X. and Santos, S.C. (2018) 'Sustainable business models, venture typologies, and entrepreneurial ecosystems: A social network perspective', *Journal of Cleaner Production*, 172, pp. 4565–4579. Available at: https://doi.org/10.1016/j.jclepro.2017.08.216.

Nicolopoulou, K. et al. (2017) 'An incubation perspective on social innovation: The London Hub – a social incubator', *R&D Management*, 47(3), pp. 368–384. Available at: https://doi.org/10.1111/radm.12179.

Oliveira, M. de M., Cahen, F.R. and Borini, F.M. (eds.) (2019) *Startups and Innovation Ecosystems in Emerging Markets: A Brazilian Perspective*. Cham: Springer International Publishing. Available at: https://doi.org/10.1007/978-3-030-10865-6.

Parrish, B.D. (2010) 'Sustainability-driven entrepreneurship: Principles of organization design', *Journal of Business Venturing*, 25(5), pp. 510–523. Available at: https://doi.org/10.1016/j.jbusvent.2009.05.005.

Patton, M.Q. (1990) *Qualitative Evaluation and Research Methods*. Newbury Park, CA: Sage.

Patzelt, H. and Shepherd, D.A. (2011) 'Recognizing opportunities for sustainable development', *Entrepreneurship Theory and Practice*, 35(4), pp. 631–652. Available at: https://doi.org/10.1111/j.1540-6520.2010.00386.x.

Pauwels, C. et al. (2016) 'Understanding a new generation incubation model: The accelerator', *Technovation*, 50–51, pp. 13–24. Available at: https://doi.org/10.1016/j.technovation.2015.09.003.

Ploum, L. et al. (2018) 'Toward a Validated Competence Framework for Sustainable Entrepreneurship', *Organization & Environment*, 31(2), pp. 113–132. Available at: https://doi.org/10.1177/1086026617697039.

Polzin, F., von Flotow, P. and Klerkx, L. (2016) 'Addressing barriers to eco-innovation: Exploring the finance mobilisation functions of institutional innovation intermediaries', *Technological Forecasting and Social Change*, 103, pp. 34–46.

Potts, T. (2010) 'The natural advantage of regions: Linking sustainability, innovation, and regional development in Australia', *Journal of Cleaner Production*, 18(8), pp. 713–725. Available at: https://doi.org/10.1016/j.jclepro.2010.01.008.

Randjelovic, J., O'Rourke, A.R. and Orsato, R.J. (2003) 'The emergence of green venture capital', *Business Strategy and the Environment*, 12(4), pp. 240–253. Available at: https://doi.org/10.1002/bse.361.

Rashid, L. (2022) 'Bursting the bubble: Why sustainability initiatives often lack adequate intention to action translation', *Small Business Economics*, 59(1), pp. 1–9.

Rashid, L., Alzafari, K. and Kratzer, J. (2020) 'Founder personalities, behaviors and new venture success in sub-Saharan Africa', *Technological Forecasting and Social Change*, 151, p. 119766. Available at: https://doi.org/10.1016/j.techfore.2019.119766.

Rice, M.P. (2002) 'Co-production of business assistance in business incubators: An exploratory study', *Journal of Business Venturing*, 17(2), pp. 163–187.

Sansone, G. et al. (2020) 'Are social incubators different from other incubators? Evidence from Italy', *Technological Forecasting and Social Change*, 158, p. 120132.

Sarasvathy, S.D. (2004) 'Making it happen: Beyond theories of the firm to theories of firm design', *Entrepreneurship Theory and Practice*, 28(6), pp. 519–531.

Schaltegger, S. and Wagner, M. (2011) 'Sustainable entrepreneurship and sustainability innovation: Categories and interactions', *Business Strategy and the Environment*, 20(4), pp. 222–237. Available at: https://doi.org/10.1002/bse.682.

Shepherd, D.A. and Patzelt, H. (2011) 'The new field of sustainable entrepreneurship: Studying entrepreneurial action linking "what is to be sustained" with "what is to be developed"', *Entrepreneurship Theory and Practice*, 35(1), pp. 137–163. Available at: https://doi.org/10.1111/j.1540-6520.2010.00426.x.

Shepherd, D.A., Patzelt, H. and Baron, R.A. (2013) '"I care about nature, but . . .": Disengaging values in assessing opportunities that cause harm', *Academy of Management Journal*, 56(5), pp. 1251–1273.

Shepherd, D.A. et al. (2019) 'What are we explaining? A review and agenda on initiating, engaging, performing, and contextualizing entrepreneurship', *Journal of Management*, 45(1), pp. 159–196.

Siefkes, M., Bjørgum, Ø. and Sørheim, R. (2023) 'Business angels investing in green ventures: How do they add value to their start-ups?', *Venture Capital* [Preprint]. Available at: https://doi.org/10.1080/13691066.2023.2260101.

Siefkes, M., Hamer, A. L., Haaland, G. and Bjørgum, Ø. (2024) 'Profit first, environmental impact second? Investigating hybrid institutional logics in venture capital investment approaches', *Business Strategy and the Environment* [Preprint]. https://doi.org/10.1002/bse.3902.

Sohail, K., Belitski, M. and Castro Christiansen, L. (2023) 'Developing business incubation process frameworks: A systematic literature review', *Journal of Business Research*, 162, p. 113902. Available at: https://doi.org/10.1016/j.jbusres.2023.113902.

Surana, K., Singh, A. and Sagar, A.D. (2020) 'Strengthening science, technology, and innovation-based incubators to help achieve sustainable development goals: Lessons from India', *Technological Forecasting and Social Change*, 157, p. 120057. Available at: https://doi.org/10.1016/j.techfore.2020.120057.

Terán-Yépez, E. et al. (2020) 'Sustainable entrepreneurship: Review of its evolution and new trends', *Journal of Cleaner Production*, 252, p. 119742. Available at: https://doi.org/10.1016/j.jclepro.2019.119742.

Theodoraki, C., Messeghem, K. and Rice, M.P. (2018) 'A social capital approach to the development of sustainable entrepreneurial ecosystems: An explorative study', *Small Business Economics*, 51(1), pp. 153–170. Available at: https://doi.org/10.1007/s11187-017-9924-0.

Tiba, S., van Rijnsoever, F.J. and Hekkert, M.P. (2020) 'The lighthouse effect: How successful entrepreneurs influence the sustainability-orientation of entrepreneurial ecosystems', *Journal of Cleaner Production*, 264, p. 121616. Available at: https://doi.org/10.1016/j.jclepro.2020.121616.

Vedula, S. et al. (2022) 'Entrepreneurship for the public good: A review, critique, and path forward for social and environmental entrepreneurship research', *Academy of Management Annals*, 16(1), pp. 391–425. Available at: https://doi.org/10.5465/annals.2019.0143.

Volkmann, C. et al. (2021) 'Sustainable entrepreneurial ecosystems: An emerging field of research', *Small Business Economics*, 56(3), pp. 1047–1055. Available at: https://doi.org/10.1007/s11187-019-00253-7.

Wiklund, J., Wright, M. and Zahra, S.A. (2019) 'Conquering relevance: Entrepreneurship research's grand challenge', *Entrepreneurship Theory and Practice*, 43(3), pp. 419–436.

Woolley, J.L. and MacGregor, N. (2022) 'The influence of incubator and accelerator participation on nanotechnology venture success', *Entrepreneurship Theory and Practice*, 46(6), pp. 1717–1755.
Yi, G. (2021) 'From green entrepreneurial intentions to green entrepreneurial behaviors: The role of university entrepreneurial support and external institutional support', *International Entrepreneurship and Management Journal*, 17(2), pp. 963–979.
Yin, R.K. (2009) 'How to do better case studies', in *The SAGE Handbook of Applied Social Research Methods*, vol. 2, pp. 254–282. Newbury Park, CA: Sage.
Zedtwitz, M. von (2003) 'Classification and management of incubators: Aligning strategic objectives and competitive scope for new business facilitation', *International Journal of Entrepreneurship and Innovation Management*, 3(1/2), p. 176. Available at: https://doi.org/10.1504/IJEIM.2003.002227.

6 Academic startup clinic

Applying effectuation principles to educate and support academic entrepreneurs

Basel Hammoda

Introduction

Entrepreneurship education (EE) has emerged as a reliable tool to facilitate and accelerate the production of entrepreneurs and entrepreneurial firms which benefit the economy (Matlay, 2005; Pittaway and Cope, 2007). Recently, there is a growing direction to move from traditional approaches that focus on knowledge transfer to one which equips learners with the required skills and competences through a person-centric, processual, and active approach (teaching through entrepreneurship) (Günzel-Jensen and Robinson, 2017; Mäkimurto-Koivumaa and Puhakka, 2013).

One method increasingly used in "through courses" is effectuation. As explained by Sarasvathy (2001), effectuation implies that entrepreneurs begin with a general vision, and use available resources, knowledge, and connections (who they are, what they know, and who they know). The direction is not set in advance, and they remain adaptive as they progress with their journey toward realizing their entrepreneurial aspiration, leveraging opportunities as they are made available to them and learn through their actions. Building on effectual logic, entrepreneurship educators can adopt a processual approach to teaching that revolves around the learner. This approach allows for entrepreneurs to receive tailored support while they explore multiple options, take affordable risks, leverage connections at their disposal, make use of environmental contingencies, and learn on the job through experimentation (Sarasvathy, 2001).

In the context of academic entrepreneurship, an effectual approach could prove particularly relevant. Academic entrepreneurs (AEs) typically face resource and time constraints (Alexander *et al.,* 2015), witness insufficient interest from higher educational institutions (HEIs) in their entrepreneurial endeavours (Abreu and Grinevich, 2013), lack exposure to entrepreneurial role models (Miller *et al.,* 2018), face trade-offs between their academic and entrepreneurial identities (Radosevich, 1995), and need to improve their skills and stay motivated (Miller *et al.,* 2018). Thus, Fayolle and Gailly (2008) argued that effectuation can be used effectively in developing entrepreneurial learning initiatives,

DOI: 10.4324/9781003324737-6

which should be aligned with the individual preferences, context, and available resources and connections of the learners (Rae, 2005).

In this chapter, a model for academic EE and support is conceptualized and proposed, building on effectuation principles and experiential learning concepts. Effectuation principles are synthesized, adapted, and complemented with experiential logic to be applied in an educational context, specific to nascent AEs. We first review the literature on academic entrepreneurship and effectuation, highlighting the research and practice state of affairs in each. We then present the conceptual model and explain its different components and their interlinkages.

Background

Academic entrepreneurship

In literature, the concept of academic entrepreneurship is a complex one with several subfields contributing to its scholarly development and understanding of its predeterminants and impact (Skute, 2019). These literature streams include entrepreneurial university, spin-offs, innovation, knowledge transfer, knowledge co-creation, and entrepreneurial identity, among others. We can define academic entrepreneurship as the processes and configurations that HEIs apply to establish, promote, and realize the benefits of their entrepreneurial orientation. It features a dynamic, multi-layered ecosystem with individual, organizational, and societal stakeholders (Audretsch *et al.*, 2019; Guerrero and Urbano, 2012; Hayter *et al.*, 2018).

Academic entrepreneurship has been receiving increasing attention from the scholarly community, policymakers, and industry professionals in recent years (e.g., Gümüsay and Bohné 2018; Secundo *et al.*, 2020; Skute, 2019), as science-based new ventures are judged to have a more tangible role in technological and economic development than traditional ones (Rasmussen *et al.*, 2014). Academic entrepreneurship is indeed considered an important source of innovation (Bienkowska *et al.*, 2016; Galán-Muros *et al.*, 2017), regional economic and societal development (Fini *et al.*, 2011; Perkmann *et al.*, 2013), and provides additional revenues to HEIs (Hmieleski and Powell, 2018). Recognizing that, governments and HEIs adjusted their policies and strategies to ignite an innovative drive among researchers and support them in transforming their innovations to products and services (Bienkowska *et al.,* 2016).

The changing role of academic entrepreneurship

The needle has moved, however, in recent years due to changes in government support policies, market demands, and the business models of HEIs. Universities are expected now to generate more income from private sources. Moreover, university spin-offs are becoming a competitive advantage in the higher education industry. They affect universities' rankings and play an important role in attracting students and researchers (Siegel and Wright, 2015). As a result, HEIs are encouraged to become more entrepreneurial and production hubs of innovative solutions (Bienkowska *et al.,* 2016). They are more and more regarded as the epicentre for local innovation and the fulcrum of industry and government collaboration (Hammoda, 2024; Secundo *et al.,* 2020). Hence, instead of relying on patent revenues, HEIs and AEs alike have started focusing on commercializing innovation through creating and launching research-driven start-ups (Galán-Muros *et al.,* 2017; Grimaldi *et al.,* 2011; Siegel and Wright, 2015).

This transition, however, is proving difficult. Universities have now a broader set of priorities, which can disperse their efforts. Moreover, they have inherent expertise in fulfilling their education and research roles, but not in establishing and directing an entrepreneurial organization. Universities also have to invest in physical, human, and technological capital in order to build a supportive platform for their spin-offs (Gianiodis and Meek, 2020; Grimaldi *et al.,* 2011).

While originally confined to faculty (professors) pursuing entrepreneurial projects, the scope of academic entrepreneurship has expanded lately to include graduate students, doctoral candidates, postdoctoral and early career researchers, and even alumni (Siegel and Wright, 2015). Therefore, universities are expected to play a bigger role in facilitating the equipping of a broader base of current and potential AEs with the required skills, ecosystem networks, professional experiences, and access to resources. This necessitates rethinking and reinventing the current models and approaches to support AEs, that are centred around them as individuals.

The focus on academic entrepreneurs

Several scholars turned our attention to the importance of individual level determinants of academic entrepreneurship such as Jain *et al.* (2009), who highlighted the role identity conflict that researchers with entrepreneurial intentions witness. They argued for a stronger focus on supporting the researcher as the core foundation of academic entrepreneurship. Hayter *et al.* (2018) underlined the role of graduate students in university spin-offs as in identifying market opportunities and acquiring research funding, while dealing with challenges such as finding talent with relevant scientific and business knowledge. Siegel and Wright (2015) highlighted the motivating role of funding dedicated to scientific innovation from public and private entities on AEs commercialization activity, while Grimaldi *et al.* (2011), in their review of literature on academic entrepreneurship, highlighted the individual scientist as an important factor. However, they still emphasized the strong impact of university and system-level factors on shaping researchers' entrepreneurial intentions and orientation. Moreover, Zhang *et al.* (2022) examined the factors influencing AE intentions and motivation, and posited that these factors do not exert a causal or linear effect on AEs but are rather diverse and complex in nature.

AEs and the factors impacting them are different from regular entrepreneurs, as they try to find compromises between their original research-focused and the to-be commercially driven orientations. There are several challenges that intersect their way to achieve their entrepreneurial dreams. They lack required resources and time (Alexander *et al.,* 2015; Müller-Wieland *et al.,* 2019). HEIs tend to deprioritize their entrepreneurial interests (Abreu and Grinevich, 2013). They are isolated in the university without much interaction with startups, industry, or markets (Lubik and Garnsey, 2016; Miller *et al.,* 2018). They face high levels of uncertainty (Sinell *et al.,* 2015), consistently trying to align their academic and entrepreneurial identities (Li *et al.*, 2020). They are also hindered by a rigid academic hierarchy (Skute, 2019).

Most importantly, AEs lack the necessary means to improve their entrepreneurial skills and self-efficacy (Miller *et al.,* 2018). Despite the growth in EE in HEIs, there is a lack of courses and programs designed to address the specific learning and training needs of scientific researchers (Pittaway *et al.,* 2023; Siegel and Wright, 2015). It therefore comes as no surprise that the literature has concluded that a significant proportion of research-driven entrepreneurial projects fail at conception or dwindle as the time goes by (Fini *et al.,* 2017; Fisher *et al.,* 2016). This finding is shared with more "regular" startups, with some studies finding that the firm closures are at a higher rate than the new firms' establishment (Metzger, 2014), with a remarkably high failure rates among startups (92%) reported in the Startup Genome project (Marmer *et al.*, 2012). The universities face similar consequences, with the majority of technology transfer offices (TTOs) showing little (Fini *et al.*, 2017) or even negative return on investment (Lafuente and Berbegal-Mirabent, 2019; Puntillo *et al.,* 2022).

Academic entrepreneurship education

A key element in achieving the desired outcomes of academic entrepreneurship is to equip AEs with the relevant business knowledge, skills, and experiences. While AEs might exhibit high degrees of scientific and technological knowledge, they suffer from a lack of relevant education and training on opportunity identification and exploitation (Skute, 2019). In addition, universities are expected to broker their connections with the wider entrepreneurial ecosystem and industry (Secundo *et al.*, 2016). EE is regarded a viable option to provide academics with necessary mindset and competences in support of their entrepreneurial aspirations (Bienkowska *et al.,* 2016; Rippa *et al.,* 2022). EE can prepare researchers for exploring business opportunities and adapting their innovations to market needs (Pittaway *et al.,* 2023; Munoz *et al.,* 2020). Moreover, Gianiodis and Meek (2020) argue for the bigger impact that EE can have on universities toward achieving their desired technology transfer and commercialization outcomes.

However, current research on the pedagogical approaches to academic EE among researchers is scarce and displays a fragmentation among HEIs approach

(Bienkowska *et al.,* 2016; Rippa *et al.,* 2022). Bolzani *et al.* (2021), for example, found that the majority of TTOs that are tasked with research commercialization participate in the provision of EE to university scientists. They do so either directly by offering EE programs to faculty and students or through collaborating with departmental EE programs. Gianiodis and Meek (2020) argued for incorporating diverse stakeholders in academic EE and proposed a modular framework for supporting innovation and assessing it. Hence, a promising area of research is investigating the development of entrepreneurial competences by academics (Gümüsay and Bohné, 2018; Oosterbeek *et al.,* 2010) through applying specialized approaches to entrepreneurial learning (Guerrero and Urbano, 2012), as they advance through the entrepreneurial process.

Effectuation in academic entrepreneurship

Given the challenges and uncertainty that AEs face and the lack of attuned approaches and programs to upskill them, Li *et al.* (2020) suggest that an effectual logic could be suitable for addressing those shortcomings that AEs face. This is especially true for the educational part of their development (Fayolle and Gailly, 2008) as AEs face a conundrum between their academic career in doing research and teaching students, and the entrepreneurial one in marshaling resources and transforming their innovation into a viable business (Müller-Wieland *et al.,* 2019; Villani *et al.,* 2018).

Moreover, such transformation requires acquisition of new (entrepreneurial) behaviors, while they maintain their existing (academic) roles (Jain *et al.,* 2009). Effectuation as a heavily behavioral model advocates for entrepreneurs to enact several attitudes such as fomenting existing resources, leveraging contingencies as they occur, capitalizing on connections, and containing and managing risks (Sarasvathy, 2001). In addition, the effectual logic supports emergent decision making within academic entrepreneurship context. It advocates for a bootstrapping approach to mapping and mobilizing resources (Politis *et al.,* 2012), idea discovery, evaluation, testing (Lubik and Garnsey, 2016), flexibility in adjusting the developing model to the changing circumstances (ibid.), navigating around bottlenecks and critical events, and emphasizing and the positive role of the connections an entrepreneur makes along the way. These explicit effectual activities are synonymous to the process of scientific innovation and commercialization.

Effectuation

Effectuation was proposed by Sarasvathy (2001) as a behavioral model to provide a complementary alternative to causation (Agogué *et al.,* 2015; Reymen *et al.,* 2017), which often follows a linear logic to entrepreneurship (Mäkimurto-Koivumaa and Puhakka, 2013). Following a causal approach to venture creation, the entrepreneur sets a goal, procures the required resources to achieve it, researches the market, and forecasts returns and possible risks. Effectuation, however, explores the unpredictive decision-making process of entrepreneurs when they are faced by uncertainty, through leveraging available resources, knowledge, and connections (Dew *et al.*, 2009; Read and Sarasvathy, 2005; Sarasvathy, 2009). Hitherto, it rhymes with the entrepreneurial premise of making use of available means and exploiting opportunities (Racat *et al.*, 2023). Given the increasing degree of environmental and market dynamism and uncertainty, there has been a growing interest in effectuation as a decision-making approach in business and entrepreneurship recently as an alternative logic to causation (Frese *et al.*, 2020; Hauser *et al.*, 2020).

Having studied on experienced entrepreneurs, Sarasvathy (2001) established four main principles of applying an effectual logic. These are affordable loss, which limits resource sacrifice and hemorrhage rather than chasing expected returns; leveraging industry connections as alliances rather than viewing them as competitive forces; exploiting contingencies along the way instead of deliberate planning and precise goal setting; and controlling uncertainty rather than adopting a predictive analytical behavior (Sarasvathy, 2001). Effectuation thus advocates for adopting resource preservation, partnerships building, business model flexibility, and experimentation in entrepreneurial activities (Chandler *et al.*, 2011). We elaborate on effectuation principles in the following sections.

Effectuation principles

Means: Effectual entrepreneurs start with available resources and proceed from there, instead of defining goals and planning backwards. In this way, effectuation draws parallels from the core logic of bricolage (Senyard *et al.*, 2009). The rationale is that entrepreneurs should focus on the resources they already have access to and control over, instead of wasting effort in acquiring distant resources to attain their predefined goals. Hence, in the effectual approach, the goals are shaped as the proposition becomes clearer and remains flexible pertinent to the evolvement of the business model (Honig, 2004). Moreover, in practice, entrepreneurs constantly update and adjust their strategies and goals to the changing resources and circumstances (Alvarez and Barney, 2007; Read and Sarasvathy, 2005). These means include knowledge; industry experience; skills; connection; and the financial, human, and material assets they can capitalize on.

Affordable loss: The concept of affordable loss directs the effectual entrepreneurs' focus to resource containment when evaluating ideas and projects to pursue, instead of basing their decisions on potential future returns (Sarasvathy, 2009). Available means are identifiable and quantifiable (ibid.), in comparison to the guesswork involved in estimating expected returns. Effectuation then directs entrepreneurs to commit only resources they are ready to relinquish, thus minimizing their losses.

Partnerships: The effectual logic views other individuals and organizations having similar or related businesses as potential collaborators and partners. This opposes the causal and strategic views of the business environment as a competitive battlefield. Hence, an effectual entrepreneur leverages existing and new connections to build strategic alliances that provide him with further resources and opportunities (Sarasvathy, 2001), rather than adopting a defensive or an aggressive stance.

Contingencies: Exploiting contingencies entails exploring opportunities as they arise rather than viewing challenges as merely obstacles (Fisher, 2012). This mindset can be supported by adopting a flexible approach to defining goals, based on available means. It thus leads to the adoption of a controlling approach to risks rather than trying to predict them.

Control: Navigating the emerging firm through the troughs and heights of the turbulent seas of entrepreneurship is an essential concept in the effectual logic (Sarasvathy, 2009). Instead of businesses spending time upfront trying to predict and scenario-plan their responses to every possible risk, the effectual approach applies a guiding principle, more or less of a firm hand, to risk contingency.

The building blocks of effectuation do not exist in isolation and are not entirely linear. The exploitation of the means and the connections develops artefacts that can then be adjusted and adapted based on evolving contingencies. The knowledge and resources acquired through alliances feed back into the means and aspirations of the entrepreneur. Similarly, as the entrepreneur adjusts their mental and business model along the process, new alliances are thought. This view reflects a dynamic nature of the effectual process that resembles entrepreneurial realities (Dew *et al.*, 2009).

Effectual logic in entrepreneurship education

Current approaches to EE lean toward a causation-based logic (Mäkimurto-Koivumaa and Puhakka, 2013). They fall short of equipping students with real-life skills. In recent years, there has been a growing trend to follow a "through" experiential approach to EE, which can provide students with the practical skills they need for entrepreneurship. Despite an abundance of trials at theorizing the practice-based approach through several lenses, there is yet to be a concept that can be unequivocally aligned with a learning "through" approach that resembles real-life entrepreneurship (Fayolle and Gailly, 2008). A "through" approach to EE aligns with the dynamic nature of entrepreneurship as a practice (Blenker *et al.*, 2012). This is true for effectuation, as a learning model, which emphasizes the learn by doing approach, in contrast to linear cause-effect-based approaches such as business planning, which are less likely to influence the daily behaviors of entrepreneurs (Politis, 2005). Hence, several scholars (e.g., Fayolle and Gailly, 2008; Günzel-Jensen and Robinson, 2017) argued that effectuation is a suitable paradigm to be applied in designing and conducting experiential entrepreneurship programs.

Moreover, EE in its broad definition of developing an entrepreneurial learner helps develop students' knowledge, skills, mindset, and intentions. This contrasts with the traditional narrow causation-based focus of EE on promoting firm creation among students. However, following an effectual approach translates to an EE that directly contributes to the venture creation process, without compromising on the other aims. Effectuation calls for an educational pedagogy that reflects the opportunity identification and exploitation phenomena of entrepreneurship (Sarasvathy, 2003; Shane and Venkataraman, 2000). Its principles can be more widely conceptualized as pedagogical guidelines to improve the delivery of EE and achieving its broad range of desired outcomes (Günzel-Jensen and Robinson, 2017; Mäkimurto-Koivumaa and Puhakka, 2013).

However, there are several limitations in effectuation. As a theory, it needs more clarity on the explanation of its building blocks and their configurations in different applications. Similarly, there has been limited theorizing in literature to advance our understanding of effectuation and its dispositions. Moreover, the original model stemmed from an examination of established entrepreneurs' decision-making logic. Hence, its projection on nascent entrepreneurs and entrepreneurial learners needs to be further established and might require some alterations to the original model.

A few researchers applied effectuation to academic entrepreneurship (e.g., Agogué *et al.,* 2015; Li *et al.,* 2020; Villani *et al.,* 2018) or EE in general (Günzel-Jensen and Robinson, 2017). Agogué *et al.* (2015) explored the application of effectuation and causation logics in decision-making by nascent student technology entrepreneurs, as they analyze an existing platform and developed new applications for it, using C-K diagrams.

Li *et al.* (2020) investigated the adoption of effectual logic among AEs and its impact on firm performance, and whether their pursuit of a role innovation methodology improves the consequences. They found that, in general, adopting an effectual logic and conjoining it with role innovation leads to improved prospects of academic entrepreneurship endeavors. However, AEs applying the affordable loss principle, that is, investing limited resources, indented their entrepreneurial chances. It is worth noting, however, that science-based entrepreneurship is resource intensive, especially in the early stages of the business development, which can provide some rationale to their findings. They also found that even when AE manage to transform their roles, it does not seem to help them become more flexible to a degree that can influence their enterprise prospects positively.

Villani *et al.* (2018) examined the antecedents for using effectuation and/or causation by AEs, based on (fs/QCA) of a longitudinal startup dataset in the United States. They found that AEs can exhibit some inclination toward risk-taking, apply their industry and startup experience, conduct deliberate planning and market research, and leverage partnerships. But they mostly lack the required flexibility compared to regular entrepreneurs, denoting a lack of effectual logic preparedness. The causal goal-defined planning approach is especially relevant among risk-averse AEs who lack enough industry and startup experience. They called for more research on understanding the causal and effectual approaches among AE.

Günzel-Jensen and Robinson, (2017) structured and delivered an undergraduate course using effectuation over six months. They inductively identified three barriers to its application among to-be entrepreneurs. The first is their noviceness. While effectuation was developed among expert entrepreneurs, students lack the required means, or an understanding of what resources are required. Secondly, the encompassing context was still "educational" and not realistic, which affected their commitment to the process. Thirdly, they suffered from a lack of legitimacy as the educator was not an entrepreneur or a mentor and thus the effectuation-based methods and processes could not be substantiated by real-world narratives.

In summation, despite the growing interest in academic entrepreneurship from all involved stakeholders, there are still several unique challenges impeding AEs' pursuit of their science-based startups. In addition, current approaches to EE are still unable to present the ideal model for a learning "through" approach that supports nascent entrepreneurs' enaction in entrepreneurial realities. By deduction from literature, I have shown that effectuation might represent the missing link between the two juxtaposing aims of EE; venture creation and entrepreneurial competencies development. This duality is of critical importance to AEs as it covers their true needs of competence development while navigating their relevant industry networks.

Academic startup clinic

Background and setup

The developed model synthesized effectuation principles and adapted their application to an educational context, while leveraging linkages between effectuation and experiential pedagogies for developing a model for academic EE. The original effectuation model was designed based on expert entrepreneurs' decision-making behaviors (Sarasvathy, 2001; Perry *et al.,* 2012). Hence, it needs to be adjusted for entrepreneurial learning among AEs, who can be considered as novice entrepreneurs. AEs also have certain characteristics and face specific challenges in their pursuit of an entrepreneurial career, compared to regular entrepreneurs.

The term "clinic" was selected for two reasons. First, we believe that developing academic entrepreneurship is an ongoing process that requires initial assessment of the idea, business model, AE capabilities, with several support "follow-ups" spaced by a few weeks' intervals. Hence, it resembles the remedial process followed in some medical practices. Secondly, the personalized approach and connections, which resemble health care provision, are essential in supporting AEs due to the relative uniqueness of their scientific innovation, their time constraints, and their social support exigency.

The clinic should ideally be managed by a team with the following competences: EE expertise, ecosystem and industry connections, experiences in startup mentoring, as well as academic research. Participation is open to all current and aspiring AEs from all disciplines with a basic idea or a general understanding of what they want to achieve. Hence, they represent a heterogenous group, with differing backgrounds, ideas, and expertise, but share a common purpose, which is becoming an entrepreneur.

This multidisciplinary organization of EE helps enrich discussions, collaborative learning, and knowledge transfer among participants (Volkmann and Audretsch, 2017), following a T-shaped educational approach to academic EE (Rippa *et al.,* 2022). It can improve AEs' capabilities, intentions, and self-efficacy (Fayolle and Gailly, 2008; Rippa *et al.,* 2022). Moreover, it can equip the novices among them with diverse set of skills and perspectives, complementary to their expertise, to effectively address complex real-life problems, which often require an understanding of multiple disciplines (Pittaway *et al.,* 2023).

Academic startup clinic model components

In this part, we explain the different components of the proposed Academic Startup Clinic model as illustrated in Figure 6.1 in detail, delineating their relationships and value flow.

Group meetups

The backbone of the model is the monthly group meetups. These take place in-person, and those who cannot attend can join the meetup online. The meetup typically lasts between 2 and 3 hours only, given the limited time available to AEs (Alexander *et al.,* 2015). It starts with a round of progress updates from the AEs. This is a chance to exhume challenges, worries, and upsets, and reflect on them (Kolb and Kolb, 2005). In return, AEs receive support and advice from other members in the social circle which resembles a community of inquiry (COI). COI has proved to expand the knowledge and social capital of entrepreneurs and

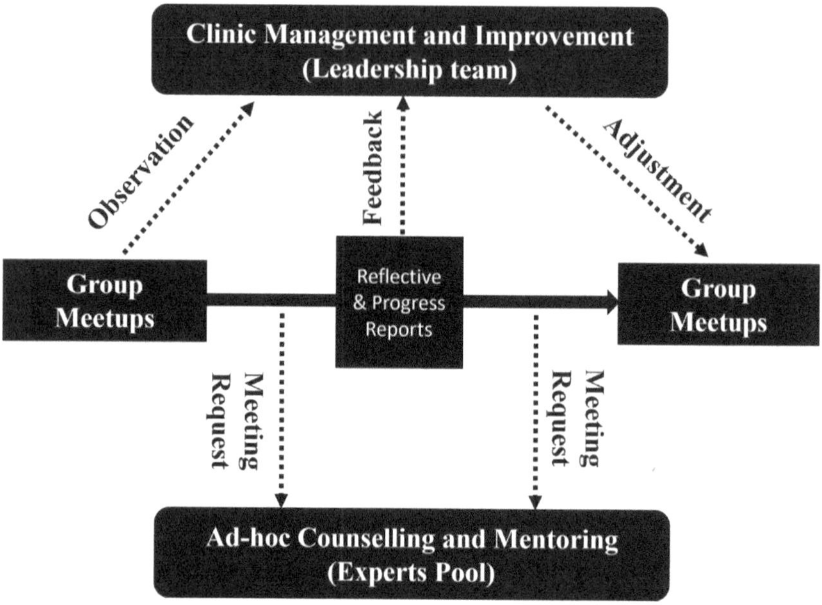

Figure 6.1 Academic Startup Clinic model

provide required emotional support (Garrison *et al.*, 2010). It also resembles the group therapy approach followed in other disciplines, which have demonstrated benefits with regard to the motivation, perseverance, goal pursuit, and mental strength of small business leaders (Saraf *et al.*, 2019).

After the initial grumbling and peer feedback cycle subside, one of the entrepreneurial topics is explained by a member of the clinic leadership team. The subject is tailored to become more relevant to research commercialization. This is done through the inclusion of apropos topics, in addition to common EE themes, models, examples, and activities. For example, topics such as university spin-offs, patenting, and industry labs operations are discussed, which do not commonly form part of standard entrepreneurship curricula. Also, alternative models are utilized such as the sustainable business model canvas (Joyce and Paquin, 2016), which advocates for a triple bottom line emphasis in business, instead of the standard Osterwalder and Pigneur (2010) canvas. When explaining entrepreneurial teams, in-class activities using multidisciplinary members are implemented, leveraging the diversity in participants' academic backgrounds and expertise. This is one of the beneficial features of the Startup Clinic, as they improve knowledge transfer and collaborative learning (Volkmann and Audretsch, 2017).

The monthly meetups aim primarily at improving the "means" available to AEs (Sarasvathy, 2001). Through the explained topics, which are tailored to academic entrepreneurship, they can develop entrepreneurial and business knowledge, more specific to their needs. In addition, the initial exhuming and reflection help them develop a better awareness of themselves, their capacities, and their connections (Who I am? What I have? Whom do I know?). The initial group therapy-like activity can also help build their social capital and knowledge relevant to precise scenarios and challenges, and learn from other experiences, thus replenishing their means.

Ad-hoc counselling

The second feature of the Startup Clinic is the mentoring spaces. These are set up on a need to basis, according to the AEs' requests. They would typically ask for them to acquire additional or specific knowledge about a certain topic; receive advice on a situation or an aspect of managing their entrepreneurial project; or ask to be connected or introduced to an industry figure, potential partner, client, or investor. When the request is received, the clinic leadership team initially "triage" it, to assess whether it could be fulfilled directly by them or will require an external support. If the latter, then relevant figures from the pool of experts that signed up to support the clinic are contacted and a meeting is facilitated between the AE and the relevant expert.

The ad-hoc meetings thus help AEs supplement their means. This could happen through access to specific industry or entrepreneurial knowledge or the connections they get introduced to. They also get to build partnerships, either new ones or leverage existing relationships, guided by the mentors in the ad-hoc meetings. Most importantly, whenever they face a contingent scenario or an unexpected event, the mentor is able to discuss with them possible strategies to respond to it, thus improving their resilience and opportunity recognition. This last role of the ad-hoc counselling is significant to AEs given their lack of business knowledge and experience (Miller *et al.*, 2018), and being traditionally risk-averse individuals who follow a systematic (causal) approach in their research.

Reflective and progress notes

An essential part of the learning process is reflecting on oneself, capabilities, mental models, and attitudes (Kolb and Kolb, 2005). This is especially important for entrepreneurs as they learn through experiences in a contextually relevant social circle (Corbett, 2005), which is an integral part of the Startup Clinic proposition. AEs would be able to reflect on their progress on the previously mentioned aspects. They will become more aware of their evolving needs and resources as they acquire more means, adjust their expectations, build stronger partnerships, face contingencies, and try to control uncertainty. Hence, they can apply their conclusions from those reflective notes to adjust the course of their entrepreneurial project.

Moreover, the AEs are required to include a brief description of their progress on regular intervals, in addition to their reflective notes. This is crucial not to adrift or fall behind, which is common in academic entrepreneurship (Miller *et al.,* 2018). It will also form a guiding document that can enable them to exert a controlling behavior over their emerging venture, as they navigate an uncertain environment (Sarasvathy, 2009).

Clinic improvement

The progress notes of AEs will establish the basis for the clinic leadership team, together with their observations from the group meetups and the ad-hoc meetings, to reflect on its progress and adjust its structure, topics, experts' pool, and connections accordingly. This will enable the leadership team to maintain the inherent flexibility of the Startup Clinic. Hence, the model becomes more responsive to the participating AEs' characteristics and requirements, the evolving contextual factors within the respective academic institution, and the changes in external environment. The Startup Clinic model thus embodies an effectual approach to academic entrepreneurship learning and support.

Conclusion and implications

Supporting the development of competences and entrepreneurial projects among academics requires following a more tailored methodology, rather than the standard approaches to EE. Although they exhibit significant technological knowledge and professional maturity, they lack enough business acumen. These characteristics, when combined with the specific challenges and the resource constraints they suffer from, mandate the application of a more social and behavioral approach to supporting their entrepreneurial decision-making junctures.

Following an effectual approach to educating and supporting them, hence, seems logical, which is complemented by the inclusion of external agents from the entrepreneurial ecosystem (Bischoff *et al.,* 2018) and academics with diverse backgrounds (Fiore *et al.,* 2019). The description of the model provided earlier aims to replenish the "means" of AEs, help them understand their "affordances", build effective "partnerships", navigate "contingencies" more successfully, and exert a guided "control" over uncertainty.

The effectuation-based model offers an alternative approach to traditional methods as well as accelerators/incubators for educating and supporting nascent and to-be AEs. It answers better to their specific needs, challenges, and situational factors than formal entrepreneurship courses (Politis, 2005). The model allows for personalized learning, mindset development, and self-awareness, which are critical aspects of entrepreneurial learning (Rae, 2005). From a theoretical perspective, it extends our limited understanding of effectuation process applications by adapting it to an educational context and extending it to an understudied field, academic entrepreneurship. It also advances the research on EE as a process.

By focusing on novice and aspiring entrepreneurs, the model provides an additional layer to the original logic of Sarasvathy (2001) that was built on interactions with expert entrepreneurs. In addition, it adds to the scarce research on the changing role of AEs from selling patents to founders of innovative economic entities (Miller *et al.,* 2018). Moreover, integrating effectuation in processual EE among AEs opens new avenues for research to build on our work through further empirical studies to validate and improve our model, apply it to other EE settings, and experiment its implementation through various activities and approaches to EE.

Startup Clinic offers a model entrenched in effectuation and experiential principles to cater for a broader range of EE outcomes, from competences development to social capital enrichment and venture creation. Given its inherent flexibility, universities can apply it to their specific contexts and use it as a platform to integrate the different stakeholders concerned with academic entrepreneurship and provide better support to their burgeoning AEs, thus cementing their role as the fulcrum of innovation-based local and regional economic development.

References

Abreu, M. and Grinevich, V. (2013) 'The nature of academic entrepreneurship in the UK: Widening the focus on entrepreneurial activities.' *Research Policy*, 42(2), pp. 408–422.

Agogué, M., Lundqvist, M. and Middleton, K.W. (2015) 'Mindful deviation through combining causation and effectuation: A design theory-based study of technology entrepreneurship.' *Creativity and Innovation Management*, 24(4), pp. 629–644.

Alexander, A.T., Miller, K. and Fielding, S. (2015) 'Open for business: Universities, entrepreneurial academics and open innovation.' *International Journal of Innovation Management*, 19(06), p. 1540013.

Alvarez, S.A. and Barney, J.B. (2007) 'Discovery and creation: Alternative theories of entrepreneurial action.' *Strategic Entrepreneurship Journal*, 1(1–2), pp. 11–26.

Audretsch, D.B., Cunningham, J.A., Kuratko, D.F., Lehmann, E.E. and Menter, M. (2019) 'Entrepreneurial ecosystems: Economic, technological, and societal impacts.' *The Journal of Technology Transfer*, 44, pp. 313–325.

Bienkowska, D., Klofsten, M. and Rasmussen, E. (2016) 'PhD students in the entrepreneurial university-perceived support for academic entrepreneurship.' *European Journal of Education*, 51(1), pp. 56–72.

Bischoff, K., Volkmann, C.K. and Audretsch, D.B. (2018) 'Stakeholder collaboration in entrepreneurship education: An analysis of the entrepreneurial ecosystems of European higher educational institutions.' *The Journal of Technology Transfer*, 43, pp. 20–46.

Blenker, P., Frederiksen, S.H., Korsgaard, S., Müller, S., Neergaard, H. and Thrane, C. (2012) 'Entrepreneurship as everyday practice: Towards a personalized pedagogy of enterprise education.' *Industry and Higher Education*, 26(6), pp. 417–430.

Bolzani, D., Munari, F., Rasmussen, E. and Toschi, L. (2021) 'Technology transfer offices as providers of science and technology entrepreneurship education.' *The Journal of Technology Transfer*, 46, pp. 335–365.

Chandler, G.N., DeTienne, D.R., McKelvie, A. and Mumford, T.V. (2011) 'Causation and effectuation processes: A validation study.' *Journal of Business Venturing*, 26(3), pp. 375–390.
Corbett, A.C. (2005) 'Experiential learning within the process of opportunity identification and exploitation.' *Entrepreneurship theory and practice*, 29(4), pp. 473–491.
Dew, N., Read, S., Sarasvathy, S.D. and Wiltbank, R. (2009) 'Effectual versus predictive logics in entrepreneurial decision-making: Differences between experts and novices.' *Journal of Business Venturing*, 24(4), pp. 287–309.
Fayolle, A. and Gailly, B. (2008) 'From craft to science: Teaching models and learning processes in entrepreneurship education.' *Journal of European Industrial Training*, 32(7), pp. 569–593.
Fini, R., Fu, K., Mathisen, M.T., Rasmussen, E. and Wright, M. (2017) 'Institutional determinants of university spin-off quantity and quality: A longitudinal, multilevel, cross-country study.' *Small Business Economics*, 48, pp. 361–391.
Fini, R., Grimaldi, R., Santoni, S. and Sobrero, M. (2011) 'Complements or substitutes? The role of universities and local context in supporting the creation of academic spin-offs.' *Research Policy*, 40(8), pp. 1113–1127.
Fiore, E., Sansone, G. and Paolucci, E. (2019) 'Entrepreneurship education in a multidisciplinary environment: Evidence from an entrepreneurship programme held in Turin.' *Administrative Sciences*, 9(1), p. 28.
Fisher, G. (2012) 'Effectuation, causation, and bricolage: A behavioral comparison of emerging theories in entrepreneurship research.' *Entrepreneurship Theory and Practice*, 36(5), pp. 1019–1051.
Fisher, G., Kotha, S. and Lahiri, A. (2016) 'Changing with the times: An integrated view of identity, legitimacy, and new venture life cycles.' *Academy of Management Review*, 41(3), pp. 383–409.
Frese, T., Geiger, I. and Dost, F. (2020) 'An empirical investigation of determinants of effectual and causal decision logics in online and high-tech start-up firms.' *Small Business Economics*, 54, pp. 641–664.
Galán-Muros, V., van der Sijde, P., Groenewegen, P. and Baaken, T. (2017) 'Nurture over nature: How do European universities support their collaboration with business?.' *The Journal of Technology Transfer*, 42, pp. 184–205.
Garrison, D.R., Anderson, T. and Archer, W. (2010) 'The first decade of the community of inquiry framework: A retrospective.' *The Internet and Higher Education*, 13(1–2), pp. 5–9.
Gianiodis, P.T. and Meek, W.R. (2020) 'Entrepreneurial education for the entrepreneurial university: A stakeholder perspective.' *The Journal of Technology Transfer*, 45(4), pp. 1167–1195.
Grimaldi, R., Kenney, M., Siegel, D.S. and Wright, M. (2011) '30 years after Bayh–Dole: Reassessing academic entrepreneurship.' *Research policy*, 40(8), pp. 1045–1057.
Guerrero, M. and Urbano, D. (2012) 'The development of an entrepreneurial university.' *The Journal of Technology Transfer*, 37, pp. 43–74.
Gümüsay, A.A. and Bohné, T.M. (2018) 'Individual and organizational inhibitors to the development of entrepreneurial competencies in universities.' *Research Policy*, 47(2), pp. 363–378.
Günzel-Jensen, F. and Robinson, S. (2017) 'Effectuation in the undergraduate classroom: Three barriers to entrepreneurial learning.' *Education+ Training*, 59(7/8), pp. 780–796.
Hammoda, B. (2024) 'Please "bridge" the gap! Conceptualizing "Practicality" as a field of inquiry.' *The International Journal of Entrepreneurship and Innovation*, 0(0), An OnlineFirst paper. https://doi.org/10.1177/14657503241245555.

Hauser, A., Eggers, F. and Güldenberg, S. (2020) 'Strategic decision-making in SMEs: Effectuation, causation, and the absence of strategy.' *Small Business Economics*, *54*, pp. 775–790.

Hayter, C.S., Nelson, A.J., Zayed, S. and O'Connor, A.C. (2018) 'Conceptualizing academic entrepreneurship ecosystems: A review, analysis and extension of the literature.' *The Journal of Technology Transfer*, 43, pp. 1039–1082.

Hmieleski, K.M. and Powell, E.E. (2018) 'The psychological foundations of university science commercialization: A review of the literature and directions for future research.' *Academy of Management Perspectives*, 32(1), pp. 43–77.

Honig, B. (2004) 'Entrepreneurship education: Toward a model of contingency-based business planning.' *Academy of Management Learning & Education*, 3(3), pp. 258–273.

Jain, S., George, G. and Maltarich, M. (2009) 'Academics or entrepreneurs? Investigating role identity modification of university scientists involved in commercialization activity.' *Research Policy*, 38(6), pp. 922–935.

Joyce, A. and Paquin, R.L. (2016) 'The triple layered business model canvas: A tool to design more sustainable business models.' *Journal of Cleaner Production*, 135, pp. 1474–1486.

Kolb, A.Y. and Kolb, D.A. (2005) 'Learning styles and learning spaces: Enhancing experiential learning in higher education.' *Academy of Management Learning & Education*, 4(2), pp. 193–212.

Lafuente, E. and Berbegal-Mirabent, J. (2019) 'Assessing the productivity of technology transfer offices: An analysis of the relevance of aspiration performance and portfolio complexity.' *The Journal of Technology Transfer*, 44(3), pp. 778–801.

Li, Y., Zou, B., Guo, F. and Guo, J. (2020) 'Academic entrepreneurs' effectuation logic, role innovation, and academic entrepreneurship performance: An empirical study.' *International Entrepreneurship and Management Journal*, pp. 1–24.

Lubik, S. and Garnsey, E. (2016) 'Early business model evolution in science-based ventures: The case of advanced materials.' *Long Range Planning*, 49(3), pp. 393–408.

Mäkimurto-Koivumaa, S. and Puhakka, V. (2013) 'Effectuation and causation in entrepreneurship education.' *International Journal of Entrepreneurial Venturing*, 5(1), pp. 68–83.

Marmer, M., Hermann, B. J., Dogrultan, E. and Berman, R. (2012) 'Startup genome report.' Retrieved March 5, 2024, from https://cdn.startupgenome.com/sites/62c58b4d00b3f50043b92724/content_entry62c58c4b00b3f50043b92770/62c59def61a37b0042c28e59/files/Startup_Genome_-_Why_Startups_Succeed.pdf

Matlay, H. (2005) 'Researching entrepreneurship and education: Part 1: What is entrepreneurship and does it matter?.' *Education+ Training*, 47(8/9), pp. 665–677.

Metzger, G. (2014). 'Gründungstätigkeit wiederbelebt – Impuls aus dem Nebenerwerb.' Retrieved March 05, 2024, from https://www.kfw.de/PDF/Download-Center/Konzernthemen/Research/ PDF-Dokumente-Gr%C3%BCndungsmonitor/KfW-Gr%C3%BCndungsmonitor-2014.pdf

Miller, K., Alexander, A., Cunningham, J.A. and Albats, E. (2018) 'Entrepreneurial academics and academic entrepreneurs: A systematic literature review.' *International Journal of Technology Management*, 77(1–3), pp. 9–37.

Müller-Wieland, R., Muschner, A. and Schraudner, M. (2019) 'Academic entrepreneurship: Phase-specific constraints and needs.' *Journal of Enterprising Communities: People and Places in the Global Economy*, 13(3), pp. 353–371.

Munoz, C.A., Guerra, M.E. and Mosey, S. (2020) 'The potential impact of entrepreneurship education on doctoral students within the non-commercial research environment in Chile.' *Studies in Higher Education*, 45(3), pp. 492–510.

Oosterbeek, H., Van Praag, M. and Ijsselstein, A. (2010) 'The impact of entrepreneurship education on entrepreneurship skills and motivation.' *European Economic Review*, 54(3), pp. 442–454.
Osterwalder, A. and Pigneur, Y. (2010) *Business model generation: A handbook for visionaries, game changers, and challengers* (Vol. 1). John Wiley & Sons.
Perkmann, M., Tartari, V., McKelvey, M., Autio, E., Broström, A., D'este, P., Fini, R., Geuna, A., Grimaldi, R., Hughes, A. and Krabel, S. (2013) 'Academic engagement and commercialisation: A review of the literature on university–industry relations.' *Research Policy*, 42(2), pp. 423–442.
Perry, J.T., Chandler, G.N. and Markova, G. (2012) 'Entrepreneurial effectuation: A review and suggestions for future research.' *Entrepreneurship Theory and Practice*, 36(4), pp. 837–861.
Pittaway, L., Brush, C., Corbett, A. C., & Tantawy, M. M. (2023) 'Doctoral programs in entrepreneurship: Building cognitive apprenticeships.' *Entrepreneurship Education and Pedagogy*, 6(4), pp. 608–642.
Pittaway, L. and Cope, J. (2007) 'Entrepreneurship education: A systematic review of the evidence.' *International Small Business Journal*, 25(5), pp. 479–510.
Politis, D. (2005) 'The process of entrepreneurial learning: A conceptual framework.' *Entrepreneurship Theory and Practice*, 29(4), pp. 399–424.
Politis, D., Winborg, J. and Dahlstrand, Å.L. (2012) 'Exploring the resource logic of student entrepreneurs.' *International Small Business Journal*, 30(6), pp. 659–683.
Puntillo, P., Rubino, F. and Veltri, S. (2022) 'Transferring knowledge to improve university competitiveness: The performance of technology transfer offices.' *Governance and Performance Management in Public Universities: Current Research and Practice*, pp. 129–147.
Racat, M., Ricard, A. and Mauer, R. (2023) 'Effectuation and causation models: An integrative theoretical framework.' *Small Business Economics*, pp. 1–15.
Radosevich, R. (1995) 'A model for entrepreneurial spin–offs from public technology sources.' *International Journal of Technology Management*, 10(7–8), pp. 879–893.
Rae, D. (2005) 'Entrepreneurial learning: A narrative-based conceptual model.' *Journal of Small Business and Enterprise Development*, 12(3), pp. 323–335.
Rasmussen, E., Mosey, S. and Wright, M. (2014) 'The influence of university departments on the evolution of entrepreneurial competencies in spin-off ventures.' *Research Policy*, 43(1), pp. 92–106.
Read, S. and Sarasvathy, S.D. (2005) 'Knowing what to do and doing what you know: Effectuation as a form of entrepreneurial expertise.' *The Journal of Private Equity*, pp. 45–62.
Reymen, I., Berends, H., Oudehand, R. and Stultiëns, R. (2017) 'Decision making for business model development: A process study of effectuation and causation in new technology-based ventures.' *R&D Management*, 47(4), pp. 595–606.
Rippa, P., Landi, G., Cosimato, S., Turriziani, L. and Gheith, M. (2022) 'Embedding entrepreneurship in doctoral students: The impact of a T-shaped educational approach.' *European Journal of Innovation Management*, 25(1), pp. 249–270.
Saraf, P., Rahman, T. and Jamison, J.C. (2019) 'Group-based cognitive behavioral therapy (CBT) training improves mental health of SME entrepreneurs: Experimental evidence from conflict-affected areas of Pakistan.' World Bank Policy Research Working Paper, 8872.
Sarasvathy, S.D. (2001) 'Causation and effectuation: Toward a theoretical shift from economic inevitability to entrepreneurial contingency.' *Academy of Management Review*, 26(2), pp. 243–263.

Sarasvathy, S.D. (2003) 'Entrepreneurship as a science of the artificial.' *Journal of Economic Psychology*, 24(2), pp. 203–220.
Sarasvathy, S.D. (2009) *Effectuation: Elements of entrepreneurial expertise.* Edward Elgar Publishing.
Secundo, G., De Beer, C. and Passiante, G. (2016) 'Measuring university technology transfer efficiency: A maturity level approach.' *Measuring Business Excellence*, 20(3), pp. 42–54.
Secundo, G., Ndou, V., Del Vecchio, P. and De Pascale, G. (2020) 'Sustainable development, intellectual capital and technology policies: A structured literature review and future research agenda.' *Technological Forecasting and Social Change*, 153, p. 119917.
Senyard, J., Baker, T. and Davidsson, P. (2009) 'Entrepreneurial bricolage: Towards systematic empirical testing.' *Frontiers of Entrepreneurship Research*, 29(5), p. 5.
Shane, S. and Venkataraman, S. (2000) 'The promise of entrepreneurship as a field of research.' *Academy of Management Review*, 25(1), pp. 217–226.
Siegel, D.S. and Wright, M. (2015) 'Academic entrepreneurship: Time for a rethink?.' *British Journal of Management*, 26(4), pp. 582–595.
Sinell, A., Heidingsfelder, M. and Schraudner, M. (2015) 'Entrepreneurship and academic employment-more alike than you'd think.' *Journal of Technology Management & Innovation*, 10(3), pp. 1–10.
Skute, I. (2019) 'Opening the black box of academic entrepreneurship: A bibliometric analysis.' *Scientometrics*, 120(1), pp. 237–265.
Villani, E., Linder, C. and Grimaldi, R. (2018) 'Effectuation and causation in science-based new venture creation: A configurational approach.' *Journal of Business Research*, 83, pp. 173–185.
Volkmann, C. and Audretsch, D. (2017) *Entrepreneurship education at universities* (pp. 1–10). International Studies in Entrepreneurship, Springer International Publishing AG.
Zhang, Y., Wang, P. and Zhao, Y. (2022) 'Big five personality, academic entrepreneurial motivation, and academic entrepreneurial intention: A research method based on fuzzy set qualitative comparative analysis.' *Frontiers in Psychology*, 12, p. 799770.

7 Reflective practice as continuing professional development for entrepreneurs and intrapreneurs

Russ Hepworth-Sawyer and Mike Wilson

Reflective practice, as a term, did not emerge as academic parlance and certainly was not in vogue until the works of Schön, Dewey, Kolb, Gibbs and others in academic fields were bought forward and placed into sharper focus during the 1980s and 1990s. As a result, reflective practice is considered 'central to transforming experience and knowledge into expertise' (Vallance, 2019 in Hamblin & Crisp, 2022). Despite the fanfare and widespread adoption within the fields of healthcare (nursing specifically), sport and teacher training, business management, specifically entrepreneurship, has lacked weighty consideration of systematic reflective practice as something of value to the individual and to wider organisations.

In this chapter, we explore how reflection is practised by established entrepreneurs and business owners, usually with a personalised, unsystematic technique. Through qualitative interviews with experienced entrepreneurs, business owners and consultants from Northern England, we explore how much reflective practice, consciously or subconsciously, has been employed in their success, when and how they conceived it as *reflective practice*, and how they practice it today.

This chapter displays that reflective practice has been a keystone to each of the interviewees, and most interestingly, has been a practice developed and honed by each interviewee individually. No respondent initially 'adopted' a system from a third-party source until perhaps later in one instance. Most have developed their own system, and we discuss those here. This chapter also reports the importance of reflective practice to the interviewees and how it has helped them proceed with their chosen careers and lives, and those of others, as we shall learn. We conclude with a further question for the future as to whether a systematised form of reflective practice would benefit entrepreneurs of the future.

Introduction and backdrop

A superficial search of the wealth of literature about reflective practice will demonstrate its prominence in the fields of healthcare (nursing in particular), sport and teacher training (herein referred to as just *education*). Even a search

DOI: 10.4324/9781003324737-7

for *reflective practice and professional development* produces more results that reside predominantly in the education field. In the field of business, reflective practice emerges in articles around education in the form of business school and enterprise teaching (McGivern & Thompson, 2012; Lang & McNaught, 2013; Kimberley, 2019; Clarke et al., 2020, for example), yet 'reflection, as a key component . . . has received little attention in the project management and leadership literature' (Ollila, 2000). However, more research is needed in the direct use of reflective practice as a means of continuing professional development (CPD) in enterprise and entrepreneurship specifically.

To many, the notion of reflecting upon one's own work is left to 'intuition' (Tikkamäki et al., 2016) or perhaps conceived as a personal burden too far to be valuable enough to dedicate the necessary time to and adds negatively to the contemporary 'work-life balance' and time poor paradigms (Raelin, 2002). 'Despite [reflection's] power to improve learning and practice, reflection does not seem to be a spontaneous activity in our professions or everyday life as we need to actively dedicate time and effort to make reflections' (Gelter, 2003). Reflective practice gains 'short shrift in society' and is needed to 'prove to a deeper than trial-and-error experience' and is essentially 'thinking about thinking' (Raelin, 2002).

Marshall et al. (2022) note that natural 'reflective practice is an inherently personal and relational process, occurring privately within people' but that 'they may be ineffective or unaware of using it' (Black & Plowright, 2010; Marshall et al., 2022). This, to the authors, launches a discussion about the lack of systematisation in the practice. Brookfield (2017) challenges 'common sense assumptions' that those who are most senior in their roles (teaching) will have the best instincts, and notes that the length of service 'does not automatically confer deepened insight and wisdom'. In fact, Brookfield asserts that 'ten years of practice can be one year's worth of distorted and poorly interpreted experience repeated ten times' and to counter this, systematised reflective practice offers 'accuracy and validity' (Brookfield, 2017). Equally, Gray (2007) citing Daudelin (1996) notes that 'one explanation for this is that [business] managers themselves have always placed a higher premium on action than reflection' (Gray, 2007). Adding difficulty to this is the ability to shy away from something difficult because 'the premise [is] that the nature of [business] "management" is complex, ambiguous, contradictory and uncertain' (McGivern & Thompson, 2012).

In the field of business management, to assert reflection is baron would be unfounded. Important, mainstream, books such as Kaufman's *The Personal MBA* resigns reflection to a set of good self-exploratory questions about personal improvement to the appendices and not more centrally (Kaufman, 2020). However, perhaps something is lost, as it is interesting that Joseph Schumpeter (1883–1950), one of the forefathers of entrepreneurship, so early on, endorsed discovery, evaluation and exploitation of opportunities to create new goods and services (Sobel & Clemens, 2020). The evaluative skills of the entrepreneur, the 'thinking about thinking', enlightened the entrepreneur (Raelin, 2002). It can be interpreted that reflection still lingers in popular entrepreneurial consideration, but to the authors' knowledge, no shared vision of what that practice looks like is on offer.

Therefore, we further posit reflective practice to be undervalued by enterprise colleagues and employers as a form of CPD. The dissonance between this perceived nonchalant view and the widespread adoption of reflective practice within other fields such as education and healthcare is of interest. For the authors, this dissonance is most evident when applied to senior leaders within organisations.

Both authors contribute and deliver upon our institution's Senior Leader Apprenticeship Programme. This Post-Graduate Diploma is then enhanced by a further large module graduating apprentices through to a full Executive MBA programme. As the title suggests, these participants are mature students and senior leaders who undertake a structured, blended qualification over 22 months to reach the apprenticeship standard for a senior leader (see https://www.instituteforapprenticeships.org/apprenticeship-standards/senior-leader-v1-2). The 'top-up' distance-learning module that extends a further six months to reach the Executive MBA qualification is a module completely centred around reflective practice. As Jarvis (2004), the famed professional educationalist, stated, we move the apprentice from a 'front-end model of education . . . to formulate [an]other approach . . . to the subject' (Jarvis, 2004). In delivering this module, we have noticed that participants unlock unexpected outcomes and, in return, permit their roles and employers to gain improvements from their sole revelations. Most have found the experience extremely rewarding and have been able to 'work through' through difficult work-related issues they face throughout the process.

It is curious why a module of study is required (or is forcing) to trigger necessary reflective practice to make such a positive impact. This is especially important because we identify that it is certainly not our ability to teach (or in this case facilitate) reflective practice – it is purely the participants' new-found ability to solely adopt and employ reflective practice, with its models and strategies, to reach a revelatory outcome that permits change, understanding, and beyond this, a personal development plan for their future.

The transformation of these apprentices is the driver for this particular chapter and provides a backdrop to the power of reflective practice within business management, specifically enterprise and entrepreneurship. However, we wished to assess how those without the MBA experience had adopted and utilised reflective practice to their businesses, and, therefore, this chapter focuses on how five entrepreneurs and business owners consider *reflective practice* and use their own methods (both created and adopted) to engage.

Organising this chapter

Observing the positive impact that reflective practice had upon those involved in the Executive MBA top-up module led us to a fundamental question first – how is reflective practice currently employed in the field of business management? Furthermore, considering the focus of this volume, how important is reflective practice within the wider enterprise and entrepreneurial community, and in what form, and how does it manifest? We also wished to explore any aforementioned dissonance between those who undertake reflective practice in the enterprise sector and those within higher education who traipse it out, but may not provide the necessary nuances that make it impactful for the intrapreneurial or entrepreneurial professional within a CPD context.

To achieve this, we initially make an introduction through the literature relating reflective practice to the field of business management – within which entrepreneurship and enterprise reside. We then discuss literature relating to reflective practice more generally, then leaning into a focus on enterprise and entrepreneurship. Later we discuss how reflective practice is written about as a form of CPD.

Through qualitative interviews with a range of entrepreneurs and consultants, we aim to understand, in detail, what reflective practice means to them, how they introduce it into their practice, and what difference it continues to make. We expressly ask them how they broadcast the benefits of reflective practice in their work.

To conclude, we posit that reflective practice is a positive and necessary process to ensure that entrepreneurs are true and faithful to their mission and able to improve and refine their roles, or indeed pivot or reposition themselves and their enterprises due to the wealth that reflective practice offers them. Given entrepreneurs are often charting new territory, there could be little or no roadmaps for them to follow, and in order to look forward, they might benefit from looking backwards.

Reflective practice and its relationship to pedagogy, andragogy and heutagogy

Schön's PhD was a critique of John Dewey's *Logic: The Theory of Inquiry* (Bauer, N.J., 1991). Dewey (1933) defined the concept of reflection as 'turning a subject over in mind and giving it serious and constructive consideration'. Schön's similarly titled paper 'The Theory of Inquiry: Dewey's Legacy to Education' in 1992 promotes reflection within the needs of 'professional knowledge and education' (Schön, 1992).

Schön did not limit the fields to which his work could be applied. In fact, within his 1974 book *Theory in Practice* Schön asserts that the practice is to increase 'professional effectiveness' and therefore not just the effectiveness of higher education practice (or nursing). In his 1987 book *Educating the Reflective Practitioner* Schön speaks specifically to fields such as architecture (his initial field), design, music, psychoanalytic practice, counselling and consulting. Most specifically he explores how reflective practice can (and we'd argue should) 'bridge the worlds of University and Practice', with the important subtitle 'redesigning professional education' (Schön, 1987).

Professional education, as a term, was coined for the education of 'the learned professions' which historically were law, medicine and theology (Neumann, 2019). Neumann (2019) updates 'the professions' in contemporary times to include 'architecture, education, psychotherapy, dentistry, veterinary medicine, engineering, accountancy, and others'. Evetts (2006), Friedson (2001) and Svensson (2006) are cited by Evans (2008), who coins the phrase of 'new' professionalisms to cater for this redefinition and expansion of the professions. Neumann (2019) continues to distinguish between the higher education leaver and professional competence, and the education required within is what creates the professional within their 'new' professions, and hence the term 'professional education' (Evans, 2008; Neumann, 2019).

Peter Jarvis, in his seminal work on professional education, wrote in 1983 that it is about the education of adults for their professional lives and work (Jarvis, 2018). Sockett (1993, 1996), although centred around teaching, identifies that the term 'professionalism' 'is about the quality of practice . . . and the public state of a job' (profession). Sockett relates the responsibility of the 'job' with its professionalism. In other words, the 'accountability' of the role is based on moral professionalism and that leads to terming the role one of the professions (Sockett, 1996). As Evans (2008) notes, professionals need to take 'greater responsibility for defining the nature and content of their work'. Whether it be professionalism, accountability, responsibility, quality of the work, or simply independence, there appears to be an acknowledgement that there's a distance to travel between the university graduation ceremony and professional competence, something coined as the 'void' (Hepworth-Sawyer, 2021).

This independence, especially when it comes to learning for the adult, is one of Malcolm Knowles's principles of andragogy (1975). We introduce Knowles's term 'andragogy' here as it concerns the education of the adult and is separate from the term 'pedagogy' as being the 'science and art of teaching' as introduced by Kinnaman (1902). The rationale behind Kinnaman's paper was to highlight the importance of the didact (teacher), and in doing so he was predominantly meaning the school teacher arguing that teaching ought to be considered as important as the other professions. Kinnaman's paper does, interestingly, draw out the connection between the term 'pedagogy' and higher education recounting that Johns Hopkins University started events where 'lecturers from other departments were called in to discuss the teaching of their own subjects' (Kinnaman, 1902). In other words, the specialist pedagogues were not considering the teaching of those in receipt of true pedagogy – those in schools. Despite this anomaly, modern-day parlance now situates pedagogy as university teaching, rather than just school teaching as presumably it was initially intended.

Taking andragogy and pedagogy at their original meanings, it could be argued that they are largely different artforms to quite different audiences. Nevertheless, we use these terms constructively and contemporarily here to differentiate between formal undergraduate university delivery (pedagogy) and adult-focused delivery (andragogy), the latter of which can be in many forms from university-led to purely personal development. Knowles was particularly interested in the 'principles of andragogy' which are foundational to understanding the reasons why adults learn, and therefore we can then extend this to their professional learning. These are the notions of: self-concept as learners (self-directed learners); need to know the information on offer; role of experience in the learning process to deepen learning; readiness to learn demonstrates in being motivated and dedicated to the process; orientation to learning means that adults seek to apply their learning in their roles; and adult learners are motivated to learn for professional growth (Knowles et al., 2014). Some of these attributes are explored and exuded by each of our interviewees later in this chapter.

Meanwhile, heutagogy (Hase & Kenyon, 2000, 2013; Kenyon & Hase, 2001), a more modern definition, explores more specifically 'self-determined learning' and as such relates to autodidactic professional education – something that is central to day-to-day personal development. Heutagogy is different to pedagogy where 'it was the teacher who decided what the learner needed to know . . . and how' (Hase & Kenyon, 2000). Andragogy, however, *continues* the 'teacher-learner' relationship, but there is some agency in the learner being in the room outside of just a receipt of a qualification (Hase & Kenyon, 2000). Extrapolating for the purposes of this chapter, andragogic and heutagogic principles apply to the entrepreneur here, especially in the context of the authors' delivery on the aforementioned qualifications.

Understanding Knowles' and Schön's positions provides an intersection between andragogy and professional education (each their own foci in this debate). Both posit that motivation of the professional 'student' needs to come from within and we conclude that reflection is inherently needed, to explore the skills and understanding to permit that to be professionally important. Heutagogy, of course, explores those who learn for themselves and are reflected within the interviews that follow.

Reflective practice fundamentals, the entrepreneur and the desire for a systematised approach

Schön's work is perhaps the most influential in laying down the fundamental concepts of reflective practice. For this chapter, we're going to focus on two of Schön's main considerations of reflection. The first is his concept of the cliff top and the swamp. In essence, Schön (1983) provided a tale to explain his concept about why reflective practice was necessary. As Hargreaves and Page (2013) noted, Schön (1983) accepted the notion of the scientific method and acknowledged the indisputable positivity this brought to humanity but argued that 'scientific methods seemed more important than any other sort of knowledge' (Hargreaves & Page, 2013). The 'tale' Schön told was called the swampy lowlands and demonstrates a different approach to gathering knowledge. In essence there is the 'high, hard ground where practitioners can make effective use of research-based theory and technique' and consider this as a hill or clifftop where the vantage point looking out below is clear far into the distance. Meanwhile, 'there is a swampy lowland where situations are confusing "messes" incapable of' a simple and clear solution, or path (Schön, 1983).

The high grounds represent the scientific method, where clarity and prescribed approaches to highly defined practice are expected. The lowlands, meanwhile, represented by 'the swamp [where] the problems of greatest human concern' reside, and are considered 'messy' and rely on intuition, trial and error, and muddling through (Schön, 1983). Schön discussed the two approaches as either 'rigor or relevance', and it is generally conceived that a mixture of both is also possible. To make sense of the swamplands, we must apply reflective practice principles to our experiences. Therefore, in order to navigate the messy approaches to actions and events, Schön developed three stages of reflection in relation to an event (coined by John Flanagan in 1954 as a *critical incident*). These were *reflection-on-action, reflection-in-action* and *reflection-through-action.* In essence, Schön was delineating between whether the professional reflects during doing something (in) or after doing something (on), or indeed in the future by reflecting before doing something (for). In other words, Schön just describes the notion of reflection upon something we've done or reflecting during something and preparing for the future based on our experiences, feelings and judged outcomes. The field of reflective practice has developed considerably since and a number of models exist that relate to reflection, but also learning styles, or cycles, such as Gibbs (1998) or Kolb (1984) and many others. These have been amply applied in the fields of nursing and teacher training, and by the authors within their MBA-reflective practice module.

Applying Schön's principles to enterprise, the entrepreneur might seek to design their enterprise from a place of rigour on the highlands, but as noted by Read et al. (2016, p. 2) it is a 'fairytale journey'. In essence, the entrepreneurial journey is that of the relevance idea depicted in Figure 7.1 and could be conceived to be mapped to the 'relevance' of the swampy lowlands, where the setbacks and changes of direction make the outcome of the enterprise what it becomes.

As a result, Read et al. indirectly argue the need to intertwine reflective practice with entrepreneurial activity. Whilst, certainly, in the authors' teaching, this symbiosis is promoted, there continues to appear to be a lack of systematic approach both to teach reflective practice and to engage in it as a practice.

Academic writing about reflective practice within entrepreneurship specifically appears to be somewhat lacking, despite reflective practice clearly being employed by many business schools, including our own. Lawless et al. (2015) demonstrate that business schools have been influenced 'by a discourse holding that reflective practice [of managers] provides real value to the organisation in which [the students] operate' and that 'reflection is now enshrined in most professional and postgraduate management programmes' (Lawless et al., 2015).

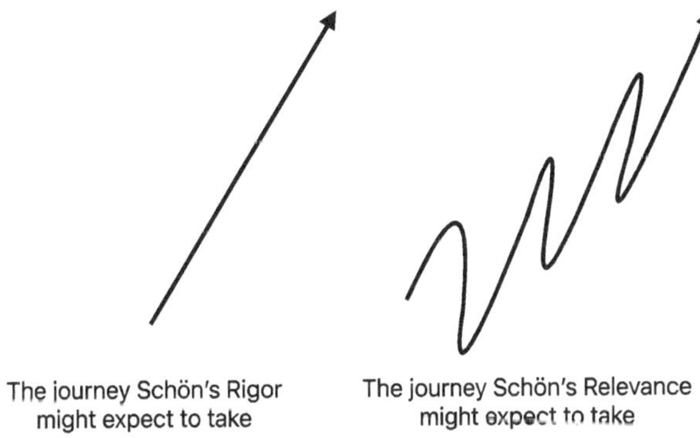

Figure 7.1 'Mythical' entrepreneurial journeys mapped to Schön's Rigour and Relevance concept.

Source: Adapted from Read et al. (2016) and Schön (1987)

Lawless et al. cite Mann et al. (2007) suggesting that the evidence for this 'curriculum intervention . . . remains largely theoretical'. Our experiences to date would appear to challenge this assertion. Mann et al. also note that there is little 'to guide educators in their work in understanding and developing a reflective capability in their learners' which we could chime with (Mann et al., 2007; Gray, 2007). There may not be a collective view of educating the business management professional or entrepreneur in reflective practice, but perhaps there ought to be. In fact, Cheetham and Chivers (1998) called for a 'need for a comprehensive model' of professional competence in which reflection would be a 'vital element' and be 'central' to the professional.

Brookfield's contribution to this particular aspect of the debate is interesting in that he investigates the link between critical reflection and executive business as being disconnected, on purpose. The terminology used in contemporary business is centred around a means of justifying actions by somewhat dehumanising, which in turn suggests that to reflect is possibly bad (being human). Brookfield's terminological explanation makes a link with capitalist business methods and contends that terms such as 'downsizing' and 'rightsizing', for example, make the executive's actions 'palatable' and thus a move away from previous moral codes in society. Reflective practice, through this capitalist lens, would only humanise the 'reality of people losing their livelihoods, homes, marriages' and so on (Brookfield, 2009). If Brookfield's assertion is to be taken as read, then this could explain the perceived canyon with the positivity within self-reflection on one bank, and the business entrepreneur and owner on the other with the canyon representing some form of capitalist conditioning (Jensen, 2011). Despite this, it is clear that reflective practice is ongoing. For example, Tikkamäki et al. (2016) interestingly explore the positive aspects of stress (eustress) among entrepreneurs and how reflective practice is used to deal with and learn from this. In their analysis, Tikkamäki et al. link the entrepreneur's response to stress as being dependent based upon whether their interpretation is positive or negative'. To that extent . . . reflective practice is potentially a tool for entrepreneurs seeking to harness the benefits of eustress'. Concepts such as *learning to learn, thinking outside the box* and challenging routines are the benefits to the entrepreneur (Tikkamäki et al., 2016). To consider a system for this, Tikkamäki et al. created their 'Toolset and tools for reflective practice'. Their six tools are quickly summarised here: studying oneself; changing one's point of view; putting things into perspective; harnessing a feeling of trust; regulating resources; and engaging in dialogue (Tikkamäki et al., 2016). This is echoed by Partington et al. (2015), who found that reflecting in a structured manner is important to question their own beliefs but also to discuss with others (the collective) to open new insights and continually progress (Partington et al., 2015).

Leggett's work in 2014 is the closest to addressing the same territory as this chapter, where she interviewed 24 management trainees on a development programme for middle and senior managers, all within a public sector organisation. Leggett's *Management Effectiveness Program* has some similarities to our own MBA module in reflective practice in that there was no prescribed system by which to undertake the reflection other than Argyris and Schon's (1996) Methods of Inquiry. However, the main difference is that our module is arranged as a distance-learning module in general and that one of the echoed positives from-Leggett's work was the ability to 'work collaboratively with peers . . . and a safe space . . . has supported them in embedding reflective practice behaviours'. Leggett's conclusion, however, chimes with our interpretations in that participants have increased levels of self-awareness and self-esteem despite this fundamental difference (Leggett, 2014).

As part of this chapter, we wished to see whether self-generated approaches to reflective practice reaps the same rewards as our somewhat-structured MBA module does for its participants. As we will introduce, each of the interviewees below is, to some degree or another, involved in providing consultancy, business advice, apprenticeship or mentoring. Puutio et al. (2009) believe that, from their own consultancy practice, reflective practice and giving advice are somewhat synonymous. In fact, they conceive that a request for advice can initiate reflection (Puutio et al., 2009). In the interviews that follow, we explore how reflection is initiated, considered and undertaken.

The interviews

Instead of delving into the valuable experiences of our MBA participants (perhaps a future project for consideration), we felt that to look to experienced business personnel away from the programme would permit a broader understanding and appreciation of what is considered reflective practice, away from the methods and constraints that pedagogic methodology 'imposes' on our apprentices. As such, we interviewed five interviewees from Northern England who speak to the use of reflective practice within their work. As experienced by Tikkamäki et al. (2016), we observe that some act 'mainly on their intuition' and 'others regularly used reflective ways of thinking . . . and believed this practice to be beneficial'.

Our intention was to gain some further qualitative depth through the semi-structured discussions with our interviewees. In the interviews, we explore not only the individual careers of the interviewees and how they became entrepreneurs, consultants and business owners, but to what level they use and systematise reflective practice.

Tikkamäki et al. (2016) also noted, importantly, that entrepreneurs had internalised their reflective practice to help analyse experiences, themselves, and to develop future practice. In response to this, Tikkamäki et al. introduced their aforementioned Reflective Practice Toolset which has similarities to Phil Crowshaw's *12 segments model* we'll discuss later. This suggests that what follows, in terms of varied experiences and applications of reflective practice, is a natural expectation, and why future research needs to further systematise a process for entrepreneurs.

In order to understand the importance and impact of reflective practice, it has been necessary to remain quite open to the flow of the discussion, and as such, interviewees' discussions differ, as do their approaches to reflective practice, which are all discussed here. All the interviewees embrace reflective practice, or 'self-reflection' as some prefer to describe it. We asked them when they chose to reflect and how they reflected.

The interviewees, an introduction

Wendy Bowers is the founder of ROLE, her consultancy company. As an experienced business mentor and coach and with considerable board-level experience at regional and national level, Wendy employs her 30 years of experience building businesses across all industry sectors. Working with leaders to create vision, strategy and growth alongside positive and happy owners and employees, Wendy is passionate about leadership reflection, wellbeing and stress management. Wendy is a HeartMath-registered practitioner and Courage and Renewal Facilitator, offering business leadership coaching and training which incorporate both resilience and reflective practice. Wendy is the author of *Words, Walks, Wisdom* and her work can be viewed at https://role.uk.com/

Rachel Kay is the proprietor of Love Local Solutions Limited, which supports and promotes local Lancashire businesses. As a proud Lancashire business owner, Rachel connects, supports, celebrates and educates businesses across our county. Her networking and speaker and expo events help businesses to meet, source growth advice, build relationships, inspire and support each other and generate new business. Rachel's award programmes celebrate businesses and communities across Hyndburn, Pendle and the Ribble Valley. Rachel also provides small group interactive training on how to network effectively, resilience, change management and improve team communication. For more information, please visit https://lovelocalnetworking.co.uk/

Phil Crowshaw is a highly accomplished, consultant, coach, trainer, non-executive director and event speaker who is passionate about business development with a key emphasis on digital media, innovation, and online strategies and tactics. As an internet entrepreneur Phil's strength as a leader also allows him to obtain buy-in and engagement from small and large teams alike to achieve the identified goals and objectives. Phil is the co-author of *How To Make Your Business Work For You* and is an accredited coach and training provider for government-backed business development programmes. Phil is an active podcast and livestream host and has his own channel, The Passions Project, accessible at www.youtube.com/@thepassionsproject.

Richard Few is the founder of Sales Geek and claims that they 'are changing the way the world perceives sales. One day sales people will be proud of what they do, buyers will confidently engage with sales departments and sales will be a conscious career choice for young people in education'. Sales Geek helps more people ethically sell more products and services by better understanding their product, their customer and themselves. More about Richard and his work can be gleaned from www.salesgeek.co.uk

Phil Myerscough is a professional (some may say veteran) with getting on for 25 years' experience in eCommerce management and digital marketing. After his student years in London writing drum and bass and trying to get into the music production industry, Phil started at the coal face selling hi-fi at Richer Sounds before quickly becoming eCommerce Manager there. Phil returning to Yorkshire worked for a mail order business, managing and growing their eCommerce arm. Phil then had a brief foray into the luxury sector as Head of eCommerce for cashmere brand, N. Peal. Phil now manages pjm:digital – an eCommerce-focused micro agency based in Bradford – acting as a consultant for some clients, and a Shopify and digital marketing agency for others. Phil has trained several apprentices in his company. In Phil's spare time he is an entrepreneur through SoundShirts.com as well as supporting Alliance Française de Leeds and Yorkshire's Brain Tumour Charity as a trustee. More about Phil can be found at https://pjmdigital.co.uk/

Beginning reflective practice

We'd like to start with Wendy Bowers, due to her sudden jolt to a deeper form of reflective practice than the norm. This was not as a form of obvious CPD, but from another vantage point completely. As a result of this, Wendy now runs an organisation dealing with woman's leadership but has a history of serving as a board-level executive at many firms, in addition to running her own firms. In fact, Wendy explains that she's had '40 years in business that really started when I created my first business directly after leaving college with my [then partner] which was a furniture manufacturing business'. Wendy then left to create her own business.

Interestingly, Wendy is the only interviewee with a dedication to journal continuously since the age of 11. She has developed a 'real habit' that 'enables [her] to figure things out, to get things down' and overcome what Wendy considers to be her 'poor memory'. What is interesting is that despite this exceptional commitment to journaling, the time necessary to decompress and take stock of the captured moments may have not manifested themselves to meet the term 'reflective practice' used here. For example, Wendy recounts:

> [I]f you'd asked me [about reflective practice as a topic] about seven years ago, I wouldn't have known very much about [it], because my life was all about 100 miles an hour going from meeting to meeting, sitting on a couple of national boards, running my own business, trying to balance that with quite significant family issues and honestly never having a minute to myself.

Wendy describes a work-life balance which she acknowledges many will chime with in contemporary enterprise.

For Wendy, this lifestyle came to a head in 2016 when it was clear to family members that she was burning out. As the president of the local chamber of commerce, and a member of the national board of chambers, they attended a significant dinner event. Wendy and her husband stayed overnight in a hotel. Wendy is keen to point out that she never indulged in alcohol when on business trips. However, she woke her husband at five o'clock in the morning saying she felt 'really, really ill' followed by a rush to the hospital thinking it might be a heart attack. The tests, during a 4-day stay in hospital, did not produce any obvious results although a diagnosis of internal shingles, brought on by stress, was returned several weeks later.

Meanwhile, once home, with Wendy still poorly, her daughter took matters in her own hands and drove Wendy to a Buddhist Monastery in Scotland, leaving her there to 'sort herself out before she killed herself'. Once there, Wendy was forced to reflect on what on earth she was doing and what was a success. What Wendy commented on was that 'other people saw me as a success', but this did not resonate with her once there was time to reflect. Instead, Wendy observed that she wished to slow down and build in 'time for, initially, mindfulness' but later she acknowledges she was seeking 'resilience on how to keep healthy and reduce her stress levels'. Wendy's recovery is interesting, and this introduces her heightened level of reflective practice.

The outcome of the monastery trip and 'falling off the hamster wheel' led to positive outcomes, not just within Wendy, as she altered her approach to her commitments professionally and elsewhere, but also in terms of the things she chose to put her energy into. One culmination of this was the book she ended up self-publishing called *Words, Walks, Wisdom* (Bowers, 2019). Another result of this period of reflection was how she'd been, like so many CEOs and senior managers, linking herself to her diary (not her aforementioned journal) believing that she had fallen 'into the trap of thinking [I] have to go to every single meeting' and not embracing delegation. 'You've put people into a senior leadership team position, and you've done it because you trust them' and Wendy makes the point that you should trust them and therefore you don't need to be at 'everything'. That could be time to use to reflect otherwise there's 'no time to decompress'. You're in a 'hamster wheel' like that! These pivotal events for Wendy have fundamentally shifted her view on reflection as we'll learn a little later.

Meanwhile Richard Few, whilst working in a golf club shop as a teenager, saw his future lay bare before him. He'd made the link between being stuck at the club's shop as the installed professional later in life along with the long hours and 'occasional lesson' to teach. Richard decided that, despite his absolute love of golf, this was not the future for him and decided to explore his already observed skill in sales from his time at the club's golf shop. He progressed in various roles at various companies achieving the nickname 'sales geek' and it stuck. This is now the name of his company.

Richard's entrepreneurial mindset is interesting in that he 'realised [he] could build a business, a brand and a product around what [he] knew . . . and just needed the courage to step into the unknown as it were'. This came through the reflections of a sales person and that sales somewhat has a bad name, noting not many career officers at school would propose it as an option for their leavers, for example. Richard is somewhat on a mission to change the perception of sales.

Richard Few says he 'probably first came across [reflective practice] at quite a young age and . . . probably didn't call it that'. As mentioned earlier, Richard wanted to be a professional golfer during his formative years, and like with any sport, you'll be 'reflecting on and reviewing . . . and providing that feedback to yourself on performance and breaking things down to what went well and what didn't go well . . . [in a] feedback loop in order to drive improvement'. Richard realised the importance of being positive about his reflections noting that we must 'recognise the good things that we do and build up a positive memory bank . . . not just the bad shots'. Focusing on the 'negative stuff . . . can get yourself in a bit of a bad headspace' and is a 'trap' where you can't 'make them better'. Richard, uniquely, has continued this into business and his area of sales. It must be noted that reflective practice is keenly considered in these terms within the field of sport.

Rachel Kay, an NLP (neurolinguistic programming) master practitioner and entrepreneur in her own right, now runs a decade-old business which focuses on networking, speaker engagements, awards and expo events. Upon asking about her reflective practice, Rachel, like many of us, explains that she does 'it all the time' and is adamant that she would not be as successful without reflective practice. This reflection is, it could be argued, the normal reflective process all professionals may employ after a critical incident (considering Black & Plowright, 2010; Marshall et al., 2022). However, upon enquiring further, it is clear that Rachel scrutinises the critical incidents in her business much more frequently, as we'll find out, and seemingly in more depth than one might 'normally' expect. In fact, she noted at the start some 'disastrous partnerships' where collaboration was not the basis of the relationship and increasing her reflexivity permitted her to refine the core mission of her business which she believes has led to the longevity of the business.

Phil Myerscough, once an employee working in eCommerce and digital marketing, had not taken too much time to engage in formal reflective practice until beginning his current business. 'If I look back to the start and how I pitched to companies, it's no wonder it's rubbish'. Reflective practice has been thrust upon Phil as he's 'literally refined and refined it, even the branding, the little yellow underline I now use to tie the design of everything up'. Phil realised by looking at how both competitors, and allied industries alike, were presenting themselves and then reflecting upon his own approach, undertaking refinement to aid the progress and sustainability of this business, he would succeed more often. Through the use of networking and collaboration, Phil continues this quest for improvement, or refinement.

Phil Crowshaw has what he calls a 'potted history' which started with a mainly corporate background, growing up the 'greasy pole so to speak', but morphed into an entrepreneur. What Phil's 'potted history' does not expose is Phil's significant role as a mentor and business advisor. Through both his ability to get promoted and his work of advising others on their profession, he has had to reflect, and teach others how to reflect. As with the other interviewees, Phil's approach is not one from the expected canon, but something more bespoke, yet extremely powerful. Reflective practice for Phil came from being ambitious and notes that 'I don't really know where it came from because my dad was a bank manager and my mum was a librarian'. Phil identified that personal development was key to the growth he was yearning for. Phil just knew that if he 'waited for the company to teach and train [him]. . .[he'd] be waiting a long time'. 'I took the responsibility for getting the latest books'. This is what Phil calls taking 'personal responsibility' – something that is covered in his personal reflective model we'll cover later.

Undertaking reflective practice

Richard Few explains 'for me I don't follow any models per se. Well, if I do, it's not by design. It's by accident'. 'I don't even see it as a as a thing that I deliberately do, it's just it's just a normal part of my life' . . . taking time 'either side of meetings you know' to engage in reflection.

> I'll get off this call, I'll go and make myself a brew in the time I've got before my next meeting, and I will reflect on is there anything I didn't say to [you] or did I say a thing that I kind of wish I hadn't said. I just do. I just do it automatically.

Richard also explains that there are longer periods of time where the whole day will be reflected upon, say during a run or a long drive and he 'will reflect on the day'.

Perhaps Richard is underplaying his 'by design' statement. In Sales Geek (his company) 'sometimes . . . reflection will involve other people as well. . . . Reflection is a shared process as well, and we do this at Sales Geek'. This is akin to collective reflection (Boud et al., 1985; Raelin, 2001; Tikkamäki et al., 2016). 'We we debrief a lot which I suppose is kind of the same thing really'. Richard explains how this group reflection happens.

> It's quite common practice here [at Sales Geek] when certain events have happened, certain big meetings or big calls that we've had . . . we'll grab each other, jump in a room for 10 minutes and go 'right. OK. What do we think? How did that go? What went well? . . . we try and do that even at the end of meetings.

Richard states that he'll direct these meetings as a 'big thing'. The importance being that it is too easy to be 'learning and then moving on' without gaining the benefit from reflection. Richard, in these circumstances, has stated that he's 'had to become disciplined on . . . because reflection can rumble on a little bit'.

The positivity of reflection, Richard says, is that

> you spend a lot of time living in the future, but so therefore you can't spend too much time living in the reflection of past events because at some point you've got to take the learning and move on. My biggest gripe with anybody and myself is when you reflect, learn some stuff and then do nothing about it – it's like reflection without action. It's kinda pointless really. . . . If you're gonna reflect, commit to doing the things, the actions that you took away from the reflection that you did, because nothing will change if you don't take action and hold yourself accountable to that.

Rachel Kay says of her approach 'I do a lot of self-reflection and I thought about it [prior to this discussion] and I do it all the time'. Rachel's depth of reflection is akin to that of Richard Few and is a reactionary process to an event (or critical incident in reflective practice parlance).

> When I've done something, when I've had a conversation with somebody, perhaps if things didn't go to plan or it didn't kind of go quite as I'd thought

> it might do, then I reflect on that and think, OK, how did I handle that? How did they handle that? How can I handle it better but also within [the] business? I'm constantly looking at what I'm doing and then what I've done to see how I can make it better.

Rachel's reflection is naturally stimulated by an event and, similar to Richard Few, a personal reflective practice emerges. Few's approach in his business was to huddle with his team and discuss the potential things that could be learnt. As Rachel is a mainly a sole entrepreneur, her reflection is somewhat a solo affair and is internally systematised. When asked when this 'system' of reflection kicks in, Rachel responds that

> I sort of think about it as soon as something's happened. I'm kind of processing it already, thinking . . . what could I have done better? And so it's kind of an immediate thing, but then maybe a few days, or a week later, I'll put aside time depending on how big the [critical incident] is.

When asked about an example, Rachel used an awards event series she organises, where she has ran with

> '. . . three this year . . . it's a bit of an iterative process and interesting things can happen that you never foresee . . . and then say how do I stop that happening in the future [especially] with so many moving parts?'.

The example revolved around the sponsor presenters involved overstepping their time slots and rather than giving one sentence about their entries, giving five minutes each, taking the whole event off schedule. Rachel explained that the most natural way to overcome this in the future would be to prevent the sponsors writing their own speeches. However, initial reflection gave Rachel concern for whether this was meeting the mission and values of the awards she was running. Whilst this example might appear simple to overcome from a scheduling point of view, and if that were just the case, then the correction would not require much reflection. However, the buy-in from the participants and the longer-term reputation of her company would be at stake if her approach to correcting this was to be seen to eradicate this value-led position, or too interventionist. As such, the 'iterative' process of reflection led Rachel to altering the approach and as such allowing her to script, with the presenters, their lines, ensuring that the length is kept to the correct schedule, to great success.

Rachel recounts her NLP training and that it has made it possible for her to identify the large numbers of those who perhaps don't self-reflect enough to temper or moderate their communications at events through emotional intelligence. Meanwhile, those who are shy in business or who are not actively engaged in reflective practice may not necessarily be the best communicators and in doing so may miss out on personal, and professional, connections that permit business to flourish. In many ways, opportunities and referrals only happen through those you know, like and trust.

Phil Myerscough practices reflective practice, much like Rachel Kay, based upon reactionary opinions of an event or outcome. These will manifest immediately after a pitch (for new work) or an interaction. Like Richard Few and Rachel, Phil has internally systematised the approach. His approach is mostly alone (as a solo business), and his purpose for doing so is to 'see iterative improvement'. To track and plan 'stuff like that is literally ending up on a spreadsheet. And it's what's coming in and what work is on, what retainers we have and the bigger projects on top'. Myerscough employs an annual planner on a spreadsheet as a structure. For the purposes of this chapter, Phil is exerting reflection-on-action and reflection-for-action in his development process. In keeping with Rachel Kay, Myerscough employs his short drive to the office to reflect on the things that have happened and what needs to happen (reflection-on-action and reflection-for-action).

Further outcomes for Wendy from the monastery trip and realignments of her commitments also led her to the Center for Courage and Renewal (www.couragerenewal.org), a US-based organisation which Wendy has supported and brought access to professionals within the British Isles. Courage and Renewal work is practised using a set of guidelines called Touchstones. These act as a foundation for individual Reflective work which is carried out in groups called Circles of Trust™. The Touchstones quickly build trust and enable sharing by invitation in a safe and confidential space. The Touchstones relate to 'define clear boundaries in a circle of trust' and include giving and receiving the same welcome; being present as much as possible; invitation not demand; speak your truth in ways that respect other's truths; no fixing, saving, advising or correcting; respond to others with honest open questions (https://couragerenewal.org/library/courage-renewal-touchstones/).

Phil Crowshaw, like Wendy, has a systematised format for prompting self-reflective thought and consideration which is well developed and is a form Phil trains in his coaching, mentoring and courses. His system relates to 12 segments.

1. Motivation – 'have I got a strong enough reason why or motivation to do this thing I want to do'. Phil explains that if there are any doubts, then when things get tough, and in the entrepreneurial journey they will, then 'there's a good chance you'll fall by the wayside'.
2. Clear aims – 'have I got clear objectives and goals for this? If I haven't, I reflect on what those objectives and goals should look like' (Phil employs SMART – Specific, Measurable, Achievable, Relevant and Time-bound).

3. Creativity – 'what I call possibility thinking, and this is really key, and where I would argue creativity comes in'. Understanding Phil, this creativity comes in the form of visioning the product, service or system and designing new, USP-like aspects which would excite the marketplace and engage the business.
4. Planning – which is the obvious one. Again, there's a tendency, I think, for younger entrepreneurs, to park the planning because it is not the sexy bit. The planning is the organisation. It's the process. It's the procedure . . . So, there's a lot of reflection in planning [reflection-for-action], because you're thinking about what resources do I need, what money do I need . . . what people do I need to make it happen? All the different elements of planning you need in order to achieve [it].
5. Being Committed – 'it's basically personal responsibility. Am I going to take personal responsibility to make this happen and I usually do that on a scale of 1–10.'
6. Networking – 'which is involving other people. The reflection here is who else could I involve in getting to this point, getting to this goal?'
7. Taking Action – 'Am I taking enough action here? So again . . . a . . . whole self-reflection question – am I doing enough? Am I taking enough action?'. Phil recounted an experience of interviewing Sahar Hashemi, the co-founder of Coffee Republic, where she recounts being mentored at the time of the startup. She was getting weary of not getting the funding necessary, as the banks and investors could not quite understand how anyone might pay £3 for a cup of coffee at a time when hot drinks were much cheaper. She'd been to 'about ten banks' and the mentor said 'come back and talk to me when you've approached 50' and you're in the same place. 'And, that's the whole idea of taking in, and taking on enough action'.
8. Embracing change – 'in terms of self-reflection this is what's changing in the market, what is changing in technological terms, that is going to help me to get where I want to go . . . and that's about research basically?' In terms of this Phil discusses PESTLE, STEEPLE, Porter's 5 Forces and barriers to entry and so on – all the business management diet for students.
9. Monitoring – I spoke . . . to an investor a few years back and they said the worst thing that they can ever see is an entrepreneur, a young entrepreneur in particular, turning up in a flash car. They want them to be working from a shed in a back garden with a battered old Mini in the driveway and a great idea. That shows [the investor] that they understand the importance of cost control . . . And monitoring performance is a big one because that is very relevant to reflection. 'Yeah, how are we doing?'
10. Sacrifice – Am I sacrificing enough to make this happen. A lot of these things link together, so they're designed in a wheel format when I teach this.

If you think about them as segments, as a like . . . Trivial Pursuit type pie, you know, or a pie? Yeah. And sacrifice, then again, comes back to personal responsibility and commitment . . . So people will say I haven't got time and then I'll say, OK, be honest with me, how many hours have you spent watching either soaps or box sets in the last month? Or, just being on your phone, just, you know, Tik Toking up and down.

11. BHW (Bloody Hard Work) – 'Am I putting enough work into this? And that links very much into motivation – I'm gonna work a lot harder at it if I've got high motivation to achieve it'.
12. Confidence – What Phil refers to as 'self-belief to make this thing happen'.

Benefits of reflective practice

In considering the benefits of reflective practice, the interviewees have differing observations starting with Wendy Bowes:

> [Reflective practice] has absolutely changed my life. And that's why I build it in. I build it into whatever it is I'm doing, whether I'm mentoring, coaching, delivering a culture change programme, or delivering a women's programme. And you know, I've even delivered it at a leaders' group in the village here. It has absolutely changed me and my 4 kids have said that they can see differences in my behaviours at home. I speak quite a lot slower, and I don't nag as much and I listen much better now as well.

Wendy notes the irony in her life-long practice and the revelations her children have told her.

> And yet I wrote a journal for all those years, but it was only when I combined the journaling with reflective practice, following particular guidelines, that it all started to really make sense.

Richard Few notes that reflective practice has helped him with what he now identifies as Imposter Syndrome. Richard explains how this manifested for him through his success and natural skill in sales:

> Throughout my career, and when I was very young and I had some pretty senior roles, I really struggled with, I suppose people call it impostor syndrome now, but it kind of didn't really have a name back then. Impostor syndrome and self-confidence [are linked] and I had to really catch and monitor my negative self-talk on some of these things because I remember being 26 or 27, you know, and the head of sales taking on a sales team

> where every single person in that team was older than me, had more experience than me. And equally starting the business and getting going and speaking to customers. Most of our customers in that first year before we launched the training business were business owners in their own right. And there were times where I caught myself sitting there going, who am I to tell these people how to do stuff better like these guys are up on a pedestal for me and until I got those first, you get 3, 4, 5, 6, then 7 customers on board and could tangibly see the value that I had. It is a really a really, really struggle with it and then.

Richard has since moved his Sales Geek business into a franchise model spreading the brand internationally. He continues to combat the syndrome by creating a feedback loop for a start where customers, colleagues and others can feed back on what work they do.

> There'll be a flurry of feedback forms that we collate and gather all of that information together. We . . . get the anecdotal feedback. We give that back to the individual franchisees. We turn that back into learning about the content and how we can make it better. We get feedback from clients as we off-board them as well. How was the experience, did you did you get what you wanted from it? How would you talk about Sales Geek externally kind of get that feel so for me feedback is the breakfast of champions?

Rachel Kay recounts the informal way in which she reflects noting the things that went well 'I'm going to keep doing, or you know, I'm going to do more of that' and so it recirculates as a 'sort of roadmap'. It is only later, during more critical reflection, that 'if you just leave it and do the same thing again next time, you're going to get the same outcome', which leans towards the lack of criticality as to whether an improvement could be made. Rachel notes, too, that things that went well can also be improved upon, and reflection is the key to this iterative progress – 'it's giving you ways to improve . . . in a nutshell'. Furthermore, her approach to reflective practice is initially based around a lot of independent thought, but after some percolation, things would get written down on paper, before systems and models come into focus. Rachel discusses that this is mainly a task-based approach rather than a unique system, which results in 'do I need to update my process' or 'do I need to speak to somebody about something'. For Rachel it's the 'process of continuous improvement' that requires the time dedicated to reflection.

Phil Crowshaw recounts how his 12-segment reflective practice model is 'ingrained in my head . . . so I'll automatically whizz around all the 12 segments with a client'. Phil speaks about his clients, whether they are entrepreneurs or podcast hosts gaining training, and recounts to them that

> they're starting from Ground Zero – if they compare their first episodes to their 30th [during a process] of self-reflection and reflecting in the [12 segment] way . . . then they will look at theirs and notice the improvement and it will get better. What holds people back is that they look at somebody who's been doing it for years and they think, they can do that easily – it's easy, but when they come to do it, it's more difficult than they thought.

Phil importantly notes that critical reflective practice tends to 'always going to be 100% critical, a bit like electricity, in terms of moving forward. . . . It's not a choice – it's a given'. So Crowshaw suggests that reflective practice is to handle 'the truth and you can handle the feedback'.

Conclusions and further research

Defining a specific system or process of reflective practice for many of our interviewees was unique to them, from a spreadsheet (clearly linked to ongoing business engagements and sales) all the way through to a personally developed system within 12 segments. Not one thread of reflective practice commonality existed between the interviewees except for the 'incidental' approaches they all adopt, as business owners. It was evident that all the interviewees relied on and utilised reflective practice in their own business, and beyond it – in the interactions, training and teams they work within, and for. In many ways this heutagogic approach demonstrated autodidactic behaviour which, to most interviewees, has been sub-conscious, or 'incidental'.

Interestingly, the one person engaged in the journalling aspect of reflective practice was Wendy Bowers. As a serial journalist, Wendy says that she had the resources to reflect all along, but like so many we observe in this chapter, the system for reflection was never fully systematised to gain the best benefit. Ironically, in business culture, it is common to find project management or time management software that promises new powers of achievement, or pressure from videos suggesting how you need to work harder to create your future opportunities. However, there are few articles, videos, or applications that support the systematisation of reflective practice, and so it is no surprise that there is more to consider aiding enterprises and entrepreneurs gain the most from reflective practice.

We acknowledge, from our interviews and research, that reflective practice is not only a naturally occurring process, but is something that, when enhanced, provides a useful systematic approach to many business interactions, entrepreneurial decisions and successes. The key example of this is Phil Crowshaw's 12 segment system which has been conceived as a personal tool, but one that can be disseminated.

It is the authors' intention to begin to further this research by considering reflective practice systems and models in detail and consider the threads between them, and their applications (sectors), in a longer-term quest for a systematised entrepreneurial-related reflective model. The dream would be that this could be applied to all andragogic business management programmes and perhaps beyond.

References

Argyris, C. and Schon, D. (1996). *Organisational Learning*. Reading, MA: Addison-Wesley Publishing.

Bauer, N.J. (1991). *Dewey and Schön: An Analysis of Reflective Thinking*. Paper presented at the Annual Meeting of the American Educational Studies Association (Kansas City, MO, October 23–26, 1992).

Black, P.E. and Plowright, D. (2010). A multi-dimensional model of reflective learning for professional development. *Reflective Practice*, 11(2), pp. 245–258.

Boud, D., Keogh, R. and Walker, D. (1985). What is reflection is learning? In D. Boud, R. Keogh and D. Walker (Eds.), *Reflection: Turning Experience into Learning* (pp. 7–17). London: Kogan Page.

Bowers, W. (2019). *Words, Walks, Wisdom*. Amazon. https://www.amazon.co.uk/Words-Walks-Wisdom-Wendy-Bowers/dp/1671172353

Brookfield, S. (2009). The concept of critical reflection: Promises and contradictions. *European Journal of Social Work*, 12(3), pp. 293–304.

Brookfield, S.D. (2017). *Becoming a Critically Reflective Teacher*. San Francisco: John Wiley & Sons.

Cheetham, G. and Chivers, G. (1998). The reflective (and competent) practitioner: A model of professional competence which seeks to harmonise the reflective practitioner and competence-based approaches. *Journal of European Industrial Training*, 22(7), pp. 267–276.

Clarke, A.P., Cornes, C. and Ferry, N. (2020). The use of self-reflection for enhanced enterprise education: A case study. *Education + Training*, 62(5), pp. 581–598.

Daudelin, M.W. (1996). Learning from experience through reflection. *Organizational Dynamics*, 24(3), pp. 36–49.

Dewey, J. (1933). *How We Think*. Boston: Heath.

Evans, L. (2008). Professionalism, professionality and the development of education professionals. *British Journal of Educational Studies*, 56(1), pp. 20–38.

Evetts, J. (2006). Introduction: Trust and professionalism: Challenges and occupational changes, *Current Sociology*, 54(4), p. 5.

Flanagan, J.C. (1954). The critical incident technique. *Psychological Bulletin*, 51(4), p. 327.

Friedson, E. (2001). *Professionalism: The Third Logic*. London: Polity Press.

Gelter, H. (2003). Why is reflective thinking uncommon. *Reflective Practice*, 4(3), pp. 337–344.

Gibbs, G. (1988). Learning by Doing: A guide to teaching and learning methods. *Further Education Unit*. Oxford Polytechnic: Oxford.

Gibbs, G. (1998). *Learning by Doing, Further Education Unit*. Oxford Polytechnic. Available at https://dsdweb.co.uk/wp-content/uploads/2021/10/learning-by-doing-graham-gibbs.pdf (last accessed 30/06/2024)

Gray, D.E. (2007). Facilitating management learning: Developing critical reflective through reflective tools. *Management Learning*, 38(5), pp. 495–517.

Hamblin, M. and Crisp, P. (2022). Negative focus, self-doubt, and issues of 'tool proficiency': Beginner-coaches' reflections on reflective practice. *Physical Culture and Sport. Studies and Research*, 95(1), pp. 1–13.
Hargreaves, J. and Page, L. (2013). *Reflective Practice*. John Wiley & Sons.
Hase, S. and Kenyon, C. (2000). From andragogy to heutagogy. *Ultibase Articles*, 5, pp. 1–10.
Hase, S. and Kenyon, C. eds. (2013). *Self-determined Learning: Heutagogy in Action*. A&C Black.
Hepworth-Sawyer, R. (2021). Mastering the void: A missing link in UK audio education?. In *Audio Engineering Society Conference: 2021 AES International Audio Education Conference*. New York: Audio Engineering Society.
James, B.P. and Crowshaw, P. (2008). *Make Your Business Work for You: The Secrets of Success*, 2nd edition. Great Ideas Publishing.
Jarvis, P. (2004). *Adult Education and Lifelong Learning: Theory and Practice*. London: Routledge Falmer.
Jarvis, P. (2018). *Professional Education (1983)*. Routledge.
Jensen, C. (2011). Conditional contraction: Globalisation and capitalist systems. *European Journal of Political Research*, 50(2), pp. 168–189.
Kaufman, J. (2020). *The Personal MBA 10th Anniversary Edition*. London: Penguin.
Kenyon, C. and Hase, S. (2001). 'Moving from Andragogy to Heutagogy in Vocational Education', *Proceedings of the Australian Vocational Education and Training Research Association (AVETRA) Conference*, Adelaide, 28–30 March 2001.
Kimberley, A. (2019). 'Critical Reflective Practice as a Means to Encourage Critical Thinking and Strengthen Confidence and Self-efficacy of Undergraduate Business Students', *International Journal of Arts and Sciences*, 9(1), pp. 243–260.
Kinnaman, A.J. (1902). Pedagogy in our colleges and universities. *The Pedagogical Seminary*, 9(3), pp. 366–373.
Knowles, M.S. (1975). Self-directed learning: A guide for learners and teachers. *The Adult Education Company* (New York).
Knowles, M.S., Holton III, E.F. and Swanson, R.A. (2014). *The Adult Learner: The Definitive Classic in Adult Education and Human Resource Development*. Routledge.
Kolb, D.A. (1984). *Experiential learning: Experience as the source of learning and development*. Englewood Cliffs, NJ: Prentice-Hall.
Kolb, D.A. (2014). *Experiential Learning: Experience as the Source of Learning and Development*. NJ: FT Press (New Jersey).
Lang, R. and McNaught, K. (2013). Reflective practice in a capstone business internship subject. *Journal of International Education in Business*, 6(1), pp. 7–21.
Lawless, A., Holden, R.J., Griggs, V. and Rae, J. (2015). Reflective practice in management practice: A systematic review. In *UFHRD Conference Archives* (No. 2015). London, UK: University Forum for Human Resource Development.
Leggett, R. (2014). *Developing Reflective Practice in Managers: Exploring the Contribution of Management Training*. London, UK: University Forum for Human Resource Development (UFHRD).
Marshall, T., Keville, S., Cain, A. and Adler, J.R. (2022). Facilitating reflection: A review and synthesis of the factors enabling effective facilitation of reflective practice. *Reflective Practice*, 23(4), pp. 483–496.
Mann, K., Gordon, J. and MacLeod, A. (2007), Reflection and reflective practice in health professions: A systematic review. *Advances in Health Science Education*, 14, pp. 595–621.
McGivern, J. and Thompson, J. (2012). Teaching management through reflective practice. In *Thinking about Management* (pp. 81–97). London: Routledge.

Neumann Jr, R.K. (2019). The professions and professional education. In Rury, J.L. and Tamura, E.H. (Eds.), *The Oxford Handbook of the History of Education*. Oxford, UK: Oxford University Press.
Ollila, S (2000). Creativity and innovativeness through reflective project leadership. *Reflective Project Leadership*, 9(3), pp. 195–200.
Partington, M., Cushion, C.J., Cope, E. and Harvey, S. (2015). The impact of video feedback on professional youth football coaches' reflection and practice behaviour: A longitudinal investigation of behaviour change. *Reflective Practice*, 16(5), pp. 700–716.
Puutio, R., Kykyri, V.L. and Wahlström, J. (2009). The process and content of advice giving in support of reflective practice in management consulting. *Reflective Practice*, 10(4), pp. 513–528.
Raelin, J.A. (2001). Public reflection as the basis of learning. *Management Learning*, 32(1), pp. 11–30.
Raelin, J.A. (2002). "I don't have time to think!" versus the art of reflective practice. *Reflections: The SoL Journal*, 4(1), pp. 66–79.
Read, S., Sarasvathy, S., Dew, N. and Wiltbank, R. (2016). *Effectual Entrepreneurship*. Routledge.
Schön, D.A. (1983). *The reflective practitioner: How professionals think in action*. Temple Smith (London).
Schön, D.A. (1987). *Educating the Reflective Practitioner. Toward a New Design for Teaching and Learning in the Professions*, The Jossey-Bass Higher Education Series. San Francisco, CA: Jossey-Bass Publishers.
Schön, D.A. (1992). The theory of inquiry: Dewey's legacy to education. *Curriculum Inquiry*, 22(2), pp. 119–139.
Svensson, L.G. (2006). New professionalism, trust and competence: Some conceptual remarks and empirical data. *Current Sociology*, 54(4), pp. 579–593.
Sobel, R.S. and Clemens, J. (2020). *The Essential Joseph Schumpeter*. Vancouver, Canada: Fraser Institute.
Sockett, H.T. (1993). *The Moral Base for Teacher Professionalism*. New York: Teachers College Press.
Sockett, H.T. (1996). Teachers for the 21st Century: Redefining Professionalism, *NASSP Bulletin*, May, 22–29. USA: Sage Publishing (Thousand Oaks, USA).
Tikkamäki, K., Heikkilä, P. and Ainasoja, M. (2016). Positive stress and reflective practice among entrepreneurs. *Journal of Entrepreneurship, Management and Innovation*, 12(1), pp. 35–56.
Vallance, P. (2019). A critical review of the role of reflective practice in the development of sport coaches. *Applied Coaching Research Journal*, 4(1), 24–33.

8 Value hidden in plain sight – an allied health professional case study

Andrew P. Clarke, Claire E. Mercer and Paulina A. MacKrell

Introduction

This chapter derives from personal experiences and insights gained whilst considering if *commercial acumen has value as a stream of enterprise and entrepreneurship education (EE).* On first view, it would seem obvious that commercial acumen does have value in enterprise and EE; if so, it would seem wise to consider why EE education is delivered mainly in business schools within higher education institutions (HEIs) to only students taking business degrees. This chapter aims to demonstrate, through a case study approach, how entrepreneurial attributes and behaviours have value within occupations not primarily considered to be business, and deserve their place in the wider curriculum.

The authors' collective experiences stem from teaching the application of entrepreneurial skills and behaviours in real-world scenarios, which then add value to the employee and the employer. The three authors have experience within academic delivery and the workplace, so they view value from the lens of the educator and the employer.

This chapter will open the discussion about how value is viewed and recognised within enterprise and EE in UK HEIs. This chapter explores the current focus on new venture creation, and if that focus is because EE is held mainly within a business school in an HEI (Jamieson, 1984; Shane and Venkataraman, 2000; Sirelkhatim and Gangi, 2015). It will consider potential neglect of areas of value from entrepreneurial actions due to the direct focus on business school education. This business school focus was noted in a study by Turner and Gianiodis (2018) evaluating blended entrepreneurial taught courses where an inventory of entrepreneurship taught material was carried out. The focus will then move to how value is viewed; we view 'value' as something that contributes a gain to an employer or employee through an enhanced human capital (Clarke, 2024). We link that gain to company performance, those potentially neglected entrepreneurial actions and analyse how the value in those actions can be recognised.

The chapter will move beyond the current sole focus of EE on new venture creation and discuss a potential link between commercial acumen, human capital,

DOI: 10.4324/9781003324737-8

sense of value in the person and in the company, and company performance. The chapter proposes to move away from the traditional ways of measuring new venture creation through quantitative methodologies, and offers exploration to employ qualitative ontological and epistemological perspectives to investigate the value of entrepreneurial actions to human capital. A case study approach will be used to further enhance this exploration.

Background

The roots of the chapter stem back to around 2016, when two of the authors of this chapter were asked to teach 'business' to science post-graduate students in a UK university. The request was vague; this could have been because the science students sat within a science school, the associated academics were experts in their discipline and business was not part of their fields. The students requested content to be business focused or business related; however, they were unsure as to what exactly this should be. Whilst eager to share our knowledge we had no clear picture of expectations or requirements. As we had broad experience within varied careers, we had the ability to notice and appreciate the link between business, science and engineering as well as the commercial drivers within the laboratory. This request required us to consider 'business' from the point of view of the learner. To ensure we had engagement and offered 'value' to the learner, we needed to understand what was important to the learner and crucial to the business owner(s) who will potentially employ that learner in the future.

A search through the literature indicated that approximately 10% of students intend to start a business (Jones and Penaluna, 2013). Engagement with the student cohort was key; the learners were science students and not business students, and it would be important to adapt our learning techniques accordingly to successfully engage the whole cohort, not just the 10% that may be interested.

In preparation, a study was carried out on current enterprise and EE. The work demonstrated that, in the main, teaching was delivered within business schools, to students who signed up for business-related degrees (Clarke *et al.*, 2020). Considering the results of the study (ibid, 2020), the approach and focus have been shifted to prepare content that would be valuable to the students. An ethnographic stance was utilised as it allowed us to reflect, build on and share their own experiences from different fields of materials engineering, social science, business and management, and academia. It is evident that further research is required to uncover a *common* understanding of value in entrepreneurship education and consequently, what should be offered to add such value.

Definitions

It is first important to examine existing definitions of enterprise and entrepreneurship, and analyse their potential meaning. The Quality Assurance Agency (QAA,

2018) defines enterprise as "the generation and application of ideas, which are set within practical situations during a project or undertaking", and entrepreneurship as "the application of enterprise behaviours, attributes and competencies into the creation of cultural, social or economic value. This can, but does not exclusively, lead to venture creation". *Value* is of importance here and it would be important for further consideration. For example, what *value* means to different stakeholders (such as students) and how can *value* be added in different contexts (such as enhancement of employability prospects).

The QAA paper (2018) continues to define enterprise education as "the process of developing students in a manner that provides them with an enhanced capacity to generate ideas, and the behaviours, attributes, and competencies to make them happen", and entrepreneurship education as "to build upon the enterprising competencies of students who are capable of identifying opportunities and developing ventures, through becoming self-employed, setting up new businesses or developing and growing part of an existing venture". There are various interpretations of what constitutes 'enterprise'; however, the very definition of enterprise and entrepreneurship is often regarded as confusing and convoluted; the two terms are routinely interchanged (Pittaway and Cope, 2007).

The following discussion will focus not on the traditional areas of new venture creation, but aims to operationalise the QAA definitions given earlier and focus on taught content which enhances 'enterprise behaviours, attributes and competencies' and develop 'a capacity to generate ideas, . . . build upon the enterprising competencies, . . . identifying opportunities, . . . developing and growing part of an existing venture'. Entrepreneurial orientation was noted by Lumpkin and Dess (1996) to link to firm performance when five behaviours were noted: autonomy, risk-taking, innovativeness, competitiveness and proactiveness.

The term 'commercial acumen' within this chapter was chosen to define this taught content; this is because commercial acumen allows researchers to step back from the convoluted term EE with the aim of trying to simplify definitions and meaning. For the purposes of this chapter, we define commercial acumen as having an understanding of the facets of business, such as ideas generation, opportunity identification, business planning, brands and branding, and the importance of building trust and confidence.

An example of such variation in understanding and operationalising enterprise-related terminology was highlighted within previous research (Clarke *et al.,* 2020). A senior academic mentioned once that staff in their discipline include enterprise 'throughout their curriculum' because their students write a CV and make a social media profile. That team of academics were trying to offer the best learning experience they could, but their experience and understanding of enterprise meant they viewed it as a task that had a start and finish point; enterprise can be 'done' by completing a task, in this case the form of creating a social media profile. This demonstrated that the fundamental view of enterprise and entrepreneurship varied according to the individuals involved. Enterprise can therefore be viewed as a project rather than a subject (Clarke *et al.*, 2020). This could potentially mean that some individuals (including academics) regard enterprise activity as something that has a finish and an end: 'I've done some enterprise this week as I submitted a tender application', for example.

It is proposed that there is some confusion around what constitutes enterprise. If being an entrepreneur or performing enterprise is viewed as a project, which has a start and an end, it should, therefore, be measurable. However, there is no common indication, nor understanding, of which parameters should be used or how these parameters should be measured. Such examples, confusions and lack of clarity between the terms of enterprise and entrepreneurship are often merged and used interchangeably and therefore are not held to the QAA definitions (QAA, 2018). This is possibly because success and failure in entrepreneurship are often viewed from the lens of the funding bodies. For example, European Union–funding projects require project managers to report back on metrics such as 'number of enterprises receiving support' or 'number of visits to supported sites' (Nigohosyan and Vutsova, 2018); these are quantifiable and consider value from the point of view of the funder rather than the employer or employee. Most funded projects require a thorough justification and breakdown of the expenses (Herzog *et al.*, 2013), and one way of doing that is by using quantitative data.

As such, this has resulted in definitions such as new venture creation being used, because the success or failure of a business can be measured and defined. Although the monetary value and quantitative methods of exploring entrepreneurship are appreciated and realised, there is a gap in understanding entrepreneurship and its value amongst different stakeholders (not just the lenders or funders). Consequently, we propose that the meaning of value be explored differently with qualitative value, such as case studies, in which individuals could share their experiences, thoughts and beliefs regarding their engagement with the company they work for, what they feel about the value they bring, and how they consider their own accumulated skills and experiences frame that sense of value.

The value of enterprise and entrepreneurship education

EE is increasingly becoming part of the HEI offer and curriculum design (Turner and Gianiodis, 2018). As Hannon (2006) points out, EE has been rather inserted instead of integrated into HEI because of a breadth of drivers, including political, ideological, institutional and educational reasons. Turner and Gianiodis (2018) note one driver for this change is economic; in the United States some doctoral programmes are integrating elements of EE, in areas such as medicine and veterinarian studies, for instance. This could be seen as a challenge as not all HE institutions, or academics, have been instructed on how this should be achieved or what the exact requirements are. Trying to embed EE across different fields, especially outside the business school, could be seen as problematic; the Turner and Gianiodis (2018) study continues to note that including EE into non-business school subjects is complicated, as different subjects view EE in different ways. This concurs with the study by Clarke *et al.* (2020) who noted value in reflection on the part of the educator when delivering EE to students from different disciplines. As Hannon (2006) maintains, when subjects are formalised for teaching they are often maximised with content, and as a result enterprise education becomes peripheral. By taking an ethnographic approach to our teaching, our experience explained earlier in this chapter was similar – we focused on helping the students understand the commercial acumen skills which underpin their science, enabling them to appreciate the relevance of those skills to their future work and encouraging them to engage with their scientific backgrounds, whilst at the same time appreciate (or learn the value of) how their work enhanced the agenda of the business they could work for or start. This approach diverged from the traditional new venture creation method taught as part of the traditional enterprise and EE (Bellotti *et al.,* 2012), and feedback was obtained to deepen our understanding, leading to research-informed teaching which was contextual dependent on the experiences of the student body. We further developed educational resources and teaching of EE to other specialisms (Clarke *et al.,* 2020), some examples of which were arts and media, allied health professionals, and students with sports backgrounds.

We have demonstrated (Clarke *et al.,* 2020) that the term 'enterprise' in 'business' means different things to different people; as the students pointed out within the feedback received, 'an artist might struggle to put a monetary value on their art because they are so emotionally invested in it'; 'a healthcare professional might see caring for people as their primary aim but drugs cost money – there is a commercial element to healthcare which raises ethical questions such as the cost of care'. Students have shared multiple examples through feedback, and as a result, support an individualised and contextualised approach based on the group and subject that EE is delivered to. A toolkit of elements of enterprise and EE is required, together with educational reflection to ensure that the right elements are delivered to support effective delivery for the group (Clarke *et al.,* 2020). Presenting and context is key to be able to deliver the usual approaches to EE (marketing, buyer behaviour, stocks and shares, business planning) but demonstrate relevance to the students for them to appreciate the associated value.

Case study

To illustrate the value of commercial acumen, an ethnographical approach using a case study example was taken to look at the impact of value on the individual and organisation in terms of actions and behaviours. The case study chosen for this chapter will illustrate the added value approach within one Allied Health Professional (AHP) role. This will allow the entrepreneurial activity of an AHP to be identified and valued in concert with, and complimentary to, their skills in healthcare, in addition to recognising the impact to the service user and potential commercial aspects to the provider.

For context, an allied health professional is a healthcare practitioner who is not a doctor, dentist, or nurse, but who works collaboratively with these and other healthcare providers in the delivery of health services. Allied health professionals typically specialise in areas such as physiotherapy, occupational therapy, speech therapy, radiography, dietetics, podiatry, as examples. They play a crucial role in supporting patient care, rehabilitation, prevention and management of various health conditions.

Technological and digital skills are now, more than ever, an essential part of healthcare education, and radiography is a discipline which is naturally at the forefront of these developments. Within the medical imaging field, there is a workforce crisis which has been ongoing for many years. Although increasing the workforce through improvements and expansion in education is essential, identifying areas to improve workflow through supporting the wellbeing of staff and service users, digital advancements, and workflow solutions is key to respond to this crisis. One area of diagnostic radiography sits the specialism of breast imaging (mammography). Mammography supports the early detection of benign breast conditions and malignant breast disease, and is considered as the gold standard of screening though it is highly dependent on the production of high-quality mammography images. This is the field where the case study for the ethnographic reflexive analysis will be focused from. Working as a clinical mammographer undertaking an MSc alongside their career, one practitioner's research in 2013 identified inadequate breast compression during a mammogram and a lack of standardised positioning technique (Mercer *et al.*, 2013). This was the catalyst for more research within the industry and was the impetus for a further mammography practitioner to develop their research and together publish new positioning standards (Hogg *et al.,* 2013; Mercer *et al.,* 2015; Smith *et al.,* 2015). These standards for practice are now embedded in the UK breast screening services for around 2,000,000 clients per annum supporting a change to clinical practice. This has had a positive effect on clients' experiences, with a potential reduction in pain levels during mammography and improvements in detecting benign and malignant disease. This unique research has also led providers outside of the UK (Norway, the Netherlands) to update their practice and policy, resulting in standardisation of approach and improved client experiences for another 500,000 clients. This has then spurred the publication of a book (Hogg *et al.,* 2015), now in its second edition (Mercer *et al.,* 2022). Additionally, the first edition of *Clark's Essential Guide to Mammography* (Borrelli and Mercer, 2023) saw further publication of these guidelines to support improvements in practice. This AHP then developed within academia and formed a collaboration with an external company to develop enterprise and entrepreneurship within the HEI. Using the LUCID Window Relationship Model (Clarke and Deacon, 2015), the AHP was able to focus on the stages of listening, understanding, co-designing, involving and delivering to enable enhanced relationships with stakeholders. LUCID allows the user to identify and understand the main factors which determine successful collaboration and relationship building.

This collaboration was further developed by forming the unique industry partnership where the radiography facilities within the HEI could then be used other than the purposes of education, supporting shared educational delivery, staff training for industry partners, the development of industry placements and renting of the imaging facility. The Centre for Medical Imaging at this HEI was the first in the UK to have this unique arrangement within a radiography department, and this was spurred through the enterprise and entrepreneurship actions of the individual within this case study; development work was grounded from a research approach, working with industry to ensure impact and value.

Within this case study, this particular individual's education did not include enterprise and EE within a taught module in a UK HEI, nor was it seen as a value. It was only when this individual within the case study moved into academia that they saw relevance to EE further within their field, as discussed earlier. Recently, with the development of the multi-professional framework (Health Education England, 2017), entrepreneurial activities are given value within AHPs with the development from enhanced, advanced and consultant practice. This is a huge leap forward in seeking value to this recognition and requires input from HEIs into learning outcomes within modules. The four pillars of practice are clinical practice, leadership and management, education and research, and mapping standards to Health Education England's 2017 Multi-Professional Framework for advanced clinical practice in England, which sets minimal standards for working at these levels. The NHS Clinical Entrepreneur Programme (2016) was created by NHS England and Health Education England in 2016 for clinicians and NHS staff who want to develop clinical innovations to improve patient care and support service redesign through commercial and non-commercial enterprises. It is targeted at all AHPs and has recruited over 360 AHPs so far including doctors, dentists, health care scientists, nurses, midwives and pharmacists from a diverse range of backgrounds. Unfortunately, it is not widely publicised. Entrepreneurship has always been an uphill task but never an impossible one if done with the right attitude and ethical values.

The advanced and consultant practitioner in radiography will now often be an entrepreneur with business ventures often alongside their main job roles; for example, some will develop an image reporting business alongside their primary role. Outside of the UK, within the radiologist's role over a decade ago, there was an "urgent need for entrepreneur radiologists to set up financially viable radiology practices and run them successfully" (Jakhere, 2011). One could consider then that there is educational value in embedding entrepreneurship within educational modules for enhanced and advanced practice within radiographers in the UK. The multi-professional framework, whilst not specifically recognising the term 'entrepreneur', does explicitly state that the leader should demonstrate 'the values of their organisation/place of work'; 'lead new practice and service redesign solutions'; 'working across boundaries and broadening sphere of influence'; 'continually develop practice in response to changing population health need' and 'engaging in horizon scanning for future developments' (Health Education England, 2017, p. 9). All of this could be classed as learning outcomes for the developing entrepreneur.

The AHP in this case study demonstrates attributes such as a person-centred approach; a strong work ethic, good communication skills; commercial and business development skills; networking; an ability to adopt to new technologies and adaptability. Looking back at the definitions in this chapter to the five entrepreneurial behaviours of autonomy, risk-taking, innovativeness, competitiveness and proactiveness noted in entrepreneurs (Lumpkin and Dess, 1996) and comparing these to the skills required of an AHP on the UK Government National Careers Service website (NCS, 2020), there is a difference in the lexicon but a similar meaning where the attributes demonstrated by the AHP clearly follow those of the entrepreneur:

- *Autonomy*: patient-centred approach, thorough and detail-oriented clinical decision-making.
- *Risk-taking and risk awareness:* adopting new techniques, thinking and reasoning skills.
- *Innovativeness*: technology adoption, knowledge of medical procedures and opportunity identification.
- *Competitiveness*: networking, *the ability to work with others and work well under pressure.*
- *Proactiveness*: a desire to help people and opportunity identification.

From these, it is clear to see how entrepreneurial attributes enhance the ability of the AHP, and, therefore, the value that the AHP brings to their employer.

Human capital and company performance

Within this chapter we are proposing a link with the subject matter being taught, how the value of that is recognised in the individual person, and the impact of that value on the company that the person works for. This shows a relationship between the entrepreneurial nature of the individual, their human capital and the firm performance. To better understand that relationship, some discussion on what human capital is in its fundamental form is necessary to explore.

Human capital is viewed as *knowledge in the individual, organisation or nation* (Kwon, 2009). This human capital can be seen as an *individual's* accumulated skills and experience such as networking, interpersonal skills, role specific and technical skills; the collective competencies and culture for an *organisation such as project management, crisis management and response to change*; and the culture and political position in terms of the *nation*. With this definition, there is a clear link between human capital and society (Clarke, 2024). Kwon (2009) continues by arguing that human capital can be divided into general (accumulated knowledge and skills) and specific (contextual education and training on specific tasks). If one accepts that an organisational culture comes from its staff and the human factors within the staff are critical to the success of the company, then well-being and human capital must mean that the employee needs the tools required to be able to do their job to the best of their ability, and the employees' knowledge and experience contribute to the culture and feeling in the company (Galabova and McKie, 2013). For example, a business owner who has a greater understanding of the entrepreneurial intent and work-life balance of the employees of that company will have a greater opportunity to realise how to gain an enhanced firm performance from the skills and experiences of their employees: ergo, if the business owner of a company appreciates and values the human capital of their employees, the company will be more successful. If the value that the employee brings, in terms of their entrepreneurial behaviours, is recognised, the company can foster an ethos where developing those skills in each individual is encouraged. This will potentially lead to better outcomes for the company (Clarke, 2024; Mawson and Casulli, 2024). Though it is important to recognise that the outcome/s may be different for each company and industry sector, the principle remains the same: someone understanding their own entrepreneurial traits and behaviours, and understanding how those behaviours are valuable, should incur a positive outcome for their company. This can be correlated with our case study illustration, where the HEI recognised the potential of a particular employee and consequently provided support for the enhancement of their entrepreneurial abilities. As a result, the employee established a new centre for medical imaging, leading to financial gains for the university through the provision of continuing professional development activities and renting out the facility.

Sweetland (1996) defined human capital theory as the economic benefits that individuals and society gain from investments in people. Nafukho *et al.* (2004) state that Human resource development (HRD) is a process which develops an employee's work-based knowledge for the benefit of an organisation. Thus, human capital theory is focused on an investment in people with the outcome of enhanced performance. In reflexive terms, it involves an evaluation of one's accumulated human capital and the resultant impact on the value of an individual who displays entrepreneurial behaviours. We suggest a positive link between human capital and company performance. It is necessary to explore how strategic entrepreneurship connects with human capital. 'Strategic entrepreneurship' is a term used to show a company's ability to operate in an entrepreneurial way (Barringer and Bluedorn, 1999). In terms of entrepreneurship, this means how a company recognises opportunities; reacts to those opportunities; and encourages, measures and rewards entrepreneurial behaviours in its staff. The level of this is known as its *entrepreneurial intensity*, and is a result of the way a company and its employees recognise opportunities, evolve and change in line with those opportunities, the level of employee involvement in those changes and in the workplace culture, and how innovation is stimulated (Barringer and Bluedorn, 1999). Following on from the case study example used earlier, strategic entrepreneurship would be the way the hospital recognises and rewards staff who look for ways to change and improve practice, in a safe and established way. This is also the way in which each company and industry sector views the skills and experiences of its staff – the human capital in its employees.

There is a clear development of the notion of human capital, and the way it is being viewed in terms of the individual, but also of the company and the company culture. Indeed, that culture is a result of the collective individuals, so this notion of human capital and how it relates to the performance of the business is a relationship between the entrepreneurial intensity of the company, the way that culture and those accumulated skills are managed by the leaders of the company, and the resultant performance. This leads to *strategic entrepreneurship* as the mediator variable between entrepreneurial orientation of the employees and the company, and the performance of that company. If the leadership team can identify and recognise the value in employees with commercial acumen skills, and manage those skills effectively, the company performance can potentially be increased.

Conclusion

This chapter derives from personal experiences and insights, and offers an alternate way of viewing value within enterprise and EE by asking the question of *if commercial acumen has value as a stream of enterprise and EE*. By using a case study and learning from the authors' lived experiences, we have added to the current sole focus on viewing value in terms of the qualitative metrics of profit in new venture creation; we have taken an ethnographic approach and have shown that the term 'business' means different things to different people. We have used a case study example to look at the impact of value on the individual and organisation in terms of actions and behaviours. The case study chosen was of an Allied Health Professional (AHP), and a comparison was made in the recognised entrepreneurial behaviours and the behaviours exhibited by the AHP, with the similarities indicated. We then link this value in the person to its related impact on the value to the company, showing a relationship between the entrepreneurial nature of the individual, their human capital and the firm performance. Finally, we show that there is a relationship between human capital and firm performance, and, therefore, the relationship between the entrepreneurial intensity of the company, the way that culture and those accumulated skills are managed by the leaders of the company, and the resultant performance.

It will be crucial to expand this work to have a clearer understanding of how such entrepreneurial attributes and skills could be identified, recognised and appreciated.

References

Barringer, B. R., & Bluedorn, A. C. (1999). The relationship between corporate entrepreneurship and strategic management. *Strategic Management Journal*, 20, 421–444. doi: https://doi.org/10.1002/(SICI)1097-0266(199905)20:5<421::AID-SMJ30>3.0.CO;2-O.

Bellotti, F., Berta, R., Gloria, A. D., Lavagnino, E., Dagnino, F., Ott, M., Romero, M., Usart M, & Mayer, I. S. (2012). Designing a course for stimulating entrepreneurship in higher education through serious games. *Procedia Computer Science*, 15, 174–186. doi: 10.1016/j.procs.2012.10.069

Borrelli, C., & Mercer, C. (2023). *Clark's Essential Guide to Mammography*. London, UK: CRC Press.

Bourdieu, P. (1986). The forms of capital. In J. G. Richardson (Ed.), *The Handbook of Theory and Research for the Sociology of Education* (pp. 241–258). New York: Greenwood Press.

Clarke, A. P. (2024). *Entrepreneurial Attributes: Accessing Your Inner Entrepreneur for Business and Beyond* (1st ed.). London, UK: Routledge. doi: 10.4324/9781003401087-6

Clarke, A. P., & Deacon, J. C. (2015). *LUCID Window Relationship Model*. Salford, UK: University of Salford.

Clarke, A. P., Ferry, N., & Cornes, C. (2020). The use of self-reflection for enhanced enterprise education: A case study. *Education + Training*, 62(5), 581–598.

Galabova, L., & McKie, L. (2013). "The five fingers of my hand": Human capital and well-being in SMEs. *Personnel Review*, 42(6), 662–683. doi: 10.1108/pr-01-2012-0017

Hannon, P. D. (2006). Teaching pigeons to dance: Sense and meaning in entrepreneurship education. *Education + Training*, 48(5), 296–308. doi: 10.1108/00400910610677018

Health Education England (2017). *Multi-Professional Framework for Advanced Clinical Practice in England*. London: Health Education England. Advanced Practice – Website Content – multi-professionalframeworkforadvancedclinicalpracticeinengland (1).pdf

Herzog, C., Richter, A., Steinhüser, M., Hoppe, U., & Koch, M. (2013). Methods and metrics for measuring the success of enterprise social software – what we can learn from practice and vice versa. The 21st European Conference on Information Systems (ECIS); 2013, Utrecht, ECIS.

Hogg, P., Kelly, J., & Mercer, C. (2015). *Digital Mammography* (pp. 1–307). London, UK: Springer.

Hogg, P., Taylor, M., Szczepura, K., Mercer, C., & Denton, E. (2013). Pressure and breast thickness in mammography – an exploratory calibration study. *The British Journal of Radiology*, 86(1021), 20120222–20120222.

Jakhere, S. G. (2011). The entrepreneur radiologist. *Indian Journal of Radiology and Imaging*, 21(02), 159–160.

Jamieson, I. (1984). Schools and Enterprise. *Education for Enterprise*, 1(1), 7–18.

Jones, C., & Penaluna, A. (2013), Moving beyond the business plan in enterprise education, *Education + Training*, 55(8/9), 804–814.

Kwon, D.-B. (2009). Human capital and its measurement. The 3rd OECD World Forum on "Statistics, Knowledge and Policy" Charting Progress, Building Visions, Improving Life, 27–30.

Lumpkin, G. T., & Dess, G. G. (1996). Clarifying the entrepreneurial orientation construct and linking it to performance. *Academy of management Review*, 21(1), 135–172.

Mawson, S. & Casulli, L. (2024). *Entrepreneurial Thinking: Mindset in Action*. London, UK: SAGE Publications Ltd.

Mercer, C. E., Hogg, P., & Kelly, J. (Eds.). (2022). *Digital Mammography: A Holistic Approach*. London, UK: Springer Nature.

Mercer, C. E., Hogg, P., Lawson, R., Diffey, J., & Denton, E. R. E. (2013). Practitioner compression force variability in mammography: A preliminary study. *The British Journal of Radiology*, 86(1022), 20110596.

Mercer, C. E., Szczepura, K., Kelly, J., Millington, S. R., Denton, E. R., Borgen, R., Hilton, B., & Hogg, P. (2015). A 6-year study of mammographic compression force: Practitioner variability within and between screening sites. *Radiography*, 21(1), 68–73.

Nafukho, F. M., Hairston, N., & Brooks, K. (2004). Human capital theory: Implications for human resource development. *Human Resource Development International*, 7(4), 545–551. doi: 10.1080/1367886042000299843

National Careers Service (2020). National careers service. Available at: https://nationalcareersservice.gov.uk (Accessed 20 March 2024)

NHS Clinical Entrepreneur Programme (2016). The programme – NHS clinical entrepreneur programme (nhscep.com) www.aru.ac.uk

Nigohosyan, D., & Vutsova, A. (2018). The 2014–2020 European Regional Development Fund indicators: The incomplete evolution. *Social Indicators Research*, 137(2), 559–577. doi: 10.1007/s11205-017-1610-8

Pittaway, L., & Cope, J. (2007). Entrepreneurship education: A systematic review of the evidence. *International Small Business Journal*, 25(5), 479–510. doi: 10.1177/0266242607080656

QAA (2018). *Enterprise and Entrepreneurship Education: Guidance for UK Higher Education Providers* (pp. 1–33). Gloucester, UK: QAA.

Saunders, M., Lewis, P., & Thornhill, A. (2019). *Research Methods for Business Students* (8th ed.). Harlow: Pearson Education Limited.

Shane, S., & Venkataraman, S. (2000). The promise of entrepreneurship as a field of research. *Academy of Management Review*, 25(1), 217–226. doi: 10.5465/amr.2000.2791611

Sirelkhatim, F., & Gangi, Y. (2015). Entrepreneurship education: A systematic literature review of curricula contents and teaching methods. *Cogent Business & Management*, 2(1), 1–11.

Smith, H., Szczepura, K., Mercer, C., Maxwell, A., & Hogg, P. (2015). Does elevating image receptor increase breast receptor footprint and improve pressure balance?. *Radiography*, 21(4), 359–363.

Sweetland, S. R. (1996). Human capital theory: Foundations of a field of inquiry. *Review of Educational Research*, 66(3), 341–359. doi: 10.3102/00346543066003341

Tett, G. (2021). *Anthro-Vision: How Anthropology Can Explain Business and Life*. London, UK: Penguin Random House.

Turner, T., & Gianiodis, P. (2018). Entrepreneurship unleashed: Understanding entrepreneurial education outside of the business school. *Journal of Small Business Management*, 56(1), 131–149. doi: 10.1111/jsbm.12365

9 Social capital and entrepreneurial loneliness

Mapping the startup journeys of London-based fashion entrepreneurs

Beki Gowing and Ashley Evenson

Introduction

The creative industries are essential to many modern economies, yet creative entrepreneurs are increasingly lonely and burnt out. In recent years, the prevalence of entrepreneurial loneliness and its negative impact on business sustainability and founder wellbeing have become apparent (Agarwal, 2018), with 30% of UK founders identifying isolation as a concern (Deane, 2016). Researchers have observed entrepreneurial burnout influencing loneliness, and loneliness as a predictor for business success or failure (Fernet et al., 2016; Omrane et al., 2018). The role of social capital in new venture creation is well documented, and the possession of social capital is widely agreed to contribute to entrepreneurial success (Greve and Salaff, 2003; Kleinhempel et al., 2020). Early-stage studies have linked social capital and loneliness, predominantly focusing on loneliness among young people (Nyqvist et al., 2016) and in later life (Hagan et al., 2020). A relationship between founder social capital and entrepreneurial loneliness has not been examined elsewhere and is explored for the first time in this chapter, focusing on the experiences of startup fashion entrepreneurs in London. By mapping the startup journeys and experiences of loneliness and burnout for early-stage founders, this chapter explores the relationship between entrepreneurial loneliness and social capital and offers preliminary suggestions for further research and potential support.

Approximately 98,500 creative businesses are based in London (ONS, 2022), with many additional part-time and full-time freelancers (Creative Industries Council, 2021a). UK creative businesses have been severely impacted by the pandemic (Khlystova et al., 2022), and the *Financial Times* found London-based startups are most likely to fail (Nilsson, 2017). Despite the UK's active Enterprise Support Organisations (ESOs) (Cunningham and Fraser, 2022), research by Bandera and Thomas shows that easy access to social capital development opportunities does not guarantee entrepreneurs engage with them (2017). Research shows entrepreneurs experience considerable stresses and constraints

DOI: 10.4324/9781003324737-9

in their novitiate years (Omrane et al., 2018), and entrepreneurial wellbeing is an increasingly important focus for research (Stephan, 2018; Wiklund et al., 2019), making this study timely and with potential for significant impact.

Using a phenomenological methodology to collect founder startup stories, this research develops a general composite description of the lived experience of solo-founders behind London-based fashion product businesses. This contributes to the study of entrepreneurial loneliness by using social capital as a theoretical framework to understand the creative startup journey. Zaheer et al.'s Five-Stage New Venture Creation (NVC) framework is used to structure this mapping and identifies significant triggers for loneliness and burnout occurring when trading begins. Khlystova et al. write that post-pandemic, 'The resilience of the creative industries is important for their ability to survive, sustain their level of operations or workforce, and adapt in order to grow' (2022, p. 1204). This resilience must include the wellbeing of the founders running the creative businesses. Findings reveal a link between certain types of social capital and entrepreneurial loneliness. Bonding social capital can reduce entrepreneurial loneliness, while bridging social capital offers benefits but has limited impacts on loneliness. The authors share suggestions to develop founders' bonding social capital, potentially reducing entrepreneurial loneliness, improving wellbeing and business sustainability.

Literature review

The startup journey

Solo-founders are common in the fashion and creative industries (Creative Industries Council, 2021a), and mean one person has sole responsibility and management of the enterprise. This can compromise solo-founders as support or resources may not be available without a co-founder (Greenberg et al., 2018). Founders may be further impacted by systemic contexts, such as female founders or those from diverse backgrounds experiencing reduced access to resources, funding, or support such as mentoring, advice, training, market research, and awards (Hruskova et al., 2022; Motoyama and Knowlton, 2017; Spigel, 2020). The systemic context is considered within this research, as the selected entrepreneurs are majority female and many come from diverse backgrounds. Despite these challenges, gaining external support is becoming more accessible. With the latest burst in ESOs, entrepreneurs can access incubators, accelerators, and university programs to support business launch and growth (Hruskova et al., 2022). This research explores the startup journey for solo-founders who have and have not accessed ESO support to draw comparisons and explore how these impact social capital and loneliness.

An NVC process is 'a new, independent venture's journey from initiation to completion of its creation' (Davidsson and Gruenhagen, 2021). Zaheer et al.

propose the process can be organized into five stages: (1) conceptualizing, (2) resourcing, (3) developing, (4) resourcing for scaling, and (5) scaling (2022). Their framework allows for evolution, iteration, or progression to be led by anyone, including large organizations or individuals. Despite being created to describe digital entrepreneurship, Zaheer et al.'s Five-Stage NVC framework is used in this research due to its flexibility and similarity to the fashion industry. Researchers including Gieure et al. and Townsend et al. have explored the entrepreneur's journey from the perspective of skills, intentions, and personal attitudes (2020), and decision making, industry changes, access to resources, and time lags (2008). However, as entrepreneurship changes, there is encouragement for more research mapping what startup journeys can look like and how it is similar and different across industries and entrepreneurs (Zaheer et al., 2022).

Creative entrepreneurship and fashion

Creative entrepreneurs differ from other industries, as they utilize business and creative mindsets and balance sometimes conflicting creative and business outputs. They are often solo-founders running micro businesses (employing less than nine people), require complex skills-sets, and demonstrate a value chain that 'embraces the entire process from creating the artifact to its marketing, retailing and consumption' (Henry, 2007, p. 56). Organizations such as Nesta have focused on researching and supporting international creative entrepreneurship. Their 2015–2020 Creative Enterprise Programme builds on their 2007 Creative Enterprise Toolkit, which found that creative entrepreneurs benefit from sector-specific enterprise support (2020). Creative entrepreneurship is normally defined as startup and enterprise activity within nine interlocking industries outlined by The Creative Industries Federation. These include crafts, design (including fashion), music, and performing arts. They contribute over £115 billion to the UK economy and employ over 2 million people (Creative UK, 2021), highlighting their importance to many individuals, the wider economy, and their obvious cultural impact on society (Henry, 2007). Approximately 98,500 creative businesses are based in London (ONS, 2022), annually generating over £58 billion (Creative UK, 2021). Despite London's prominence, London-based startups are most likely in the UK to fail (Nilsson, 2017) and London's creative sector was severely impacted by the pandemic (Khlystova et al., 2022). London's precarious yet 'powerhouse' role in the UK creative industry explains the authors' decision to focus on London-based businesses and the London enterprise ecosystem.

Fashion plays an integral role in the UK creative sector, with over 34,000 fashion and textile businesses in the UK. Approximately 85% of these are micro-businesses (including freelancers) (*UKFT's Compendium of Industry Statistics and Analysis 2020*, 2021) and prior to 2019 the industry was growing 5% per year (Creative Industries Council, 2021b). The fashion industry has faced severe disruption from Brexit, and the pandemic and increased enterprise support is recommended to support sustainability and growth (Bulman and Solomon 2023; *UKFT's Compendium of Industry Statistics and Analysis 2020*, 2021). This research explores the startup journey from a product-based fashion business perspective, informed by the understanding that the innovation process is different for products and services (Shin et al., 2022). Social capital plays an important role in the fashion industry, as a majority of businesses are launched by solo-founders who may have limited access to other forms of capital.

Social capital and entrepreneurship

Since the 1980s, social capital has been defined as the social networks available to develop financial assets (Bourdieu, 1986). Coleman furthered this theory by exploring the role of trust, obligations, norms, and expectations in developing social relationships and proposed positive outcomes beyond financial gains (1988). Our research borrows Putnam's exploration of bonding and bridging social capital, where bonding describes ties between homogenous groups and bridging describes ties between heterogeneous groups (2000). Social capital theory established that social relationships unlock support, resources, and information, and recent enterprise research has explored the nuances of social capital benefits in business. Among entrepreneurs, bonding relationships may offer empathy and understanding, while bridging relationships offer new opportunities and perspectives (Todd, 2012). Both are needed, particularly during the NVC process (Kariv, 2013), although Kleinhempel et al. outline the dynamic nature of the startup journey and suggest social capital offers differing value during different stages (2020). Founders with higher social capital can positively impact business outcomes (Greve and Salaff, 2003; Kariv, 2013). While the link between social capital and loneliness among entrepreneurs has not previously been established, recent research is often more founder-centered, considering founder wellbeing as a moderator for business success (Agarwal, 2018; Fernet et al., 2016; Omrane et al., 2018; Stephan, 2018; Wiklund et al., 2019).

This study uses the terminology of weak and strong ties to describe the quality of relationships. Putnam's original theory proposes bonding social capital offers emotional support from strong ties with family and close friends, while bridging social capital offers information sharing from weak ties with business associates and acquaintances (2000). Research now suggests the internet has changed social relationships and it is common to seek emotional support from a larger, more heterogeneous network (Krämer et al., 2021). This is seen in entrepreneurship communities, where founders offer emotional support despite having limited common ground (Gowing, 2023). Therefore, this research separates weak and strong ties from the concept of bonding and bridging social capital to better understand which types of social capital might impact entrepreneurial loneliness.

Loneliness, isolation, and burnout

The entrepreneurial journey can lead to moments of extremity, meaning the high stressors experienced by entrepreneurs can cause mental health difficulties. This can lead to loneliness, social isolation, and burnout (Cardon and Arwine, 2023; Lerman et al., 2020). Loneliness is defined as a self-perceived relational deficiency felt when people have a lack of desired social interactions or personal relationships (Cardon and Arwine, 2023). Described as 'a silent killer', (Zhu et al., 202, p. e00368), loneliness can particularly affect solo-founders (Fernet et al., 2016), whose entrepreneurial journey is solely reliant on them, leading to poor mental health and failures in business prosperity (Cacioppo et al., 2014). Solo-founders facing other systemic challenges are especially disadvantaged. Many solo-founders interviewed are working in isolation and away from native homes or support systems, reducing their mental or psychological capital and further draining their resources (Zhu et al., 2023; Gao et al., 2021).

An important but deficient resource for solo-founders is time, leading to lack of socialization, connection, and social support. Often entrepreneurs find connecting with others difficult, due to being solely responsible for their enterprise and its mental and physical time requirements (Cardon and Arwine, 2023; Kuratko et al., 2023). Without proper resources, solo-founders may experience burnout, which can be defined as 'a state of physical, emotional, and mental exhaustion' (Pines and Aronson, 1988; Schaufeli and Greenglass, 2001, p. 501; Fernet et al., 2016). Time factors causing burnout for entrepreneurs include excessive work hours and limited or no annual leave, and work stressors such as being the main strategist and lead decision-maker advancing the enterprise (Fernet et al., 2016). Another element of burnout is the 'Conservation of Resources' theory, which depicts burnout as 'resource loss' (Hobfoll, 1989). This suggests it is not only loss of resources, but the *threat* of loss of resources, which can manifest in poor mental health practices, leading to burnout, loneliness, and isolation.

Causes and prevention

Compacted stress is a fundamental cause of loneliness, isolation, and burnout. This stress comes from three main components: (1) lack of resources and skills; (2) the tension of varying roles, priorities, and risks associated with running an enterprise; and (3) complex relationships with collaborators, customers, or key suppliers in the business (Omrane et al., 2018). These components combine to create ambiguity, risk, and future uncertainty. Previous literature on entrepreneurial loneliness and burnout has suggested that some conditions could be eased by stress or time management training (Omrane et al., 2018). Alternatively, Cardon and Arwine suggest wellbeing routines and access to social connections are needed (2023). Yet the current options in contemporary research do not specifically explore or address solo-founders' needs for more time as a resource to reduce burnout, and more social capital as a resource to reduce loneliness.

Methodology

This work used qualitative semi-structured interviews with 11 solo-founders to answer the research questions:

1. What is the lived experience of loneliness for successful London-based fashion solo-founders?
2. What is the relationship between social capital and entrepreneurial loneliness during startup journeys?
3. What can solo-founders and ESOs do to navigate entrepreneurial loneliness?

A phenomenological strategy was applied to the research design to develop a general composite description of launching a fashion business as a solo-founder. Moustakas approach to phenomenology describes two descriptive levels: (1) collecting original interview data and (2) analyzing and interpreting data to describe the experience (1994). This allowed researchers to identify commonalities to map the startup journey. Bracketing, or identifying personal bias, is important in phenomenology, although there will always be elements of subjectivity (Tufford and Newman, 2012). Before commencing research, interviewers shared their personal experiences and potential biases. They agreed to self-reflect before and after interviews to set aside personal judgements and knowledge. During the 60- to 90-minute individual interviews, founders were guided through topics, encouraging them to describe their experience of launching a business. Topics covered business ideation; founder health; social interactions; family/cultural views of enterprise; and engagements with customers, ESOs, and other entrepreneurs. As questions sometimes required founders to share difficult memories, care was taken to finish interviews with questions encouraging positive reflections on values and impact.

To access a wide range of potential interviewees, founders were recruited from London-based incubators, ESOs, and personal networks. Researchers shared adverts asking for participants and purposively approached suitable entrepreneurs who engaged with ESOs at different stages and had different levels of experience and social capital. This ensured research considered and compared ESO impact. Table 9.1 summarizes the participants. Personal support is defined as support from family, friends, neighbors, or social community, and professional support is from ESOs, fellow entrepreneurs, mentors, or professional networks. All participants were required to have been:

- Operating for at least 2 years (to avoid collecting data which may not support business success).
- Started by a solo-founder.
- Primarily based in London or accessing London ESOs.
- Creating fashion products (e.g., garments, textiles, fashion accessories).

Table 9.1 Summary of participants, industry experience, social capital available at startup, and the NVC stage they accessed an ESO

	Participant Summary	*NVC Stage They Accessed ESO*
Participant 1	Female founder of an accessories business, running for 5 years. Some prior fashion industry experience. No personal support, some professional support.	Conceptualizing
Participant 2	Female founder of a clothing business, running for 2 years. Some prior fashion industry experience. Strong personal support, some professional support.	Resourcing
Participant 3	Female founder of a clothing business, running for 3 years. Some prior fashion industry experience. No personal support, some professional support.	Conceptualizing
Participant 4	Female founder of a clothing business, running for 13 years. Extensive prior fashion industry experience. Some personal support, some professional support.	Developing
Participant 5	Female founder of an accessories business, running for 2 years. Extensive prior fashion industry experience. Some personal support, some professional support.	ESO support not accessed
Participant 6	Male founder of a clothing business, running for 3 years. Extensive prior fashion industry experience. Limited personal support, some professional support.	Developing
Participant 7	Female founder of a textile business, running for 2 years. Some prior fashion industry experience. No personal support, limited professional support.	ESO support not accessed
Participant 8	Female founder of a clothing business, running for 3 years. No prior fashion industry experience. Strong personal support, no professional support.	ESO support not accessed
Participant 9	Female founder of a clothing business, running for 2 years. Some prior fashion industry experience. Some personal support, strong professional support.	Resourcing
Participant 10	Female founder of a clothing business, running for 6 years. Extensive prior fashion industry experience. Some personal support, some professional support.	Conceptualizing
Participant 11	Female founder of a clothing business, running for 4 years. No prior fashion industry experience. Some personal support, strong professional support.	Conceptualizing

While the sample size is relatively small, participants represent a wide range of ages, socio-economic backgrounds, professional experience levels, and attitudes to enterprise. The length of the interviews and variety of topics discussed enabled researchers to build a rich and detailed understanding of their individual startup journeys.

Interview transcriptions were read to generate inductive codes. The codes broke the separate stories into 'units', which were grouped to form a sense of the 'essence' (Moustakas, 1994) of the startup journey. Units were interrogated to uncover further meaning and find links with theory, and ordered to describe the 'universal nature' (von Eckartsberg, 1998) of launching a fashion product business. This answered the first research question (What is the lived experience of loneliness for successful London-based fashion solo-founders?). Next, researchers reviewed this structure to uncover links between loneliness and social capital. This answered the second research question (What is the relationship between social capital and entrepreneurial loneliness during startup journeys?). With this new understanding, transcriptions were re-read to identify activities and processes that answered the final research question (What can solo-founders and ESOs do to navigate entrepreneurial loneliness?).

Findings and discussion

After analyzing in-depth semi-structured interviews with 11 fashion entrepreneurs, findings were grouped according to three themes based on the research questions: the lived experience of the startup journey for fashion entrepreneurs, the impact of social capital on entrepreneurial loneliness during startup, and recommendations for support to reduce founder loneliness and burnout.

Mapping the startup journey

Table 9.2 maps the generic composite fashion startup journey created by analyzing interview transcripts against Zaheer et al.'s Five-Stage NVC framework (2022). It demonstrates the flexibility of this framework, showing it not only describes digital entrepreneurship but can also describe fashion entrepreneurship and potentially other product-based creative enterprises. While Kleinhempel et al.'s research explores the value of social capital at different points in the startup journey (2020), our findings suggest social capital does not significantly impact loneliness until the business begins trading in stage 3 (developing). Despite an initial 'boost' from positive feedback and initial sales, this is often when the reality of running a business becomes apparent and entrepreneurs report feeling increased pressure to meet external expectations. These expectations require a time commitment which can trigger burnout, and without a suitable support network entrepreneurs may experience isolation and loneliness. Table 9.2 also uses findings to identify points during the 2nd and 3rd stages when interventions to tackle loneliness and burnout may be most beneficial.

Table 9.2 The fashion startup journey mapped against Zaheer et al.'s Five-Stage NVC framework (2022), showing loneliness and burnout triggers and potential intervention points.

Zaheer et al.'s NVC Framework Stage	*Fashion Startup Journey Findings*	*Burnout/Loneliness Triggers and Interventions*
1. Conceptualizing	Ideation and identification of an opportunity Catalyst triggering business initiation Research and exploration	
2. Resourcing	Business strategy development[1] Making business connections[2] Pre-launch	Potential burnout intervention Potential loneliness intervention
3. Developing	Operational processes and systems[3] Accessing/developing a support network[4] Launch and initial sales[5]	Potential burnout intervention Potential loneliness intervention Loneliness trigger Burnout trigger
4. Resourcing for scaling	Concept adaption/ development	Loneliness trigger
5. Scaling[6]		

[1] Participants who included this stage often reported lower levels of burnout later.

[2] This stage predominantly refers to making connections with potential suppliers, stockists, and/or collaborators. While not necessarily a source of emotional support, this is a potential point where entrepreneurs may reflect on their current support network and identify gaps.

[3] Most participants developed operational processes and systems after launch, often amplifying burnout. Findings suggest if entrepreneurs begin this before trading introduces added time pressures, burnout may be reduced.

[4] Many participants did not experience loneliness until after launch. Those who did not have an existing support network then sought one out after launch, after feelings of isolation began. Again, findings suggest if support networks are developed before trading begins, entrepreneurial loneliness may be reduced.

[5] Participants reported that that after making initial sales, feelings of empowerment and validation decreased, and that loneliness briefly decreased as they developed connections with their customer base. However, this rapidly declined as the pressure to meet external expectations (e.g., continued sales, social media content, supplier payments, customer service queries) increased feelings of burnout and isolation. The expectation to develop and improve the business (into stage 4 – resourcing for scaling) can become overwhelming if the entrepreneur does not have enough social capital to access a support network.

[6] The last NVC stage (scaling) is not explored as few participants had reached this stage. Therefore, stages 1–4 can be described as the startup journey, and stage 5 demonstrates progression beyond startup.

Social capital and entrepreneurial loneliness

Studies by Hagan et al. (2020) and Nyqvist et al. (2016) identified a preliminary relationship between social capital and loneliness among young people and older people. Qualitative analysis of data aligns with their findings, suggesting that this link also appears among entrepreneurs. A limited support network can contribute to feelings of loneliness and isolation, while a sense of community, trustworthy relationships, and a supportive personal or professional network can reduce an entrepreneur's feelings of loneliness and isolation. However, results show that not all social capital is equal and different forms of social capital offer different levels of impact on entrepreneurial loneliness. Putnam's work on bonding and bridging social capital (2000), and Krämer et al.'s work on the strength of social ties (2021), helps categorize and explore the forms of social capital and their impact. For example, high bridging social capital, observed when founders had extensive industry experience and a high number of professional contacts, appears to have little impact on loneliness. Founders experienced other benefits from this social capital such as knowledge and resource sharing, but found their network of contacts working for large-scale established businesses could not understand or empathize with the issues facing a solo-founder. Founders with high bridging social capital and low bonding social capital still reported high levels of loneliness. In comparison, founders with high bonding social capital from supportive family, friends, or professional relationships with other creative founders reported lower levels of loneliness. Some participants described initial feelings of loneliness that reduced after finding a supportive network of creative founders. This suggests founder social capital at venture creation does not determine founder wellbeing for the entire startup journey and shows the potential impact appropriate entrepreneurial support can have.

Although strong ties generally offer more noticeable impact, reported loneliness is reduced regardless of the strength of ties between individuals. A weak bonding tie, such as joining a WhatsApp group for early-stage fashion entrepreneurs, delivered similar reported benefits as a strong bonding tie, such as a close collaborative and accountability relationship with another similar-stage entrepreneur or receiving emotional support from a family member or friend. This supports Krämer et al.'s development of Putnam's original definitions, proposing the internet has taught us to access emotional support through weak ties. Therefore, the authors offer the following summary (Table 9.3) to develop Hagan's

Table 9.3 Summary of the impact of different types of social capital on reported feelings of loneliness among London-based fashion entrepreneurs

	High Bonding Social Capital	*High Bridging Social Capital*
Weak Ties	**Reduced loneliness** (e.g., community WhatsApp groups, neighbors)	**No impact** (e.g., ex-colleagues, wider professional network)
Strong Ties	**Reduced loneliness** (e.g., close family, close friends, collaborator, accountability partner)	**No impact** (e.g., mentor)

2020 and Nyqvist's 2016 theories of social capital and loneliness when considering entrepreneurship and the fashion startup journey.

These findings suggest that solo-founders with pre-existing high bonding social capital may be less likely to experience loneliness during the startup journey. However, it also found that developing bonding social capital by reconnecting with friends, family, and neighbors, and building new relationships with similar-stage entrepreneurs, can reduce loneliness at any stage of the startup journey. While participants reported bridging social capital having no impact on their feelings of loneliness, it does not mean this form is worthless. Participants with high bridging social capital reported many benefits observed in past research such as access to knowledge, resources, opportunities, and feedback.

Support to reduce loneliness

The benefits of enhancing social capital for entrepreneurs and reducing loneliness among founders are widely known (Agarwal, 2018; Fernet et al., 2016; Gowing, 2023; Kleinhempel et al., 2020; Omrane et al., 2018), and recommendations are evident in ESOs' current offers. However, offering entrepreneurs opportunities to develop social capital does not always ensure engagement or deliver the expected benefits (Bandera and Thomas, 2017; Hughes et al., 2007). This research suggests founders and support organizations can decrease founder loneliness, improve founder wellbeing, and positively impact entrepreneurial success by creating opportunities to specifically develop bonding social capital. Useful bonding social capital development opportunities mentioned by participants included:

- Joining WhatsApp groups without hierarchy or gatekeepers where similar-stage and similar-sector entrepreneurs can share advice and experiences.
- Attending informal and unstructured face-to-face interactions with other entrepreneurs.
- Attending markets and showcases for startups to sell or show ideas in progress, interact with customers, and meet other entrepreneurs.
- Finding a collaborator or accountability partner.
- Discussing the business and their positive and negative experiences with close friends and family.

While online interactions can deliver value, face-to-face interactions were consistently mentioned as delivering higher impact. The final list item comes from our learning that even entrepreneurs with minimal professional networks reported low levels of loneliness if they had a strong personal support network from family and friends. Many participants relied on their family and friends for emotional support despite them not understanding the nuances of starting a business. One participant commented 'I don't think they realized what they were doing for me . . . they were carrying me but they didn't know it'. The emotional support from bonding social capital contrasts with that from high bridging social capital. One such participant commented, 'There's a lot of people that want to give advice but have never run a small business . . . there's no way [they can] understand what this feels like'. Therefore, the value of close personal relationships should not be overlooked. Entrepreneurs should avoid closing off from friends and family, and support organizations could offer tools and activities to help entrepreneurs reflect and share their feelings. Enacting practices that encourage bonding social capital, such as those listed earlier, may help to navigate entrepreneurial loneliness and isolation and develop effective entrepreneurial support ecosystems.

Burnout does not appear to be explicitly linked to social capital as participants with high/low social capital still reported symptoms of burnout. However, our findings show loneliness can amplify burnout, and Fernet et al.'s work shows burnout may then increase loneliness (2016), potentially creating a negative feedback loop. Increasing social capital may not reduce burnout, but neglecting it may make situations worse, risking founder wellbeing and business sustainability. Kuratko's research highlights time as a resource to reduce burnout, and a lack of time was mentioned by most participants. One mentioned, 'as you develop processes in your business, things become easier'. ESOs should consider how to offer support for entrepreneurs to increase their time resources and reduce burnout, such as sharing time-saving systems and processes. Templates, guides to generic processes, and training on automation may mean entrepreneurs can avoid 'reinventing the wheel' and can reduce time spent on tasks, potentially reducing the risk of burnout and, therefore, loneliness.

Conclusion

This work takes research by Nyqvist et al. (2016) and Hagan et al. (2020) as a starting point to explore the relationship between social capital and loneliness among a diverse group of London-based fashion entrepreneurs. As the creative industries focus on recovery after the pandemic, this work is necessary as social capital and entrepreneurial loneliness can impact founder wellbeing and business success (Fernet et al., 2016; Greve and Salaff, 2003; Kleinhempe et al., 2020; Omrane et al., 2018). The authors found that solo-founders who already possessed or learnt to develop high bonding social capital reported decreased feelings of loneliness, while high levels of bridging social capital did not impact loneliness. Participants' lived experiences were used to map the fashion startup journey against Zaheer et al.'s Five-Stage NVC framework (2022), and this identified the 'developing' (3rd) stage when businesses begin trading as high risk for experiencing loneliness and burnout. Findings provide a template to support entrepreneurs' awareness of potential challenges and mitigation strategies and for ESOs to develop support programs. Research limitations include the small sample size, reliance on qualitative data, and focus on a specific industry niche. These could be addressed in further research to develop the findings by repeating the methodology in alternate industries or locations, testing the theory using quantitative methods, or employing a practice-based approach to develop and measure a loneliness support program's impact.

References

Agarwal, D.P. (2018) 'It is time we acknowledged loneliness in entrepreneurs and did something about it', *Forbes*. Available at: https://www.forbes.com/sites/pragyaagarwaleurope/2018/07/12/loneliness-as-an-entrepreneur-heres-something-we-can-do-about-it (Accessed: 10/12/2022).

Bandera, C., Thomas, E. (2017) 'Startup incubators and the role of social capital', 2017 IEEE Technology and Engineering Management Conference. https://doi.org/10.1109/TEMSCON.2017.7998368.

Bourdieu, P. (1986) 'The forms of capital', in Richardson, J.G. (ed.), *Handbook of Theory and Research for the Sociology of Education*. New York: Greenwood Press, pp. 241–258.

Bulman, S., Solomon, L. (2023) *Impact of Brexit and COVID-19 on the UK Fashion, Textiles and Technology Ecosystem*. University of the Arts London and the University of Leeds.

Cacioppo, S., Capitanio, J.P., Cacioppo, J.T. (2014) 'Toward a neurology of loneliness', *Psychological Bulletin*, 140(6), pp. 1464–1504. https://doi.org/10.1037/a0037618.

Cardon, M.S., Arwine, R.P. (2023) 'The many faces of entrepreneurial loneliness', *Personnel Psychology*. https://doi.org/10.1111/peps.12614.

Coleman, J.S. (1988) 'Social capital in the creation of human capital', *American Journal of Sociology*, 94, pp. S95–S120. Available at: http://www.jstor.org/stable/2780243 (Accessed: 18/08/2023)

Creative Industries Council (2021a) 'Employment figures – The creative industries', Available at: https://www.thecreativeindustries.co.uk/facts-figures/uk-creative-overview-facts-and-figures-employment-figures (Accessed: 01/09/2022).

Creative Industries Council (2021b) 'How fashion fuels the UK economy, the creative industries', Available at: https://www.thecreativeindustries.co.uk/facts-figures/industries-fashion-fashion-facts-and-figures-how-fashion-fuels-the-uk-economy (Accessed: 15/09/2023).

Creative UK (2021) 'UK Creative Industries 2021', *The Creative Industries Federation*. Available at: https://drive.google.com/file/d/118K7yiift1cTosufulxa1NxcYLKAzjuU/view?usp=sharing (Accessed: 08/10/2023).

Cunningham, J., Fraser, S. (2022) 'Images of entrepreneurship: Divergent national constructions of what it is to "do" entrepreneurship', *Entrepreneurship and Regional Development*, 34, pp. 7–8, 567–581. https://doi.org/10.1080/08985626.2022.2071997.

Davidsson, P., Gruenhagen, J.H. (2021) 'Fulfilling the process promise: A review and agenda for new venture creation process research', *Entrepreneurship Theory and Practice*, 45(5), pp. 1083–1118.

Deane, J. (2016) *Self-Employment Review: An Independent Report*. Department for Business, Innovation and Skills. Available at: https://www.gov.uk/government/uploads/system/uploads/attachment_data/file/529702/ind-16-2-self-employment-review.pdf (Accessed: 10/09/2022).

Fernet, C., Torres, O., Austin, S., St-Pierre, J. (2016) 'The psychological costs of owning and managing an SME: Linking job stressors, occupational loneliness, entrepreneurial

orientation, and burnout', *Burnout Research*, 3(2), pp. 45–53. https://doi.org/10.1016/j.burn.2016.03.002.
Gao, J.L., Li, D.S., Conway, M.L. (2021) 'Family support and entrepreneurial passion: The mediating role of entrepreneurs' psychological capital', *Social Behavior and Personality*, 49(3), pp. 1–15.
Gieure, C., del Mar Benavides-Espinosa, M., Roig-Dobón, S. (2020) 'The entrepreneurial process: The link between intentions and behavior', *Journal of Business Research*, 112, pp. 541–548. https://doi.org/10.1016/j.jbusres.2019.11.088.
Gowing, B. (2023) 'Building online communities to support women creative entrepreneurs during lockdown', in Hill, I., Jones, P., Elias, S., Dobbs, S. (eds.), *Creative (and Cultural) Entrepreneurship in the 21st Century*. Contemporary Issues in Entrepreneurship Research, 18 Part B. Leeds: Emerald Publishing Limited.
Greenberg, J. and Mollick, E.R. (2018) 'Sole survivors: Solo Ventures versus founding teams', *SSRN Electronic Journal [Preprint]*. https://doi.org/10.2139/ssrn.3107898.
Greve, A. and Salaff, J.W. (2003) 'Social networks and entrepreneurship', *Entrepreneurship Theory and Practice*, 28(1), pp. 1–22. https://doi.org/10.1111/1540-8520.00029.
Hagan, R., Manktelow, R., Taylor, B. (2020) 'Loneliness, cumulative inequality and social capital in later life: Two stories', *Irish Journal of Sociology*, 28(2), pp. 192–217. https://doi.org/10.1177/0791603520908764.
Henry, C. (2007) *Entrepreneurship in the Creative Industries*. Cheltenham, UK: Edward Elgar.
Hobfoll, S.E. (1989) 'Conservation of resources: A new attempt at conceptualizing stress', *American Psychologist*, 44(3), p. 513.
Hruskova, M., Mason, C., Herzog, S. (2022) 'Mapping entrepreneurship support organisations: An examination of the "cluttered landscape" critique', *Local Economy*, 37(7), 541–563. https://doi.org/10.1177/02690942231173655.
Hughes, M., Ireland, R.D., Morgan, R.E. (2007) 'Stimulating dynamic value: Social capital and business incubation as a pathway to competitive success', *Long Range Planning*, 40, pp. 154–177. https://doi.org/10.1016/j.lrp.2007.03.008.
Kariv, D. (2013) *Female Entrepreneurship and the New Venture Creation: An International Overview*. New York: Routledge.
Khlystova, O., Kalyuzhnova, Y., Belitski, M. (2022) 'The impact of the COVID-19 pandemic on the creative industries: A literature review and future research agenda', *Journal of Business Research*, 139, pp. 1192–1210. https://doi.org/10.1016/j.jbusres.2021.09.062.
Kleinhempel, J., Beugelsdijk, S., Klasing, M.J. (2020) 'The changing role of social capital during the venture creation process: A multilevel study', *Entrepreneurship Theory and Practice*, 46(2), pp. 297–330. https://doi.org/10.1177/1042258720913022.
Krämer, N.C., Sauer, V., Ellison, N. (2021) 'The strength of weak ties revisited: Further evidence of the role of strong ties in the provision of online social support', *Social Media + Society*, 7(2). https://doi.org/10.1177/20563051211024958.
Kuratko, D.F., Burnell, D., Stevenson, R., Neubert, E., Fisher, G. (2023) 'Enacting entrepreneurial hustle', *Business Horizons*, 66(2), pp. 237–249. https://doi.org/10.1016/j.bushor.2022.06.007.
Lerman, M., Munyon, T., Carr, J. (2020) 'Stress events theory: A theoretical framework for understanding entrepreneurial behavior', in *Entrepreneurial and Small Business Stressors, Experienced Stress, and Well-Being*. Leeds: Emerald Publishing Limited, pp. 35–63. https://doi.org/10.1108/S1479-355520200000018003.
Motoyama, Y., Knowlton, K. (2017) 'Examining the connections within the startup ecosystem: A case study of St. Louis', *Entrepreneurship Research Journal*, 7(1), pp. 1–32.
Moustakas, C. (1994) *Phenomenological Research Methods*. CA: SAGE Publications, Inc. https://doi.org/10.4135/9781412995658.

Nesta (2020) 'Creative enterprise programme', *Nesta*. Available at: https://www.nesta.org.uk/project/creative-enterprise-programme/ (Accessed: 4/10/2023).
Nilsson, P. (2017) 'London start-ups are most likely to fail', *Financial Times*, 12 October. Available at: https://www.ft.com/content/e3c745c4-88d8-11e7-afd2-74b8ecd34d3b (Accessed: 11/09/2022).
Nyqvist, F., Victor, C.R., Forsman, A.K., Cattan, M. (2016) 'The association between social capital and loneliness in different age groups: A population-based study in Western Finland', *BMC Public Health*, 16(1), p. 542. https://doi.org/10.1186/s12889-016-3248-x.
Omrane, A., Kammoun, A., Seaman, C. (2018) 'Entrepreneurial burnout: Causes, consequences and way out', *FIIB Business Review*, 7(1), pp. 28–42. https://doi.org/10.1177/2319714518767805.
ONS (2022) 'Creative industries by region', *Office for National Statistics*. Available at: https://www.ons.gov.uk/businessindustryandtrade/business/activitysizeandlocation/adhocs/14171creativeindustriesbyregion (Accessed: 06/09/2022).
Pines, A., Aronson, E. (1988) *Career Burnout: Causes and Cures*. New York: Free Press.
Putnam R.D. (2000). *Bowling Alone: The Collapse and Revival of American Community*. New York: Simon and Schuster.
Schaufeli, W.B., Greenglass, E.R. (2001) 'Introduction to special issue on burnout and health', *Psychology and Health*, 16(5), pp. 501–510.
Shin, J., Kim, Y.J., Jung, S., Kim, C. (2022) 'Product and service innovation: Comparison between performance and efficiency', *Journal of Innovation & Knowledge*, 7(3). https://doi.org/10.1016/j.jik.2022.100191.
Spigel, B. (2020) *Entrepreneurial Ecosystems: Theory, Practice and Futures*. Cheltenham, UK: Edward Elgar Publishing, pp. 46–86.
Stephan, U. (2018) '"Entrepreneurs" Mental Health and Well-Being: A Review and Research Agenda', *Academy of Management Executive*, 32, pp. 290–322. https://doi.org/10.5465/amp.2017.0001.
Todd, R. (2012) 'Young urban Aboriginal women entrepreneurs: Social capital, complex transitions and community support', *British Journal of Canadian Studies*, 25(1), pp. 1–19, 149.
Townsend, D.M., Busenitz, L.W., Arthurs, J.D. (2008) 'To start or not to start: Outcome and ability expectations in the decision to start a new venture', *Journal of Business Venturing*, 25(2), pp. 192–202. https://doi.org/10.1016/j.jbusvent.2008.05.003.
Tufford, L., Newman, P. (2012) 'Bracketing in qualitative research', *Qualitative Social Work*, 11(1), pp. 80–96. Available at: https://doi.org/10.1177/1473325010368316.
UKFT's Compendium of Industry Statistics and Analysis 2020 (2021) *UKFT*. Available at: https://ukft.s3.eu-west-1.amazonaws.com/wp-content/uploads/2021/11/24095453/UKFTs-Compendium-of-Industry-Statistics-and-Analysis-2020-Executive-Summary.pdf (Accessed: 6 October 2024).
von Eckartsberg, R. (1998) 'Existential-phenomenological research', in Valle, R. (ed.), *Phenomenological Inquiry in Psychology*. Boston, MA: Springer. https://doi.org/10.1007/978-1-4899-0125-5_2.
Wiklund, J., Nikolaev, B., Shir, N., Foo, M., Bradley, S. (2019) 'Entrepreneurship and well-being: Past, present, and future', *Journal of Business Venturing*, 34(4), pp. 579–588. https://doi.org/10.1016/j.jbusvent.2019.01.002.
Zaheer, H., Breyer, Y., Dumay, J., Enjeti, M. (2022) 'The entrepreneurial journeys of digital start-up founders', *Technological Forecasting and Social Change*, 179, p. 121638.
Zhu, F., Yu, W., Fan, S.X., Jonathan, J.G. (2023) 'Should I stay or should I go? The impact of entrepreneurs' loneliness on business exit intentions through entrepreneurial passion', *Journal of Business Venturing Insights*, 19, p. e00368.

10 Innovation in sports

Institutional entrepreneurship at play

Amy Gresock

Introduction

Entrepreneurship is crucial to the sports sector, as it allows for evolving consumer demands to take shape and increased emphasis on innovation (Ball, 2005). Ratten (2011) proposes sports-based entrepreneurship as a category of entrepreneurship that promotes economic development in the sports management field, defining it as enterprise or entrepreneurship within a sports context. Institutional entrepreneurship encompasses the actions of agents who disrupt existing social institutions or create new ones (DiMaggio, 1988; Tiberius et al., 2020). However, as institutional entrepreneurship has emerged as an important research theme (Battilana et al., 2009), the literature lacks illustration of how activities that comprise institutional entrepreneurship vary in different contexts (Maguire et al., 2004). Thus, in this chapter, attention is given to the prevalence and influence of institutional entrepreneurship within the context of sports management.

An institutional field refers to the organizations that collectively compose a recognized area of institutional life (DiMaggio and Powell, 1983). These are steeped in established rules, norms, and routines so formidable that organizations and individuals are obligated to comply and display behaviors consistent with them (DiMaggio and Powell, 1991). Professional hockey can be considered an established organizational field, comprised of teams, suppliers, and professional organizations (e.g., National Hockey League) for which there are accepted standards, policies, and norms. However, such constraints of institutional fields are apt to evolve over time (Barley and Tolbert, 1997). In hockey, these have changed as the sport developed, an example being in the adaptation (and then regulation) of protective masks for goalies. They weren't in common use until the mid-twentieth century after Montreal Canadiens goaltender Jacques Plante, who after being hit with a shot, returned to the ice with a custom-made fiberglass mask he had used in practice (Wulf, 2009). Although it was controversial and he was ridiculed, soon other goalies started donning their own models and iterations occurred, resulting in greater protection to the head and neck. Eventually, the innovation was used across teams, and something viewed as cowardly progressed

DOI: 10.4324/9781003324737-10

to being considered necessary and nowadays, even artistic (USA Hockey, n.d.). Thus, a now standard item in the field had been ultimately accepted as it became further institutionalized. When initiatives for new standards are introduced to a field, they must defy the inertia related to the adherence to embedded standards that support the functioning of existing fields (Garud et al., 2002). To defeat this initial inertia, institutional entrepreneurs must organize a collective in favor of the innovative standard. For Jacques Plante, attaining buy-in from other goaltenders in support of wearing masks helped bring legitimacy to this equipment so it was ultimately standardized as an extension of their uniforms.

Initiatives to shape institutions in new ways signify acts of institutional entrepreneurship (Fligstein, 1997). Institutional entrepreneurs have both shaped the face of sports considerably and adapted their strategies when operating in less institutionalized fields. An example is a sports entrepreneur using strategic tactics to establish "legitimacy" with the few others in their area; together, they engage in developing emerging fields characterized by a low degree of institutionalization. They aim to formulate a vision that tries to establish a common identity specific to only the actors who will be part of the new field (Markowitz, 2007). This might take the form of the creation of an exclusive sports association. A recent illustration was in 2023, when American businesswoman Michele Kang (see *Michele Kang: Founder and Chief Executive Officer*, n.d.) signed an agreement with OL Groupe to create the first-of-its-kind global multi-team women's soccer organization (New York Times, 2023). She became the majority owner and CEO of the newly formed entity, making this the first women-owned, women-led multi-soccer organization (Businesswire, 2023; Kassouf, 2023; Linehan, 2023).

Those existing in less institutionalized fields may also need to legitimize the field from the perspective of major stakeholders on whom they are likely to depend (DiMaggio and Powell, 1991; Koene, 2006). Investors, coaches, players, or even the public may push for more standardization in a field that is not fully institutionalized, and standards may be hazy. As a new sport grows and starts to institutionalize, such as the emerging sport of fullball (*Fullball the origin*, n.d.), there may be strong pressures from stakeholders on finding ways to institutionalize. An emerging sport may eventually legitimize in the eyes of these stakeholders when norms and common practices are firmly in place and known. Consider sport climbing, which as a sport made its Olympic debut in Tokyo (2021) and for its second time at the Olympic games is returning with a "fresh format" with changes to competition (Brief, 2024; International Federation of Sport Climbing, 2024). Fields that are emerging often favor institutional entrepreneurs' use of strategies that exploit the fascination with novelty (Zimmerman and Zeitz, 2002). Institutional entrepreneurs set the standard in creating new fields that attract different field members, and simultaneously legitimize the field with centrally positioned actors in neighboring fields. This may involve setting rules for a novel sport or taking an established sport and revamping it for a new market.

The goal is to provide an understanding of how institutional entrepreneurship operates in sports by considering theoretical foundations and the perspective of institutional fields unique to this context. The chapter addresses issues associated with innovation in sports by proposing a view of institutional entrepreneurs in sports as visionaries who change the rules, transforming existing institutions or creating entirely new ones. The concept of institutional fields, as well as the potential for institutional entrepreneurs to be lifestyle entrepreneurs, will be discussed. The case of Albert Spalding is introduced as an institutional entrepreneur within the realm of baseball. There is also consideration provided to factors that give rise to the development of institutional entrepreneurship in sport, despite institutional pressures for maintaining the status quo. Since institutional entrepreneurs initiate changes that fracture from existing institutions, they deal with challenges arising from others' embeddedness and potential opposition. In addition, the importance of social capital is mentioned, and the role of mascots is discussed, with insight provided by the examples of Handsome Dan, Mr. Celery, and current controversies affecting institutions. Finally, further research directions are proposed for the intersection of sports management with institutional entrepreneurship, as there are theoretical and practical implications for these fields as well as organizational theory.

Entrepreneurship for sports

The modern forms of sports have evolved over the years along with other key institutional forms of contemporary life (Smart, 2005). Entrepreneurial forces are at work and continue to be a main source of energy for sport-related industries today (Santomier, 2002). Sport transcends cultural and social settings and is played in multiple contexts across the world (Ratten, 2011). The area of sport entrepreneurship is evolving and affects several management areas including business strategy, new sport development, product innovation, promotional strategies, social issues, sustainability concerns, and technological developments. Ratten (2011) proposes sport-based entrepreneurship as a category within entrepreneurship that promotes economic development in the sports management field.

Sports-based entrepreneurship is defined as a sports-related organization performing innovatively in a business context, and appropriately a sports-based entrepreneur is someone who organizes, operates, and shoulders risk for a business venture that is sports related (Ratten, 2010). The formal recognition of entrepreneurial activity has been frequently lacking in this field, and subsequently, many entrepreneurs don't view themselves as such (Dobson and McLuskie, 2020). Entrepreneurs may be driven by forces other than financial gain, such as social goals or community (Hemme et al., 2017). They choose a business that corresponds with their way of life and hobbies (i.e., lifestyle entrepreneurs), or work in pursuit of legitimacy for institutional factors of a field. In sports-based ventures, there does not always have to be a necessity for profit generation, nor does profit have to be the chief aim of the enterprise (Ratten 2010). They may also innovate to problem-solve. Such was the case with the popular pastime of Wiffle Ball, developed by David Mullany as a way to combat soreness arising from throwing small balls in makeshift backyard baseball games (Wulf, 2009). The lightweight plastic Wiffle Ball was patented in 1957 as a solution to undue stress on the arms of young players; it also spurred an enduring game unto itself for which there is a World Wiffle Ball Championship (Kindy, 2019; worldwiffleball.org, 2024).

Sport and institutional fields

Sport is a worldwide activity that has been influenced throughout its history by changing environmental factors. These factors occur on a global level (Ratten, 2010), and may include economic and social shifts that affect how we play sports, or the businesses affiliated with sport. Sport over the years has been influenced by technological factors as well. For example, outdoor display technology has innovated to become larger and has more detailed resolution that even classic ballparks such as Fenway Park and Wrigley Field (which still also use traditional hand-operated scoreboards) have incorporated (Fisher, 2018). Harvard University claims to have used the first scoreboard on American Thanksgiving Day 1893 when its team played the University of Pennsylvania (Beck and Wilkinson, 2013). Since then, technology has improved this standard component of professional parks and arenas, as dot-matrix-based scoreboards have been replaced by massive state-of-the-art video boards able to display high-end video and intricate animations (Fisher, 2018). Now, such scoreboards are expected at large stadiums and are the institutional standard. Some have questioned what makes sport organizations so similar and why organizations' institutional fields have adopted practices that are seemingly irrational (Robertson et al., 2022), and it is interesting to consider how certain practices have been legitimized.

As Smart (2005) describes, in England and America starting in the mid-nineteenth century, customary leisure activities were steadily being replaced by the emergence of modern sports. During this time, agreed-upon rules concerning how specific sports should be played were articulated in several institutional contexts, governing bodies in sports fields were established, and the frequency of competition increased dramatically given easier railway travel. Thus, recreational games became subject to transformation through the institutional process of formalization, as folk games that had been played fitting local customs and traditions were modernized. Along this process, governing bodies served to create and administer rules of conduct that regulated different sports and created consistency for ways of playing. The widespread compliance of such rules and standards makes competition fair between teams. Sports today apply such parameters of play to specify permitted physical and behavioral parameters within which competitive activity takes place.

Institutional theory has served as an important framework in the field of sport management (Washington and Patterson, 2011), as some researchers have acknowledged that sport can be a unique context for exploring relevant institutional issues in view of the prominence of emotions and interconnected identities often found within athletics. It is essential for sport management to be at the forefront of engaging institutional theory (Nite and Edwards, 2021). As fields continue to evolve, researchers can consider how institutional forces work and what pressures may be forcing agents to conform to existent field norms.

Some sports entrepreneurs participating in institutional entrepreneurship processes are disrupting institutional environments and participating in creative destruction (see Schumpeter, 1934), whereby innovativeness has the capacity to not just alter existing institutions, but to dismantle the market they are a part of and create something anew (Beckert, 1999). Institutional creation work has received increased attention in a range of sports contexts, especially within emerging sports and sport organizations where regulatory structures are deficient. Governing bodies for specific sports have played a substantial role in not only determining the rules under which players may compete, but also who may not be included in official competition (Smart, 2005). Since Washington and Patterson's (2011) review of institutional theory in sport management and their appeal to researchers for the examination of the creation of institutions in sport, work from this perspective has gained popularity; however, there is a gap in the sport management literature examining institutional disruption at work, which warrants further study in order to advance our understanding of institutional change within sports management (Nite and Edwards, 2021).

Few studies have assumed the institutional entrepreneurship perspective in sports. Researchers have applied the sport context to offer detailed analysis of the micro foundational level of how entrepreneurs operate, and how they function to ultimately change existing institutional practices. Such studies have influenced the field to help describe how institutions are created, maintained, and disrupted (Robertson et al., 2022). Important to these institutions are the norms and traditions which are allowed and what they signify. Take the accepted tradition of cutting down the nets following the victory of an important basketball game. NC State University basketball coach Everett Case was the first to cut down a net as a souvenir of a significant win in 1947; now it is a recognized act for certain situations (i.e., a player would not do this after a loss) and there is etiquette to the tradition (ensuring the team captains and the coach go last; Wulf, 2009). This act is a celebratory performance of basketball culture and has become so standardized that the National Collegiate Athletic Association (NCAA) has an official ladder and scissors to accomplish it (Wilco, 2024). This is dissimilar from different institutional fields in sports, where celebrations and post-game rituals take other forms. One such unique celebratory act is that since 1956 the winner of the Indianapolis 500 automobile race consumes a bottle of chilled milk in Victory Lane, inspired from the practice of driver Louis Meyer drinking buttermilk in the

1930s (Skiver, 2024). In 1993 when winner Emmerson Fittipaldi drank orange juice before milk, he was booed and later issued a formal apology letter, which demonstrates how important field norms and traditions are to institutional stakeholders (*Associated Press*, 1993; Taranto, 2022).

The institutional entrepreneurship perspective is especially appropriate for the study of agents working to legitimize new or unpopular sport fields. In developing a field, sport clubs are required to have specific facilities and must employ professional staff (e.g., coaches, athletes, team management), have sizable financial resources for costs in institution building (e.g., athletes' contracts), and have the proper infrastructure (i.e., should facilities not meet institutional requirements, it cannot participate in the league or must use infrastructure in another town that does) (Mankowski, 2018). Nite et al. (2020) sought to understand how institutional entrepreneurs established a new professional sport league by examining two efforts to launch professional rugby union football leagues within the United States. Their work points to the importance of sport managers in recognizing how the institutions impact effective implementation and long-term continuance of new sport efforts (Nite et al., 2020). Institutional entrepreneurship helps us to also consider the processes through which informal entrepreneurs have been able to bring about successful change.

Institutional theory in practice

Rules characterize sports such as football, basketball, and hockey, for without them the games would be chaos (Littlefield, 2007). Every sport has written and unwritten rules. Breaking a written rule will result in a penalty, whereas breaking an unwritten rule could make an athlete the target of aggression from an opponent (Wulf, 2009). Sport is typically organized by associations that stipulate structure and rules for competition, regulate transactions among organizations, and provide structures for understanding within a certain sport's context; governance of these associations tends to become institutionalized as the actual governing bodies become institutions of their own (Nite et al., 2019). When member organizations do not adhere to a field's institutional norms, the legitimacy of their actions is questioned, and performance is liable to be affected (Cunningham and Nite, 2020).

Institutions identify and endorse both formal and informal social arrangements and behaviors by incorporating taken-for-granted, culturally engrained beliefs (Garud et al., 2007). An organization's culture is made pervasive in performances by sport mascots, T-shirts adorned with pictures or numbers of sports stars, and through collectible items such as player baseball cards (Slowikowski, 1993). Institutions also constrain and inhibit behaviors that do not fit with established norms. Consider the act of hitting a home run in baseball, where calling excessive attention to oneself on the field will invite retribution toward that player or the next batter in the lineup (Wulf, 2009). Organizational scholars have often concentrated on the essential function that institutions have in offering continuity and stability in organizational practices. In a context such as sports, institutional arrangements reduce ambiguity, lessen opportunistic behavior that may arise with negotiations, grant legitimacy to new technologies, and promote standards for new organizations looking to join an established league. Standards function to symbolize the structure of practices into voluntary rules that can steer the evolution of fields (Pacheco et al., 2010).

One governance association that has evolved into an institution with rules and standards is the NCAA, which regulates appropriate activities and relationships in intercollegiate sports within the United States (Nite et al., 2019). In December 1905 U.S. President Theodore Roosevelt called for a conference at the White House to discuss violence in American football following numerous serious injuries and even death caused by the sport; as a result, the Intercollegiate Athletic Association of the United States (which changed its name to the NCAA in 1910) was formed with 62-member institutions (Beck and Wilkinson, 2013). The evolution of the NCAA provides understanding of how an association shapes institutional structures and maintains them (Nite et al., 2019). Over time, the NCAA transformed itself to maintain control over field structuration by expanding membership criteria to contend with a competing institution (Washington, 2004). Findings by Nite et al. (2019) indicate that although in its early years it struggled to establish legitimacy, the NCAA changed its manner for controlling institutional boundaries, practices, and cognitions to create dominance (Nite et al., 2019).

Framing of heroes

Institutional entrepreneurs can employ framing techniques, where they try to portray their institutional arrangement as the most attractive for as large of an audience as possible. The use of framing tactics can link the goal of establishing legitimacy for new practices by incorporating innovative ideas and processes with institutionally accepted procedures and norms. The entrepreneurial story is an important antecedent of venture legitimation (Taeuscher et al., 2021). The application of discourse and stories has been widespread in the attempts of institutional entrepreneurs in creating institutional change (Zilber, 2007). They may use legends of heroes or recount games of the past to try to legitimize something for the future and may even draw upon the current celebrity appeal of a sports star. Those who have achieved celebrity in sports are recognized by judgements accrued in public discourse and the media as having done something significant in their field – for example, Venus Williams as a tennis player (Stewart and Giles, 2020). As one of the most recognizable figures in the history of the sport who have advocated for gender equity in sports, she has not only achieved championships but has even been honored with a doll created in her likeness for a new Role-Model line of Barbie dolls, which celebrates female sporting icons (Binswanger, 2024; Polacek,

2024). Some researchers regard entrepreneurs as heroic individuals who succeed by conquering overwhelming obstacles (Garud and Karnøe, 2003). The sporting hero has become a sports star and ever more a celebrity (Smart, 2005) who needs to be relevant for today's fans and modern marketers. *Sports Illustrated* opined in 2023 that if a marketing company were to design the modern athlete influencer from scratch, they would build one with all the elements of Kansas City Chiefs' quarterback Patrick Mahomes, who has prowess on the field, career success, relatability to fans, and a role as a powerful influencer. The publication's author believes that given this, the subsequent generation of successful quarterbacks will follow his example behaviorally (Bishop, 2023).

The category of achieved celebrity refers to those who have earned their celebrity status through apparent accomplishments in each field, where value is unique from field to field, and over time, to boost celebrity status (Stewart and Giles, 2020). It is apparent how accomplishments in one field do not have the same value in creating celebrity for another (e.g., boxing versus swimming). Also, since value changes over time, achievements that are considered extraordinary and confer value for celebrity status in the early days of a sport may be unremarkable as the field matures and a larger number of athletes with greater capabilities are competing.

Celebrity status operates within and relating to the fields that celebrities inhabit and move between (Stewart and Giles, 2020). They legitimize an institutional project and in championing it, they galvanize forces for collective action and create strategies for establishing entirely new institutions (Garud et al., 2002). The mythical idea of the entrepreneur conjures images of heroic individuals amassing wealth rather than collective action toward more egalitarian goals or projects of institutional transformation (Levy and Scully, 2007). Wright and Zammuto (2013) highlight the potential for lone hero institutional entrepreneurs to learn from failure in working in isolation and embrace more collective tactics. Their case study follows an institutional entrepreneur, Colonel Rait-Kerr, in creating opportunities that led to the 1963 introduction of a novel mass-market category, a Knock-Out Cup to the field of First-Class County Cricket in England. The Colonel's progress demonstrates that actors who identify opportunities for new categories in mature fields may evolve from isolationist to collaborative approaches for institutional entrepreneurship (Wright and Zammuto, 2013).

Although changes in sports are benefited by collective action, it is important to recognize that at the same time the field may be a mix of competitors (Mankowski, 2018). Institutional entrepreneurs may prompt action by creating the impression of a collective versus an unliked incumbent; this is consistent with explanations in institutional theory research on how change can generate momentum by evoking the image of a common foe (Garud et al., 2002). Researchers should consider how this might be the case especially in sports contexts as certain games and athletic areas have legitimized over time through the efforts of multiple actors led by someone considered a heroic figure in the field.

Leaders are important in institutional processes, and work has demonstrated that the executive immigration of leaders with distinctive backgrounds (and likely different values/experiences) is a major aspect of the process through which existing institutions are transformed (Kraatz and Moore, 2002). There are many examples of how an institution can change with the addition of a new star athlete or a revolutionary coach. One notable case is David Stern, who, during a thirty-year tenure as commissioner for the National Basketball Association (NBA), built a major international presence and prosperity for a league whose finals had been on tape delay (Sports Business Journal, 2018). When he assumed the role in 1984, he was expected to repair the league's damaged image. Ultimately, he not only brought sophistication to the sport but greatly expanded its influence and is therefore considered by many to be one of the most impactful commissioners in professional sports history (Gregory, 2020). Such migration of innovative leaders is key in creating shifts in institutional elements, at the level of both individual organizations and institutional fields (Kraatz and Moore, 2002).

Michael Jordan and Nike

Michael Jordan, whose influence extends beyond his existence as a skilled athlete but as a brand, exemplifies the way in which sport celebrity culture is tied to commodity culture (Smart, 2005). In 1984, Michael Jordan signed a rewarding deal with Nike which included a signature series of apparel and shoes (Turner, 2019). Nike began much of what is considered sports marketing, specifically regarding individual athletes (Sports Business Journal, 2018). During that time, the company chose to focus its promotional spending on a handful of elite athletes such as Jordan (Turner, 2019). They invested substantial resources into making him their signature athlete (Smart, 2005).

The connection between elite sport and spectator desirability was brought to light by the Air Jordan shoe, a product that played a significant part in Nike's success (Turner, 2019). Brand aficionados are loyal to the brand built by Phil Knight, which is one of sport's most prosperous (Sports Business Journal, 2018). By the mid-1980s Nike's shoes outnumbered adidas on basketball courts across the United States, and the red and black Nike Air Jordan was the must-have casual shoe of that era (Turner, 2019). The Jordan Brand stands out in sneaker culture, and the legendary Jumpman logo is still prominent on many sport jerseys and fan merchandise (Bishop, 2023).

Decades after he played in his final NBA game, Jordan remains one of sport's most recognizable and enduring figures (Bishop, 2023) and Nike continues to be influential after more than half a century (Sports Business Journal, 2018). Jordan bestowed celebrity appeal upon Nike products, and Nike institutionalized new standards for not just the design but the marketing as well (Turner, 2019).

Institutional entrepreneurs in sports as lifestyle entrepreneurs

One type of entrepreneur who an institutional entrepreneur may identify as is the lifestyle entrepreneur. When entrepreneurs engage in lifestyle entrepreneurship, they align their entrepreneurial activity to match their way of life and fit with their personal circumstances (Morrison, 2006). The literature on lifestyle entrepreneurship includes research on sport entrepreneurship (Ivanycheva et al., 2023). Some entrepreneurs build businesses to seize benefits they may acquire from taking part in sport activities they find fulfilling, and it is understood that economic goals are secondary (Ratten, 2010). For many of these lifestyle entrepreneurs in sport ventures, it may be a sport that they are passionate about, one they have played for much of their life, a game/team that they are an avid spectator or fan of, or a fitness hobby. To them, the lifestyle benefit is paramount. Some athletes, even at elite levels, claim they do it for the love of the sport even when financial rewards are lacking (*BBC Sport*, 2024). They may engage in organizational commitment behaviors that are unique to sports such as helping teammates, performing community service, recruiting, and being social with fans (Love and Kim, 2019). The term organization commitment behaviors refer to individual behaviors that are not formally required or recognized in the formal reward system but that contribute to the effective functioning of the organization (Organ, 1997; Organ and Ryan, 1995). Institutional entrepreneurs in sports may engage in these behaviors irrespective of rewards because of their firm commitment to the sport and desire to advance it as an institution.

The case of Spalding as an institutional entrepreneur

It is plausible to view institutional entrepreneurs in sports as visionaries who change the rules, whereby they transform existing institutions or construct entirely new ones. They not only create products or start businesses, but they change the scope of the playing field, so to speak. There are several examples of this in sports management. When considering just a single sport, such as baseball, one should take into account that the evolution of baseball took place as much off the field as it did on. Fans today may not realize that the sport as we know it didn't surface fully formed. It has been transformed over the years by different agents, and the institutional environment has been disrupted by them; this includes iterations to policies, expectations, equipment, and norms. For example, in terms of fundamental playing rules, strikes didn't exist until 1858, called balls came into being five years after, and overhand pitching wasn't allowed until 1884 (Weber, 2011). Such aspects of the game were not just changes in technique, but substantial impacts upon how the game was played and understood that influence it today. Thus, the history of baseball is not simply the history of the greatest players; it is also the history of the pastime's rules, traditions, and the place it has held in society (Morris, 2010). Much of that has to do with the institutional factors in effect.

As much as any other dominant figure in the history of the sport of baseball, Albert Goodwill Spalding (1850–1915), the star pitcher, manager, and owner of the Chicago White Stockings (predecessors of current-day Chicago Cubs), an organizer of the National League, and founder of a powerful sporting goods company bearing his name, was perhaps most responsible for making professional baseball what it is today (Melville, 2020). Spalding was a notable character in the first few decades of Major League Baseball, and his career demonstrated that baseball was certainly a business that could be expertly managed for profit (Lewis II, 2011).

In the late 1850s, organized baseball existed in America as a club-based pastime supported by the local culture of teams, but by the mid-1870s, it had started to become a more significant profitmaking enterprise contingent on sound business management, attendance, and the paid labor of players (Goldstein, 2009). One of the modernizers of the game, Albert Spalding opened a business known initially as the A.G. Spalding & Bros. Sporting Goods Company. The entire firm was capitalized with $800 in 1876 by Spalding and his brother J. Walter with a loan from Spalding's mother (Light, 2005; Rielly, 2000). The growth of the firm was rapid, and in early 1885 the first store in New York was launched. Industry competitors Reach, Peck & Snyder, and Wright & Ditson were eventually bought out by Spalding. By 1892, the company stock value was already worth $4 million. Throughout the next few decades, Spalding commanded baseball production and created equipment for other sports well into the twentieth century (Light, 2005).

Early on, he began manufacturing sporting goods to supply his retail business. The pitcher and manager was among the first stars on the diamond who established his own name as a brand, thereby creating the convention of celebrity-endorsed products in sports (Lewis II, 2011). Such a feat changed the institutional field and is prevalent today. The rising sporting goods entrepreneur received the right to manufacture the National League's ball and official guide (Light, 2005). This type of uniformity had been lacking in the early years of the sport, when balls were either homemade or produced on a custom basis by cobblers or tanners (Jogendra and Bhalla, 2021), with some containing fish-eye cores (Stamp, 2013). In the early 1870s the standard for the baseball's weight and size was determined and the production became standardized, which Spalding profited from (Jogendra and Bhalla, 2021). Spalding constructed baseballs and paid $1 per dozen that he supplied to the league to advertise his merchandise as the approved ball. By having his product serve the certified baseball for official play, it was legitimized by the institution (i.e., an endorsement by the league). By the turn of the century, Spalding was marketing four baseballs in children's size and eight at regulation size, ranging from four cents to a dollar (Jogendra and Bhalla, 2021). Subsequent sports items created by Spalding included bats, gloves, hats, uniforms, and various rule books. Spalding had crafted the game, as much as anyone, into a beloved pastime (Rielly, 2000). In the process, he legitimized many of its rules, practices, and traditions via his role as an institutional entrepreneur and, in effect, codified much of the institution.

Spalding was a true pioneer in the field of sport marketing. His sporting goods company and baseball teams dominated the sport industry in the early years following Civil War in the United States (Santomier, 2002). Consider how the trademark became a visible component of the baseball bat. When Spalding received the contract to manufacture the official bats for the National League, he added the trademark to all his bats, asserting that it was stamped on each to ensure genuineness. It also signified that every player at bat from the National League had such a stamp advertising Spalding's sporting goods company (Morris, 2010). Also, as mentioned earlier, his brand's baseball was the official ball of the National League, and remained so until 1976 (Lewis II, 2011; Stamp, 2013). The few iterations to its design included changing cores from rubber to cork and replacing horsehide covers with ones made of cowhide (Jogendra and Bhalla, 2021). Furthermore, in an era when not many players wore gloves (and those who did opted for flesh-colored ones to conceal the fact), Spalding wore a conspicuous black glove that was essentially a clever way of advertising his equipment (Morris, 2010). Additionally, he swiftly bound his firm to the future of the National League by gaining the right to publish the official league book, titled *Spalding's Official Baseball Guide* (Rielly, 2000). This would have also been his way of further institutionalizing the field, and in the public's mind would create the inseparability of the Spalding name from interest in baseball (Levine, 1985).

Viewing himself as a captain of the industry, Spalding deemed baseball a systematic business and he followed the scientific management principles championed by industrial engineer Frederick Taylor. Peter Levine (1984) considered him a flamboyant entrepreneur who recognized baseball's basic principle as subordination to the rule. Managing double roles as team owner and businessperson, Spalding became an example for future owners who also established complementary businesses in the field (Lewis II, 2011); he ultimately legitimized this practice as well.

Spalding has been described as the "father of baseball" not because he invented the game, but as a player, manager, and owner of a sporting-goods business, he did so much to represent, standardize, and popularize the game in the United States and abroad (Rielly, 2000). This standardization was essential toward institutionalization. Spalding helped steer the league through its early organizational obstacles, and diligently labored to advance the game into a pastime desirable of the patronage, support, and appreciation of a greater breadth of the population (Levine, 1984). During much of his Chicago baseball career, Spalding was also linked with another, much less well-known sport in America: cricket. This connection not only highlights the uncertainty of baseball's public image during the late 1800s, but also indirectly influenced Spalding's own conceptions of what baseball should be in American society (Melville, 2020). He helped to shape and institutionalize the sport. Spalding recognized the possibilities in the promotion of sport and acted in a way that encouraged the commercialization of sport as well as its emergence into an important social institution (Levine, 1985). Ultimately, his passion as a player and president paired with his acumen as a sporting-goods magnate and a relentless promoter of the game resulted in Spalding emerging as one of the innovators most responsible for baseball's becoming the pastime that it exists as today (Weber, 2011).

Factors for institutional entrepreneurship in sport

Those who engage in institutional entrepreneurship in sport also may do so because they see the potential for institution building in emerging sports. Different sports become popular over time, and institutional fields must evolve for each of them as a result. Take, for example, the rise of adventure sports which may include mountain-biking, surfing, skateboarding, and BMX (Dobson and McLuskie, 2020). These might not have institutional fields as firmly set in place, and an institutional entrepreneur may be able to easily change norms or set rules.

Institutional entrepreneurs assess institutional environments to find ones suitable for their opportunities. The work of Lok and De Rond (2013) explores how highly institutionalized practices in a sports context are maintained by examining how the institutional inhabitants restore performance breakdowns (disruptions of the taken-for-granted system when things don't go as expected) in institutionalized practice. This analysis, done via Cambridge University's preparation for the 2007 annual boat club race, reveals that institutions can be protected against breakdowns through maintenance work. Institutional maintenance work represents actors' deliberate attempts to preserve existing institutions (Colombero and Boxenbaum, 2019) and can be done via socialization, rule monitoring, and enforcement activities (Dacin et al., 2010). Institutional entrepreneurs should anticipate what conditions would lower institutions' stability and imperil them to breakdown if maintenance work is overlooked.

Institutional entrepreneurship may surface in attempts to remedy problems that sports fields face or to modify existing policy. In the 2000s, several developments in the field of concussions in sports indicated institutional change (Lu and Heinze, 2021). Heinze and Lu (2017) investigated changes in how a formidable sport governing body responded to institutional transformation in a case study of the National Football League's (NFL's) responses to player concussions. They discovered that the NFL altered its responses to this institutional change as the field itself evolved. These findings help in understanding sport governing bodies' reactions to institutional change and have consequences for organizational stakeholders (Heinze and Lu, 2017). In a later study, they analyze how two coalitions that functioned as institutional entrepreneurs in the states of Washington and Oregon established the first youth sport concussion legislation in the United States (Lu and Heinze, 2021). Given the results, they developed a model of the mechanisms by which institutional entrepreneurs create and promote new policy in sports (Lu and Heinze, 2021).

The rising of institutional entrepreneurship can coincide with corporate social responsibility initiatives. Sports can be a conduit for instituting environmental causes such as conservation, as the benefits derived from fan identity can extend to initiatives that teams may decide to employ. For example, the University of Missouri-Columbia (MU) formed their *Mizzou Tigers for Tigers* program with the help of organizations like the World Wildlife Federation to build conservation efforts for their mascot, who is an endangered species. As a result of MU's efforts, other schools with tiger mascots have joined together in this mission to save wild tigers from extinction (Sartore-Baldwin and McCullough, 2021).

Social capital

The institutional perspective permits for the assessment of how novel plans gain social approval (i.e., legitimacy) for critical stakeholders and their interaction with current institutional arrangements (Hinings et al., 2018). Institutional entrepreneurs can achieve this approval with the help of social capital. Enhancing social capital is key for institutional entrepreneurs. Social capital can be defined as the goodwill available to individuals and groups (Adler and Kwon, 2002; Kwon and Adler, 2014). It is the value obtained from resources embedded in social ties that an individual has with others (Lin, 2008). Its sources lie in the social relations among individuals, and these social relations are different from relations having to directly deal with market exchange and hierarchical authority (Kwon and Adler, 2014). Sports entrepreneurs depend upon social capital and their social networks to assemble stakeholders and facilitate innovation (Ratten, 2010). Within the environment of sport, social capital allows entrepreneurship to rise from reciprocity that develops when short-term sacrifices are made in the anticipation and hope of long-term gains. A community, such as those within sports, is composed of scattered networks of personal relationships in which social capital can be viewed as the value those relationships add to individuals' lives (de Zúñiga et al., 2017). Sport organizations possessing high levels of social capital may place importance on trust and willingness to take risks with the expectation that other organizations within the institutional field will react similarly. Social networks among sports players function as a bridging activity to entrepreneurial sport endeavors. By having access to a sport network, entrepreneurs can cultivate their social capital since they are learning, absorbing, and innovating to be appropriate for market conditions. Institutional entrepreneurs advocating for changes in sport policy may need to influence or mobilize stakeholders including government officials, athletes, and sport governing bodies, all while operating within the legal parameters (Lu and Heinze, 2021). Those who have social capital and effective social skills (e.g., reading the environment) become leaders and set new paths since this enables one to take the right steps within an organization and push forward change (Mankowski, 2018). It is crucial that institutional entrepreneurs have the social network support their strategy and that the actions to reach the strategic goal are agreed upon.

The role of mascots

Advantages of celebrity from sport or usage of mascots leads to benefits for the sports brand involving recall, trust, image, identity, purchase intentions, and likability (Srivastava, 2021). Sports organizations in their institutionalization must create a powerful brand. These types of brands, like all brands, must create authentic emotional connections with consumers that surpass common interactions (Quan et al., 2024). Schultz and Sheffer (2018) observed that there is a deep relationship between mascot loyalty and fan identification, especially related to one's perceptions of belonging to the sports family. Within sports institutions, a mascot is an animal, person, or object that behaves as a symbolization of an athletic team (Knoester and Rockhill, 2021). The person or animal who acts as a mascot will often be visible on the sideline or in the stands interacting with fans at prominent athletic events (Sweitzer, 2009).

Starting with baseball's initial codification in the 1840s, superstitious players embraced a variety of charms and curiosities that they imagined might help fate on the diamond, including a rabbit's foot, a tailless dog, and even a four-legged chicken (Abel, 2022). Sports teams used animals and even children as informal mascots in the nineteenth century (Shea, 2018). As sport institutions grew, many professional and amateur teams and individual athletes across the United States employed figures they deemed unique to tend to the players' equipment and serve as a human talisman believed to be gifted enough to bring victory "by virtue of oddity, deformity, race, and the brightness of his smile" (Abel, 2022, p. 53). Logo characters generally arrived in the twentieth century; it wasn't until the 1970s that the leading modern-era character mascots were developed, generating a surge of mascot creation (Shea, 2018). Some sports institutions add new informal mascots over their existence (while keeping original ones) to energize marketing efforts, to take advantage of extra merchandising opportunities, and sometimes accidentally, as is the case when they arise spontaneously in the zeal of playoffs or an enthusiastic season (Jacobsen, 2013). Mascots frequently become the symbol of identification of the entire institution, not simply its current athletic team (Sweitzer, 2009).

Mascots are beyond mere characters, as they personify the soul of the teams they symbolize. They serve as physical and emblematic representations of sports teams to which strong attachments are formed (Sartore-Baldwin and McCullough, 2021). The process for creating a sports mascot is a mixture of team identity, local culture, and creative design (Bennett, 2024). Mascots are points of attachment between fans and their favorite teams, whereby their usage is handled by sport institutions to deepen fan commitment, promoting fan identification (Sartore-Baldwin and McCullough, 2021). Some have been in existence in their institutions for more than a century (Sweitzer, 2009) and are firmly engrained in the norms and traditions associated with a team. History and culture are accessible to supporters in diverse forms via the sport mascot (Slowikowski, 1993). They often occupy anthropomorphic animal forms, making them visually unique and emotionally appealing for fans (Quan et al., 2024). Several mascots are icons representative of a team's location such as Penn State's Nittany Lion for Mt. Nittany, (Penn State, 2024), while others have been chosen via fan vote (Sweitzer, 2009). Some football clubs in the United Kingdom have mascots that are somehow connected to the club crest (BBC, 2022). While mascots can be planned to fit with the institutional field, they also surface out of conditions such as passion during playoffs or the purpose of offering entertainment at games (Jacobsen, 2013). Throughout history, mascots have organically arisen from their institutional environments while more recently, they are strategically planned to fit in with and strengthen the existing institution. Designers begin by pinpointing the top features that exemplify the team, which can include its colors, symbols, and location, and they apply these to create a distinctive character that the team's fanbase can identify with and which stands apart from competitors (Bennett, 2024). It is important that the mascot's behavior fits in with existing standards and fan expectations (Wolff and Stone, 1995). There are institutional policies and procedures, as mascots have established guidelines, standards, and behavior whereby there are three essential elements of mascotting: entrance, exaggeration, and emotion (Thomas, 2002).

The effect of celebrities on branding is documented, and in sports this can include mascots in advertising for the brand of a team (Srivastava, 2021). Their marketing influence is well recognized, as mascots function as bridges between users and products, communicate messages to users, and transmit visual cues (Quan et al., 2024). Given the reach of social media, sports teams have more platforms for utilizing their mascots beyond games and events, as mascots in the digital age have evolved into multifunctional tools for sales, promotions, team communications, and fostering loyalty (Shea, 2018). From a business perspective, mascots work to earn fan allegiance, build a collective identity among fans, provoke emotional responses, and ultimately construct competitive advantage (Sartore-Baldwin and McCullough, 2021).

Handsome Dan setting a precedent

In the early days of mascots, it wasn't uncommon for teams in different sports to use live animals as an emblem (BBC, 2022). Yale University is said to be the first instance of adopting a live animal mascot in 1889, and today their Olde

English Bulldogge mascot, Handsome Dan, is considered the most renowned (Beck and Wilkinson, 2013; LaRue, 2019). A dog belonging to a student was brought across the field before baseball and American football matches, and the appearance became so cherished that Yale now has the nineteenth embodiment of Handsome Dan (BBC, 2022). This ritual developed into a tradition at the university's major sporting events, intended to impart confidence and success upon their athletes (LaRue, 2019). Although Uga, the University of Georgia's royal line of blue-blooded English bulldogs, is another popular canine live animal mascot (Beck and Wilkinson, 2013), Handsome Dan led the way institutionally.

Native American controversy: changing institutional norms

Different controversies have illuminated the power of imagery imbedded in mascots (Bever, 2011). The issue involving Native American mascots is a controversy which involves many viewpoints (King, 2003). The meaning of Native American mascots and their impact on Native American people have been debated in the media and scholarly literature for more than fifty years (Burkley et al., 2017). The increase in Native American political activism in the 1960s and 1970s, together with greater awareness of the cultural representation of minorities, caused increasing discomfort with using "Indian" mascots for sports teams (Jones, 2007; King et al., 2006). Concerns about their descriptions in sport have further challenged the status quo of sports practices more recently (Knoester and Rockhill, 2021).

Teams were commonly represented by a person dressed in a stereotypical warrior costume akin to the image of Hollywood Westerns (e.g., headband and feathers, war paint on the face, with a bow and arrows or spear); this mascot might ride onto the playing field on horseback or perform a war dance, using antagonistic body language to suggest that the team would "massacre" opponents during the game (Jones, 2007). Supporters claim that they are honoring and celebrating Native American culture (Sweitzer, 2009). Others stress symbols such as these mascots cause harm and dehumanize Native Americans because the characters are often cartoonish, stereotypical depictions and because their domain in sports is alongside mostly animal symbols as mascots (Knoester and Rockhill, 2021). Institutional change is occurring in that the usage and acceptance of Native American imagery within the context of sports is evolving. Bresnahan and Flowers (2008) opine that sports organizations have a responsibility to take into consideration any potential negative audience effects of the mascot imagery that are utilized for the promotion of their teams.

Institutional change with Mr. Celery

The field of mascots has been shifting with the popularity of unconventional characters. Mr. Celery is the anthropomorphic celery stalk mascot who comes out to celebrate after every Wilmington Blue Rocks run and has been voted as a best minor league mascot in the 2024 *USA TODAY* 10Best Readers' Choice Awards for baseball (Tresolini, 2024). In 2000, this accidental mascot captured the interest of fans of the Blue Rocks minor league baseball team (Jacobsen, 2013). He currently dances in celebration of runs scored, a popular tradition that has been imitated by Blue Rocks fans and visitors to games (Tresolini, 2024). Mr. Celery was a success with fans from the first instance he ran out during a game (Hill, 2017).

According to Jacobsen (2013), the notion of having a celebratory mascot for the Blue Rocks emerged during the 1999 California League All-Star game. The Blue Rocks' general manager, who was in attendance, saw a mascot in the form of a bunny celebrating runs scored by the Lake Elsinore Storm. He found this humorous, and desired to similarly incorporate a celebratory mascot for his team in Wilmington, Delaware. In early 2000, an intern encountered several old costumes which a concessions operator had previously used between innings to promote food offerings. The only undamaged costume of the lot was the celery stalk. Blue Rocks' management enlisted an intern to don the costume and perform on the field when the Blue Rocks scored. Mr. Celery's debut was unannounced and a surprise for fans attending, but after first watching him with curiosity, the crowd exploded with laughter as his appearance was a resounding success. Thus, his entrance was made a recurring event for every time a Blue Rocks player crossed home plate (Jacobsen, 2013).

Mr. Celery isn't a mere publicity stunt; the mascot is an established tradition who fans share the fun of the game with. Almost immediately, he was a bona-fide ballpark celebrity complete with his own cheering section (Hill, 2017). A Celery Squad of loyal fans was formed, donning wigs of green hair, and creating a web presence, for whom prohibitions on outside food were relaxed to allow the bringing of celery stalks into the stadium to wave while Mr. Celery danced (Jacobsen, 2013). He now has a Frawley Stadium concourse drinking establishment named in his honor as well as a Wilmington Brew Works specialty beer with cans depicting his image (Tresolini, 2024). The popularity of Mr. Celery as an unofficial mascot took off. This also included the marketing of official merchandise bearing Mr. Celery's likeness, including stuffed replicas, key chains, T-shirts (Jacobsen, 2013), and even baseball jerseys with his image on them (Cormier, 2021). On the concourse, one can see celery-themed artwork and signage (Hill, 2022) signaling that he has become institutionalized.

Mr. Celery as a mascot fanatically and economically impacts the Blue Rocks and their fans (Jacobsen, 2013). A mascot such as Mr. Celery plays a significant role to the institution, as fans of athletic teams often identify with mascots, which is a key component in arousing emotion among supporters of the team (Sweitzer, 2009). Though the organization capitalizes on Mr. Celery's popularity at the park, there are intentional restrictions on Mr. Celery's use, as the unofficial mascot only emerges when the team scores or at special events at the stadium (Jacobsen, 2013). When he does appear, fans only see him for around fifteen seconds and then he hides away again (Cormier, 2021). He does not roam the stadium during games to interact with fans, as this is the work of Rocky Bluewinkle, whose duties as the official mascot include crowd visits and appearances on behalf of the team (Jacobsen, 2013). Mr. Celery's appearance is always accompanied by the 1997 hit "Song 2" by the English band Blur with its refrain, "Woo-hoo!", which has become his slogan and is featured on Mr. Celery merchandise (Cormier, 2021). Thus, fans know what to expect from him and he becomes deep-rooted in their traditions of the institution.

One reason why Mr. Celery works well for the Blue Rocks is that he is the star of a unique sideshow that has become a norm for the team. "We're not just baseball. We have to entertain through marketing", explains Blue Rocks official Kevin Linton (Cormier, 2021). Currently, Mr. Celery has been entertaining fans for a quarter of a century (Tresolini, 2024). The magic of this mascot rests in his restricted, unique use, and fans seem to value Mr. Celery because of it (Jacobsen, 2013).

Future directions

Organizations cannot be fully understood without considering the dynamics of their institutional context (Hinings et al., 2018). Research on institutional theory has emerged to examine how firms emulate innovators to legitimize and, therefore, institutionalize new domains (Ferreira et al., 2017). This is especially true in the context of sport, where we see the strong influence of institutional environments on organizations. Within this field, institutional entrepreneurship involves the creation of novel activities relating to sports (Ratten, 2010). Although the institutions may inhibit or enable entrepreneurial actions, ultimately, they do not determine them (Pacheco et al., 2010), for the institutional entrepreneur has the agency to create or destroy.

It is essential for an institutional entrepreneur to envision the consequences of their institutional changes. Khan et al. (2007) investigated what they call a "darker" side of institutional entrepreneurship by considering how the institutional practice of child labor was eliminated from the world's largest soccer ball manufacturing cluster in Pakistan. It became apparent that this occurrence of institutional entrepreneurship had unplanned consequences resulting from its successful implementation, such as disruption to family life, income losses, and detrimental effects to women. Sports fields have many stakeholders, and an institutional entrepreneur should consider how changes can directly and indirectly affect these groups before they engage in change processes.

Knowledge of the adventure sports area of sports entrepreneurship as a sub-field of the general area of sports management is very limited (Dobson and McLuskie, 2020). Researchers of institutional entrepreneurship should investigate emerging sports fields such as these and Esports as they change in scope and their institutional fields are more defined. It is suggested that sport management scholars as well as those involved in this Esports should define field boundaries with regard to this new field (Nite et al., 2019). There can also be possible studies of how product- versus service-based innovations vary in their impact on institutions. For example, in Major League Baseball, institutional entrepreneurship has included innovative baseball uniforms (Ratten, 2010). Consider that on June 19, 1858, Harvard University's crew team wore red silk bandanas, distinguishing itself from competition and marking the first time a team featured an identifying mark, and in 1908 the University of Pittsburgh was the first team to wear numbers on their American Football jerseys (Beck and Wilkinson, 2013). What athletes wear as a team has changed and institutionalized into what we see today. The equipment used in sports is constantly being modified for performance and safety (Smart, 2005). Equipment innovations and/or equipment rules adjustments may lower the risk of injury, but such changes may change the style of play of a sport, and potentially increase the potential for injury (Krauss, 2014). How are those legitimization effects different from other innovations occurring in the institutional field around the same time? Furthermore, it might be worthwhile to spotlight the creativity aspect of entrepreneurship and how it plays a role for entrepreneurs in modifying institutions in sports.

It is also beneficial to investigate how social changes affect institutional change. Sport organizations are creating strategies to actively recruit and attract LGBTQIA+ fans and employees to a greater extent (Cunningham and Nite, 2020). However, regardless of legislative headway concerning equity and inclusion, considerable challenges persist in addressing historically embedded prejudices and discriminations encountered by the LGBTQIA+ population within sports organizations (Robertson et al., 2019). The work of Cunningham and Nite (2020) indicates that LGBTQIA+ inclusiveness can attract employees or customers for whom equality is important, and it is associated with performance improvements when institutional logics are such that inclusion is apparent. Additionally, by taking an institutional perspective of inclusion in Australian cricket, Robertson et al. (2019) examined social change at the intersection of gender and sexuality inclusion. Research can further investigate this intersection in other sports contexts.

The eminence of sport in modern culture has resulted in an abundance of narratives dealing with sporting performance and heroes (Smart, 2005). Research going forward can also examine how sports celebrities impact institutional fields, especially given the usage of pervasive social media outlets. Celebrity status is earned based on myriad approvals and disapprovals made by individuals but expressed with others, collectively through groups and established through institutions (Stewart and Giles, 2020). In contemporary sports fields, a limited number of elite athletes become instant heroes/celebrities, and, with the assistance of sports agencies, are the recipients of huge endorsement contracts. Today's sport star is the result of a historical progression involving the rise of formally structured and profit-driven professional sports from traditional recreational games, the expansion of media interest, and an upsurge in the value of sponsorship and endorsement contracts (Smart, 2005). Soccer star David Beckham has had commitments for sunglasses, clothing, soft-drinks, and razors, while golfer Tiger Woods has been a spokesperson for foods, cars, watches, and even laser eye surgery (Smart, 2005). The most visible hero/celebrities become international icons capable of endorsing a wide range of products and services and have a role in determining the marketability of the sport that they represent (Santomier, 2002). This visibility, their following, and their power have the possibility to influence sport, but in what ways? How is the institutional field altered until the next charismatic athlete comes along? These are all interesting questions that have implications not just for sports marketing but for the sports themselves.

Institutional entrepreneurs alter existing institutional arrangements (DiMaggio, 1988). While scholars have investigated this phenomenon in prior work (see Battilana et al., 2009; Tiberius et al., 2020; Pacheco et al., 2010), the field of institutional entrepreneurship would benefit from future efforts that explore different contexts, particularly those relating to the field of sports management. Over time, as scholars learn more regarding entrepreneurs' capacity to break with existing institutional norms in sports, it becomes evident that the consequences of institutional change are significant in the context of sports management and for understanding its continued evolution.

References

Abel, A. (2022) 'Mascot memories: The phenomenon of the sports team mascot had theatrical, sometimes demeaning origins', *American History*, 57, pp. 50–57.

Adler, P. S. and Kwon, S.- W. (2002) 'Social capital: Prospects for a new concept', *Academy of Management Review*, 27, pp. 17–40.

Associated Press (1993) *Fittipaldi issues belated apology for swigging OJ instead of milk*. Available at: https://www.newspapers.com/article/the-indianapolis-star/24452722/ (Accessed: 24 May 2024).

Ball, S. (2005) 'The importance of entrepreneurship to hospitality, leisure, sport and tourism', *Hospitality, Leisure, Sport and Tourism Network*, 1, pp. 1–14.

Barley, S. R. and Tolbert, P. S. (1997) 'Institutionalization and structuration: Studying the links between action and institution', *Organization Studies*, 18(1), pp. 93–117.

Battilana, J., Leca, B., and Boxenbaum, E. (2009) 'How actors change institutions: Towards a theory of institutional entrepreneurship', *Academy of Management Annals*, 3(1), pp. 65–107.

BBC (2022) *BBC Bitesize: A short history of sporting mascots*. Available at: https://www.bbc.co.uk/bitesize/articles/zby4wsg (Accessed: 22 May 2024).

Beck, S. and Wilkinson, J. (2013) *College sports traditions: Picking up butch, silent night, and hundreds of others*. Scarecrow Press, Inc.

Beckert, J. (1999) 'Agency, entrepreneurs, and institutional change: The role of strategic choice and institutionalized practices in organizations', *Organization Studies*, 20(5), pp. 777–799.

Bennett, P. (2024) *Sports mascots: A lighthearted exploration of the history, design, and impact of beloved sports mascots*. Available at: https://fordhamram.com/2023/06/13/sports-mascots-a-lighthearted-exploration-of-the-history-design-and-impact-of-beloved-sports-mascots/ (Accessed: 22 May 2024).

Bever, M. L. (2011) 'Fuzzy memories: College mascots and the struggle to find appropriate legacies of the Civil War', *Journal of Sport History*, 38(3), pp. 447–463.
Binswanger, J. (2024) *Tennis icon Venus Williams scores her own Barbie doll.* Available at: https://www.msn.com/en-us/lifestyle/lifestyle-buzz/tennis-icon-venus-williams-scores-her-own-barbie-doll/ar-BB1mRMuK?ocid=BingNewsSearch (Accessed: 25 May 2024).
Bishop, G. (2023) *The power list 2023: The 50 most influential figures in sports*. Available at: https://www.si.com/sports-illustrated/2023/07/13/the-power-list-50-most-influential-figures-in-sports (Accessed: 23 May 2024).
Bresnahan, M. J. and Flowers, K. (2008) 'The effects of involvement in sports on attitudes toward Native American sport mascots', *The Howard Journal of Communications*, 19(2), pp. 165–181.
Brief, S. (2024) *In with the new: What are the new sports and events at the 2024 Paris Olympics?* Available at: https://www.nbcolympics.com/news/new-what-are-new-sports-and-events-2024-paris-olympics (Accessed: 23 May 2024).
Burkley, M., Burkley, E., Andrade, A., and Bell, A. C. (2017) 'Symbols of pride or prejudice? Examining the impact of Native American sports mascots on stereotype application', *The Journal of Social Psychology*, 157(2), pp. 223–235.
Businesswire (2023) *OL Groupe and Michele Kang form global multi-team women's football group.* Available at: https://www.businesswire.com/news/home/20230516005928/en/OL-Groupe-and-Michele-Kang-Form-Global-Multi-Team-Women%E2%80%99s-Football-Group/ (Accessed: 23 May 2024).
Colombero, S. and Boxenbaum, E. (2019) 'Authentication as institutional maintenance work', *Journal of Management Studies*, 56(2), pp. 408–440.
Cormier, R. (2021) *This is how Mr. Celery was born. And why he's more popular than ever on his 21st birthday.* Available at: https://www.delawareonline.com/story/news/2021/09/07/how-mr-celery-more-popular-than-ever-his-21st-year/7979213002/ (Accessed: 22 May 2024).
Cunningham, G. B. and Nite, C. (2020) 'LGBT diversity and inclusion, community characteristics, and success', *Journal of Sport Management*, 34(6), pp. 533–541.
Dacin, M. T., Munir, K., and Tracey, P. (2010) 'Formal dining at Cambridge Colleges: Linking ritual performance with institutional maintenance', *Academy of Management Journal*, 53(6) pp. 1398–1418.
de Zúñiga, H. G., Barnidge, M., and Scherman, A. (2017) 'Social media social capital, offline social capital, and citizenship: Exploring asymmetrical social capital effects', *Political Communication*, 34(1), pp. 44–68.
DiMaggio, P. J. (1988) 'Interest and agency in institutional theory', in L. G. Zucker (ed.), *Research on institutional patterns: Environment and culture.* Ballinger Publishing Co, pp. 3–22.
DiMaggio, P. J. and Powell, W. W. (1983) 'The iron cage revisited: Institutional isomorphism and collective rationality in organizational fields', *American Sociological Review*, 48(2), pp. 147–160.
DiMaggio, P. J. and Powell, W. W. (1991) *New institutionalism in organizational analysis*. University of Chicago Press.
Dobson, S. and McLuskie, P. (2020) 'Performative entrepreneurship: Identity, behaviour and place in adventure sports enterprise', *International Entrepreneurship and Management Journal*, 16(3), pp. 879–895.
Ferreira, M. P., Reis, N. R., and Pinto, C. F. (2017) 'Schumpeter's (1934) influence on entrepreneurship (and management) research', *Revista de Empreendedorismo e Gestão de Pequenas Empresas*, 6(1), pp. 4–39.

Fisher, E. (2018) *Technologies that have revolutionized the sports industry*. Available at: https://www.sportsbusinessjournal.com/Journal/Issues/2018/04/30/Technology/Tech-milestones.aspx?publicationSource=SBJ (Accessed: 27 May 2024).

Fligstein, N. (1997) 'Social skill and institutional theory', *The American Behavioral Scientist*, 40(4), pp. 397–405.

Fullball the origin (n.d.) Available at: https://officialfullball.com/ (Accessed: 24 May 2024).

Garud, R., Hardy, C., and Maguire, S. (2007) 'Institutional entrepreneurship as embedded agency: An introduction to the special issue', *Organization Studies*, 28(7), pp. 957–969.

Garud, R., Jain, S., and Kumaraswamy, A. (2002) 'Institutional entrepreneurship in the sponsorship of common technological standards: The case of Sun Microsystems and Java', *Academy of Management Journal*, 45(1), pp. 196–214.

Garud, R., and Karnøe, P. (2003) 'Bricolage versus breakthrough: Distributed and embedded agency in technology entrepreneurship', *Research Policy*, 32(2), pp. 277–300.

Goldstein, W. J. (2009) *Playing for keeps: A history of early baseball*. Cornell University Press.

Gregory, S. (2020) *How David Stern rescued the NBA and turned basketball into a global force*. Available at: https://time.com/5757570/david-sterm-rescued-nba/ (Accessed 25 May 2024).

Heinze, K. L. and Lu, D. (2017) 'Shifting responses to institutional change: The National Football League and player concussions', *Journal of Sport Management*, 31(5), pp. 497–513.

Hemme, F. Morais, D. G., Bowers, M. T., and Tod, J. (2017) 'Extending sport-based entrepreneurship theory through phenomenological inquiry', *Sport Management Review*, 20(1), pp. 92–104.

Hill, B. (2017) *On the road: Becoming Mr. Celery in Wilmington*. Available at: https://www.milb.com/news/how-mr-celery-became-a-wilmington-blue-rocks-legend-251686270 (Accessed: 22 May 2024).

Hill, B. (2022) *Explore Wilmington's frawley stadium*. Available at: https://www.mlb.com/news/featured/explore-frawley-stadium-home-of-the-wilmington-blue-rocks (Accessed: 22 May 2024).

Hinings, B., Gegenhuber, T., and Greenwood, R. (2018) 'Digital innovation and transformation: An institutional perspective', *Information and Organization*, 28(1), pp. 52–61.

International Federation of Sport Climbing (2024) *Olympic games Paris 2024*. Available at: https://www.ifsc-climbing.org/olympics (Accessed: 23 May 2024).

Ivanycheva, D., Schulze, W. S., Lundmark, E., and Chirico, F. (2023) 'Lifestyle entrepreneurship: Literature review and future research agenda', *Journal of Management Studies*, pp. 1–36.

Jacobsen, K. A. (2013) 'The accidental mascot: How Mr. Celery reached his salad days with the Wilmington Blue Rocks', *NINE: A Journal of Baseball History and Culture*, 22(1), pp. 130–136.

Jogendra, S. T. and Bhalla, S. (2021) 'Field of play and equipment for baseball game: An overview', *International Journal of Physical Education, Sports and Health*, 8(4), pp. 219–222.

Jones, L. E. (2007) 'Sports mascot controversies', in C. A. Barrett (ed.), *American Indian history, Volume 2*. United States: Salem Press, pp. 518–520.

Kassouf, J. (2023) *After buying into Lyon, Washington Spirit, Michele Kang charts a new course for women's soccer*. Available at: https://www.espn.com/soccer/story/_/id/37871183/michele-kang-interview-nwsl-lyon-ol-reign-future-plans (Accessed: 23 May 2024).

Khan, F. R., Munir, K. A., and Willmott, H. (2007) 'A dark side of institutional entrepreneurship: Soccer balls, child labour and postcolonial impoverishment', *Organization Studies*, 28(7), pp. 1055–1077.
Kindy, D. (2019) *How the Wiffle Ball came to be*. Available at: https://www.smithsonianmag.com/innovation/how-wiffle-ball-came-to-be-180972900/ (Accessed: 24 May 2024).
King, J. (2003) 'The sports mascot controversy', *The Review of Communication*, 3(2), pp. 158–160.
King, C. R., Davis-Delano, L., Staurowsky, E., and Baca, L. (2006) 'Sports mascots and the media', in A. Raney and J. Bryant (eds.), *Handbook of sports and media*. Routledge, pp. 626–645.
Knoester, C. and Rockhill, C. (2021) 'Multiculturalism and antiracism in sports? U.S. public opinions about Native American team names and mascots and the use of hijabs in sport', *Socius: Sociological Research for a Dynamic World*, 7, pp. 1–16.
Koene, B. A. S. (2006) 'Situated human agency, institutional entrepreneurship and institutional change', *Journal of Organizational Change Management*, 19, pp. 365–382.
Kraatz, M. and Moore, J. (2002) 'Executive migration and institutional change', *Academy of Management Journal*, 45(1), pp. 120–143.
Krauss, M. D. (2014) 'Equipment innovations and rules changes in sports', *Current Sports Medicine Reports*, 3(5), pp. 272–276.
Kwon, S. W. and Adler, P. S. (2014) 'Social capital: Maturation of a field of research', *The Academy of Management Review*, 39(4), pp. 412–422.
LaRue, J. (2019) *Handsome Dan: A 130-year-old legacy*. Available at: https://news.yale.edu/2019/07/03/handsome-dan-130-year-old-legacy (Accessed: 25 May 2024).
Levine, P. (1984) *A. G. Spalding: A flamboyant entrepreneur, empire builder*. Available at: https://sabr.org/journal/article/a-g-spalding-a-flamboyant-entrepreneur-empire-builder-business-missionary-motives-behind-1888-89-world-tour/ (Accessed: 23 May 2024).
Levine, P. (1985) *A. G. Spalding and the rise of baseball: The promise of American sport*. Oxford University Press.
Levy, D. and Scully, M. (2007) 'The institutional entrepreneur as modern prince: The strategic face of power in contested fields', *Organization Studies*, 28(7), pp. 971–991.
Lewis II, R. F. (2011) 'Spalding, Albert', in S.A. Riess (ed.), *Sports in America from colonial times to the twenty-first Century: An encyclopedia*. Taylor & Francis Group, pp. 844–846.
Light, J. F. (2005) 'Spalding Sporting Goods', in *The cultural encyclopedia of baseball*, 2nd ed. McFarland and Company, Incorporated Publishers, p. 863.
Lin, N. (2008) 'A network theory of social capital', in D. Castiglione, J. W. Van Deth, and G. Wolleb (eds.), *The handbook of social capital*. Oxford University Press, pp. 50–69.
Linehan, M. (2023) *Spirit owner Michele Kang sets vision for future of women's soccer with new global football group*. Available at: https://www.nytimes.com/athletic/4525051/2023/05/16/spirit-nwsl-michele-kang-lyon-global/ (Accessed 25 May 2024).
Littlefield, B. (2007) *Only a game*. Lincoln: University of Nebraska Press.
Lok, J. and De Rond, M. (2013) 'On the plasticity of institutions: Containing and restoring practice breakdowns at the Cambridge University Boat Club', *Academy of Management Journal*, 56(1), pp. 185–207.
Love, A. and Kim, S. (2019) 'Organizational citizenship behavior in sport: A perspective from athletes', *Journal of Sport Management*, 33, pp. 25–36.
Lu, L. D. and Heinze, K. L. (2021) 'Examining institutional entrepreneurship in the passage of youth sport concussion legislation', *Journal of Sport Management*, 35(1), pp. 1–16.

Maguire, S. Hardy, C., and Lawrence, T. B. (2004) 'Institutional entrepreneurship in emerging fields: HIV/AIDS treatment advocacy in Canada', *Academy of Management Journal*, 47(5), pp. 657–679.

Mankowski, D. J. (2018) 'Sport organizations and environmental pressures: An institutional analysis', *Society Register*, 2(1), pp. 155–170.

Markowitz, L. (2007) Structural innovators and coreframing tasks: How socially responsible mutual fund companies build identity among investors', *Sociological Perspectives*, 50(1), pp. 131–153.

Melville, T. (2020) 'Cricket and Mr. Spalding', in B. Nowlin, M. Armour, S. Bush, L. Heaphy, J. Pomrenke, C. Tan, and J. Thorn (eds.), *SABR 50 at 50: The society for American Baseball research's fifty most essential contributions to the game*. Lincoln: University of Nebraska Press, pp. 213–219.

Michele Kang: Founder and Chief Executive Officer (n.d.) Available at: https://cognosante.com/leadership/michele-kang (Accessed: 23 May 2024).

Morris, P. (2010) 'What ever happened to baseball history?: Keynote speech to the Sixteenth Annual *NINE* Spring training conference', *NINE: A Journal of Baseball History and Culture*, 18, pp. 1–10.

Morrison, A. (2006) 'A contextualisation of entrepreneurship', *International Journal of Entrepreneurial Behaviour and Research*, 12(4), pp. 192–209.

Nite, C., Abiodun, I., and Washington, M. (2019) 'The evolving institutional work of the National Collegiate Athletic Association to maintain dominance in a fragmented field', *Sport Management Review*, 22(3), pp. 379–394.

Nite, C. and Edwards, J. (2021) 'From isomorphism to institutional work: Advancing institutional theory in sport management research', *Sport Management Review*, 24(5), pp. 815–838.

Nite, C., McLeod, C. M., Beldon, Z., and Nauright, J. (2020) 'Establishing a professional Rugby Union Football league in the USA: Managing institutional pluralism in sport entrepreneurship', *Sport Management Review*, 23(5), pp. 883–897.

New York Times (2023) *Spirit owner Michele Kang joins OL Groupe to create new global women's football organization* Available at: https://www.nytimes.com/athletic/4524551/2023/05/16/michele-kang-ol-groupe-lyon/ (Accessed: 23 May 2024).

Organ, D. W. (1997) 'Organizational citizenship behavior: It's construct clean-up time', *Human Performance*, 10(2), pp. 85–97.

Organ, D. W. and Ryan, K. (1995) 'A meta-analytic review of attitudinal and dispositional predictors of organizational citizenship behavior', *Personnel Psychology*, 48(4), pp. 775–802.

Pacheco, D. F., York, J. G., Dean, T. J., and Sarasvathy, S. D. (2010) 'The coevolution of institutional entrepreneurship: A tale of two theories', *Journal of Management*, 36(4), pp. 974–1010.

Penn State (2024) *The origin of the Nittany Lion*. Available at: https://www.psu.edu/news/campus-life/story/origin-nittany-lion/ (Accessed: 26 May 2024).

Polacek, S. (2024) *Tennis legend Venus Williams among athletes to be honored with Barbie dolls*. Available at: https://bleacherreport.com/articles/10122332-tennis-legend-venus-williams-among-athletes-to-be-honored-with-barbie-dolls (Accessed: 24 May 2024).

Quan, Z., Qian, W., and Mao, J. (2024) 'The impact of mascot attributes on sponsorship effectiveness the case of "Bing Dwen Dwen" at the Beijing winter Olympics', *Asia Pacific Journal of Marketing and Logistics*, 36(4), pp. 1024–1042.

Ratten, V. (2010) 'Developing a theory of sport-based entrepreneurship', *Journal of Management and Organization*, 16(4), pp. 557–565.

Ratten, V. (2011) 'Sport-based entrepreneurship: Towards a new theory of entrepreneurship and sport management', *International Entrepreneurship and Management Journal*, 7(1), pp. 57–69.

Rielly, E. J. (2000) *Baseball: An encyclopedia of popular culture.* ABC-CLIO, pp. 280–281.

Robertson, J., Dowling, M., Washington, M., Leopkey, B., Ellis, D. L., and Smith, L. (2022) 'Institutional theory in sport: A scoping review', *Journal of Sport Management*, 36(5), pp. 459–472.

Robertson, J., Storr, R., Bakos, A., and O'Brien, D. (2019) '"My ideal is where it is just Jane the cricketer, rather than Jane the gay cricketer": An institutional perspective of lesbian inclusion in Australian Cricket', *Journal of Sport Management*, 33(5), pp. 393–405.

Santomier, J. (2002) 'Sport business entrepreneurship', *New England Journal of Entrepreneurship*, 5(1), pp. 5–7.

Sartore-Baldwin, M. and McCullough, B. (2021) 'Examining sport fans and the endangered species who represent their affiliated team mascots', *Society and Animals*, 29(3), pp. 268–86.

Schultz, B. and Sheffer, M. L. (2018) 'The mascot that wouldn't die: A case study of fan identification and mascot loyalty', *Sport in Society*, 21(3), pp. 482–496.

Schumpeter, J. A. (1934) *The theory of economic development.* Harvard University Press.

Shea, B. (2018) 'Money-making mascots; the cute, sweaty secret weapon for pro sports teams', *Crain's Detroit Business*, 34(36), pp. 10–20.

Skiver, K. (2024) *Indy 500 milk tradition, explained: Why does the Indianapolis 500 winner drink milk?* Available at: https://www.msn.com/en-us/sports/other/indy-500-milk-tradition-explained-why-does-the-indianapolis-500-winner-drink-milk/ar-AAXQtCD?ocid=BingNewsSerp (Accessed 24 May 2024).

Slowikowski, S. S. (1993) 'Cultural performance and sport mascots', *Journal of Sport and Social Issues*, 17(1), pp. 23–33.

Smart, B. (2005) *The sport star: Modern sport and the cultural economy of sporting celebrity.* SAGE Publications.

Sports Business Journal (2018) *Twenty for 20: Most influential sports executives.* Available at: https://www.sportsbusinessjournal.com/Journal/Issues/2018/04/30/People-and-Pop-Culture/Most-Influential.aspx (Accessed: 27 May 2024).

Srivastava, R. K. (2021) 'Effectiveness of films, sport, celebrity or mascot to content in the advertising – a dilemma for global brands', *Journal of Promotion Management*, 27(5), pp. 716–739.

Stamp, J. (2013) *A brief history of baseball.* Available at: https://www.smithsonianmag.com/arts-culture/a-brief-history-of-the-baseball-3685086/ (Accessed: 23 May 2024).

Stewart, S. and Giles, D. (2020) 'Celebrity status and the attribution of value', *European Journal of Cultural Studies*, 23(1), pp. 3–17.

Sweitzer, K. (2009) 'Sports mascots', in E. F. Provenzo Jr. and A. B. Provenzo (eds.), *Encyclopedia of the social and cultural foundations of education 2.* Thousand Oaks, CA: SAGE Publications, pp. 751–754.

Taranto, S. (2022) *Indy 500: How the tradition of the winner drinking milk in Victory Lane began.* Available at: https://www.cbssports.com/motor-sports/news/indy-500-how-the-tradition-of-the-winner-drinking-milk-in-victory-lane-began/ (Accessed: 24 May 2024).

Taeuscher, K., Bouncken, R., and Pesch, R. (2021) 'Gaining legitimacy by being different: Optimal distinctiveness in crowdfunding platforms', *Academy of Management Journal*, 64(1), pp. 149–179.

Thomas, J. D. (2002, March 24). 'Choking, groping and emoting: You think it's easy being a jester?' *The New York Times.*

Tiberius, V., Rietz, M., and Bouncken, R. B. (2020) 'Performance analysis and science mapping of institutional entrepreneurship research', *Administrative Sciences* 10(3), pp. 1–21.

Tresolini, K. (2024) *Celebrate the stalk: Blue Rocks 'Mr. Celery voted a top mascot*. Available at: https://www.delawareonline.com/story/sports/2024/03/21/mr-celery-the-dressed-as-a-stalk-mascot-who-pops-out-from-behind-the-backstop-after-every-rocks-run/73044584007/ (Accessed: 22 May 2024).

Turner, T. (2019) *The sports shoe: A history from field to fashion*. Bloomsbury Publishing.

USA Hockey (n.d.) *History of the goalie mask*. USA Hockey Magazine. Available at: https://www.usahockeymagazine.com/article/history-goalie-mask (Accessed: 23 May 2024).

Washington, M. (2004) 'Field approaches to institutional change: The evolution of the National Collegiate Athletic Association 1906–1995', *Organization Studies*, 25(3), pp. 393–414.

Washington, M. and Patterson, K. D. W. (2011) 'Hostile takeover or joint venture: Connections between institutional theory and sport management research', *Sport Management Review*, 14(1), pp. 1–12.

Weber, B. (2011) *The prehistory of baseball*. Available at: https://www.nytimes.com/2011/04/10/books/review/book-review-baseball-in-the-garden-of-eden-by-john-thorn.html (Accessed: 28 September 2023).

Wilco, D. (2024) *Why basketball teams cut down the nets*. Available at: https://www.ncaa.com/news/basketball-men/article/2019-03-30/why-basketball-teams-cut-down-nets (Accessed: 24 May 2024).

Wolff, A. and Stone, C. (1995) 'Mascot mayhem', *Sports Illustrated*, 82(8), February 27.

World Wiffle Ball Championship. (no date) Available at: https://worldwiffleball.org/ (Accessed: 24 May 2024).

Wright, A. L. and Zammuto, R. F. (2013) 'Creating opportunities for institutional entrepreneurship: The colonel and the cup in English county cricket', *Journal of Business Venturing*, 28(1), pp. 51–68.

Wulf, S. (2009) *ESPN: The mighty book of sports knowledge*. Random House Publishing Group.

Zilber, T. B. (2007) 'Stories and the discursive dynamics of institutional entrepreneurship: The case of Israeli high-tech after the bubble', *Organization Studies*, 28, pp. 1035–1054.

Zimmerman, M. A. and Zeitz, G. J. (2002) 'Beyond survival: Achieving new venture growth by building legitimacy', *The Academy of Management Review*, 27(3), pp. 414–431.

11 Entrepreneurship in the arts and cultural sectors

The role of the intermediary

James Cunningham

Introduction

The creative industries provide a context of entrepreneurship which is both economically important and culturally complex. While broader definitions of the creative industries include any enterprise with its origin in individual creativity, skill, and talent (Department for Digital, Culture, Media & Sport, 2022), this can often cast the net so wide that understandings of creative entrepreneurial processes become generic and meaningless. Instead of contenting with such a broad scope, this chapter specifically considers arts and cultural production, as a site of unique entrepreneurial tension and contextual sensitivity within the creative sectors. The nature and role of entrepreneurship in the arts and cultural sectors is investigated, as we look to uncover how entrepreneurial processes manifest to establish economic and societal impact.

The Centre for Economics and Business Research estimates that arts and cultural activities contribute £13.5 billion to the UK economy through direct taxation and employment (CEBR, 2020). However, much of the literature looking to the arts sectors posits a conflict between the idealized craft of artistic endeavor and the economic management of artistic output (Eikhof & Haunschild, 2006; Phillips, 2011). Entrepreneurship in this context becomes a mechanism to bridge the artistic and the economic (Swedberg, 2006). Often, this is framed as a skills issue, where the burden is put on the artist to develop entrepreneurial skills such as marketing, sales, and the identification of trending opportunities (Thom, 2016; Fillis, 2004). Such a focus on the individual creator is intuitive, evoking parallels between an artist's career trajectory and what we consider archetypal entrepreneurs (Fillis & Rentschler, 2010). We expect both artist and entrepreneur to take risks, to build distinctive identity, and to produce for an imagined future state (Shepherd & Haynie, 2009). But there is tension here. Chaston and Sadler-Smith (2012) point out that conventional thinking on entrepreneurship does not take account of the contextual pressures and social complexities commonly faced in the creative sectors. If we argue for individual artists-as-entrepreneurs, we are led to linear economic explanations (Anderson, 2015), convincing us to look

DOI: 10.4324/9781003324737-11

for evidence of entrepreneurial growth and opportunity exploitation. However, such a singular value construction does little to help us understand how complex social arrangements are navigated by those engaging with artistic creation.

In this chapter, I argue that an economic and individualized approach to understanding entrepreneurship in the arts and cultural sectors is limited, as it does not take account of the unique character of this form of enterprise. I look to more recent understandings of entrepreneurship, which consider the networked and social context of entrepreneurial situations (Anderson et al., 2010), to examine how entrepreneurial processes unfold in the arts and cultural sectors. In elucidating the arguments, I identify the role of the 'intermediary', presented as an entrepreneurial agent which straddles the worlds of the artistic and the commercially economic. This is not necessarily an artist, but a role which works with artists to sustain the broader sector. Such figures play an important part in creative production; beyond individualized motivations and a desire for economic gain, they provide both a compass and a vehicle for artistic production (Cunningham & Tolonen, 2019).

The chapter offers three practical examples of the intermediary: *the retailer*, *the festival* organizer, and *the gallery* owner. Ethnographic insight from one spatial location, a small rural town, provides empirical data on the variety of intermediary activities in the community. Importantly, this chapter does not focus on the creators of artistic work themselves, but instead looks to the socialized mechanisms that bring artistic work to broader society. The chapter explains that economic imperatives are often far from the minds of our entrepreneurial intermediaries (Caves, 2000), but that relational and cultural considerations are what bring the role into being. Framed as such, artistic and cultural entrepreneurship is not something which happens in, or is generated from, one individual, but is instead a phenomenon embedded within a community of shared values. These learnings join calls for a more nuanced understanding of entrepreneurship in all creative contexts. When entrepreneurial activity is characterized by craft, passion, and a unique sense of cultural importance, traditional views on economic growth and opportunity exploitation do little to help us understand it. By foregrounding the social connections of artistic production, we better see the implications and processual dynamics of entrepreneurship in this sector (Steyaert, 2007).

Entrepreneurship in the arts and cultural sectors

Before we begin a discussion on arts and cultural entrepreneurship, we must first address a definitional quandary. Literature on the broader creative sectors is host to some contentious and hotly debated notions. From the contrasting economic development views of Richard Florida (2002) and David Harvey (2002) to arguments around urban (re)generation and spatial clustering (Scott, 2008), the creative industries have become highly politicized, to the point of being combative

(Flew, 2013). Part of this contestation involves how the creative sectors, including arts and cultural activities, are defined. It is not the role or intention of this chapter to enter such debates, but it is important to offer a clear definitional trajectory at the outset. Since the mid-1990s, there has been some distinction made between what is creative and what is cultural, though from a policy perspective, these descriptions are often linked. In this chapter, I follow David Throsby's (2008a) nested view of core cultural and artistic activities as a point of origin, which inform broader areas of the creative economy. This is also the model adopted by the European Union in 2006 for a major study of the cultural and creative sectors of Europe (KEA European Affairs, 2006), and is echoed in the definitions used for the 2021–2027 Creative Europe program. In the nested view, often portrayed by concentric circles (Throsby, 2008b), cultural activities are core. Hesmondhalgh and Pratt (2005) explain that cultural, in this sense, has its main interest in the production of symbolic, aesthetic, and artistic value, generating output of human expression. For instance, visual and performance arts, literature, and music would represent original cultural production. Such activities directly inform and populate the culture-based industries, such as museums, galleries, and libraries. In turn, output from these core cultural elements impacts on wider and related creative sectors, such as publishing, advertising, and media production – which are more broadly defined. The expressive value at the cultural heart of this view is set apart as "activity related to self-expression, identity, a way of expressing something deeply human and of importance to society" (EPRS, 2019, p. 2). The outcome is a conceptual separation of the cultural and the creative, where cultural production focuses on the newness and imagination of the arts, and the creative makes use of this cultural production in a mechanized and industrious manner. We end up with a form of 'culture-based creativity' (KEA European Affairs, 2009).

Following Galloway and Dunlop (2007), the discussions of this chapter reject the 'everything is creative' view of enterprise in the economy. I do not attempt to cover the spectrum of the creative industries as a homogenized value chain, but instead look intentionally at the heart of cultural production, as the main site of imaginative entrepreneurship, responsible for generating a clarity of symbolic expression before the mechanics of creative industry take over. Throughout the chapter, I refer to this as the arts and cultural sectors, though the myriad of activities within and between these sectors is acknowledged, along with the dangers of entering an overly fragmented view (Pratt, 2008). That said, for the purposes of a discussion on the role of entrepreneurship, this setting is arguably the site with most contextual tension. The production of art and cultural craft is where artistic and economic logics meet and negotiate terms, which UNESCO (2005, p. 6) refer to as often "embody[ing] or convey[ing] cultural expressions, irrespective of the commercial value". There is no straightforward logic to the complexity of cultural production (Ryan, 1991). Where previously, the lineage from artistic endeavor to commodification of cultural production was lamented as a purely market force, now a more nuanced understanding of cultural and social value is offered (O'Connor, 2009). The very notion of entrepreneurship in this realm throws up several paradoxical images. As Caves (2000) highlights, individuals working in cultural production must deal with market uncertainty while striving for uniqueness, they must acknowledge the importance of non-economic drivers alongside the need for mundane enterprise procedures, and they must also navigate the collective nature of the broader industry while maintaining individual artistic expression. Combined, these issues paint a complex, even conflicted, entrepreneurial character.

The journey of an entrepreneur in the arts and cultural sectors is contrasted against our understanding of entrepreneurship more broadly. For artists and cultural producers, perceptions of success are not seen as financial, but rather personal – for example, personal satisfaction (Kuhn & Galloway, 2015), flexibility of approach (Danson et al., 2015), and a desire for independence (Tregear, 2005). Because of these non-economic motivations, 'artisan' entrepreneurship is often compartmentalized, even dismissed, as 'lifestyle' (Ivanycheva et al., 2023). Much of this desire to separate art and culture from mainstream entrepreneurship is built on traditional distinctions made by Carland et al. (1984), looking at what should and shouldn't be considered entrepreneurial, and ultimately establishing a limited focus on growth and wealth creation. In research terms, explanations of entrepreneurship as 'artisan' and 'lifestyle' seek reasons for those who do not follow the normative economic desire to exploit profitable opportunity (Shane & Venkataraman, 2000).

Once explained, we mistakenly feel we can write off artisans' economic impact, and so, under a dominant economic framing, such entrepreneurs become less interesting. However, we should note that the 'alternative' characteristics of artisan production can just as easily be found in entrepreneurs of any business activity (Welter et al., 2017). In fact, we could argue that those entrepreneurs who are purely growth and opportunity oriented represented an uncommon form of enterprise. Family businesses, community organizations, and social enterprises are all forms of entrepreneurial activity which are more socially and cultural driven, and unexplained by linear conceptions of growth and opportunity. As such, the dominance of an opportunity-growth lens should not be considered reflective of what entrepreneurship truly is, but instead reflective of what we, as researchers, have decided to look for in entrepreneurship. We have chosen to prioritize the economic and to explain away anything which does not fit this as different from our normalized expectations; in doing so, we neglect the deeper understandings necessary to see entrepreneurship in more complex settings, such as the arts and cultural sectors.

Entrepreneurship in the social context

For arts and cultural entrepreneurship, characterized as lifestyle, we tend to see the enterprise as rooted in the circumstances of the individual. This individualized approach neglects the very aspects which make entrepreneurship in this setting interesting, the cultural and social interactions which constitute value (Morrison, 2006). There is a social meaning attached to the arts and cultural industries (Markusen et al., 2008). Identities beyond that of the individual entrepreneur coalesce around cultural production due to its aesthetic and symbolic value (Hesmondhalgh & Pratt, 2005). As opposed to being characterized by individual lifestyle, artists and cultural producers are informed by the setting and reception of their work. Pret and Cogan (2019, p. 601) explain, "a place's culture, history, policies, and landscape play significant roles in shaping artisan entrepreneurship and vice versa". In this sense, entrepreneurs in the arts and cultural sectors must engage with the social setting, due to the very nature of their business offering.

As a result, Hoyte (2019) argues that art-based entrepreneurship is more exposed to community mindsets than the individualized notions of lifestyle choice would have us believe. Much of this comes down to the relationships which allow entrepreneurship to happen *in situ*. Left to their own devices, producers of art and cultural goods may not have the capacity to bring their products to market; it is the surrounding social structures which support and provide a vehicle for artistic creation. As such, our understanding of how entrepreneurship happens should move beyond individualized notions of artists-as-entrepreneurs and instead foreground the role of culture in how entrepreneurship is organized (Lounsbury et al., 2019). This brings us to the spatial setting of entrepreneurial activity and the close relationships held among those involved. It could be argued that arts and cultural markets are more spatially grounded than other sectors (Drake, 2003). Cultural factors form relational 'scenes', constructing a creative milieu (Lange, 2009). These scenes are made up of multiple actors, not the artist alone. Galleries, collectives, agents, event organizers, and related and non-related industries, all coalesce around collective expectations of what art should look like in the spatial setting. This forms what Cunningham and Tolonen (2019) see as a maintenance structure, socially constructing how activities are accepted and encouraged in the evolving entrepreneuring of a creative place (Anderson & Gaddefors, 2016).

For its part, the field of entrepreneurship has begun to loosen its methodological individualism and focus on how entrepreneurship is formed in context (Steyaert, 2007). Part of this considers the relational view, the interactions of the entrepreneur, and their social surroundings (Jóhannesson, 2012). These relational aspects are perhaps most clearly seen outside of the expected urban locations, in rural areas where formal support ecosystems and linear growth trajectories are limited, an entrepreneurship of the periphery (Anderson, 2000). For instance, rural entrepreneurship is found to interact with spatial context as a social space, optimizing the use of resources in the rural area, leveraging a re-connection with place through the entrepreneurial activities. The setting is not a passive backdrop, but an active element in the formation of entrepreneurial activities and character (Korsgaard et al., 2015). With this understanding, entrepreneurship is best viewed as nested in the complex and dynamic relationships of the locale (McKeever et al., 2015). It is in understanding these relationships that knowledge of entrepreneurship can be gained.

The remainder of this chapter looks to just that, the relational processes of arts and cultural production in place. A vivid picture is constructed of how entrepreneurship occurs as a relational process, clearer and more holistic than that which can be achieved through individualized views alone. In particular, the role of the intermediary in the arts and cultural sectors is highlighted as crucial in the process, enabling entrepreneurial activity, and ensuring art and cultural production is brought to the broader community.

The place-based intermediaries

To introduce and understand the role of arts and cultural sector intermediaries, in the following sections I present three distinct examples: *the retailer*, *the festival*, and *the gallery*. These roles have been identified through ethnographic-style observation of arts and cultural production in a small rural town on the coast of north–east Scotland, UK (population of just over 10,000 and 15 miles outside of the nearest urban district). Empirical materials are taken directly from key stakeholders within each of the intermediary roles, along with informal observation data and any relevant documentary evidence available, such as web content and press coverage – pseudonyms are used to preserve anonymity of town, businesses, and individuals. The analysis is interpretivist in approach, drawing on the reflexive traditions of qualitative field-research (Alvesson & Kärreman, 2007; Alvesson & Sköldberg, 2018). As the main researcher, I have spent time in the research site, focusing on the presentation of arts and cultural production and the various relationships which exist. Over a four-year period, I maintained close interactions with each of those involved. Once the three articulations of the intermediary were identified, this led to focused interviews with key stakeholders. In such a way, this work may be seen as a case study of place. The setting of a rural and coastal town offers a location on the periphery of entrepreneurial support and infrastructure, a location in which entrepreneurial activities are especially shaped by the character of the local context (Gaddefors & Anderson, 2019). Additionally, as a coastal town of seasonal tourism, arts and cultural production are at the heart of the cyclical enterprise activity experienced each year (Guerreiro et al., 2019). In such a setting, individual entrepreneurs are found to rely on bricolage behaviors to mobilize and develop the resources local to them (Yachin & Ioannides, 2020; Korsgaard et al., 2021), forcing them into relational interactions.

The following three sections take each intermediary role in turn. While the presentation of these roles makes use of empirical ethnographic data, this is supplemented with broader theoretical insight in a constant-comparative manner (Anderson & Jack, 2015). This follows recent ethnographic work in rural settings (e.g., Haugh, 2022) by seeking plausible articulations of the role each intermediary plays in the broader system of arts and cultural production. The chapter argues for the applicability of 'the intermediary' as a socialized theoretical construct in arts and cultural production, seen most clearly in this tightly held empirical setting.

The retailer: Adored Oasis

Adored Oasis is a small independent store in the town, run by Paula and her husband Stuart. Both the store and Paula were featured in the local press, in the summer of 2023, where it was described as a "hub for local crafters", a "treasure trove" of pottery, trinkets, paintings, fabric items, and even some artisan food stuff. A large part of the store is dedicated to products created by Paula, bespoke earrings, but the rest of the store space is made available for other producers who either rent shelves at a fixed cost or have their work displayed in the store on a commission basis. The physical location of the store is adjacent to the town center, outside of the normal pedestrian routes. Paula puts a lot of their custom down to "word of mouth spreading", but also, there is an artisan coffee shop and a candlemaker on the same street, creating a draw for those seeking crafted products.

Small-scale retail may be the most traditional medium of the arts to market interface, yet there appears scant literature on how this form of entrepreneurship functions. Where the concept of retail is in focus, discussions tend to highlight an increasing need for artists to develop retail and marketing skills of their own; for example, Baym (2015) and Whitson et al. (2021) consider the demands placed on independent music producers to undertake each element of the industry value chain. This newly pragmatic and self-contained approach to artisan production puts creators in charge of their own output (Booth & Røyseng, 2022), however, it also adds responsibility to artists, who are often ill-equipped to deal with such expectations (Win, 2014). From such conversations, one would be forgiven for thinking retailers in the arts and cultural sectors have been made redundant. However, for Paula and her store, the value of the store is not solely as a retailer, but also as an empathetic support, as she explains:

> I have been what I would call a hobby crafter pretty much since I was a teenager. I always wanted to turn it into something that could support me and my family . . . I noticed especially over the last three or four years that community and shopping, shopping small, independent, local, has become a lot more important to people. . . . So, when I was in a position to open up our own shop selling my handcrafted products, I thought that it would be an ideal opportunity to showcase other talent in the area. I also didn't want the shop to be too niche.
>
> The crafting community is full of amazing, generous kind individuals who helped me and encouraged me as I started out. It was these ones that I thought

> of when I decided I wanted to share the shop space. . . . For makers, the time and effort needed to put into making a quality item can often be so high that you can't actually recoup your time in monetary value. . . . the beauty of a shop like mine is that they only need to fill a shelf or a small space with as many items as they want.

From the little research work that has been done in this area, arts and cultural retailers are found to be small and owner managed, like *Adored Oasis*, and are often classed as 'micro-retail' (Paige, 2009). As with individual producers, they are driven by a passion for the craft itself. For example, Paige and Littrell (2002) explain that measures of strategic success for such retailers emanate from an intrinsic passion and a desire to encourage this in others, along with an acute connection to localized craft traditions. Paula mirrors this drive with *Adored Oasis*.

Here we have something of a bridge between artistic and cultural creation, normally rooted in artistic ideologies (Fillis, 2006), and a consumer orientation in the retailer. The intermediary role is needed to make the marketplace a success (Gupta et al., 2021). However, there is also an interdependency, an understanding that the work done will be mutually beneficial. For an artist, being stocked in *Adored Oasis* provides a legitimizing function, acting a distributor of the cultural goods of others. However, this is coupled with the need for the store to have a product range to display. Paula explains how the process works:

> With regards to those that showcase their items in our shop, I visited and still visit craft fairs and look at the quality of the items being offered, the price point they're selling at and speak to the crafters themselves to see whether they can consistently make products so that stock levels in the shop don't drop too low. . . . As much as possible, we give priority to local crafters, local makers before looking for other Scottish handmade items. We also try to limit the type of craft or product so that even within that niche there is less competition for them.

Paula is one of three self-defined independent retailers of arts and cultural goods in the town. Each follow a similar pattern, in that the store contains some of their own productions, along with those of selected others, normally local to the area. There is an optimism, in that artists will "have their products in the shop sometimes for the first time ever", and this opportunity "will also help their business grow, that they build up some kind of brand recognition".

The festival: Beag Tachartas

Beag Tachartas, a play on words from Scots Gaelic which loosely means 'small event', is a poetry festival running annually in the town. The festival was founded in 2021 and prides itself on being an open event for poets to read and perform their work, a "platform for poets", as the website information suggests. While the main event runs over two or three days in the summer, satellite events, such as workshops and monthly reading groups, run throughout the year. All of the festival's activities are located in the town, but poets travel from all parts of the UK and Ireland to take part.

Partly, the festival was born of a frustration with elitist and urban structures in the more established poetry circles. The temporary coming together of like-minded poets and poetry fans represents an evolution, and reconfiguration, of these norms (Lampel & Meyer, 2008). This produces an intensive activity with multiple contextual elements (Quinn, 2005). There is a purposeful call to poets outside of the local area, to come and visit the town and engage in the shared cultural activity, as Keith, the founder of the event, explains:

> It's a gathering of poets from all over Scotland, and as far afield as we can go. It's an open invitation for poets to take part in the festival, to read and share their work . . . we don't select the poets.

Again, an empathetic and supportive drive is noted in the origins of the enterprise, with Keith going on to reflect:

> Poetry has a history which I am trying to keep alive in this wee corner of the earth . . . [but] in my own background, the only access to poetry was in the public library, and poetry was seen as something that was done by others . . . there is a strong feeling that lots of regions in Scotland are being neglected [culturally].

More than half of the poets come from outside of the local region, bringing visitors into the area, "most of them take two days, make a weekend of it". As with *Adored Oasis*, there is a focus on those who may struggle to present their wares in other settings, "there is no type [of poet], certainly not people who earn a living, as very few do anyway, certainly [the event has] very few of the more established names in Scottish poetry – because it's not for them anyway". Duxbury and Campbell (2011) speak of how arts events can develop rural communities, which we see in the attraction of visitors, but we also see a development of the cultural field itself. Those previously excluded now have an avenue to present their work.

When speaking of the positive reaction the town has shown to a new arts festival, Keith suspects that "people were just desperate for something to happen . . . and looking for this little chink in a window whereby they could engage in the alchemy of this social communal activity". But there is also a practical consideration, which places the festival in the more conventionally economic imperatives of other businesses who rely on outside custom (Robertson & Wardrop, 2014). Keith explains the impact on other businesses as follows:

> [The main venue] tends to be the quiet place on the peripheral of the town center, it looks a bit 1970s inside, but they need their income. I think [the second venue] was just enthusiastic about expanding its activities, I think, like a lot of these places, these venues, they are very keen to be seen doing these kinds of things to justify their existence, because they are under threat.

This is the second large-scale arts festival the town holds annually, the other being a folk music festival which has taken place since 1989. Keith is clear on the need for such activities, not only to support the development of arts and cultural producers, but also to ensure a sustainable vibrancy in the town:

> I am hostage to what is available, but [if the festival doesn't happen] then you don't have a cultural phenomenon taking place, you don't have all the invisible economy that happens, you don't have all these people travelling to it, you don't have all the reputation that's generated when people go away and talk about it. The hotels don't get the pre-bookings, the bars don't get the takings, the restaurants don't get the orders. The people who do come here, they spend quite a bit of money.

The gallery: Outpost Architecture, Ltd.

Our final intermediary is a privately run business, *Outpost Architecture, Ltd. Outpost* may arguably be in the creative industries themselves (Galloway & Haniff, 2015), particularly following broader arguments that creative industry work has become subsumed into a wider knowledge economy (Foord, 2009). However, in this case, the architecture firm plays a more direct role in the arts and cultural sectors of the town. The ground floor and street-facing side of *Outpost*'s offices are made available to individual cultural producers as exhibition and/or retail space. Promoted as "an exciting pop-up venue which provides a showcase for some of the area's most talented creative businesses", exhibitors are taken in for either a week or a month, on a rental basis, within a purposefully designed space which is shared with up to three other exhibitors. Lacie, managing director of *Outpost Architecture*, explains the origins of the idea:

> We purchased the building several years ago in order to have more space for the architecture business. I never intended to have the office on the ground floor; it is too important for a small town to retain its retail space which

> contributes to the vibrancy and vitality of the high street. However, I wanted to retain control of the space and not rent it out permanently, so a pop-up venue was a good solution. I wanted the pop-up to provide space for businesses compatible with mine, ideally creative businesses who might share a similar client base to me, creating a mutually beneficial relationship.

It may be easy to cast *Outpost* as a conventional gallery, and for the purposes of this chapter, the title fits. This is a space which is offered to creators with *Outpost* acting as the gatekeeper, a sharer of resources and opportunity (Grodach, 2011). However, in contrast to what we see with cash-strapped semi-public arts institutions, *Outpost* is a successful business located in the middle of the town. Further, the normalized processes of legitimacy building, with entrepreneurial artists looking for galleries to champion them (Kackovic & Wijnberg, 2022), are more open here. It seems that *Outpost* provides the opportunity of a platform, rather than the chance of being part of a curated collection.

> In the beginning we tried to select; however, in practice we rarely turn people away so that we keep the space busy. The pop up has been used as a testing ground/launchpad for several businesses who have gone on to rent permanent bricks and mortar shops in the town. It has also allowed artists/creatives not used to exhibiting to grow their network. The most important issue for me is that the people approach their business with a professional attitude. . . . The entrance to my own business is through the shop, so it is important to me that the space looks good . . . artists have grown their network, been noticed by [established] galleries, sold work direct to the public and gained helpful feedback. Sometimes new businesses have tested the retail environment for the first time, some small businesses have tried it out and then gone on to grow their business into a permanent shop of their own.

There are echoes of entrepreneurial co-creation in how an independently successful business provides a platform for others in ostensibly unrelated industries (Shams & Kaufmann, 2016). Certainly, how arts and cultural production is being brought to the public consciousness of the town is best understood holistically. Without the prime location and space of *Outpost*, exhibitors would have limited opportunity to be in the windows of a high-street storefront. This relationship is reciprocal, and the implications are noted by Lacie:

> For my own business, the pop-up has created a lot of good will in the town, it helps to advertise my own business and so it has a marketing benefit to me. . . . The town has gained several new permanent businesses which helps the local economy. The pop up is very well supported locally and is a very popular addition to the town, helping to keep the town center vibrant and inviting.

Discussion and conclusions: contextualising arts and cultural entrepreneurship

This chapter set out to explore the socialized nature of entrepreneurship, as manifest in the arts and cultural sectors. To elucidate these arguments, the role of the intermediary is introduced and explored, highlighting the critical function of these entrepreneurial outfits, as they connect artistic creation with the broader market. Such notions have been discussed previously in the literature, where entrepreneurial activities are seen to build a bridge between idealized notions of craft and the practical realities of economic management (Eikhof & Haunschild, 2006; Swedberg, 2006). However, economic explanations of entrepreneurship in the arts and culture sectors only give us a very limited picture. As Chaston and Sadler-Smith (2012) suggest, we tend to characterize the creative industries by the value of labor inputs from individual creators, assuming some form of linear trajectory from artistic creation to market impact. This chapter argues that the liner and unilateral view of artist-as-entrepreneur is over-simplified and neglects the socialized nature of that arts and cultural sectors. The three forms of intermediary presented in this chapter do not offer such simplistic accounts. Instead, we find a role deeply embedded in cultural and spatial understanding, where the enterprise itself has emerged from a place of empathetic support for fellow artists, and an acute awareness of their impact on the spatial setting. A socialized perspective brought these relationships to the fore, through which the arts and cultural sectors operate, which in turn allows us to see more clearly contextual complexities as they are encountered in practice. By focusing on those at the intersection of artistic creation and societal reception, we address the need for more processual understanding of how entrepreneurship occurs across the broader system of artistic production, through multiple actors and at multiple levels, as called for by Steyaert (2007).

One of the first complexities offered questions the characterization of cultural producers as entrepreneurs. It can be an easy solution to classify those involved in arts and cultural productions as individual 'lifestyle' entrepreneurs (Ivanycheva et al., 2023). Entrepreneurial success is then determined by the capabilities of the individual. However, through the role of intermediaries, those who would have struggled to gain a place are offered a channel to deliver their creations. This is not always an economic arrangement, though in the case of *Adored Oasis* it is a retail location and, therefore, a more direct implication of sales. But more importantly, each of the intermediaries talks of building a platform. They look to create opportunity, not for direct economic gain, but for exposure and in some cases offering legitimacy to others through selection. *Outpost* terms this a 'showcase'. So, while not taking responsibility for individual creators' success, they assume a responsibility for opening possibilities. The importance of playing their part in an open and creative culture is clear. There is a sharing of the pressure to sustain cultural production and provide support to those who are rightfully more focused on their craft, something opportunity scholars may call a 'co-construction of opportunity' (Shepherd et al., 2019). Here, however, we see that a hybridity of artistic and market logic occurs across the social relationship, not in one entrepreneurial individual.

For the intermediaries themselves, their initiative stems from an empathetic support. Each is present in the creative industries. Both the founder of *Beag Tachartas* and the owner of *Adored Oasis* are themselves active in the same cultural domain as those they are supporting. Though *Outpost* is arguably in a more knowledge-based creative industry, architecture, there is a sympathetic understanding of the needs of their craft-focused exhibitors. Empathy with others in the same cultural scene allows the intermediaries to build appropriate support, but also, there is a developmental aspect to the role they perform. This advances what Cunningham and Tolonen (2019) found with art-based intermediaries in the urban setting, such as galleries, when they assume a responsibility for accepting, or rejecting, artistic works based on their own ideological perceptions of quality. In addition to this, here we see something else, an active support for producers which is intended to develop them further. For instance, *Outpost* expects a level of professionalism from their exhibitors, and *Adored Oasis* looks for reassurances on production volumes and quality. For *Beag Tachartas*, there are structured workshops and smaller-scale events, a form of training before potentially taking part in the main festival. It seems that, in this small-town setting, cultural intermediaries assume the position of entrepreneurial mentor, or role model (Bosma et al., 2012), tempering a fear of failure by creating both an accepting and developmental environment (Wyrwich et al., 2016). While not an explicit argument of this chapter, it is curious that without the structured entrepreneurial support ecosystems of an urban setting, the social relationships of the rural organically mimic these elements.

We have focused so far on the intermediaries' relationships with the arts and cultural producers, but given the nature of creative and cultural work, the spatial place also becomes an active element in how entrepreneurial activity occurs. Often, how this relationship takes place is framed in economic language. A festival brings bookings for hotels, a retailer serves demand for local products, a 'gallery' provides additional entrepreneurial supply, diversifying the economic mix. Each of the intermediaries shows a desire to add something to the town. Though the enterprises rely on local resources, the vibrancy and energy associated with each "cultural phenomenon" (Keith, *Beag Tachartas*) re-connects the enterprise to the spatial context (Korsgaard et al., 2015) in a reciprocal and interdependent relationship. Thus, arts and cultural entrepreneurship does not simply happen in its spatial context but becomes part of its spatial context.

Finally, from this ethnographic account of one small rural town, we cannot claim that the three intermediaries identified are exhaustive; this is not intended as a typology. But rather, as an account of the importance of relationships, we can see the socialized processes of entrepreneurship in the arts and cultural sectors. It would be unrealistic to expect entrepreneurship in this setting, and among these contexts, to exist in one person. Instead, it is in the process of entrepreneurial activities passed between individual enterprises that the arts and cultural sectors provide their impact. Future work in this area should focus less on the individual skills of artists-as-entrepreneurs and more on the social processes of cultural creativity.

References

Alvesson, M. & Kärreman, D. (2007). "Constructing mystery: Empirical matters in theory development." *Academy of Management Review* 32(4): 1265–1281.

Alvesson, M. & Sköldberg, K. (2018). *Reflexive methodology: New vistas for qualitative research*. 3rd ed. Sage Publishing, Ltd.

Anderson, A. R. (2000). "Paradox in the periphery: An entrepreneurial reconstruction?" *Entrepreneurship & Regional Development* 12(2): 91–109.

Anderson, A. R. (2015). "Conceptualising entrepreneurship as economic 'explanation' and the consequent loss of 'understanding'." *International Journal of Business and Globalisation* 14(2): 145–157.

Anderson, A. R., Dodd, S. D. & Jack, S. (2010). "Network practices and entrepreneurial growth." *Scandinavian Journal of Management* 26(2): 121–133.

Anderson, A. R. & Gaddefors, J. (2016). "Entrepreneurship as a community phenomenon; reconnecting meanings and place." *International Journal of Entrepreneurship and Small Business* 28(4): 504–518.

Anderson, A. R. & Jack, S. L. (2015). "An introduction to the constant comparative technique." In H. Neergaard & C. M. Leitch (eds.), *Handbook of qualitative research techniques and analysis in entrepreneurship*. Edward Elgar Publishing, pp. 15–20.

Baym, N. K. (2015). "Connect with your audience! The relational labor of connection." *The Communication Review* 18(1): 14–22.

Booth, P. & Røyseng, S. (2022). "Artists and online dissemination: An analysis of positions and position-takings." *The Journal of Arts Management, Law, and Society* 52(4): 266–285.

Bosma, N., Hessels, J., Schutjens, V., Van Praag, M. & Verheul, I. (2012). "Entrepreneurship and role models." *Journal of Economic Psychology* 33(2): 410–424.

Carland, J. W., Hoy, F., Boulton, W. R. & Carland, J. A. C. (1984). "Differentiating entrepreneurs from small business owners: A conceptualization." *Academy of Management Review* 9(2): 354–359.

Caves, R. (2000). *Creative industries: Contacts between art and commerce*. Harvard University Press.

CEBR (2020). *Contribution of the arts and culture industry to the UK economy*. Centre for Economics and Business Research on behalf of the Arts Council England. Available at: https://www.artscouncil.org.uk/ (Accessed: 15 November 2022).

Chaston, I., & Sadler-Smith, E. (2012). "Entrepreneurial cognition, entrepreneurial orientation and firm capability in the creative industries." *British Journal of Management* 23(3): 415–432.

Cunningham, J. & Tolonen, K. M. (2019). "Maintaining the scene: Entrepreneurship in Berlin's artistic sectors." *International Journal of Entrepreneurship and Small Business* 37(4): 492–512.

Danson, M., Galloway, L., Cabras, I. & Beatty, T. (2015). "Microbrewing and entrepreneurship: The origins, development and integration of real ale breweries in the UK." *The International Journal of Entrepreneurship and Innovation* 16(2): 135–144.

Department for Digital, Culture, Media & Sport (2022) "DCMS sector economic estimates methodology." Available at: https://www.gov.uk/government/publications/dcms-sectors-economic-estimates-methodology/dcms-sector-economic-estimates-methodology (Accessed: 10 September 2023).

Drake, G. (2003). " 'This place gives me space': Place and creativity in the creative industries." *Geoforum* 34(4): 511–524.

Duxbury, N. & Campbell, H. (2011). "Developing and revitalizing rural communities through arts and culture." *Small Cities Imprint* 3(1).

Eikhof, D. R. & Haunschild, A. (2006). "Lifestyle meets market: Bohemian entrepreneurs in creative industries." *Creativity and Innovation Management* 15(3): 234–241.

EPRS (2019). *Employment in the cultural and creative sectors*. European Parliament: Briefing. Available at: https://www.europarl.europa.eu/RegData/etudes/BRIE/2019/642264/EPRS_BRI(2019)642264_EN.pdf (Accessed: 20 September 2023)

Fillis, I. A. N. (2004). "The internationalizing smaller craft firm: Insights from the marketing/entrepreneurship interface." *International Small Business Journal* 22(1): 57–82.

Fillis, I. A. N. (2006). "Art for art's sake or art for business sake: An exploration of artistic product orientation." *The Marketing Review* 6(1): 29–40.

Fillis, I. A. N. & Rentschler, R. (2010). "The role of creativity in entrepreneurship." *Journal of Enterprising Culture* 18(1): 49–81.

Flew, T. (2013). "Introduction: Creative industries and cities." In T. Flew (ed.), *Creative industries and urban development*. Routledge, pp. 1–14.

Florida, R. (2002). *The rise of the creative class*. Basic Books.

Foord, J. (2009). "Strategies for creative industries: An international review." *Creative Industries Journal* 1(2): 91–113.

Gaddefors, J. & Anderson, A. R. (2019). "Romancing the rural: Reconceptualizing rural entrepreneurship as engagement with context (s)." *The International Journal of Entrepreneurship and Innovation* 20(3): 159–169.

Galloway, L. & Haniff, A. (2015). "Managing projects in architecture: A study of leadership in a creative industry." *Open Economics and Management Journal* 2(1).

Galloway, S. & Dunlop, S. (2007). "A critique of definitions of the cultural and creative industries in public policy." *International Journal of Cultural Policy* 13(1): 17–31.

Grodach, C. (2011). "Art spaces in community and economic development: Connections to neighborhoods, artists, and the cultural economy." *Journal of Planning Education and Research* 31(1): 74–85.

Guerreiro, M. M., Henriques, C. & Mendes, J. (2019). "Cultural and creative tourism: The case of 'celebrations' in the Algarve Region." *Journal of Tourism, Sustainability and Well-being* 7(4): 320–338.

Gupta, R., Sinha, P. K., Sahu, A. & Sood, V. (2021). "Success drivers of urban haats selling craft products." *International Journal of Rural Management* 17(1): 120–139.

Harvey, D. (2002). *Spaces of capital: Towards a critical geography*. Routledge.

Haugh, H. M. (2022). "Changing places: the generative effects of community embeddedness in place." *Entrepreneurship & Regional Development* 34(7–8): 542–566.

Hesmondhalgh, D. & Pratt, A. C. (2005). "Cultural industries and cultural policy." *International Journal of Cultural Policy* 11(1): 1–13.

Hoyte, C. (2019). "Artisan entrepreneurship: A question of personality structure?" *International Journal of Entrepreneurial Behavior & Research* 25(4): 615–632.

Ivanycheva, D., Schulze, W., Lundmark, E. & Chirico, F. (2023). "Lifestyle entrepreneurship: Literature review and future research agenda." *Journal of Management Studies*. https://doi.org/10.1111/joms.13000

Jóhannesson, G. T. (2012). ""To get things done": A relational approach to entrepreneurship." *Scandinavian Journal of Hospitality and Tourism* 12(2): 181–196.

Kackovic, M. & Wijnberg, N. M. (2022). "Artists finding galleries: Entrepreneurs gaining legitimacy in the art market." *Entrepreneurship Theory and Practice* 46(4): 1092–1116.

KEA European Affairs (2006). *The economy of culture in Europe*. European Commission. Available at: https://ec.europa.eu/assets/eac/culture/library/studies/cultural-economy_en.pdf (Accessed: 17 September 2023).

KEA European Affairs (2009). *The impact of culture on creativity*. European Commission. Available at: https://keanet.eu/wp-content/uploads/2019/09/impactculturecreativityfull.pdf (Accessed: 17 September 2023).

Korsgaard, S., Müller, S. & Tanvig, H. W. (2015). "Rural entrepreneurship or entrepreneurship in the rural–between place and space." *International Journal of Entrepreneurial Behavior & Research* 21(1): 5–26.

Korsgaard, S., Müller, S. & Welter, F. (2021). "It's right nearby: How entrepreneurs use spatial bricolage to overcome resource constraints." *Entrepreneurship & Regional Development* 33(1–2): 147–173.

Kuhn, K. M. & Galloway, T. L. (2015). "With a little help from my competitors: Peer networking among artisan entrepreneurs." *Entrepreneurship Theory and Practice* 39(3): 571–600.

Lampel, J. & Meyer, A. D. (2008). "Field-configuring events as structuring mechanisms: How conferences, ceremonies, and trade shows constitute new technologies, industries, and markets: Guest editors introduction." *Journal of Management Studies* 45(6): 1025–1035.

Lange, B. (2009). "Accessing markets in creative industries – professionalization and social-spatial strategies of culturepreneurs in Berlin." *Creative Industries Journal* 1(2): 115–135.

Lounsbury, M., Gehman, J. & Ann Glynn, M. (2019). "Beyond homo entrepreneurus: Judgment and the theory of cultural entrepreneurship." *Journal of Management Studies* 56(6): 1214–1236.

Markusen, A., Wassall, G. H., DeNatale, D. & Cohen, R. (2008). "Defining the creative economy: Industry and occupational approaches." *Economic Development Quarterly* 22(1): 24–45.

McKeever, E., Jack, S. & Anderson, A. (2015). "Embedded entrepreneurship in the creative re-construction of place". *Journal of Business Venturing* 30(1): 50–65.

Morrison, A. (2006). "A contextualisation of entrepreneurship." *International Journal of Entrepreneurial Behavior & Research* 12(4): 192–209.

O'Connor, J. (2009). "Creative industries: A new direction?" *International Journal of Cultural Policy* 15(4): 387–402.

Paige, R. C. (2009). "Profiles of successful craft micro-retailers." *Journal of Developmental Entrepreneurship* 14(4): 393–412.

Paige, R. C. & Littrell, M. A. (2002). "Craft retailers' criteria for success and associated business strategies." *Journal of Small Business Management* 40(4): 314–331.

Phillips, R. J. (2011). "Arts entrepreneurship and economic development: Can every city be austintatious?" *Foundations and Trends® in Entrepreneurship* 6(4): 239–313.

Pratt, A. C. (2008). "Cultural commodity chains, cultural clusters, or cultural production chains?" *Growth and Change* 39(1): 95–103.

Pret, T. & Cogan, A. (2019). "Artisan entrepreneurship: a systematic literature review and research agenda." *International Journal of Entrepreneurial Behavior & Research* 25(4): 592–614.

Quinn, B. (2005). "Arts festivals and the city." *Urban Studies* 41(5/6): 927–42.

Robertson, M. & Wardrop, K. (2014). "Festivals and events, government and spatial governance." In J. Mair (ed.), *The Routledge handbook of events*. Routledge, pp. 500–517.

Ryan, B. (1991). *Making capital from culture: The corporate form of capitalist cultural production*. Walter de Gruyter.

Scott, A. J. (2008). *Social economy of the metropolis: Cognitive-cultural capitalism and the global resurgence of cities*. Oxford University Press.

Shams, S. R. & Kaufmann, H. R. (2016). "Entrepreneurial co-creation: A research vision to be materialised." *Management Decision* 54(6): 1250–1268.

Shane, S. & Venkataraman, S. (2000). "The promise of entrepreneurship as a field of research." *Academy of Management Review* 25(1): 217–226.

Shepherd, D. A. & Haynie, J. M. (2009) "Birds of a feather don't always flock together: Identity management in entrepreneurship." *Journal of Business Venturing* 24(4): 316–337.

Shepherd, D. A., Williams, T. A. & Zhao, E. Y. (2019). "A framework for exploring the degree of hybridity in entrepreneurship." *Academy of Management Perspectives* 33(4): 491–512.

Steyaert, C. (2007) "'Entrepreneuring' as a conceptual attractor? A review of process theories in 20 years of entrepreneurship studies." *Entrepreneurship & Regional Development* 19(6): 453–477.

Swedberg, R. (2006). "The cultural entrepreneur and the creative industries: Beginning in Vienna." *Journal of Cultural Economics* 30: 243–261.

Thom, M. (2016). "Crucial skills for the entrepreneurial success of fine artists." *Artivate* 5(1): 3–24.

Throsby, D. (2008a). "Modelling the cultural industries." *International Journal of Cultural Policy* 14(3): 217–232.

Throsby, D. (2008b). "The concentric circles model of the cultural industries." *Cultural Trends* 17(3): 147–164.

Tregear, A. (2005). "Lifestyle, growth, or community involvement? The balance of goals of UK artisan food producers." *Entrepreneurship & Regional Development* 17(1): 1–15.

UNESCO (2005). "Convention on the protection and promotion of the diversity of cultural expressions." Available at: http://unesdoc.unesco.org/images/0014/001429/142919e.pdf (Accessed: 20 September 2023).

Welter, F., Baker, T., Audretsch, D. B. & Gartner, W. B. (2017). "Everyday entrepreneurship – a call for entrepreneurship research to embrace entrepreneurial diversity." *Entrepreneurship Theory & Practice* 41(3): 311–321.

Whitson, J. R., Simon, B. & Parker, F. (2021). "The missing producer: Rethinking indie cultural production in terms of entrepreneurship, relational labour, and sustainability." *European Journal of Cultural Studies* 24(2): 606–627.

Win, T. S. (2014). "Marketing the entrepreneurial artist in the innovation age: Aesthetic labor, artistic subjectivity, and the creative industries." *Anthropology of Work Review* 35(1): 2–13.

Wyrwich, M., Stuetzer, M. & Sternberg, R. (2016). "Entrepreneurial role models, fear of failure, and institutional approval of entrepreneurship: A tale of two regions." *Small Business Economics* 46: 467–492.

Yachin, J. M. & Ioannides, D. (2020). ""Making do" in rural tourism: The resourcing behaviour of tourism micro-firms." *Journal of Sustainable Tourism* 28(7): 1003–1021.

12 Change via institutional entrepreneurship

Amy Gresock

Introduction

Entrepreneurship deals with the discovery and exploitation of valuable opportunities (Shane & Venkataraman, 2000) and is a critical component in promoting economic growth (Nissan et al., 2011). Actions that sustain economic growth involve constructing an enduring institutional policy (Galindo-Martín et al., 2020). Institutional rules behave as myths that organizations incorporate, which lead to increased legitimacy, stability, and resources and firm longevity (Meyer & Rowan, 1977). The acceptance of a policy or program by an organization is influenced by the extent to which it is institutionalized (Tolbert & Zucker, 1983). As a consequence, organizations, and the people within them, are caught in a network of values, norms, rules, beliefs, and taken-for-granted assumptions, that are partially of their own design (Barley & Tolbert, 1997). Institutionalization may prohibit certain responses to new conditions, openly supporting the preservation of the institutional status quo and preventing the notion of institutional change (Kraatz & Moore, 2002).

Given that institutions are entrenched in established rules, norms, and routines which are so powerful that organizations and individuals are likely to conform to them, how can new institutions ultimately emerge and existing ones change? (DiMaggio & Powell, 1991; Seo & Creed, 2002). Although institutions represent constraints on the choices that individuals and collectives are likely to make, these constraints are subject to change over time (Barley & Tolbert, 1997). Institutionalist theorists have contributed insights on the relationship between organizational structures and the broader social environments in which organizations are positioned (Beckert, 1999). The institutional theory perspective of institutional entrepreneurship regards the entrepreneur as an institutional innovator or agent of institutional change, who may be compelled by a variety of motivations and conducts change in diverse contexts (Pacheco et al., 2010). Scholars investigating entrepreneurship have called this new category of actors "institutional entrepreneurs" (Aldrich, 2011). These individuals frame issues, gain support, assemble resources, and create institutional change in a strategic

DOI: 10.4324/9781003324737-12

manner (Lee & Hung, 2014). The uniting of institutional and entrepreneurial forces into the single concept of institutional entrepreneurship creates possibilities for understanding how and why particular novel solutions such as new practices or organizational forms materialize and eventually become established (Garud et al., 2007).

Actors (i.e., those who engage in institutional entrepreneurship) may have sufficient resources to impose change on an institutional field. For example, once John D. Rockefeller had acquired most of the oil refineries in the United States, he was easily able to change how the oil market operated, and given his position, those in the institutional field had to accept his changes to the established way of doing things (Dorado, 2005). This concept of institutional field refers to the organizations that collectively compose a recognized area of institutional life (DiMaggio & Powell, 1983). Rockefeller's Standard Oil Company was able to rapidly take control and set institutional norms in this field that had uncertain conditions at the outset (Bolanos, 2019). Also, although Standard Oil was not the first corporation to engage in public relations, it is one of the earliest to reject secretive Gilded Age business practices (Leccese, 2017). This exemplifies that through initiating institutional entrepreneurship processes, organizations and entire institutional fields can evolve radically. It is a noteworthy concept for understanding innovation and processes of change in our world.

Given its relevance to sociology, management, and entrepreneurship, institutional entrepreneurship theory has received interest from researchers delivering scholarly work in this area (Tiberius et al., 2020). Institutions limit accessible choices, since better options than the status quo may be available, but these are only obtainable by means of violation of the established institutional structure (Beckert, 1999). This chapter provides insight into this violation of recognized institutional structures enabled by institutional entrepreneurs. To do this, institutional theory will be introduced and the essential relation of legitimacy to institutions will be discussed. Legitimacy is socially constructed since it displays a similarity between activities of the legitimized entity and the shared beliefs of a particular social group (Suchman, 1995). This is important for understanding homogenization and congruence to institutional standards. The concept of institutional entrepreneurship is introduced as an institutional change process and differentiated from traditional forms of entrepreneurship. Ideas are linked to Schumpeter's work on creative destruction. The chapter continues by discussing who institutional entrepreneurs are, and factors that give rise to institutional entrepreneurship. Institutional entrepreneurship is then applied in the context of the development of the academic field of entrepreneurship at large. Finally, strategic steps are recommended for institutional entrepreneurs engaging in institutional change, including the clear articulation of strategic vision, change processes, and buy-in from stakeholders in support of the strategy. To conclude, future directions in this area are discussed. Throughout, the significance of institutional entrepreneurship as a way for providing institutional transformation is considered.

Entrepreneurship as change

Economically and socially, entrepreneurs are innovative rebels who tamper with the status quo. These individuals are compelled to deviate or escape from generally accepted cultural norms (Morrison, 2006). Entrepreneurial agency is within individuals who possess the ability to discover and exploit opportunities that are beyond the scope of others (Garud & Karnøe, 2003). Their affinity for market disturbance and their ability to pursue opportunities also entail creatively disrupting existing systems. However, with this interference comes extraordinary energy and novelty. Through innovation, unique products and services are made available, new markets open, and entrepreneurs create real value that is necessary for economic and social well-being (Smilor, 1997).

New ventures establish themselves within the context of an existing institution. Institutions rely on a cultural foundation to facilitate effectiveness. If a society chooses rules that conflict with its deep beliefs or values, those rules will not be taken seriously and thus be difficult to enforce unless applied with significant coercive power (Mokyr, 2023). Entrepreneurs may destroy these taken-for-granted rules if they recognize this will be productive (Beckert, 1999). Cultures and institutions evolve together and affect one another in many complex ways.

Institutions matter

Institutions afford entrepreneurship the financial resources and human capital to carry out objectives as well as the appropriate structure and framework in which to enact entrepreneurial activity (Galindo-Martín et al., 2020). Strong institutions can inspire trust among people at the interpersonal and inter-organizational level (Fulgsang & Jagd, 2015). They also lower uncertainty by forming expectations of others' behavior (Beckert, 1999). Institutionalization involves the processes through which social processes, obligations, or actualities eventually take on a rule-like status in social thought and action (Meyer & Rowan, 1977). When intense institutionalization occurs, patterns of behavior are taken for granted (Dorado, 2005). Longevity and stability are the essence of institutionalization (Kraatz & Moore, 2002).

Although institutions propel change and influence the nature of change across levels and contexts, it is acknowledged that they themselves also may change in their roles and effectiveness over time (Dacin et al., 2002). Institutions and actions are interconnected, and institutionalization is recognized as a dynamic, ongoing process (Barley & Tolbert, 1997). The extent of institutionalization may affect actors' agency and the process of resource mobilization most probable for facilitating institutional change (Dorado, 2005).

Routinized organizational behaviors are the result of ideas, values, and beliefs that commence in the institutional context (Greenwood & Hinings, 1996;

Meyer & Rowan, 1977). Institutional opportunities can be considered as the likelihood that an organizational field will allow actors to recognize and introduce a novel institutional combination and enable the mobilization of necessary resources to make it long-lasting (Dorado, 2005). Novel ideas can be converted into practice via habitualization, a key component of institutionalization (Reay et al., 2013). Mimicry occurs when rules gradually emerge and are evaluated (Bouncken et al., 2020). These aspects of the institution are set in place and may be imitated by other organizations that want to emulate it and legitimize themselves in the context of new institutional norms.

Institutional maintenance work refers to actors' purposeful efforts to maintain existing institutions (Colombero & Boxenbaum, 2019). Institutional fields vary in their level of insulation from other fields, as some fields lack permeability (i.e., they are relatively closed off to, or not exposed to ideas from other institutional fields), whereas others are more open and thus prone to allowing change (Greenwood & Hinings, 1996). Actors utilize authentication (i.e., the relational constitution of an artefact as original or as a genuine expression of a particular type, style, or person) to achieve institutional maintenance work (Colombero & Boxenbaum, 2019). Organizational field transparency is also a consideration, as generally the more institutionally developed a field, the more unclear opportunities are likely to be for actors (Dorado, 2005).

Institutional theory

Institutional theory has emerged as a powerful and accepted explanation for individual as well as organizational action (Dacin et al., 2002). Institutions relate to social configurations that endure over time and are secured in distinctive cultural perspectives (Tumbas et al., 2018). Institutional theory suggests that organizations are deeply influenced by the institutions in which they exist. An organization's behaviors are therefore determined by the necessity to be regarded as legitimate within the appropriate institutional environment (DiMaggio & Powell, 1983). When institutional theory was used to account for observed organizational homogeneity within fields, it emphasized the criticality of the environment in which organizations are entrenched. Additionally, this theory described isomorphism among organizations exposed to comparable institutional pressures.

An organizational field refers to those organizations that together comprise an established area of institutional life, including main suppliers, resource and product consumers, regulatory agencies, and other organizations that create comparable services or products (DiMaggio & Powell, 1983). Institutionalization describes the system through which mechanisms of formal structure become broadly accepted as appropriate and necessary for the field, and function to legitimize organizations (Tolbert & Zucker, 1983). The need for changes often will be determined by the lack of consensus or degree of conflict within the organization. When organizational elements are institutionalized (i.e., when they are widely recognized as appropriate and necessary components of efficient, rational organizations), firms are under substantial pressure to integrate these elements into their formal structure to uphold perceived legitimacy. When a field develops and is ultimately well established, there is inevitable movement toward homogenization (DiMaggio & Powell, 1983). Fields only exist to the extent that they are structurally defined. The concept that accounts for this process of homogenization is isomorphism. This is ultimately a constraining process in a population that forces one unit to resemble other units that face similar environmental conditions (DiMaggio & Powell, 1983; Haveman, 1993; Meyer & Rowan, 1977).

Encompassing taken-for-granted, culturally ingrained beliefs, institutions specify and validate formal and informal social arrangements and behaviors (Garud et al., 2007). They also constrain and inhibit behaviors that do not fit with established norms. During their initial stages, organizational fields exhibit substantial diversity with their approach and form, but once a field matures into one that is well established, there is relentless pressure for homogenization (DiMaggio & Powell, 1983). All organizations exist within an institutional environment that defines their social reality (Scott, 1987). Organizational scholars have often concentrated on the essential function that institutions have in offering continuity and stability in organizational practices.

Over time, change may occur in established institutions. Institutional theory may help account for divergent change that occurs within organizations (D'Aunno et al., 2000). Many people cannot conceive that small, unplanned, and incremental alterations can ultimately amount to great consequences. Because established and massive multifaceted structures may seem incontrovertible and resistant to change, they can be taken for granted (Aldrich, 2011). Change for these existing institutions may be stimulated from social pressures resulting from transformations in social norms and opportunities that arise from social conflict (Pacheco et al., 2010). As society evolves, entrepreneurs may create pressures to disrupt entire institutions to reflect the changing dynamics of society. Institutional change is a difficult concept since a critical component of institutions is that they are resistant to change, and other options or alternatives may be unimaginable at the time (Nite & Edwards, 2021).

Legitimacy

Organizations are competitive not only in hopes of gaining customers and resources, but also for political prowess and institutional legitimacy, which affect social and economic strength (DiMaggio & Powell, 1983). Legitimacy is a key component of institutional theory (Trittin-Ulbrich & Böckel, 2022) and is defined as "a generalized perception or assumption that the actions of an entity are desirable, proper, or appropriate within some social constructed system of norms, values, beliefs, and definitions" (Suchman, 1995, p. 574). As such, it is possessed objectively, yet produced subjectively (Suchman, 1995). An institutional perspective allows for the examination of how new arrangements attain social approval (i.e., legitimacy) by important stakeholders and their coaction with existing institutional arrangements (Hinings et al., 2018).

Legitimization is a multifaceted social process (Fligstein, 1997), involving both entrepreneurial organizations and prospective resource providers, such as customers, investors, media, and other interested audiences, in the creation of organizational identities and perceptions about the practicality of the business model (Navis & Glynn, 2010). Central to papers in the field of institutional theory is the notion that certain organizations adopt new structures and practices not because they are necessarily effective or efficient, but rather, because they bestow to the organization a certain degree of legitimacy (Alvesson & Spicer, 2019).

This achieved legitimacy comes at a price. If organizations must behave in an appropriate manner within their socially constructed system (Suchman, 1995), they may encounter punishments for deviation from institutionally accepted norms. As a result, the choice of strategic options and the degree of individual agency available to an organization are constrained (Manolova et al., 2008). Legitimacy is especially impactful for new ventures, as it is a vital resource for the acquisition of other resources, with such resources being critical for growth, and legitimacy can be heightened by strategic actions of new ventures (Zimmerman & Zeitz, 2002). Legitimacy thus represents an essential requirement for a new venture's resource acquisition, evolution, and ultimate survival (Taeuscher et al., 2021). Hence, the institutional environment has substantial influence on entrepreneurial entry rates as well as the resulting trajectories of entrepreneurial initiatives (Manolova et al., 2008). However, distinctiveness can be important for new firms too. A level of distinctiveness matters as it enables unknown ventures to attract interest and garner attention from resource-providing audiences (Taeuscher et al., 2021). Institutional theorists have emphasized that distinctiveness can derail the attainment of legitimacy in fields (DiMaggio & Powell, 1991).

Achieving normative legitimacy

An expectation of institutional theory is that compliance with institutional norms increases the symbolic performance of organizations (Heugens & Lander, 2009). Legitimacy is gained through the approval of normative institutions, which typically manifest in standards such as those established by professional and trade associations, and business groups (Manolova et al., 2008). Normative legitimacy relates to an organization's perceived congruence with normative expectations within its institutional environment (Scott, 2001). Organizations achieve normative legitimacy when audiences perceive them as engaging in the correct standards and doing the right things in accordance with normative expectations (Taeuscher et al., 2021). An example of an institution gaining normative legitimacy, which is discussed later in the chapter, involves the scholarly field of entrepreneurship as it evolved to be recognized as credible in academia.

Institutional entrepreneurship defined

The concept of institutional entrepreneurship focuses on the process of introducing divergent changes to an institution and the agents who break the status quo via transformative activities, thereby disrupting existing institutions or creating new ones. Institutional entrepreneurship confronts the change of social phenomena that generally do not change with ease (Tiberius et al., 2020). Institutional entrepreneurship is often difficult, as various fields face different barriers when establishing legitimacy. This can have considerable impact on the existing institutional arrangements (e.g., Trittin-Ulbrich & Böckel, 2022). Institutional change results from adjustments in the logic by which legitimacy is measured (Suddaby & Greenwood, 2005). It has been suggested that institutional change requires some sort of jolt to destabilize established practices (Reay et al., 2006).

Institutional entrepreneurs are defined as change agents who, whether they initially envisioned changing their institutional environment or not, introduce and actively participate in the implementation of changes that diverge from prevailing institutions (Battilana et al., 2009). To be considered institutional entrepreneurs, actors do not have to be successful in the full implementation of this change. Actors may organize the necessary resources to establish a new practice but might fail in convincing prospective adopters to shift routines. They would still be deemed institutional entrepreneurs even though the change was not adopted.

Thus, to qualify as institutional entrepreneurs, actors must commence changes as well as work on implementing them in their situation. Establishing unfamiliar institutionalized arrangements takes substantial struggle, and institutional entrepreneurs are described as skillful actors who must cultivate influential arguments that will enable them to gain support and persuade others to unite with their vision (Tumbas et al., 2018). Research indicates that individuals' background, experience, and social capital may influence whether they engage in institutional entrepreneurship or not (Pacheco et al., 2010).

Battilana et al. (2009) argue that institutional entrepreneurs are indeed change agents, but not all change agents are institutional entrepreneurs. To be such, they must initiate what are considered divergent changes and should actively participate in the implementation of such changes. Non-divergent changes are aligned with the existent institutions in a field, whereas divergent changes sever ties with them. Only when the changes introduced are divergent regarding the institutional environment in which they are embedded does the change agent qualify as an institutional entrepreneur. The institutional entrepreneur must also have active participation and work on the implementation of the institutional changes. Therefore, the actor must actively organize resources to implement change to be regarded as an institutional entrepreneur. Institutional entrepreneurship highlights the significance of skillful and forceful agency by these actors who strategically align resources for realizing institutional change and innovation (Lee & Hung, 2014).

The primary activities in which institutional entrepreneurs participate when employing this change that deviates from institutional norms involve the articulation of a novel vision and the organization of allies to support this vision. Since these individuals are launching divergent changes that split from prevailing institutions, institutional entrepreneurs encounter specialized obstacles occurring from other actors' institutional embeddedness and potential political opposition (Battilana et al., 2009).

Collective institutional entrepreneurship

The type of actor is not limited to individuals but also includes organizations and social movements. A collective nature of institutional entrepreneurship exists, and institutions are not just changed by individuals but also by larger groups and organizations. Collective institutional entrepreneurship is defined as the process of defeating collective action problems and accomplishing cooperation with dispersed actors to create or change institutions (Pacheco et al., 2010). Aldrich (2011) urges us to apply the concept of institutional entrepreneurship to represent the collective action of individuals and other entities (e.g., professional associations) that revolutionize institutions, and stresses that institutional entrepreneurship is often accomplished by entrepreneurs via collective action.

Framing

Institutional entrepreneurs often engage in framing, whereby they seek to portray their chosen institutional arrangement as appealing to the broadest potential audience. Framing tactics correspond to the objective of establishing legitimacy for new forms and practices by carefully incorporating novel ideas and processes with generally accepted narratives (Pacheco et al., 2010). The application of discourse and stories has been prevalent in the attempts of institutional entrepreneurs to benefit their positions through drawing out institutional change (Zilber, 2007). Institutional entrepreneurs' agency does not just take place within a given structure, but also transforms and thus surpasses it (Tiberius et al., 2020).

Differences from traditional entrepreneurship forms

The constructs of traditional entrepreneur and institutional entrepreneur partially overlap (David et al., 2013). To qualify as institutional entrepreneurs, actors must pioneer changes and execute them in their context (Leca & Naccache, 2006). As described by David et al. (2013), some (but not all) traditional entrepreneurs are also institutional entrepreneurs, and the same classification goes for institutional entrepreneurs engaging in traditional entrepreneurship (Phillips & Tracey 2007; Tracey et al., 2011; Tolbert et al., 2011). While some institutional entrepreneurs may participate in institutional change without actually founding new organizational entities (e.g., Maguire et al., 2004), others may create new organizations that alter the institutional field and therefore are also entrepreneurs in the traditional sense. Institutional entrepreneurs are thus socially skilled actors who serve to justify and legitimize innovative types of social arrangements, whereas traditional entrepreneurs are considered as those who found new organizations, not all of which are novel (David et al., 2013).

Tracey et al. (2011) suggest that although they may occur in tandem, the processes of entrepreneurship and institutional entrepreneurship are dependent upon separate forms of action. Their findings indicate that the commercial skills required in creating a business venture are wholly different from the type of institutional work necessary to influence and change an institutional environment (Tracey et al., 2011). The target of institutional entrepreneurs' efforts can vary. Institutional entrepreneurs can advance innovative sub-organizational elements, including roles, practices, or procedures. On the other hand, institutional entrepreneurs can work to create and build entirely novel forms of organizations that project original identities (David et al., 2013).

Institutional entrepreneurship is also different from intrapreneurship, which is an important sub-field of entrepreneurship studies (Blanka, 2019). Intrapreneurship has elicited research attention considering its key role in innovation and organizational performance (Huang et al., 2021). Intrapreneurship is essentially conducting entrepreneurship in the confines of an existing organization (Adachi & Hisada, 2017; Antoncic & Hisrich, 2001). This process occurs inside the existing firm, regardless of its size, and can result in not just a new firm but also the development of original products, services, strategies, and administrative techniques (Antoncic & Hisrich, 2001). Although intrapreneurship and institutional entrepreneurship have the potential to be innovative, they are different concepts. The predominant focus of intrapreneurship is on the creation of new ventures (Antoncic & Hisrich, 2003). This is not the case for institutional entrepreneurship, which is focused on building and changing institutions, either within the organization, as a new organization, or for an entire field. The label "institutional entrepreneurship" refers to the actions of actors who are attracted to certain institutional arrangements and who leverage resources to construct new institutions or to alter existing ones (Garud et al., 2007). Also termed corporate entrepreneurship and corporate venturing, intrapreneurship seeks to exploit a new opportunity and generate economic value for the existing organization (Parker, 2011). According to Pandey et al. (2021), intrapreneurship is an important precursor of firm performance. This process enables managers to innovate and enhance overall business performance (Parker, 2011). The intrapreneurship concept is based on the belief that valuable human capital lies within employees in current organizations (Blanka, 2019). With this process, intrapreneurial employees often generate and pursue new ideas, and through information sharing with peers, the organization becomes more competitive (Huang et al., 2021). In contrast, institutional entrepreneurs may not be concerned with traditional organizational performance outcomes.

Engaging in creative destruction

Many entrepreneurs engaging in institutional entrepreneurship are disrupting institutional environments and participating in creative destruction. Although institutional theory literature has embraced the entrepreneurship moniker, there is modest reference to entrepreneurship theory in this field of research (Pacheco et al., 2010). Their innovativeness has the capacity to not just alter existing institutions, but to dismantle the market they are a part of and create something anew.

The entrepreneur is ultimately an agent who destroys markets with innovations. In order to understand this process, we use economist Joseph Schumpeter's theory of creative destruction. Generations since the book's publication, *The Theory of Economic Development* is still regarded as one of the most influential books in economics and is highly referenced in the field of entrepreneurial studies. It is Schumpeter's seminal work, and his reputation has been cemented as a promoter of innovation (Croitoru, 2012). During the Industrial Revolution, the basic cultural view that propelled creative destruction was a solid belief in progress (Mokyr, 2023). The Schumpeterian entrepreneur is not an inventor but rather, an innovator. Entrepreneurial activity is considered totally distinct from the routine administration of a firm (Croitoru, 2012). The works of Schumpeter provide general theories of economic development propelled by the entrepreneur and innovator as the dominant force for creating opportunities (Filser et al., 2023).

Schumpeter advocated for the function of the entrepreneur in economic development and endures as one of the first scholars to take into account the relevance of the role of entrepreneurs in the economic growth process (Nissan et al., 2011). He accomplished this in his influential work first published in 1912, *Theorie der Wirtschaftlichen Entwicklung* and later translated to English (Schumpeter, 1934). In Schumpeter's work, innovation and successful entrepreneurship were regarded as being deeply connected (Estrin et al., 2022). The original concepts of Schumpeter still influence the discipline, especially that of generating innovative opportunities through the process of creative destruction. According to Schumpeter, the entrepreneur powers economic growth by pioneering innovations (Ferreira et al., 2017).

Even though Schumpeter's theory originated in economics, the influence on entrepreneurship and management research is noteworthy. With the advent of the formal discipline of entrepreneurship, these works became foundational to entrepreneurship as a field. Schumpeter proposed that economic progress would warrant shifts or ruptures based on something new entering the system such as an innovation to existing markets. The entrepreneur drove economic change as they disturbed the equilibrium by launching innovations. The critical component was creative destruction, and transformation could surface from the individual and from innovations in established organizations (Ferreira et al., 2017). This coincides with institutional entrepreneurship. Emerging substitute institutions can be the innovation prompted by the entrepreneurial undertaking of creative destruction (Beckert, 1999). One can regard this in relation to the example of consumption of music via different formats, and how novel forms replace previous ones. Consider the launch of the compact disc, and the corresponding disappearance of the vinyl record, as just one of many illustrations of Schumpeter's creative destruction process; other examples where this has been a factor include automobiles, electricity, aircraft, and personal computers (Sobel, 2008).

Following the logic of Schumpeter's work, entrepreneurial activity is viewed as spurring new industries and substantial structural shifts within the economy, which have significant effects on economic growth and social welfare (Galindo-Martín et al., 2020). The Schumpeterian vision implies that entrepreneurs are innovators who destroy prevailing structures (Nissan et al., 2011). Schumpeter regards entrepreneurship activity as entailing innovation through the development of a new product, organization, or process and generating a destruction process; however, these actions are established in an environment in which institutions have a critical role (Galindo-Martín et al., 2020).

The changing of institutionalized structures, rules, and strategies through creative destruction will only be successful if those preferring the status quo either do not have means available or don't use available means, to counteract the ruin of established practices (Beckert, 1999). Institutions that support creative destruction should provide incentives for entrepreneurs and ensure that they have the resources to execute their designs (Mokyr, 2023).

Institutional entrepreneurs – who are they?

Opportunity recognition is fundamental to the process of institutional entrepreneurship. To identify these institutional entrepreneurship opportunities, certain traits may be advantageous. As with all types of entrepreneurship, opportunity recognition in institutional entrepreneurship is likely to demand creativity, social networks, and relevant prior knowledge and experience (Phillips & Tracey, 2007). Institutionalized rules may be viewed as constraints by observers, but not from the perspective of the organization and those within it (Beckert, 1999). Therefore, an institutional entrepreneur must be aware of these constraints before they can take advantage of the opportunities available for change and gain the support of others. One may even consider how prior opportunity recognition in institutional entrepreneurship may affect certain traits and potentially enhance an actor's propensity for engaging in such processes again for future change. Incorporating the concept of opportunity recognition into institutional entrepreneurship research offers a constructive avenue for explaining the role of actors involved in institutional change at various levels of analysis (Phillips & Tracey, 2007).

Research demonstrates that characteristics such as the background, experience, and social capital of individuals may influence their participation in institutional entrepreneurship (Dorado, 2005; Pacheco et al., 2010; Seo & Creed, 2002).

Existing literature has identified a range of such skills, such as analytical skills and political skills (Beckert, 1999; Garud et al., 2002). Perkmann and Spicer (2007) examined skills used by institutional entrepreneurs and determined that they are multiskilled rather than possessing specific skills as traits.

Battilana (2006) proposed that individuals' social position is an essential variable for understanding how they may be able to emerge as institutional entrepreneurs despite the presence of strong institutional pressures. Battilana's (2011) study examines the relationship between social position (within both the field and the organization) and the prospect of individual actors instigating organizational changes that deviate from institutional status quo. The results illustrate that social position within both contexts influences actors' propensity to introduce organizational changes that diverge from the institutional norms. These include changes that depart from the institutionalized template of role division among organizations as well as those among professional groups in a field. The author's findings indicate that these two forms of divergent organizational change are likely to be assumed by individual actors with different types of social position within the field and the organization.

Emotions play an important part in the simultaneous distancing from established institutionalized patterns and the engagement in alternative actions (Cartel et al., 2019). It is not surprising then that the level of engagement of the actor is important when we consider institutions. The effectiveness of institutional processes is a result not only of their recurring power but also of the receptiveness of actors, which can vary over time. The work of Greenwood and Suddaby (2006) illustrates that even while institutional routines of reinforcement persist, field-level change may still happen if actors become distant and, therefore, resistant to institutional effects. Thus, if an actor's commitment level to an institution decreases, their propensity to create change and new institutional fields may increase.

Factors that give rise to institutional entrepreneurs

Institutional entrepreneurs recognize the outmodedness or undesirability of existing institutions, and so they design new institutional compositions and participate in a range of tactics to realize institutional change. As traditional practices weaken in power and innovations triumph over these practices, they succeed in their changes by concurrently presenting models of different ways of achieving goals (Beckert, 1999). Therefore, institutional entrepreneurs consider the current state of the institution, can object to existing rules and practices, and ultimately institutionalize the alternate rules and practices they are advocating (Pacheco et al., 2010). These entrepreneurs may be propelled by a variety of motives, such as social influences that may make existing institutions archaic. Research relating to the external environment and causes of entrepreneurship have earned attention because they impact entrepreneurial opportunities as well as the circumstances for unlocking essential resources in which the entrepreneur develops (Ferreira et al., 2017).

Institutional entrepreneurs may scan institutional environments to seek those that are ripe for their opportunities. These may be institutions that they have experience with, that they have a passion for, or that have gaps from existing conditions not working. This may include the recognition of institutional voids, where supportive institutions in markets are weak or absent (Mair & Martí, 2009; Mair et al., 2012; Puffer et al., 2010). An institutional entrepreneur also may be able to consider under what conditions institutions have less stability and be subject to breakdown if maintenance work is ignored within the institution.

Effective entrepreneurs are incredible learners. Entrepreneurship is an iterative process, and these individuals learn from their experiences. They learn from what ultimately does work, and sometimes more importantly, from what does not work out in their favor (Smilor, 1997). For example, they may amalgamate lessons created from experience within multiple institutional environments in their efforts for institutional change. New organizational forms can emerge through the process known as bridging institutional entrepreneurship, which entails an institutional entrepreneur merging aspects of established institutional logics and associated practices/organizational forms to produce a new form of organization supported by hybrid logic (Tracey et al., 2011). An institutional entrepreneur has likely acquired knowledge from their field and should evaluate what mechanisms succeed currently in the institutional arena. From this learning, they are better equipped to propose innovations that will break with existing norms to enhance the institutional environment.

Many of the taken-for-granted institutions of modern society have earned their place in our culture due to the efforts of institutional entrepreneurs. Hargadon and Douglas (2001) explain how Thomas Edison enabled his organization to achieve acceptance for an innovation that would eventually displace existing institutions of the gas industry. The authors discuss Edison's expansion of his system of electric lighting, a novel technology that quickly achieved common acceptance and transformed the existing institutional landscape. His system eventually supplanted many of the previous institutions and became a template for later ones. The character of Edison's design was that it took advantage of understandings developed from conventional institutions but also sustained the flexibility to progress ahead of them and foster new institutions. His system of electric lighting evolved from an innovation into an institution, composed of its own network of electric utilities companies, suppliers, investors, and customers. Through analyzing when innovations such as this first begin to alter the landscape of existing institutions, it may be possible to identify how changes displace existing institutions and suggest how future innovations might be designed to manipulate them.

Institutional entrepreneurship evolving the field of entrepreneurship

It is possible to consider the field of entrepreneurship as having actually gone through the process of institutional entrepreneurship. Within academia, entrepreneurship has grown and is considered a productive and thriving scholarly arena (Landström & Harirchi, 2018). The field of entrepreneurship is defined as "the scholarly examination of how, by whom, and with what effects opportunities to create future goods as well as services are discovered, evaluated, and exploited" (Shane & Venkataraman, 2000, p. 218). Since this field's inception, researchers have made efforts to create academic legitimacy for it (Landström & Harirchi, 2018). They have been influenced by (as well as having contributed to) a process of institutional entrepreneurship, as their work has affected the field, and the constraints of the field continually shape their work (Aldrich, 2012).

Legitimacy building is one of the major elements in creating the rise of an academic community (Hambrick & Chen, 2008). The ascent of a field builds on emergence, divergence, and convergence, and requires at least some degree of homogenization (Bouncken et al., 2020). To have an aspiring field successfully emerge and be seen as legitimate, it must differentiate itself from existent fields, demonstrating how a set of important problems cannot be solved by them (Hambrick & Chen, 2008). To establish a reputable position in the academic system, a field such as entrepreneurship must be deemed legitimate by scholars from other fields of research.

Any emergent field must construct legitimacy for the perspective of the greater academic establishment through domain-specific intellectual arguments and by adherence to the norms and standards of adjacent fields (DiMaggio & Powell, 1983; Meyer & Rowan, 1977). According to Hambrick and Chen (2008), legitimacy building is boosted if the new field leverages its ability to effectively emulate larger norms and standards of more recognized fields, thereby positioning itself as a rigorous scientific field. This has been the case over time with entrepreneurship studies. Entrepreneurship as an academic field has evolved from groups of isolated scholars undertaking research to an international community promoting studies on new firms (Aldrich, 2012). According to Landström and Harirchi (2018), during early research efforts, legitimacy was generally conferred by external forces, such as policy makers and other key external stakeholders (media, teachers, etc.), and entrepreneurship was considered a field that was relevant and practical. Over time, it has evolved as the field has been greatly dominated by robust studies, and the outcome has been that the legitimacy of the field has shifted from external stakeholders to stronger academic legitimacy. Aldrich's (2012) survey of several decades of the discipline has shown many occasions where collective action produced conditions transforming the institutional field of entrepreneurship. The substantial increase in the academic legitimacy of this field was in part sparked by the established context of business schools but also due to entrepreneurship as a scholarly field growing further institutionalized (Landström & Harirchi, 2018).

Landström et al. (2012) argue that the development of a novel field of research can be considered an entrepreneurial achievement. Scholars detect changes in society, recognize opportunities via stimulating research questions, and develop unique ideas by making these new phenomena evident. In doing this, they can draw together other researchers and over time build the field by establishing its own institutional framework which includes scientific journals, conferences, professional associations, and academic departments. The institution of entrepreneurship as an academic field has changed within the context of institutional entrepreneurship, having involved collective action by myriad scholars, agencies, organizations, and associations (Aldrich, 2012). The institutional logic of an organizational field is constructed and conveyed not just in the daily interactions of those in the field, but also through agencies and professional associations (Scott, 2001). When organizations adopt structural templates that authoritative bodies (e.g., professional associations) approve of can anticipate their perceived legitimacy by such authorities to increase within the commonly agreed to parameters of their organizational field, thereby securing the benefits of enhanced reputation (Heugens & Lander, 2009).

This field has evolved to be increasingly formalized with distinct core knowledge and research foci (Landström et al., 2012). This progression has yielded increasingly more universal and interconnected knowledge, as the field becomes further formalized and firmly anchored within a limited collection of intellectual foundations. The concept of institutional entrepreneurship is at the core of this observed change and formalization of the field (Aldrich, 2012). Hence, the institutionalization and subsequent development of the academic field of entrepreneurship is distinguished by numerous entrepreneurial initiatives by scholars who seized research opportunities and introduced innovative theories which contribute to its shaping and further its knowledge of entrepreneurial phenomena.

Steps that institutional entrepreneurs can engage in

While being an entrepreneur is challenging enough, it can be even more difficult to try starting a business when the institutional environment is not favorable. The entrepreneur will be forced to break with existing norms if they cannot conform. For example, Lee and Hung (2014) show how shan-zhai mobile phone entrepreneurs emerged from the informal economy, pursued opportunities, and changed the mobile phone market in China. Entrepreneurs who embark on these processes individually can oftentimes be overwhelmed. When an organization's size and/or complexity becomes too much for a single entrepreneur, a decision must be made. The entrepreneur realizes they can't do everything on their own, and thus team building becomes a necessary route to gain expertise through multiplying and diversifying the skills and abilities of the lead entrepreneur. Having a business development team can prove advantageous for an institutional entrepreneur. This business development team typically has a strong affinity for the lead entrepreneur and shows devotion to the vision of the business. Also, the team is likely to participate in entrepreneurially innovative and proactive efforts to expand resources and develop the venture's processes and performance (Smilor, 1997). For example, in unstable institutional contexts characterized by resource constraints and institutional transformation, actors may engage in entrepreneurial resourcefulness which enables them to combine different tangible and intangible resources (Welter et al., 2018).

In addition to expanding to a team, other strategic steps that an institutional entrepreneur can engage in include:

1. Clear articulation of strategic vision
   Every opportunity has a finite window (Smilor, 1997). Entrepreneurs can bring an opportunity to market to fit in with everything else in the environment, or they can create something that disrupts the current system. Being clear on their vision, as well as knowing when to best bring it to market to be able to create institutional transformation, is key. Unclear concepts are likely to lose interest with stakeholders and lack momentum to provide lasting change. This vision is important because a prominent driver for ultimately building consensus is to create a shared vision (Wijen & Ansari, 2006).
2. Careful management of change processes
   Change is not a sudden event but a dynamic process. Institutional entrepreneurs structure issues, assemble resources, gain support, and facilitate change strategically (Lee & Hung, 2014). Strategic action not only is about economic processes but also encompasses the social processes of creating and improving legitimacy. Instead of following the established institutional structures in place, institutional entrepreneurs mobilize resources to develop new ones or change existing institutions. Change, therefore, must be managed in a way that creates institutions which are lasting where shifts in practices are likely to be mimicked by others within the institutional environment. Skill is applied differently across organizational fields that are currently forming, become stable, and those in the process of being transformed (Fligstein, 1997). Under the guidance of skillful well-positioned agents, institutions can enable as well as restrict system change (Hung & Whittington, 2011).
3. Creating buy-in from stakeholders
   Effective stakeholder management is crucial for institutional entrepreneurs. They need to consider how to best leverage their social capital to increase buy-in and trust from those important to the institution. It is also essential that stakeholders are on board with the strategy and the objectives to attain the strategic goal are aligned similarly. Fligstein (1997) defines institutional entrepreneurs as actors who have social skills, that is, the capacity to inspire cooperation among other actors by encouraging shared beliefs. According to Fligstein (1997), "social skill can be defined as the ability to motivate cooperation in other actors by providing those actors with common meanings and identities in which actions can be undertaken and justified" (p. 398). This may involve the effective use of framing processes to create appeal for

institutional changes with already accepted narratives (Pacheco et al., 2010). In complicated institutional fields, change takes cooperation from an assortment of actors with different interests (Wijen & Ansari, 2006). Creating new or changing existing institutionalized arrangements often requires substantial effort, and institutional entrepreneurs are described as skillful actors that must cultivate convincing arguments to motivate others to join them in their institutionalization projects (Perkmann & Spicer, 2007; Trittin-Ulbrich & Böckel, 2022; Tumbas et al., 2018). This involves the use of various tactics, including the exertion of direct authority, agenda setting, brokering, negotiating, framing, maintaining ambiguity, aggregating interests, networking, and making others feel they are in control. Tactics used may ultimately depend on the audience and the purpose (Fligstein, 1997).

Conclusions and future directions

Institutional entrepreneurs break with existing institutional arrangements and are actors who push against the status quo (DiMaggio, 1988; Fligstein, 1997). Although scholars have explored this subject (see overviews by Battilana et al., 2009; Tiberius et al., 2020; Pacheco et al., 2010), there could be more context-specific work in different fields. In terms of future directions, Pacheco et al. stated in 2010 that it would be beneficial for institutional entrepreneurship research to consider mainstream entrepreneurship theories more carefully, and this is still a worthwhile concern. Work in this area can incorporate different theoretical perspectives of entrepreneurship and how they may contribute to the understanding of institutional entrepreneurship dynamics as they unfold.

Acs et al. (2018) propose that entrepreneurs, operating within productive institutional environments, supply the transmission mechanism from innovation to economic growth. Support exists for the function of the entrepreneurial ecosystem in economic growth. Furthermore, there are joint effects of entrepreneurship and institutions on economic growth. It would be worthwhile to explore this impact and the trajectory of such growth over time.

The work of Gasbarro et al. (2018) introduces sustainable institutional entrepreneurs and considers the value of sustainable innovation as a means of increasing legitimacy within institutions, thus triggering institutional change. As sustainability issues become more pronounced societally, researchers may consider how institutional change affects and is affected by initiatives relating to this.

The quantity of publications and their citations demonstrate the growing trend and mounting research interest in institutional entrepreneurship (Tiberius et al., 2020). As researchers understand more about institutional entrepreneurship and how entrepreneurs have the capacity to break with existing institutional norms, it becomes clear that the implications of institutional change are significant for understanding continued economic growth and evolution.

References

Acs, Z. J., Estrin, S., Mickiewicz, T., and Szerb, L. (2018) 'Entrepreneurship, institutional economics, and economic growth: An ecosystem perspective', *Small Business Economics*, 51(2), pp. 501–514.

Adachi, T., and Hisada, T. (2017) 'Gender differences in entrepreneurship and intrapreneurship: An empirical analysis', *Small Business Economics*, 48(3), pp. 447–486.

Aldrich, H. E. (2011) 'Heroes, villains, and fools: Institutional entrepreneurship, NOT institutional entrepreneurs', *Entrepreneurship Research Journal*, 1(2), pp. 1–4.

Aldrich, H. E. (2012) 'The emergence of entrepreneurship as an academic field: A personal essay on institutional entrepreneurship', *Research Policy*, 41, pp. 1240–1248.

Alvesson, M., and Spicer, A. (2019) 'Neo-Institutional theory and organization studies. A mid- life crisis?', *Organization Studies*, 40(2), pp. 199–218.

Antoncic, B., and Hisrich, R. D. (2001) 'Intrapreneurship', *Journal of Business Venturing*, 16(5), pp. 495–527.

Antoncic, B., and Hisrich, R. D. (2003) 'Clarifying the intrapreneurship concept', *Journal of Small Business and Enterprise Development*, 10(1), pp. 7–24.

Barley, S. R., and Tolbert, P. S. (1997) 'Institutionalization and structuration: Studying the links between action and institution', *Organization Studies*, 18(1), pp. 93–117.

Battilana, J. (2006) 'Agency and institutions: The enabling role of individuals' social position', *Organization*, 13(5), pp. 653–676.

Battilana, J. (2011) 'The enabling role of social position in diverging from the institutional status quo: Evidence from the UK National Health Service', *Organization Science*, 22(4), pp. 817–834.

Battilana, J., Leca, B., and Boxenbaum, E. (2009) 'How actors change institutions: Towards a theory of institutional entrepreneurship', *Academy of Management Annals*, 3(1), pp. 65–107.

Beckert, J. (1999) 'Agency, entrepreneurs, and institutional change: The role of strategic choice and institutionalized practices in organizations', *Organization Studies*, 20(5), pp. 777–799.

Blanka, C. (2019) 'An individual-level perspective on intrapreneurship: A review and ways forward', *Review of Managerial Science*, 13(5), pp. 919–961.

Bolanos, J. A. (2019) 'Energy, uncertainty, and entrepreneurship: John D Rockefeller's sequential approach to transaction costs management in the early oil industry', *Energy Research and Social Science*, 55, pp. 26–34.

Bouncken, R. B., Kraus, S., and Martinez-Perez, J. F. (2020) 'Entrepreneurship of an institutional field: The emergence of coworking spaces for digital business models', *International Entrepreneurship and Management Journal*, 16(4), pp. 1464–1481.

Cartel, M., Boxenbaum, E., and Aggeri, F. (2019) 'Just for fun! How experimental spaces stimulate innovation in institutionalized fields', *Organization Studies*, 40(1), pp. 65–92.

Colombero, S., and Boxenbaum, E. (2019) 'Authentication as institutional maintenance work', *Journal of Management Studies*, 56(2), pp. 408–440.

Croitoru, A. (2012) 'Schumpeter, J. A., 1934 (2008) The theory of economic development: An inquiry into profits, capital, credit, interest and the business cycle', translated from the German by Redvers Opie, New Brunswick (U.S.A) and London (U.K.): Transaction Publishers. *Journal of Comparative Research in Anthropology and Sociology*, 3(2), pp. 137–148.

Dacin, M. T., Goodstein, J., and Scott, W. R. (2002) 'Institutional theory and institutional change: Introduction to the special research forum', *Academy of Management Journal*, 45(1), pp. 45–56.

D'Aunno, T., Succi, M., and Alexander, J. A. (2000) 'The role of institutional and market forces in divergent organizational change', *Administrative Science Quarterly*, 45(4), pp. 679–703.

David, R. J., Sine, W. D., and Haveman, H. A. (2013) 'Seizing opportunity in emerging fields: How institution entrepreneurs legitimated the professional form of management consulting', *Organizational Science*, 24(2), pp. 356–377.
DiMaggio, P. (1988) 'Interest and agency in institutional theory', in L. G. Zucker (ed.) *Research on Institutional Patterns: Environment and Culture*. Ballinger Publishing Co, pp. 3–22.
DiMaggio, P., and Powell, W. (1983) 'The iron cage revisited: Institutional isomorphism and collective rationality in organizational fields', *American Sociological Review*, 48(2), pp. 147–160.
DiMaggio, P. J., and Powell, W. W. (1991) *New institutionalism in organizational analysis*. University of Chicago Press.
Dorado, S. (2005) 'Institutional entrepreneurship, partaking, and convening', *Organizational Studies*, 26(3), pp. 385–414.
Estrin, S., Korosteleva, J., and Mickiewicz, T. (2022) 'Schumpeterian entry: Innovation, exporting, and growth aspirations of entrepreneurs', *Entrepreneurship Theory and Practice*, 46(2), pp. 269–296.
Ferreira, M. P., Reis, N. R., and Pinto, C. F. (2017) 'Schumpeter's (1934) influence on entrepreneurship (and management) research', *Revista de Empreendedorismo e Gestão de Pequenas Empresas*, 6(1), pp. 4–39.
Filser, M., Tiberius, V., Kraus, S., Zeitlhofer, T., Kailer, N., and Müller, A. (2023) 'Opportunity recognition: Conversational foundations and pathways ahead', *Entrepreneurship Research Journal*, 13(1), pp. 1–30.
Fligstein, N. (1997) 'Social skill and institutional theory', *The American Behavioral Scientist*, 40(4), pp. 397–405.
Fulgsang, L., and Jagd, S. (2015) 'Making sense of institutional trust in organizations: Bridging institutional context and trust', *Organization*, 22(1), pp. 23–39.
Galindo-Martín, M-A., Méndez-Picazo, M-T., and Castaño-Martínez, M-S. (2020) 'The role of innovation and institutions in entrepreneurship and economic growth in two groups of countries', *International Journal of Entrepreneurial Behaviour and Research*, 26(3), pp. 485–502.
Garud, R., Hardy, C., and Maguire, S. (2007) 'Institutional entrepreneurship as embedded agency: An introduction to the Special Issue', *Organization Studies*, 28(7), pp. 957–969.
Garud, R., Jain, S., and Kumaraswamy, A. (2002) 'Institutional entrepreneurship in the sponsorship of common technological standards: The case of Sun Microsystems and Java', *Academy of Management Journal*, 45(1), pp. 196–214.
Garud, R., and Karnøe, P. (2003) 'Bricolage versus breakthrough: Distributed and embedded agency in technology entrepreneurship', *Research Policy*, 32(02), pp. 277–300.
Gasbarro, F., Rizzi, F., and Frey, M. (2018) 'Sustainable institutional entrepreneurship in practice. Insights from SMEs in the clean energy sector in Tuscany (Italy)', *International Journal of Entrepreneurial Behaviour and Research*, 24(2), pp. 476–498.
Greenwood, R., and Hinings, C. R. (1996) 'Understanding radical organizational change: Bringing together the old and the new institutionalism', *The Academy of Management Review*, 21(4), pp. 1022–1054.
Greenwood, R., and Suddaby, R. (2006) 'Institutional entrepreneurship in mature fields: The Big Five accounting firms', *Academy of Management Journal*, 49(1), pp. 27–48.
Hambrick, D. C., and Chen, M-J. (2008) 'New academic fields as admittance-seeking social movements: The case of strategic management', *The Academy of Management Review*, 33(1), pp. 32–54.
Hargadon, A. B., and Douglas, Y. (2001) 'When innovations meet institutions: Edison and the design of the electric light', *Administrative Science Quarterly*, 46(3), pp. 476–501.

Haveman, H. A. (1993) 'Follow the leader: Mimetic isomorphism and entry into new markets', *Administrative Science Quarterly*, 38(4), pp. 593–627.

Heugens, P., and Lander, M. (2009) 'Structure! Agency! (and other quarrels): A meta-analysis of institutional theories of organization', *Academy of Management Journal*, 52(1), pp. 61–85.

Hinings, B., Gegenhuber, T., and Greenwood, R. (2018) 'Digital innovation and transformation: An institutional perspective', *Information and Organization*, 28(1), pp. 52–61.

Huang, L-Y., Yang Lin, S-M., and Hsieh, Y-J. (2021) 'Cultivation of intrapreneurship: A framework and challenges', *Frontiers in Psychology*, 12, pp. 1–14.

Hung, S-C., and Whittington, R. (2011) 'Agency in national innovation systems: Institutional entrepreneurship and the professionalization of Taiwanese IT', *Research Policy*, 40(4), pp. 526–538.

Kraatz, M. S., and Moore, J. H. (2002) 'Executive migration and institutional change', *Academy of Management Journal*, 45(1), pp. 120–143.

Landström, H., and Harirchi, G. (2018) 'The social structure of entrepreneurship as a scientific field', *Research Policy*, 47, pp. 650–662.

Landström, H., Harirchi, G., and Åström, F. (2012) 'Entrepreneurship: Exploring the knowledge base', *Research Policy*, 41(7), pp. 1154–1181.

Leca, B., and Naccache, P. (2006) 'A critical realist approach to institutional entrepreneurship', *Organization*, 13(5), pp. 627–651.

Leccese, S. R. (2017) 'John D. Rockefeller, Standard Oil, and the rise of corporate public relations in progressive America, 1902–1908', *The Journal of the Gilded Age and Progressive Era*, 16(3), pp. 245–263.

Lee, C. K., and Hung, S. C. (2014) 'Institutional entrepreneurship in the informal economy: China's Shan-Zhai mobile phones', *Strategic Entrepreneurship Journal*, 8(1), pp. 16–36.

Maguire, S., Hardy, C., and Lawrence, T. B. (2004) 'Institutional entrepreneurship in emerging fields: HIV/AIDS treatment advocacy in Canada', *Academy of Management Journal*, 47(5), pp. 657–679.

Mair, J., and Martí, I. (2009) 'Entrepreneurship in and around institutional voids: A case study from Bangladesh', *Journal of Business Venturing*, 24(5), pp. 419–435.

Mair, J., Martí, I., and Ventresca, M. (2012) 'Building inclusive markets in rural Bangladesh: How intermediaries work institutional voids', *Academy of Management Journal*, 55(4), pp. 819–850.

Manolova, T. S., Eunni, R. V., and Gyoshev, B. S. (2008) 'Institutional environments for entrepreneurship: Evidence from emerging economies in Eastern Europe', *Entrepreneurship Theory and Practice*, 32(1), pp. 203–218.

Meyer, J. W., and Rowan, B. (1977) 'Institutionalized organizations: Formal structure as myth and ceremony', *American Journal of Sociology*, 83, pp. 340–363.

Mokyr, J. (2023) 'Creative destruction or destruction creation? A prelude to the industrial revolution', in U. Akcigit, J. van Reenen, and E. Macron (eds.) *The economics of creative destruction: New research on themes from Aghion and Howitt*. Cambridge, MA and London, England: Harvard University Press, pp. 714–735.

Morrison, A. (2006) 'A contextualisation of entrepreneurship', *International Journal of Entrepreneurial Behaviour and Research*, 12(4), pp. 192–209.

Navis, C., and Glynn, M. A. (2010) 'How new market categories emerge: Temporal dynamics of legitimacy, identity, and entrepreneurship in satellite radio, 1990–2005', *Administrative Science Quarterly*, 55(3), pp. 439–471.

Nissan, E., Galindo, M.-A., and Méndez Picazo, M.-T. (2011) 'Relationship between organizations, Institutions, entrepreneurship and economic growth process', *International Entrepreneurship Management Journal*, 7(3), pp. 311–324.

Nite, C., and Edwards, J. (2021) 'From isomorphism to institutional work: Advancing institutional theory in sport management research', *Sport Management Review*, 24(5), pp. 815–838.

Pacheco, D. F., York, J. G., Dean, T. J., and Sarasvathy, S. D. (2010) 'The coevolution of institutional entrepreneurship: A tale of two theories', *Journal of Management*, 36(4), pp. 974–1010.

Pandey, J., Gupta, M., and Hassan, Y. (2021) Intrapreneurship to engage employees: Role of psychological capital', *Management Decision*, 59(6), pp. 1525–154.

Parker, S. C. (2011) 'Intrapreneurship or entrepreneurship?', *Journal of Business Venturing*, 26(1), pp. 19–34.

Perkmann, M., and Spicer, A. (2007) '"Healing the scars of history": Projects, skills, and field strategies in institutional entrepreneurship', *Organizational Studies*, 28(7), pp. 1101–1122.

Phillips, N., and Tracey, P. (2007) 'Opportunity recognition, entrepreneurial capabilities and bricolage: Connecting institutional theory and entrepreneurship in strategic organization', *Strategic Organization*, 5(3), pp. 313–320.

Puffer, S. M., McCarthy, D. J., and Boisot, M. (2010) 'Entrepreneurship in Russia and China: The impact of formal institutional voids', *Entrepreneurship Theory and Practice*, 34(3), pp. 441–467.

Reay, T., Chreim, S., Golden-Biddle, K., Goodrick, E., Williams, B. E., Casebeer, A., Pablo, A., and Hinings, C. R. (2013) 'Transforming new ideas into practice: An activity based perspective on the institutionalization of practices', *Journal of Management Studies*, 50(6), pp. 963–990.

Reay, T., Golden-Biddle, K., and Germann, K. (2006) 'Legitimizing a new role: Small wins and microprocesses of change', *Academy of Management Journal*, 49(5), pp. 977–998.

Schumpeter, J. A. (1934) *The theory of economic development*. Cambridge: Harvard University Press.

Scott, W. R. (1987) 'The adolescence of institutional theory', *Administrative Science Quarterly*, 32(4), pp. 493–511.

Scott, W. R. (2001) *Institutions and organizations* (2nd ed.). Thousand Oaks, CA: Sage.

Seo, M-G., and Creed, W. E. D. (2002) 'Institutional contradictions, praxis, and institutional change: A dialectical perspective', *The Academy of Management Review*, 27(2), pp. 222–247.

Shane, S., and Venkataraman, S. (2000) 'The promise of entrepreneurship as a field of research', *The Academy of Management Review*, 25(1), pp. 217–226.

Smilor, R. W. (1997) 'Entrepreneurship: Reflections on a subversive activity', *Journal of Business Venturing*, 12(5), pp. 341–346.

Sobel, R. S. (2008) 'Testing Baumol: Institutional quality and the productivity of entrepreneurship', *Journal of Business Venturing*, 23(6), pp. 641–655.

Suchman, M. C. (1995) 'Managing legitimacy: Strategic and institutional approaches', *The Academy of Management Review*, 20(3), pp. 571–610.

Suddaby, R., and Greenwood, R. (2005) 'Rhetorical strategies of legitimacy', *Administrative Science Quarterly*, 50(1), pp. 35–67.

Taeuscher, K., Bouncken, R., and Pesch, R. (2021) 'Gaining legitimacy by being different: Optimal distinctiveness in crowdfunding platforms', *Academy of Management Journal*, 64(1), pp. 149–179.

Tiberius, V., Rietz, M., and Bouncken, R. B. (2020) 'Performance analysis and science mapping of institutional entrepreneurship research', *Administrative Sciences*, 10(3), 1–21.

Tolbert, P. S., David, R. J., and Sine, W. D. (2011) 'Studying choice and change: The intersection of institutional theory and entrepreneurship research', *Organization Science*, 22(5), pp. 1332–1344.

Tolbert, P. S., and Zucker, L. G. (1983) 'Institutional sources of change in the formal structure of organizations: The diffusion of civil service reform, 1880–1935', *Administrative Science Quarterly*, 28(1), pp. 22–39.

Tracey, P., Phillips, N., and Jarvis, O. (2011) 'Bridging institutional entrepreneurship and the creation of new organizational forms: A multilevel model', *Organization Science*, 22(1), pp. 60–80.

Trittin-Ulbrich, H., and Böckel, A. (2022) 'Institutional entrepreneurship for responsible digital innovation: The case of corporate digital responsibility', *Creativity and Innovation Management*, 31(3), pp. 447–459.

Tumbas, S., Berente, N., and von Brocke, J. (2018) 'Digital innovation and institutional entrepreneurship: Chief Digital Officer perspectives of their emerging role', *Journal of Information Technology*, 33(3), pp. 188–202.

Welter, F., Xheneti, M., and Smallbone, D. (2018) 'Entrepreneurial resourcefulness in unstable institutional contexts: The example of European Union borderlands', *Strategic Entrepreneurship Journal*, 12(1), pp. 23–53.

Wijen, F., and Ansari, S. (2006) 'Overcoming inaction through collective institutional entrepreneurship: Insights from regime theory', *Organization Studies*, 28(7), pp. 1079–1100.

Zilber, T. B. (2007) 'Stories and the discursive dynamics of institutional entrepreneurship: The case of Israeli high-tech after the bubble', *Organization Studies*, 28, pp. 1035–1054.

Zimmerman, M. A., and Zeitz, G. J. (2002) 'Beyond survival: Achieving new venture growth by building legitimacy', *The Academy of Management Review*, 27(3), pp. 414–431.

13 Cultural entrepreneurship in historical and contemporary context

Perspectives on repertoire construction and recording practice in the field of classical guitar performance

Mark Marrington

Introduction

In the context of the present volume, this chapter aims to expand the scope of the application of cultural entrepreneurship theory through consideration of a case study of the recording strategies of a single individual, the classical guitarist Andrés Segovia (1893–1987) in the early-to-mid 20th century. The chapter draws upon material garnered in the course of my own recent musicological research into the classical music recording industry as well as the field of classical guitar performance and recording per se (Marrington 2021). While a classical guitarist case study may justifiably be regarded as a niche example, its function here is to elicit an analysis of cultural entrepreneurship practice which synthesizes historical notions of the entrepreneurial nature of the classical musician with concepts recently imported into cultural entrepreneurship theory from sociology (Bourdieu). This has provided an impetus for redefining the recording classical musician as a specific type of cultural entrepreneur whose remit, in collaboration with cultural intermediaries such as the music producer, is to experiment with existing cultural forms (namely musical repertoire), with a view to eliciting 'new combinations' that can be commodified. Additionally, this chapter's focus on an account of entrepreneurial practice in the early to mid-20th century situates it within the field of entrepreneurship history per se, in the manner of seminal essays such as Dimaggio's (1982) examination of entrepreneurship in the development of musical high culture in Boston during the 19th century.[1] In these terms, the chapter may have particular value to educators who wish to consider historical models of past entrepreneurial practice within the arts through the lens of contemporary cultural entrepreneurship paradigms.

DOI: 10.4324/9781003324737-13

Problematizing the classical musician as entrepreneur: some perspectives from the literature

As a means of providing a context for this article's remit and case study focus, it is pertinent to discuss some perspectives from the literature that have problematized the relationship between the classical musician and the idea of the entrepreneur, before moving towards a consideration of how this might be resolved. Among the more significant texts to have tackled this question from the perspective of the classical musician is William Weber's (2004) foundational multi-author volume, *The Musician as Entrepreneur*, which presents a number of historical case studies of music entrepreneurship during the period 1700–1914.[2] A key point made by Weber in his introductory chapter is that the entrepreneurial activities of classical musicians have not, generally speaking, been a focus of academic enquiry:

> Music historians tend to give musicians too little credit for their central roles in shaping and re-shaping musical life on a broad social plane. We usually think of musicians either as subordinate to society – in effect menials within it – or as spiritually superior to and separate from it. We tend to lean on certain cliches: the musician as an inferior at court, as a fashionable object in public, as genius unmindful of the public, or as an avant-garde force in his or her own world.
>
> (2004: 3)

Here, Weber encapsulates several of the more cliched perceptions of the classical musician, which have been inculcated into the minds of both classical music audiences and practitioners. Of particular relevance to the present context is the persistence of the notion of the musician as 'genius unmindful of the public' and 'the avant-garde force in his or her own world' which often feeds into the view that there is somehow an unbridgeable division between the areas of art and commerce. This is something which, as Caves (2000) has observed, has its roots in the education system, in the case of classical musicians the conservatory which 'reinforces the attitude of a priestly calling to cultivate an art rather than prepare for a career', and continues to problematized by much of the recent writing on music entrepreneurship, whether in the academic arena (Bennett 2008; Bogdan 2008; Dumbreck and McPherson 2016; Radbill 2017; Nytch 2018) or in more informal online publications. Such writing often reiterates the general point that there is a need for educational establishments to teach their music students to take an entrepreneurial attitude towards developing their careers or attempts to increase entrepreneurship awareness by offering specific advice and case studies. The implication of Weber's aforementioned volume is that a reorientation of historical perspective to encompass the entrepreneurial practices of past musicians can also play an important role in addressing this deficiency and thereby provide inspiration for current and future practitioners. Weber states:

> We need instead to ask how musicians worked as active agents within musical life and thereby within society as a whole. Thus, we must start taking musicians seriously as business people and as social forces. That involves studying how they acted as entrepreneurs and how they took advantage of opportunities before them.
>
> (2004: 3)

Situating the contemporary classical musician as entrepreneur: integrating artistic idealism with entrepreneurship theory

A particular limitation of Weber's book is that the various case studies presented by its contributors do not explicitly draw upon theories deriving from the field of entrepreneurship, although many of its essays certainly imply ideas related to this context. This is unsurprising given that the primary field of Weber's scholarship is historical musicology, which has not traditionally focused on the socio-economic contexts of musical practice. What is required, therefore, is a means of reframing artistic practices of classical musicians in relation to specific concepts and themes from the entrepreneurship field that can enable us to evaluate their activities in terms of entrepreneurial behaviour. Recent developments in entrepreneurship theory have revealed considerable potential for resolving this issue by situating accounts of artists' creative activities in relation to the idea of 'cultural' entrepreneurship, which provides a means of bridging the gap between conventional economic perspectives on the entrepreneur and certain kinds of artistic endeavour in ways that can be usefully harnessed to interrogate case studies. Key to this has been the adoption of the sociological theories of Pierre Bourdieu which have drawn attention to the manner in which creative practitioners operate within a network of relationships defined by concepts of 'capital' (Bourdieu 1993). Bourdieu's ideas have been employed by Scott (2012),[3] for example, as a means of shedding light on the ways in which independent 'DIY' music producers (the 'cultural entrepreneurs' in question) demonstrate entrepreneurial agency through the mobilization of particular forms of social, cultural and symbolic capital to bring their work to the attention of 'cultural intermediaries', namely gatekeepers operative within a particular system of cultural production, in this case the music industry, who can provide access to forms of economic capital, such as record deals.

In Scott's analysis, cultural entrepreneurs, typically lacking economic resources early in their careers (operating 'sans capital'), have to find imaginative ways to generate interest in the cultural artefacts they produce such that they are perceived to have an exchange value that will permit their commodification.

Here Scott (echoing Caves 2000) acknowledges the point already made that artists typically lack predisposition towards commercial activity and do not necessarily operate first and foremost with a view to financial gain ('cultural entrepreneurs' motivations cannot be reduced to economic interest'); rather, they are primarily driven by the intrinsic values of the art form itself and focused on solving specific artistic questions, problems and issues pertinent to the evolution of their discipline. While the latter is a particular strength that the artist possesses which enables him/her to locate a potential site of innovation within the art form, this alone does not usually guarantee the recognition needed to attract cultural intermediaries. Hence, the artist needs to find a means of cultivating what Scott refers to as 'buzz', essentially an atmosphere of interest around their work, generated through collaboration with like-minded individuals (e.g., graphic designers or video makers) in a network of relationships that constitute his/her social capital. Within this system of networked 'capital mobilization', the associates of the artist both benefit from and simultaneously contribute to the latter's elevation to public significance. Hence, a particular notion of the cultural entrepreneur is posited which describes the manner in which the artist, through a networked system, actively constructs him/herself as a 'subject of value', with a view to acquiring the symbolic capital (prestige) necessary to bring them to the attention of cultural intermediaries.

Scott's utilization of Bourdieu's theory of capital as a means of locating processes that, on the part of the artist, can be regarded as entrepreneurial in nature can be usefully harnessed as a means of interrogating historically situated accounts of the activities of classical musicians. Of particular relevance to this chapter's focus, for example, is David Gramit's essay 'Selling the Serious' (2004, in Weber's aforementioned volume), discussing the German musical scene in Europe around 1800. Here, Gramit identifies processes comparable to Scott's notion of 'capital mobilization' at work in the context of the emerging European concert tradition, centred on musical repertoire – that is, the music selected to be presented (in performance) for consumption by the public – and the promotion of particular ideologies surrounding its cultural value. Specifically, Gramit demonstrates that classical musicians (both composers and performers) active at this time were engaged in cultivating a form of symbolic capital built upon the idea of 'serious' music, through the construction of a canon of musical 'works'[4] exhibiting a certain sophisticated musical pedigree and gravitas, characteristics which were commonly contrasted with competing music of a more superficial, ephemeral and frivolous nature (the word 'popular' often being used pejoratively to describe the latter). In discussing these developments, Gramit reiterates the point already made that such attitudes were at odds with commercial thinking:

> Whereas entrepreneurship is inevitably connected with the worlds of commerce and marketing, the very notion of the classical is seen to imply that

> here, at least, that music is freed of such base associations and employed to loftier ends transcending the temporally limited and the material.
>
> (2004: 81)

The espousing of such values necessitated a self-isolation from the mainstream of commercial music which was naturally problematic for the classical musician, who still needed to engage with real-world economic problems. Gramit observes that

> like the superficial and the popular over against which it defined itself, serious music still needed to be sold; if it was to exist, it would have to exist as a commercial product. And so, too, did both the discourse about the serious and the castigation of the fashionable that served to define a separate realm of serious music.
>
> (2004: 90)

To resolve this, those committed to the ideology of the serious evolved strategies for promoting the idea to the public in such a way that it could come to be accepted as desirable, thereby converting their cultural capital into a symbolic form that could be commercially exploited. Specifically, composers engaged in forms of capital mobilization which involved them in collaboration with a network of sympathetic music critics and educators to construct a discourse that would effectively generate a 'buzz' around the idea of 'serious' music. In essence, Gramit locates the origins of a particular form of cultural entrepreneurialism that has occupied classical musicians since the 19th century, namely the process of actively shaping musical taste in favour of particular aesthetic ideals, whose virtue derives from their being in opposition to popular trends. As Gramit puts it, 'we are in the presence, in short, of the entrepreneurial promotion of the anti-entrepreneurial, of the marketing of resistance to the market' (2004: 90). The re-engineering of musical taste in this manner exerted a strong influence upon the programming of music for the concert platform during the 19th century, which gradually moved from what Weber (2008) calls the 'miscellaneous' programme comprising disparate easily consumable lightweight musical tidbits, towards the presentation of approved 'self-consciously serious repertoires'. In addition to advocating the importance of composers such as Ludwig Van Beethoven, George Frideric Handel and Franz Schubert, those concerned with constructing such a repertoire also elicited a further debate which could be mobilized as a means of constructing distinctive symbolic value. This was namely the conflict between those who advocated the performance of older 'classics' versus those whose repertoire inclined towards new music by living composers ('contemporary' music), the relative merits of which were likewise brought to the attention of the public through the polemical writings of music critics such as Eduard Hanslick and Richard Pohl.

The performing classical musician, like the critic, also had a centrally important role in the promotion of new concepts of musical repertoire, occupying a position within the system of social capital that was at the nexus between the composer and their audience. Essentially a mediating presence, the classical performer functioned both as a vehicle for the delivery of musical works through their realisation in sound and, more importantly where the cultural entrepreneurial perspective is concerned, as an advocate of their aesthetic value through their decisions concerning musical programming. Historically, the classical performer's main vehicle for this purpose was the public concert, beginning with the solo recital, which began to be propagated from the 1840s by enterprising virtuosi such as Franz Liszt (often regarded as the originator of the concept), Clara Schumann and the violinist Niccolò Paganini (Weber 2008). The status of these figures, the result of marketing strategies focused on the creation of a mythology around their uncommon performing abilities, granted them a certain authority to advocate on behalf of serious repertoire ideals and cement them in the minds of the public. By the end of the 19th century, the serious repertoire paradigm centred around concepts of historical canon versus contemporary progressivism had become synonymous with the idea of 'classical' music, conditioning the aesthetic choices of those musicians who performed live on the concert stage and those who began in the early 20th century to engage with the new media-oriented modes of presentation of classical music performance, namely the gramophone record.

The classical musician as repertoire 'resource': the inception of artist-producer entrepreneurial bond in the emerging recording industry

A key point that emerges from the preceding discussion is that practitioners engaged in transforming the domain of artistic practice within which they are working require the assistance of others in their social network to bring their ideas into relation with potential consumers. This, in short, constitutes the locus of their cultural entrepreneurial activity. With the advent of recording technology in the late 19th century, new possibilities began to emerge for musicians engaged in the cultivation of such relationships as the medium began to restructure musical culture and the environment of commercial musical activity (see Gelatt 1977; Chanan 1995; Day 2000; Eisenberg 2005). Key to this transformation were the companies involved in the manufacture and distribution of the new recording media (in the early period, Victor, Edison and Columbia), who quickly began to turn their attention to the potential of their inventions for commercial music sales, establishing arms of their operations that were focused on delineating potential markets for music consumption that would inform strategies for the acquisition of musical material suitable of issuing in recorded form. In effect, these companies became the first record labels, marking the inception of the music industry and a model of music selling that still remains in place today. Not being musicians themselves, the owners of the new recording technologies typically deferred responsibility for locating potential musical subject matter to A&R (Artists and Repertoire) men. These were personnel who were charged with an essentially entrepreneurial function, namely to use their knowledge of the cultural landscape of music practice to identify and acquire content for recording. These individuals, some of whom were performers themselves, travelled widely in search of recording opportunities and were usually charismatic personalities who were skilled at persuading musicians often unfamiliar with, or averse to, the new medium to make records in a variety of social and cultural situations (see Gelatt 1977). Among the most important figures in this regard were Fred Gaisberg and Harry and Raymond Sooy, who are today commonly recognized as the first music producers (Burgess 2014).

Classical music, with its ready-made repertoire of established classics, was a natural choice for those engaged in garnering material for recording purposes, both on account of its cultural prestige and the fact that there was a well-established star system of notable performers available to be marshalled to record this music. As (perhaps surprisingly) many of the most famous classical musicians of this period were for various reasons initially resistant to recording, a key role of entrepreneurial A&R figures at this time was to convince artists to overcome their reservations and begin to regard making records as an essential aspect of their professional career portfolio. It was important in the early stages of this new collaborative relationship that such personnel did not dictate the repertoire choices of these artists when recording, but rather defer to their musical preferences, which would reflect what had already been proven on the concert stage. The mid-19th-century operatic soprano Adelina Patti (1843–1919) offers a well-known illustration. As an artist whose career had been built on the concert platform in the 1860s and 1870s, Patti initially showed little interest recording and had to be won over through persistent overtures by Fred Gaisberg and his recording team (on behalf of the Gramophone Company, later HMV), who even made the trek to camp out near her residence at Craig-Y-Nos castle in Wales. When Patti eventually acquiesced to sing before the phonograph, she exclaimed with great surprise, 'Ah! Mon Dieu! Maintenant je comprends pourquoi je suis Patti!' ('My God! Now I understand why I am Patti!'), finally being convinced of the recording medium's potential for transmitting her artistic image to the public. Subsequently, she became one of the Gramophone Company's most high-profile recording artists, cutting historically important discs of Mozart, Gounod and Bellini, composers closely associated with her operatic performing career (Ronald 1922).

By the mid-1920s with the dramatic improvement of recording techniques following the introduction of electrical process and the invention of the microphone, recording began to become a more attractive prospect to the classical musicians and an increasingly normalized aspect of their career development.

Recognizing that records could play a significant role in the construction of their public profile, the classical musician now began to cultivate new entrepreneurial strategies for promoting their artistry within the new environment engendered by the emergent technology. Of particular significance in this regard was the recognition that recordings could be more than simply a vehicle for showcasing performing prowess, but also harnessed as a means of actively shaping musical aesthetics through repertoire choice. This is an important turning point for the more enterprising recording classical musician who now began to cultivate a role within the context of their contractual obligations to the recording company that can be regarded as entrepreneurial in nature.[5] The case of the classical guitarist Andrés Segovia, whose career encompasses several decades from the early electrical period of recording through to the 1970s, provides a useful vehicle for examining this process.

The recording classical guitarist as cultural entrepreneur: the case of Andrés Segovia

Segovia's entrepreneurial activities during the 1920s constitute a particular response to the concept of the classical guitar and the musical aesthetics that had shaped its development in the early 19th century following the emergence of the modern six-string instrument. During this period, idea of a 'classical' guitar repertoire was gradually inserted into musical culture through the activities of entrepreneurially minded performers active in certain parts of Europe, including Fernando Sor, Dionisio Aguado and Mauro Giuliani. Like their contemporaries Liszt and Paganini, these guitarists made names for themselves as virtuosi and performed a self-composed solo repertoire designed to showcase the new instrument's musical potential, although the limited projection of the instrument at this time confined them to the intimate salon performance circuit. The next generation of players that emerged in the wake of these figures in the mid-late 19th century, including the Spaniards Francisco Tárrega and Miguel Llobet, now benefitting from an improved instrument which could be heard in larger auditoria, built upon these foundations by expanding the guitar repertoire to encompass a more diverse range of material derived from transcribing music written for solo instruments such as the piano and violin. Here, their repertoire programmes were clearly influenced by the movement towards the performance of serious 'classics' then being promoted by solo recitalists in Europe, including arrangements of music by sanctioned composers such as Ludwig Van Beethoven, Franz Schubert, Frederic Chopin and Felix Mendelssohn. The displays of technical prowess required to perform such material on the guitar played an important role in overturning the stereotypical view that it was a 'popular' instrument best suited to the accompaniment of singers. By shifting the emphasis to the performance of serious repertoire in a concert hall setting, performers now began to elevate the status of the guitar such that it began to be perceived as a vehicle for the performance of music of substance. Around this, there developed a narrative of the guitar's transcendence of its popular roots to the realm of the serious, reflecting the previously discussed trends in 19th-century classical music aesthetics. This later became an entrenched construct which was to be persistently employed by performers in their choices of repertoire for the instrument in the 20th century, and also became central to the recording strategy of Andrés Segovia.

Segovia's qualities as a cultural entrepreneur – principally relating to the manner in which, through his recordings, he dramatically transformed the concept of the classical guitar and its repertoire in the mid-20th century – were present from the inception of his performing career, which evolved in the context of the public concert tradition in Spain. In the early phase of his concertizing, Segovia adopted, tried and tested approaches to repertoire programming that would have chimed with Spanish audiences at this time, constructing his recitals from the repertoire of the late-19th-century Spanish guitar school and prioritizing transcriptions of 'serious' works written for instruments such as piano and violin by Tárrega and Llobet, together with miscellaneous compositions by the early 19th-century founders of the classical guitar, such as Fernando Sor. Conscious that founding his artistic identity upon such an approach would only carry him so far, Segovia began to innovate in order to expand the scope of his repertoire. Initially, this was through the inclusion of his own transcriptions of well-known works by canonical composers, such as Chopin and Mendelssohn (Segovia 1976). However, following his celebrated Paris debut in 1924, which established him as a presence on the international stage, Segovia's approach to repertoire construction began to change significantly. This was because, in the light of his increasing fame, he had now begun to gain access to a social network of high-profile musicians, including several notable composers who were interested in writing music for him to perform. Thus, the reciprocal relationship noted earlier in reference to Scott's discussion of capital mobilization was in play here, in the sense that individuals with shared artistic interests and objectives began coalescing to create a network of social capital, which benefitted and elevated all involved. In this instance, Segovia began to acquire fresh material for his concerts on the basis of which he could continue to build his progressive repertoire aesthetic, while his composer colleagues were afforded a powerful vehicle for the global dissemination of their music. The result was the establishment by the early 1950s of a distinctly Segovian classical guitar repertoire paradigm built on works by contemporary composers hailing from a wide range of national and cultural contexts, including Manuel Ponce (Mexico), Mario Castelnuovo-Tedesco (Italy), Federico Moreno Torroba (Spain), Joaquín Turina (Spain) and later, Heitor Villa-Lobos (Brazil), most of whom exhibited more fashionably '20th century'–oriented musical outlooks. A second important strategy adopted by Segovia at this time was to delve into the classical guitar's European past for repertoire opportunities – for example the music of the 16th-century Spanish vihuelists and the lute music of J.S. Bach, the latter in particular coming to represent an important repertoire calling card. By the late 1920s, as Segovia moved into the sphere of recording, he had constructed a repertoire, which while still founded within marketable 19th-century Spanish musical paradigms was beginning to reflect an increasing musical cosmopolitanism, while simultaneously becoming more deeply historically based.

After initially being resistant to recording, Segovia had by the mid-1920s begun to recognize the importance of the 78 rpm record as a vehicle for projecting his repertoire concept to the global music marketplace. Notably, his first recording contract – with the HMV label, lasting from 1927 to 1939 – was brokered by the aforementioned Fred Gaisberg, who was closely involved as a producer of Segovia's recording sessions. Gaisberg would have most likely become aware of Segovia through his appearances on the London concert circuit during this period through which he would have recognized the potential to market his performances on record, especially as the microphone was now making the recording of quieter instruments such as the guitar a realistic prospect. However, it is clear from the repertoire choices for these recording sessions that the programming decisions themselves were not being dictated by Gaisberg, who rather deferred to the musical instincts of a proven artist who had been selling out concert halls across Europe for more than a decade. Indeed, even if Gaisberg had been inclined to shape the outcome, this would have been difficult due to the fact that the classical guitar repertoire concept at this time was only superficially understood outside dedicated guitar circles. As Gaisberg's (1942) account of recording Segovia indicates, there appears to have been little more than a general expectation that it would reflect the exoticism of 'Spanish' music in some way.

Segovia naturally capitalized upon this situation, using the license he had been given through his recording contract to construct a distinctively new repertoire concept, and one which could be closely conflated with his performer image. On the one hand, the recordings reflect the traditional basis of Segovia's repertoire during this early period, encompassing the foundational material of his concert programmes, including a significant emphasis on the classic Spanish guitar repertoire of the late 19th century (including Tárrega and transcriptions of the music Enrique Granados and Isaac Albéniz). However, they also show that Segovia was actively using the recording medium as a means of promoting the new musical aesthetics that he was exploring through his developing network of contemporary composers, resulting in cuts of works by Ponce, Castelnuovo-Tedesco and Torroba, as well as a vehicle for arguing the case for pre-19th-century transcribed music which was not widely accepted at this time as 'classical guitar' repertoire, particularly the music of J.S. Bach. That Segovia's approach to repertoire programming was mould breaking (i.e., creatively destructive) even at this early point in his recording career is reflected in the reviews of his discs that appeared in the late 1920s and early 1930s, which typically expressed both surprise and incredulity with regard to his performances of Bach on the guitar and his choices of contemporary composer, a number of whom were unfamiliar to critics at this time (Marrington 2021). Thus, with Segovia we observe a situation in which the elite status of his artistry, accruing from his prestige on the concert platform, afforded him a certain amount of currency in the recording situation that enabled him to 'call the shots' when working with producers and record labels, the latter trusting him to originate new repertoire paradigms that could be marketable. This gave Segovia considerable scope for operating in the cultural entrepreneur mould, but within the safety net of the record label, the latter assisting him in constructing a narrative of his artistic evolution that could form the basis of his classical guitar brand.

After leaving HMV in 1939, and following a brief hiatus in his global performing activity due to the Second World War, Segovia resumed his recording career in 1944, securing further recording contracts with two major US labels – American Decca and Columbia – and the small short-lived independent label, Musicraft. Once again, it is clear here that Segovia's prestige was affording him considerable license to record what he wished, with his labels deferring to the repertoire concept he had already laid down with HMV. The result was further discs of music by his contemporary composer associates, including Villa-Lobos, Castelnuovo-Tedesco and Ponce, as well as new transcriptions of the music of J.S. Bach, including the landmark release (on the Musicraft label in 1946) of the composer's monumental Chaconne (a transcription from the violin), which in hindsight can be seen to have been designed specifically as a vehicle for promoting the idea of guitar as 'serious' instrument that could (in Segovia's gifted hands) field repertoire of considerable musical profundity. From 1952, Segovia began to work exclusively with American Decca, the label now providing him with a long-term vehicle for him to consolidate his repertoire concept. This coincided with the invention of one of the most important technological innovations of the era, the Long Playing (LP) record, whose increased playing time (around 20 minutes per side) dramatically transformed recording practice, freeing the musician from the limitations of the (3 minutes per side) 78 rpm format. Segovia's approach to using the new LP medium in his first recordings for the American Decca label (issued between 1952 and 1954, produced by Simon Rady) was to issue 'concert' style recital programmes which mirrored the experience of the live Segovia performance. These were presented with sleeve notes designed to reflect traditional concert programmes, often accompanied by comments relating to Segovia's innovations within the classical repertoire and his by-then familiar 'mission statement' to elevate the guitar's status. In effect, Segovia was reinforcing the narratives around his concept of the classical repertoire that had accrued since the 1920s, the LP format functioning as a vehicle for solidifying his artistic musical branding.

By the mid-1950s, however, it was clear that this model was becoming untenable, the bulk of Segovia's essential repertoire now having been fully documented in his recordings, necessitating a reconsideration of approach. It was at this point that Segovia began to work closely with a newly appointed producer at American Decca, Israel Horowitz, who – like the recording personnel he had worked with previously – initially deferred to his expertise in the matter of programming. As Horowitz commented in a later interview,

> No one goes to Segovia and says, 'This is what we want to record – go prepare it.' You don't work with him that way. There is some discretion, and very often I may have some influence when it comes down to options, but Segovia decides what he is going to record more than most artists.
>
> (Marrington 2021)

At this point, however, there was a distinct shift in the balance of relationship between producer and artist as Horowitz, through a collaborative process characterized by gentle persuasion, began to edge Segovia away from making recordings that were simply emulations of the live concert experience to a more concept-driven approach which more closely mirrored developments that were being explored in the LP format outside the classical music context (in jazz and popular music, for example). Horowitz remarked that while Segovia

> tends to look upon an album as two program segments – the way he might give them in concert . . . . I must say that this is an area where, as a record person, I would occasionally prefer to have concept albums.
>
> (Marrington 2021)

Central to this new direction was the programming of more substantial guitar works written for Segovia by members of his long-standing network of contemporary composers, namely Castelnuovo-Tedesco, Torroba and Ponce, and a more recently established contact, Alexandre Tansman. Under Horowitz's guidance, Segovia's approach, on albums such as *Five Pieces from Platero and I* (1962), *Segovia* (1965), *Mexicana* (1967) and *Castles of Spain* (1970), was to foreground particular unifying themes around this repertoire, relating to poetry and national character, which were underpinned by specially commissioned album artwork designed by close Segovia associate, Vladimir Bobri. This provided an innovative means of re-packaging Segovia's contemporary repertoire in a way that freed it from the 'recital' framing, enabling him to re-shape his profile and rejuvenate the marketplace for his recordings. The records made by Segovia during this final phase of his association with American Decca thus played an important role in transforming the classical guitar album as commercial product.

It is useful to consider Segovia's relationship of collaboration with Horowitz during this latter phase of his recording career in relation to Peterson and Berger's (1971) analysis of entrepreneurial function of the record producer. Here the authors outline, in reference to the organizational structure of the American record company during the 1960s, the strategy of designating certain areas of organizational operation (such as 'production') as sites of entrepreneurial activity in which context license could be given to certain individuals to generate new markets for music consumption. The primary purpose here was to enable the organization to respond flexibly to volatile market conditions (what they call 'environmental turbulence') at a time of rapid change in popular music style as elicited, for example, by groups such as The Beatles and other exponents of the 'rock music revolution'. At the centre of this activity is the producer who, in a similar manner to earlier A&R figures such as Fred Gaisberg, is valued for their 'presumed ability to find and produce that elusive novelty sound which will generate hit records', and in whom considerable financial resources are invested. Rather than simply capturing new artists on record, however, as would have occurred in the early A&R period, the producer during in the late 1950s and early 1960s was now beginning to be granted a certain amount of license to co-create new material in collaboration with the artist. (George Martin's work with The Beatles is perhaps the most well-known exemplar of this.) This elicited the gradual erosion of 'top-down' hierarchical relationships between recording personnel and artists (a process succinctly mapped by Kealy 1979), in which context the producer–artist relationship began to become a more reciprocal affair, with the producer now working actively with the artist to (in the Schumpeterian sense; 1949: 66) carry out 'new combinations'.

Responses to the classical guitar repertoire concept: cultural entrepreneurial practices of Segovia's successors

By the 1960s, the Segovian concept of the modern classical guitar repertoire, as expounded through his recordings, had become entrenched to such a degree that the younger generation of artists that emerged in his wake were compelled to abide by it in the construction of their performer identities. It is significant, for example, that the two most important classical guitarists to emerge in Britain during the late 1950s/early 1960s, Julian Bream and John Williams, both adopted the Segovian repertoire model to launch their performing careers, a necessity for 'proving' themselves in the eyes of cultural intermediaries now acclimatized to the classical guitar concept. However, like Segovia they then proceeded to use the recording context to carve out more individualized repertoire profiles. This was possible because the major record labels with whom they were contracted – in Bream's case RCA and in Williams', Columbia – each recognized the value of building a relationship with their respective artists that permitted an entrepreneurial approach to evolving concepts of repertoire. Regarding RCA's attitude to his recording career, for example, Bream commented in the 1980s:

> My record company, RCA, has always given me carte blanche to record just what I want and how I want. . . . They may suggest something but normally speaking they allow me to select the music to be recorded. This all comes from many years of trust, of course, and a certain amount of success.

> Obviously I know that certain records will not sell as well as others, but when I've done a record which I have really wanted to do, although I have known it was unlikely to be a great commercial success, I will then try do a more popular album next time.
>
> (Palmer 1983: 164)

Both Bream and Williams, like Segovia, benefitted from the support of their record labels which enabled them to form collaborative relationships with their producers that were highly productive (in Williams' case Paul Myers, in Bream's, James Burnett), affording them opportunities to trial new classical guitar repertoire concepts. This permitted the absorption of a wide range of musical perspectives including (then) somewhat 'uncommercial' ideas from the musical avant-garde, and popular music forms, which served to deconstruct the Segovian classical guitar repertoire concept. This model of practice – building on an existing repertoire paradigm before proceeding to elicit new combinations – has continued to govern the evolution of classical guitarists' recording careers. For example, the recording strategies of guitarists such as Xuefei Yang and Sean Shibe, in more recent years reflect the model of initially deferring to the tried and tested, before utilizing their growing status to advance new repertoire concepts which challenge or re-make the ideas of their predecessors (Marrington 2021). Indeed, it is fair to say that the notion of innovation in guitar repertoire programming has become a key component of the record label's narrativization of the classical guitarist's artistic evolution.[6]

Conclusion

This chapter has aimed, through the foregoing contextualized case study of classical music repertoire construction and the performing/recording career of Andrés Segovia, to demonstrate that certain areas of artistic endeavour whose concerns appear detached from the commercial arena can nonetheless engage with the latter via a cultural entrepreneurship process. Underlying this has been a theoretical perspective derived from Bourdieu (via Scott) concerning the mobilization of capital as a means of bringing artistic activity to the attention of cultural intermediaries, which I have related to historical examples of classical musicians' repertoire strategizing. Regarding this chapter's specific case study, the cultural entrepreneurial remit of the classical guitarist Segovia has been portrayed in terms of his role as an agent of musical innovation who is able, via the conduit of the record producer (an entrepreneur type), to forge a productive relationship with the cultural intermediary of the record company, the latter affording him an economic support system for constructively pursuing the creative imperatives of his art form. The cultural entrepreneur's specific remit in this instance is to re-shape musical culture itself, in this instance expanding (in the terms of Mihaly Csikszentmihalyi's Systems Theory) the bounds of the 'domain' of the classical guitar repertoire. The cultural intermediary co-opts the artist into the designated entrepreneurial context of the organization in a relationship of collaboration (via the producer) which is essentially intrapreneurial, thereby providing a stable as well as economically rewarding context within which this innovation can occur. Ultimately, the aim has been to show that examining such cultural phenomena in these terms can give rise to valuable insights into forms of entrepreneurial behaviour that might not otherwise be noticeable within discipline-specific framings of artistic activity that exclude consideration of such ideas, perhaps even having the potential to provide models for emerging artists to emulate in their contemporary practice.

Notes

1 As established in the 1940s in the journal *Explorations in Entrepreneurial History* (*Explorations in Economic History* since 1969).
2 As the essays in Weber's book refer to musicians active prior to 1914, they imply particular societal and cultural infrastructures that then existed to provide opportunities for remuneration for musical performance and composition, including the public concert and the sheet music publishing industry. However, they do not acknowledge the significant economic changes wrought by the emergence of the recording industry in the early 20th century.
3 Other sources that have influenced my thinking from this perspective include Naudin (2018) and McIntyre et al. (2023).
4 See Goehr (2007) for an extensive discussion of the 'work' concept and its influence on the valorization of music.
5 In this sense, the classical musician, by virtue of their position within the recording company, can also be regarded as 'intrapreneur' in the terms of the definition by Antoncic and Hisrich (2001), namely, they are undertaking 'entrepreneurship within an existing organization' that 'leads not only to new business ventures but also to other innovative activities and orientations such as development of new products, services, technologies, administrative techniques, strategies, and competitive postures'.
6 Michael O'Toole's recent book, *John Williams: Changing the Culture of the Classical Guitar* (2019), foregrounds this narrative explicitly.

Bibliography

Antoncic, B. & Hisrich, R.D. (2001) Intrapreneurship: Construct Refinement and Cross-Cultural Validation. *Journal of Business Venturing*, 16 (5), pp. 495–527.
Bennett, D.E. (2008) *Understanding the Classical Music Profession: The Past, the Present and Strategies for the Future*. Aldershot, Ashgate Publishing, Ltd.
Bogdan, V.M. (2008) *The Classical Musician and Musical Entrepreneurship: A Study Featuring Tango Music from the Public Domain*. Saarbrücken, VDM Verlag Dr. Müller.
Bourdieu, P. (1993) *The Field of Cultural Production*. Cambridge, Polity Press.
Burgess, R.J. (2014) *The History of Music Production*. Oxford, Oxford University Press.
Caves, R.E. (2000) *Creative Industries: Contracts between Art and Commerce*. Cambridge, MA, Harvard University Press.
Chanan, M. (1995) *Repeated Takes: A Short History of Recording and Its Effects on Music*. London, Verso.

Day, T. (2000) *A Century of Recorded Music: Listening to Musical History*. New Haven and London, Yale University Press.

Dimaggio, P. (1982) Cultural Entrepreneurship in Nineteenth-Century Boston: The Creation of an Organizational Base for High Culture in America. *Media, Culture & Society*, 4 (1), pp. 33–50.

Dumbreck, A. & McPherson, G. (2016) *Music Entrepreneurship*. London, Bloomsbury Academic.

Eisenberg, E. (2005) *The Recording Angel: Music, Records and Culture from Aristotle to Zappa*. 2nd ed. New Haven, CT, Yale University Press.

Gelatt, R. (1977) *The Fabulous Phonograph, 1877–1977*. New York, Collier Books.

Goehr, L. (2007) *The Imaginary Museum of Musical Works: An Essay in the Philosophy of Music*. Oxford, Oxford University Press.

Gramit, D. (2004) Selling the Serious: The Commodification of Music and Resistance to It in Germany, circa 1800. In: W. Weber, ed. *The Musician as Entrepreneur, 1700–1914: Managers, Charlatans, and Idealists*. Bloomington, IN, Indiana University Press, pp. 81–102.

Kealy, E.R. (1979) From Craft to Art the Case of Sound Mixers and Popular Music. *Work and Occupations*, 6 (1), pp. 3–29.

Marrington, M. (2021) *Recording the Classical Guitar*. New York, Routledge.

McIntyre, P., Fulton, J., Kerrigan, S. & Meany, M. (2023) Theoretical Contexts of Entrepreneurship in the Creative Industries. In: P. McIntyre, J. Fulton, S. Kerrigan, & M. Meany, eds. *Entrepreneurship in the Creative Industries: How Innovative Agents, Skills and Networks Interact*. Cham, Springer International Publishing, pp. 45–56. Available from: https://doi.org/10.1007/978-3-031-19455-9_3 [Accessed 30 June 2024].

Naudin, A. (2018) *Cultural Entrepreneurship: The Cultural Worker's Experience of Entrepreneurship*. London and New York, Routledge.

Nytch, J. (2018) *The Entrepreneurial Muse: Inspiring Your Career in Classical Music*. Oxford, Oxford University Press.

O'Toole, M. (2019) *John Williams: Changing the Culture of the Classical Guitar: Performance, Perception, Education and Construction*. Abingdon, Oxon, Routledge.

Palmer, T. (1983) *Julian Bream: A Life on the Road*. New York, Franklin Watts.

Peterson, R.A. & Berger, D.G. (1971) Entrepreneurship in Organizations: Evidence from the Popular Music Industry. *Administrative Science Quarterly*, 16 (1), p. 97.

Radbill, C.F. (2017) *Introduction to the Music Industry: An Entrepreneurial Approach, Second Edition*. New York, Routledge.

Ronald, L. (1922) *Variations on a Personal Theme*. London, Hodder and Stoughton Limited.

Schumpeter, J.A. (1949) *The Theory of Economic Development: An Inquiry Into Profits, Capital, Credit, Interest, and the Business Cycle*. Cambridge, MA, Harvard University Press.

Scott, M. (2012) Cultural Entrepreneurs, Cultural Entrepreneurship: Music Producers Mobilising and Converting Bourdieu's Alternative Capitals. *Poetics*, 40 (3), pp. 237–255.

Segovia, A. (1976) *Andrés Segovia: An Autobiography of the Years 1893–1920*. New York, Macmillan.

Weber, W. (2008) *The Great Transformation of Musical Taste: Concert Programming from Haydn to Brahms*. Cambridge, Cambridge University Press.

Weber, W. (2004) *The Musician as Entrepreneur, 1700–1914: Managers, Charlatans, and Idealists*. Bloomington, IN, Indiana University Press.

14 Regulatory institutions and productive entrepreneurship

A focus on small businesses in Iran during Covid-19

Afsaneh Bagheri and Masoud Karami

Introduction

Small firms are significantly influenced by the institutional setting wherein they operate, due to their liabilities which make them more vulnerable (LiPuma et al., 2013; Naudé, 2010). Institutional theory explains how regulatory, normative, and cognitive institutions (Scott, 2005) impact businesses in a myriad of different ways (Honig & Samuelsson, 2021; Montes & Nogueira, 2022). In this study, we focus on regulatory institutions in an emerging market to explore the critical role of government policies in shaping small firms' perceptions of uncertainty during crises and their subsequent actions and strategies to address this perceived uncertainty. This study applies institutional theory (Bruton *et al.*, 2010) and entrepreneurial opportunity literature to explain the role of regulatory institutions in supporting small firms' opportunity development and consequently their resilience and survival in the face of multiple crises. Our findings make several contributions to the underdeveloped literature on the intersection between entrepreneurship and regulations, specifically in the context of emerging markets (Fredström *et al.*, 2021) by highlighting the roles that regulatory institutions play in guiding entrepreneurs towards developing and exploiting opportunities. Additionally, this study adds to the research on the intersection between regulations and productive entrepreneurship (Fu *et al.*, 2020). The rest of this chapter is organized as follows. First, we describe the theoretical foundation of the study. Then, we detail the research methods and findings. Finally, we conclude this chapter with a discussion of the findings considering their implications for theory, and policymaking practices and research development.

Background and related work

Institutions and entrepreneurship

Institutions play a critical role in either encouraging or constraining entrepreneurial activities in different societies (Cao & Shi, 2021; Lee *et al.*, 2022)

DOI: 10.4324/9781003324737-14

due to the social context of entrepreneurship (Bruton *et al.*, 2010; Scott, 2005; Zahra *et al.*, 2014). Institutional theory (Scott, 1987, 2005) has been applied by entrepreneurship scholars to explain how different pillars of institutions help or hinder entrepreneurship in different institutional settings. Scott (2005) divides institutions into cognitive, normative, and regulatory institutions, capturing a big picture of institutional settings. North (1994, p. 360), on the other hand, defines institutions as "humanly devised constraints" and categorizes institutions into formal and informal institutions, such as culture, norms of behaviour, and social codes of conduct as informal, and constitutions, laws, and rules as formal institutions.

The socio-economic context wherein entrepreneurs are embedded influences their decision-making and actions to a great extent. Ericsson and Simon (1998) argue that the problem-solving process, including the specific heuristics that decision-makers apply, is expressed in the cultural context of the actors. North (1994, p. 359) argues that "institutions form the incentive structure of a society", which in turn determines economic performance. Advanced institutions facilitate entrepreneurship by encouraging risk-taking behaviours (Hwang & Powell, 2005). The advanced institutional setting provides supportive regulations, such as easy access to financial support (Berger *et al.*, 1993), a clear and streamlined process of starting up a new business, and minimal or no corruption (Kshetri & Dholakia, 2011). On the other hand, weak institutions leave entrepreneurs with many unanswered questions and confusion about different aspects of doing business (Junaid *et al.*, 2022). There is a huge body of research on entrepreneurship showing both the positive and negative influences of institutions in starting and running businesses by entrepreneurs and small firms (e.g., Fabowale *et al.*, 1995; Hassan & Olaniran, 2011; Romanello *et al.*, 2022).

Regulatory institutions have paid remarkable attention to entrepreneurship research (e.g., Spencer & Gómez, 2004). Regulations and policies implemented by various governments at both national and local levels play a critical role in shaping the entrepreneurial ecosystem and in either encouraging or discouraging entrepreneurs and other stakeholders from taking or avoiding risks (Davis & North, 1970). The institutional setting determines access to key resources and the quality of interactions within entrepreneurial ecosystems so that in less developed economies, entrepreneurs experience structural gaps and resource scarcity (Cao & Shi, 2021). More specifically, advanced institutional settings expose entrepreneurs to less environmental uncertainty (Denzau & North, 1994) and facilitate entrepreneurial action (Cao & Shi, 2021; North, 1990). The rule of law, regulatory quality, government effectiveness, political stability, accountability, and control of corruption provided by advanced regulatory institutions enable entrepreneurship (Kshetri & Dholakia, 2011). Whereas weak institutions constrain entrepreneurs' access to required resources and weaken their property rights and power to enforce contracts (Djankov *et al.*, 2002; Manolova *et al.*, 2008), which finally discourages new business development (Pfeffer & Salancik, 2003).

Uncertainty, institutions, and entrepreneurial resilience and success

Entrepreneurial resilience has been extensively discussed in entrepreneurship literature and has become more important since the recent pandemic (e.g., Santos *et al.*, 2023; Purnomo *et al.*, 2021). Resilience is conceptualized as stability over time despite radical uncertain and traumatic experiences (Corner *et al.*, 2017). Entrepreneurial resilience refers to the ability to stay confident and continue doing business under complex and challenging conditions (Bullough & Renko, 2013).

Resilient entrepreneurs focus on the bright side of uncertainty as it challenges the established order in the marketplace and opens new opportunities to form and establish new orders (Kirzner, 1999; Schumpeter, 1934). Entrepreneurs gain a clear understanding of their environment and the rules of the game within it, and either adapt their business practices to the existing formal and informal institutions or transform the existing institutional arrangement into a particular arrangement and establish new institutions with the help of other like-minded stakeholders (Alvarez *et al.*, 2015; Karami & Read, 2021; Maguire *et al.*, 2004). Entrepreneurs identify potential opportunities emerging from disequilibrium in the marketplace (Kirzner, 1999) and build on their social capital to extend their access to required resources through strategic partnerships (Karamia *et al.*, 2023; Sarasvathy, 2001). An advanced institutional setting facilitates networking, whereas in less developed settings, entrepreneurs choose networking to overcome institutional barriers (Aidis *et al.*, 2008). Networks provide complementary resources. Self-selected stakeholders share their understanding of the uncertain situation, including institutional uncertainties, and collectively make sense of the situation (Kerr & Coviello, 2020). The shared understanding of the situation enables the members of the network to make commitments and move forward by acting. Each action contributes to unpacking uncertainty (Sarasvathy, 2001; Wiltbank *et al.*, 2006).

Method

We incorporated insinuation theory (Scott, 2005) and the literature on entrepreneurial action to examine the role that governmental institutions and organizations play in directing entrepreneurs towards productive entrepreneurship in multiple crises. We used a multiple case-study design (Stake, 2005; Yin, 2013) due to the complexity and dynamics (Eisenhardt, 1989) of governments' and institutions' roles in supporting small businesses to successfully navigate through crises in an emerging market such as Iran. This method also enabled us to gather rich and in-depth data (Yin, 2003) about how the government supports small businesses to overcome multiple crises.

This study involved small businesses from both the manufacturing and service sectors, which are often characterized by market uncertainties in Iran (Jafari-Sadeghi *et al.*, 2021). To be selected for this study, small businesses had to have up to 50 employees and a minimum of four years of operation to ensure that they had experienced both pre- and post-Covid-19 crises. Using a purposeful sampling method and snowball sampling approach (Eisenhardt, 1989; Patton, 2014; Stake, 2005; Yin, 2009), 25 founders/CEOs of small businesses were selected to participate in this study. Table 14.1 provides further details on the founders'/CEOs' demographic characteristics of the small businesses qualified for participation in this study.

In-depth and semi-structured interviews were used to gather the data (Ryan *et al.*, 2009). Prior to carrying out the main interviews, we initially identified four cases consisting of two small business founders/CEOs from the service sector and two founders/CEOs in the manufacturing industry to participate in our pilot study (Saunders *et al.*, 2009). By doing this, we tested the robustness of our interview protocol before utilizing it for the main research and ensured that the participants were qualified for this study as suggested by Yin (2003). Based on the findings of the pilot study, we also refined the interview questions and ensured the quality of the data (Kim, 2011; Sampson, 2004). The interview protocol was developed based on the literature on government roles in directing

Table 14.1 An overview of the founders/CEOs of small businesses qualified for interviewing

No	*Age*	*Gender*	*Education*	*Business type*	*Years of running business*	*No. of employees*
1	41	Male	BA	Production	8	35
2	32	Male	BA	Production	6	50
3	54	Male	MA	Service	10	18
4	46	Male	MA	Production	6	11
5	48	Female	DBA	Service	8	50
6	35	Female	MA	Production	10	43
7	34	Male	MA	Service	9	15
8	33	Male	MA	Service	10	27
9	37	Male	MBA	Service	8	10
10	33	Male	BA	Service	6	8
11	35	Male	BA	Production	7	12
12	42	Male	MA	Production	6	14
13	39	Male	MA	Service	7	17
14	49	Male	MA	Production	9	24
15	52	Male	BA	Production	6	16
16	47	Male	MA	Production	8	28
17	45	Male	MA	Service	10	23
18	45	Male	MA	Production	8	10
19	31	Male	BA	Service	5	8
20	53	Male	MBA	Production	7	48
21	25	Male	MA	Service	6	16
22	36	Female	BA	Service	5	12
23	42	Male	BA	Service	7	23
24	26	Male	BA	Production	6	11
25	24	Male	MA	Service	5	24

small businesses (Nyarku & Oduro, 2018) and included but was not limited to questions on "How did government institutions reflect on the crises that small businesses faced?", "What were the strategies and approaches that regulatory instructions developed to face the crises?", and "How did regulatory institutions' strategies and approaches affect small businesses?" We stopped the interviews when we received no new insights (Eisenhardt, 1989; Saunders *et al.*, 2018). The process of interviewing the founders/CEOs started with a detailed briefing about what their participation in our research entails, and they were free to withdraw from the study at any point during the interview (Saunders *et al.*, 2015). We also sought permission to tape-record their narratives and promised their anonymity (Scott, 2005). We conducted the interviews between May 2020 and April 2022.

The small business founders/CEOs who participated in this study had varying ages, levels of academic qualifications, and business experiences (Table 14.1). Specifically, they aged between 54 and 24 years. Most of them were male (males = 22, females = 3), had a master's degree (MA = 15, BA = 9, DBA = 1), and had between 5 and 10 years of work experience. To capture the perspectives and experiences of founders/CEOs in diverse sectors and avoid biases towards a specific industry, we selected an almost equal number of founders/CEOs from both the manufacturing and service industries (manufacturing = 12, service = 13).

On average, the interviews with our key informants lasted between 60 and 110 minutes. Each interview was transcribed verbatim within 48 hours. For every transcribed interview, the informants were contacted to verify that the information we had reflected their account of events (Saunders *et al.*, 2015). The data collected from each founder/CEO was organized and transformed into chronological individual cases. We used both within-case and cross-case analyses as the main technique for analysing data (Miles & Huberman, 1994) because of the roles that regulatory institutions play in empowering small businesses' productive activities under multiple crises.

Findings

We organized the findings on the role of regulatory institutions in directing entrepreneurs towards productive entrepreneurship into two main categories: the role of regulatory institutions and the role of government.

Regulatory institutions

Our findings revealed two main roles that regulatory institutions play in guiding entrepreneurs towards productive entrepreneurship: an adaptive approach and a transformative approach. More specifically, most of the regulatory institutions employed an adaptive approach to empower small businesses to overcome the multiple crises in the challenging business environment of Iran. Through this adaptive approach, the regulatory institutions delegated new crisis-specific tasks to existing institutions as several of the participants stated (Table 14.2).

Table 14.2 Regulatory institutions' approaches to crises

Approaches	*Themes*	*Illustrative Quotations*
Adaptive	Delegating new crisis-specific tasks to existing institutions	*Our business education programs and professional development programs should also revise the objectives and content of their courses and include developing trainees' capabilities to face challenges very quickly. We can see in nature that, for example, ants or bees have these capabilities, when you pour water in the ants' net, they know how to immediately change their ways and react to the challenge, but we did not develop such capabilities in our people. (E12)* *It is a very good time and opportunity for the institutions to encourage business owners to remove the deficiencies in their products and improve the quality of their products. (E15)* *So, this is a very good time for the institutions to provide online training courses for business owners and teach them how to successfully go through the project. They can use their consultant and provide online consulting services for the businesses that are failing, since all of the other organizations are closed, and they cannot do any other activities. They can focus on providing trading courses and improve business owners' knowledge about the international market. (E5)*
	Creating crisis-specific sections to existing institutions	*I think we need to add a section to the existing business clinics. The new section's duty is to help SMEs in coping with emerging crises like Covid-19 or any other unpredictable crisis. The section should create the capacity in business leaders and employees on how to make urgent groups face crises. (E12)* *I think the top priority is that related institutions should think of new divisions and ways to improve the resilience and persistence of businesses to go through the crisis with less harm and costs. (E3)*

(*Continued*)

Table 14.2 (Continued)

Approaches	*Themes*	*Illustrative Quotations*
	Combine different related institutions	*We need coordinators to harmonize the actions of different instructions. We may have different related institutions, but they are in line with each other; they act more parallel to each other. So, they are targeted to help businesses, but they don't; they just waste resources. (E1)*
		I know that there are many institutions there even those many that I never know, I cannot even contact them because they are many and I don't have time to contact them. I think it is like having different tools that you never know how to use and in some cases, they conflict, and I don't see the use of that many people which is annoying. (E2)
		There are many institutions and many heads that decide for businesses like us. This makes the beauty business and the market very difficult to reach. (E7)
		I doubt even they can synchronize their activities with the needs of the businesses, mostly they lag behind the needs of businesses there, they are many, but I don't see that they are efficient enough to help businesses in crises. (E17)
		You can see there are many people there in long meetings that do not come to an efficient conclusion. (E8)
Transformative	Creating new related institutions	*At the institutional level, I think we have a long way to go. What we did in the first and second weeks of Covid-19 showed that we need to construct a lot of institutions to lead our businesses during crises and disasters. There is a huge need of developing institutions to react appropriately to crisis. (E1)*
		There were many talks and discussions about people's health; doctors, nurses, and consultants were talking day and night about how to prevent the virus, but no one talked about what businesses and specifically small businesses should do in this condition. There were no consultants who give us advice on what to do. We need responsible institutions to give us consultants to tell us how to react to crises or change the threats to opportunities. (E2)

Giving an example of ants and bees from nature, E12 explained how related institutions should take on new tasks and direct businesses:

> *We can see in nature that, for example, ants or bees have these capabilities, like when you pour water in ants' net, they know how to immediately change their ways and react to the challenge, but we did not develop such capabilities in our people. . . . Our business and trading organizations should take their new responsibilities because there is no time for us to waste here and there.* (E12)

In addition, some of the participants believed that existing regulatory institutions "should think of new divisions and ways to improve the resilience and persistence of businesses to go through the crisis with less harms and costs" (E3) and empower small businesses to navigate through multiple crises successfully.

Several of the founders discussed the various challenges they faced in overcoming crises that required a coordinated response and the development of consistent regulations across multiple regulatory bodies. Highlighting the existence of numerous different business regulatory institutions that need to be combined to effectively guide businesses through crises, founder 1 postulated that:

> *We need coordinators to harmonize the actions of different instructions. We may have different related institutions, but they are not in line with each other; they act more parallel to each other. So, they are targeted to help businesses, but they don't; they just waste resources.* (E1)

In addition to the adaptive approach, some of the founders highlighted the transformative/causal approach that regulatory institutions need to employ and create new specific instructions related to crisis management:

> *There were many talks and discussions about people's health; doctors, nurses, and consultants were talking day and night about how to prevent the virus, but no one talked about what businesses and specifically small businesses should do in this condition. There were no consultants who give us advice on what to do. We need responsible institutions to give us consultants to tell us how to react to crises or change the threats to opportunities. . . I think it [is] better to make new bodies only responsible for crises; they can better help us because they have the knowledge and expertise.* (E2)

Regulatory Institutions' Expected Roles

Our findings also revealed the roles that the founders expected regulatory institutions to play in enabling small businesses to overcome multiple crises (Table 14.3).

First, most of the founders highlighted the importance of regulatory institutions in supporting small businesses to persist and survive against multiple

Table 14.3 Regulatory institutions' roles

Themes	*Illustrative Quotations*
Support resilience and survival	*I think the first priority of restaurants and food-related institutions is to help the businesses in the industry to survive this crisis; they can provide financial packages or consultants to help the business. (E4)* *Related institutions should open new ways to stimulate the market. . . . Now we have time to think about the packaging and quality of our products. (E5)* *They need to prepare our businesses to fight against non-stop and endless problems. . . . If we can produce higher quality products and better packaging than before, we can be more competitive than other countries that didn't do anything while we were struggling with the virus. . . . So I think they need to work day and night to find a way for scraping from these conditions and we work on the quality of our products and improve our productivity. (E15)* *I think that the institutions can facilitate the processes . . . they can show us the way, but they can never force us to change the way we are doing business; this is not just giving all businesses money, which is very important but is not the whole story, but to communicate with us the ways we should go through. (E10)*
Provide crises-Specific information	*The institutions should be updated and should have enough information about all of the aspects of the business in their domain . . . they are publishing newsletters, flyers . . . online channels, and they are giving some advice. (E7)* *We are doing an electronic business, a knowledge edge business. They should find the knowledge, I don't know from where, but these institutions are connecting to here and there to find the data how we can pass these dark days. They should update their information and how all of the businesses are affected by the virus, and they can help them. (E12)* *As I see the institutions should have enough information, and they should share the information. I know no one has experience like this, but they should be in the front line. I can see that some of them like the trading and commerce chamber are having some meetings, they send the guidelines through social media, they are connecting to other organizations to find the data. (E16)*

(*Continued*)

Table 14.3 (Continued)

Themes	*Illustrative Quotations*
Create networks	*The people in the institutions should have effective links and connections in Iran and other countries. They should not stay in their comfort zone and do the minimum for businesses. . . There is no value for such things. (E6)*
	Having strong links and connections in Iran and other countries is one key . . . and connecting us to their links is another thing that is very important; they should update their information about how other businesses are affected by the virus and how they can help them by connecting them. (E17)
	I strongly believe high-technology and knowledge-based businesses need strong networks when they are facing challenges because we are working with technology and if connected, we can survive better But all the people sitting in the national trading chambers look at us like islands, like we do not need interactions. They should connect us to at least see what others are doing, how they are solving the problem. (E18)
Use new technologies to interact with businesses	*They should use new technologies to help businesses; one of the most important problems of the institutions is they do not use technologies. . . . so, they should value using new technologies. (E7)*
	I can see that they are using very old systems. They contact people like via phone call. . . . They need to think over using new tools to communicate with the business owners and people. (E8)
	The first thing is the institutions should create new ways to connect business owners, because they cannot meet the people in person, as far as I know, they are using traditional ways of long meetings and so on . . . but now they need to connect businesses more seriously and using online platforms. (E9)
Create new opportunities	*I mean they allow us to do our pilot courses in the institutions so that we can gain some experience. . . . They have many courses and can also add our courses to their previous courses. (E9)*
	They can connect businesses to the international world, but they are so slow. . . . it takes a long time for them to connect and create links with the people. . . . This is their duty that creates a chance for us to meet different people in the world and explore the opportunities for our business there. . . . Of course, I can see that with less connections and communication we have with other countries, actually they cannot do this, but they can always try. (E3)

challenges of the business environment, which were further exacerbated by the effects of Covid-19. This was evident in the statements of several business founders in this study, and specifically E15 stated:

> *They need to prepare our businesses to fight against non-stop and endless problems. . . . If we can produce higher quality products and better packaging than before, we can be more competitive than other countries that didn't do anything while we were struggling with the virus. . . . So I think they need to work day and night to find a way for scraping from these conditions and we work on the quality of our products and improve our productivity.* (E15)

Second, the founders explained, "The institutions should be updated and should have enough information about all of the aspects of the business in their domain . . . they are publishing some newsletters, flyers . . . through online channels, and they are giving some advices" (E7).

Third, several of the founders commented on the critical roles that regulatory institutions play in creating networks and connections among businesses during crises, so that they can share information and resources to persist and survive. Highlighting their vital need for networking, E18 stated:

> *I strongly believe high-technology and knowledge-based businesses need strong networks when they are in challenges because we are working with technology and if connected, we can survive more. But all the people seating in the national trading chambers look at us like islands, like we do not need interactions. They should connect us to at least see what others are doing, how they are solving the problem.* (E18)

The fourth duty of the regulatory institutions highlighted by the founders was using new technologies for fast and effective interactions with businesses during crises. This was evident in the comments of several of the founders, and E9 commented that:

> *The first thing is the institutions should create new ways to connect business owners, because they cannot meet the people in person, as far as I know, they are using traditional ways of long meetings and so on . . . but now they need to connect businesses more seriously and using online platforms.* (E9)

Finally, some of the founders highlighted the key role that regulatory institutions play in creating new opportunities for their businesses by acting as a hub and connecting small businesses to businesses in other counties. As E3 said:

> *They can connect businesses to the international world, but they are so slow,. . . it takes a long time for them to connect and create links with the*

people. . . . This is their duty that creates a chance for us to meet different people in the world and explore the opportunities for our business there. . . . Of course, I can see that with less connections and communication we have with other countries, actually they cannot do this, but they can always try. (E3)

Role of the government

We also asked the participants how the government reflected on the multiple crises. We organized the emerging themes into three phases of crises including pre-crises, during crises, and post-crises. These findings are presented in the following sections.

Pre-crises government roles

The founders explained that governments play six critical roles before crises to enable small businesses to persist and survive multiple crises (Table 14.4).

First, we found that the government plays a critical role in building trust through transparency before crises as several of the founders stated. Explaining how the lack of trust and transparency in the government caused their business to lose a lot of money, E23 stated:

The government supported the automobile companies very much. This made us very weak, and we try to acquire the knowledge for producing quality products. . . . Then, I thought that I found good opportunities in the production of car seat belts and safety parts without thinking that government will bring a new regulation that they can import all of the car accessories . . . no one knew anything about the regulation. We had invested a lot, and they ruined everything. (E23)

Second, some of the founders commented on the government's failure in using technologies for interacting with businesses, which result in "communications that are very time-consuming, slow, and inefficient" (E4). This is "One of the big problems in big and specifically public organizations that they do not have the online infrastructures and platforms, they mostly have a very weak website, so, the government can develop some circulations and update them". (E9). This was also echoed by E18:

As you can see, they are working with very old systems; they are still working with papers. . . . It takes ages in this system to do a very small thing. . . . We need new electric devices, new and fast online systems that link all of the crisis-related organizations together, like a big alarm and they work fast and easy and support different businesses all over the country. (E18)

Table 14.4 Roles of the government in empowering small businesses' productive entrepreneurship

Crises phases	*Themes*	*Illustrative Quotations*
Pre-crises	Creating trust by transparency	*The first priority of the government should be recreating the trust of the people; they should renovate peoples' trust because I believe that working in an environment where there is no trust is impossible . . . then they should create the infrastructures and mechanisms for people to work with trust. (E6)*
		The government supported the automobile companies very much. This made us very weak, and we try to acquire the knowledge for producing quality products. . . . Then, I thought that I found good opportunities in the production of car seat belts and safety parts without thinking that government will bring a new regulation that they can import all of the car accessories . . . no one knew anything about the regulation. We had invested a lot, and they ruined everything. (E23)
		Once, we almost finished a product; it was almost done . . . suddenly another company with the support of the government developed the same product. So, we couldn't deliver our product to the market on time, and they captured the market. They should not have a blind spot in the government . . . it ruined our belief that government provides the facilitating platforms for every business in the market that is already fighting against huge crises. (E24)
	Using new technologies	*They should develop related software and application to ease the process. . . . If they do not revise the rules and do not develop effective rules, we will encounter countless problems related to online businesses and infringements. (E6)*
		One of the big problems in big and specifically public organizations is that they do not have online infrastructures and platforms, they mostly have a very weak websites, so, the government can develop some circulations and update them. (E9)
		There are many unities that are using old and slow processes and procedures. They need to update their technologies if they want to meet the speed of the growing needs of businesses and specifically start-ups. (E16)
		As you can see, they are working with very old systems; they are still working with papers. . . . It takes ages in this system to do a very small thing. . . . We need new electric devices, new and fast online systems that link all of the crisis-related organizations together, like a big alarm, and they work fast and easy and support different businesses all over the country. (E18)

(*Continued*)

Table 14.4 (Continued)

Crises phases	*Themes*	*Illustrative Quotations*
	Avoiding interference	*Now our government interferes with anything . . . this reduces its effectiveness. . . . In other countries, the government does not waste its 'time to interfere with very small things . . . they delegate the responsibility to other institutions. . . . (E6)*
		So, sanctions put us in a lot of problems . . . we also didn't have support from the government or any other organizations, while other big companies importing the electronic devices have the support, so it is much easier for them to just buy the devices, like the full ready products from other countries and ship them to Iran, than working on designing and producing them with no supports. By this, the government makes the game very difficult for us. (E12)
		The economic condition of the country affects all the businesses, and we are not an exception. I can say specifically the government policies . . . one thing that affects our business is the news and when people from the government talk, the price of everything changes; why they cannot keep silent? . . . it affected our business a lot, and affected all of the other businesses . . . so, the shocks affect our business. (E24)
	Exploring ineffective rules and regulations	*The legal condition and policies are awful; they band something and tell us that we should have certificates for this and that. So, we apply for the certificate, there is a lot of bureaucracy there, it takes a long time, like one year, for them to give us the certificate to do an activity. There is no established procedure. They themselves don't know what to do; there are no rules and regulations for it, no infrastructure. Before they approve the laws and rules, they stop us from doing business. This is an issue; we should think like the policymakers. . . . This takes a lot of time from us . . . so the legal and legislative issues are very challenging for us; they are wasting our time and energy. (E16)*
		If the government has invested in new technologies to earn money than investing in oil which is not beneficial with the low oil prices now . . . we would have benefited a lot. (E7)
		We are alone there. No one even asked us how the business is going on because they think that we might put them in trouble . . . the public and governmental organizations didn't help us, and the private organizations also didn't help us . . . Sometimes, I think we should keep our business far from them because they are using the rules and procedures that do not work for today . . . in the first year of starting the business and before having an income, we had many problems with different organizations; they always came to put more problems on our shoulders,. . . . (E15)

(Continued)

Table 14.4 (Continued)

Crises phases	*Themes*	*Illustrative Quotations*
		our government can react to this new technology in two ways, either band it or facilitating using it. . . all the other countries like China, Russia and many other countries are using the technology and its benefits. . . (E17)
		We have a lot of resources, and we can have many start-ups, but the most serious obstacle is ourselves; we are the ones who make the obstacles for our businesses; why? Because we didn't define and standardize the procedures well. . . So, I think the government should invest in these and should improve the regulations. we are investing in the administrative procedures and paper works in the government which is basically wrong and takes a lot of energy and time and efforts from entrepreneurs. (E19)
	Stoping constant changes in rules and regulations	*There are new rules and regulations every month; they change the rules by day. . . they do not help us and just stop us,. they put a lot of obstacles in the way of doing a beauty business, you should take many certificates from different places, it is very time consuming and complex, some of business owners do not contact the institutions at all, they keep away from them to be safe. . . . (E7)*
		You can see that people there are making new rules and regulations constantly . . . in some cases before we get used to a new rule, they develop a new rule again and this is a big problem for us. (16)
		All these government organizations have their own rules, regulations, and bureaucracies Before starting the first steps, the organizations come to us and make different difficulties for us; sometimes, they change their rules constantly; before reaching the previous standards, they make new ones, and this creates a lot of challenges for us, while we are in the library doing our research, none of these organizations contact us, once we come to the field and we want to produce the real product, they show off and put a lot of various obstacles in our path, we overcame many of these challenges by our connections not through established and equal regulations for all. (E20)

(*Continued*)

Table 14.4 (Continued)

Crises phases	*Themes*	*Illustrative Quotations*
	Connection to international business world	*While in world stock markets, people are trading online, and there are no threats for their online trading . . . it is very simple and easy. (E6)* *We are fighting with different problems because we do not have specific and fixed regulations to connect the business in the world . . . it is very important that the government makes access to the international markets easy and fast. if not how can we understand the needs and wants of the customers in the crises conditions? (E16)* *For a high technology and knowledge-based business such as our business is vital to connect to the world; we need updated knowledge and exchange of knowledge. The government is the hub between our business and other businesses around the world by providing opportunities for us to interact with the world of business in other countries and specifically the countries which are in the edge of knowledge (E12)*
1 Post-crises	Developing crises-specific guidelines and strategies	*I think the government needs to develop some guidelines and acts, rule, and regulations for national and international crises. (E1)*
	Developing supportive strategies to direct businesses in crisis	*In the first two weeks, no one knew what to do . . . we all were very confused,. . . it is the responsibility of the top people there to seat and prepare some guidelines for us,. but you can see that it took a long time for them themselves to find out what to do,. that means we have a problem in quick response to circumstances,. . . (E11)* *We have enough rules but how to direct businesses to obey the rules and regulations in urgent situations and crises is what we need. From what I can see, there are many SMEs that totally disappeared, and their employees are jobless now. I think how many new businesses should we start to employ all these jobless people? The government should think about how to support SMEs after the virus. The government needs to develop new national and international strategies. They need to learn a lot from other countries. (E1)*

(*Continued*)

Table 14.4 (Continued)

Crises phases	*Themes*	*Illustrative Quotations*
		Regarding the priorities of the government, I think they are working on developing some new strategies, like supporting SMEs by providing them with tax exemptions or giving them some supporting packages, but as you know, the government cannot react to crises such as Covid-19 fast, it takes time, and maybe they act very late. (E2) *The government should also help with this; the government should also provide tourism businesses with financial support to pass the crisis and develops strategies and plans for after the virus. (E3)* *I heard that the government is planning to provide some packages to help businesses to survive in the crisis condition, but the problem is that the government does not have the resources . . . as you know, the oil price is around 20 dollars for each barrel; what can the government do with this . . . it is not under control of the government and the government has lost many of its financial resources. I think the government should focus on the production section to prevent them from firing their employees,. and have strong systematic control on distributing the packages and facilities to all SMEs,. . . because these packages also create corruption, so the government should have a strong system for controlling the distribution of the facilities and packages, . . . so, controlling is very important,. . . . So, they should identify the most effective place to go. (E5)* *I can see that they did not have a plan B for the crisis, I mean we are fighting with different issues, a crisis following the crisis, but we do not have effective strategies that work in directing and regulating businesses when a crisis comes. (E11)* *The government is huge and big, so they cannot act fast enough to face such big crisis. if they want to develop a specific strategy for how businesses act in crisis, it takes a lot of time. (E12)* *It doesn't work if they just give the supporting packages without targeting them to those businesses that urgently need the support, and without regulating them how to use the support to prevent their business from failure, . . . I mean they should have regulating strategies and implement the strategies effectively. (E15)*

(*Continued*)

Table 14.4 (Continued)

Crises phases	*Themes*	*Illustrative Quotations*
	Developing new specific new strategies for crises	*In terms of the security of the online services we need huge corrections. The government should investigate why monetary infringements happen. I think because those who are preparing the online trading infrastructures, look at the surface and do know it deeply. (E6)*
		Now, you can see that during the virus crisis, the government made making masks and sanitizers very fast; they give the certificates and everything for the businesses very fast; why they cannot do the same for other businesses. (E8)
		So, the government needs to create the infrastructures for online training. there are huge budgets, but they do not know how to spend the budgets. (E9)
		They are guiding small businesses so that they can find their way. They asked the very essential businesses to work under specific care. . . . These helped businesses such as our business to find their ways. We need to work with this number of employees and follow these protocols. . . (E15)
	Supporting failed businesses	*The first priority of the government should be helping the closed food businesses, to open again. If not there will be many jobless people in the industry. . . (E4)*
		What do they want to do for the businesses that existed before the crisis and now they disappeared? Do they have any plans to support them? I heard from the news that they are developing some plans to help them but when no one knows. . . it takes a lot of time, but businesses need the help very urgently. (E14)
		Look at other countries. You see they prepared so many things and doing business is very easy, why? Because the support is there, they do not leave you alone when you are bankrupted . . . they at least make your life easier by exemption of your taxes or postponing your duties. (E19)

(*Continued*)

Table 14.4 (Continued)

Crises phases	*Themes*	*Illustrative Quotations*
	Adjusting the strategies to the needs of businesses	*I think the government should look at the crisis through the eyes of business people; they should think that all businesses need to continue because the country needs the business, unless, it had not been created at all. (E6)*
		The most challenging factor is that we have no standards, for anything; we do not make things easy and simple and then standardize them. So, everything is so complicated and useless; for example, I started a smart shop, but I had to close it because of different challenges they made for me, very complex and old rules and regulations; if you want to do a simple thing, there are many procedures and the CEO of the business should do all the procedures because they do not accept anyone else on behalf of the CEO to go and do it. . . . and I think this should be changed. (E19) The second factor is the capability of the government to think and develop good ideas based on the new conditions. They cannot produce extraordinary results just by the strategies they have developed long years ago . . . people are in a new condition now, and they cannot solve our problems today by looking at the problems through the lens of hundred years ago. The government needs new approaches and policies regarding new and knowledge-based businesses. (E20)
	Developing agile crises- specific strategies	*I feel the huge gap now; we did not react to the virus properly and in time. Creating the capacity to reflect very fast on the challenges created by the environment is the responsibility of government organizations. They can react very fast to crises of seat and look at how our businesses are killed by the crises. (E2)*
		Today the power is in the speed of the government to change and develop strategies very fast. One of the key barriers is bureaucracy, we have a lot of rules and regulations that obstruct our way. So, the government should decrease bureaucracy and also generate transparency in everything . . . if the government can only do these two things, investors from all of the world will come and invest in our country. (E7)

(Continued)

Table 14.4 (Continued)

Crises phases	*Themes*	*Illustrative Quotations*
		You can see the government is still using the technologies related to 20 years ago, so, it cannot be fast. They are using old procedures . . . we have a lot of problems in releasing the technologies that we have imported from the borders . . . the government does not use the new technologies to facilitate business activities. The people in the government need to improve their skills to use new technologies to ease performing their tasks. (E13)
		Look at other countries; you see that there are very few processes and procedures; they try to make the process easy for entrepreneurs, I remember when I wanted to register my business in Germany, they gave me all the licenses in half a day. Such procedures are very easy to change; they like to make changes like in a snap; there are not so many organizations for taking the licenses and registrations. (E19)
	Provide precise and fast information	*Our business people are also suffering from not being provided with the required information, for example, they do not know the rules and regulations like the insurance and tax rules well. (E8)*
		I prefer the government to give me some information than monetary aid. . . . For example, I as a business owner do not have enough analytical and predictive capabilities . . . so, you should give me the information and guide the behaviour of all businesses. . . give me the information that enables me to predict new scenarios and select from the available methods to cope with the virus. . . . If I had a list of the suppliers or the companies producing the materials for my products and my business and whether they are active or not now, I could have better decide which one to choose among them. (E9)
		We focused on the demands of the healthcare ministry, and that was our big mistake. When they suddenly said they don't want to buy your products, we lost almost all our customers. . . . They didn't give us anything about legal procedures, laws, and regulations. If we knew more about the rules and regulations, we could survive more and did not lose that huge amount of money. (E17)

(Continued)

Table 14.4 (Continued)

Crises phases	*Themes*	*Illustrative Quotations*
	Networking and sharing resources	*So, they need to link all of the related businesses in an industry by connecting them together and creating network. (E10)* *Instead of giving money or loans to business owners, I would like the government to create some shared resources such as shared storage or resources, that all of the businesses can benefit from them. (E10)* *We are working on modems with high technology, and we need support from others. We are like some island where we work alone. . . . Some of the small businesses in our market died during the recession time, and if we were linked, we could support by just sharing some of our like things. So, we need to be connected by a hub in the hard conditions, and if we fail, other organizations are there to support us. (E12)*
Post-crises	Developing plans	*I also think the government needs to think about the problems created by the virus and how to solve them; specifically, they need to think about after the virus, what will happen to businesses after the virus and how the government can act to lessen the effects of problems created by the virus for our SMEs. (E1) Look at our plans; they need to think about what we should do for our business after all these are finished . . . they should develop strategies and plans for the days after this, the next day, they should think ahead, I think after this terrible storm, our businesses need more support than before, and they can play important roles on this. (E21)* *I don't think people in the government think of very strategic decisions to fight against this huge shock . . . they are so busy, and no one put effort and energy into thinking for strategic decisions. They should have developed plans just for this condition to give us the devices what to do, how long we should wait, and what will happen to all these businesses which are dying . . . such plans can give all the players in the market the clues where to go and why to go. (E25)*

(Continued)

Table 14.4 (Continued)

Crises phases	*Themes*	*Illustrative Quotations*
	Reviewing and rearrange strategies	*They should develop related circulations and regulations how businesses can face the crisis . . . how they help the businesses to go through the crises. If not, the government cannot go as fast as the businesses and the government will lag behind the businesses. (E8)*
		Then, they should review and replace the rules and regulations that affect all of the businesses,. there are many rules and regulations that should be reviewed and changed for the new condition, specifically in finance and exchange businesses . . . so, the government should review and change the online trading rules and regulations . . . online business rules and regulations, we can see many infringements in online businesses . . . and there is a huge need there for rules and regulations. (E16)
	Integrating different policy making organizations	*And the government should integrate all the institutions related to a business; the place to register the business, and the place to take the accreditations are now separate, and this creates many problems for businesses. We have many institutions that should be integrated and should be online and should be updated online. (E6)*
		You can see that there are many organizations, that are all working on helping businesses . . . sometimes they are in conflict, and they are not synchronized; we need to merge them. (E13)
	Developing qualified groups and structure for strategy development	*And a qualified group specifically in the technical aspects of online business should develop the rules . . . there should be an effective structure in the government related to online businesses and the group should include each and every aspect of the businesses in their rules and regulations. (E6)*

While some of the founders perceived the government to play a greater role in supporting small businesses in times of crises, others described how the government should avoid interference and allow the businesses to manage the crises. This was evident in the statement of several participants, and specifically E24 commented on this:

> *The economic condition of the country affects all businesses, and we are not an exception. I can say specifically the government policies . . . one thing that affects our business is the news and when people from the government talk, the price of everything changes; why they cannot keep silent? . . . it affected our business a lot, and affected all of the other businesses . . . so, the shocks affect our business.* (E24)

The fourth role that the founders/CEOs expected from the government was to explore ineffective rules and regulations before crises happen to effectively allocate resources, proactively prevent crises, and successfully reduce the costs and risks of fighting against crises. The majority of the participants commented on this role of the government, and specifically E15 stated:

> *We are alone there. No one even asked us how the business is going on because they think that we might put them in trouble . . . the public and governmental organizations didn't help us, and the private organizations also didn't help us. . . . Sometimes, I think we should keep our business far from them because they are using the rules and procedures that do not work for today. . . . In the first year of starting the business and before having income, we had many problems with different organizations; they always came to put more problems on our shoulders.* (E15)

In addition, the founders/CEOs explained how the constant changes in rules and regulations by the government further exacerbated their challenges while they were already struggling with the difficulties caused by the Covid-19 pandemic. Founder 20 commented on this as:

> *All these government organizations have their own rules, regulations, and bureaucracies. Before starting the first steps, the organizations come to us and make different difficulties for us; sometimes, they change their rules constantly, and before reaching the previous standards, they make new ones, and this creates a lot of challenges for us, while we are in the library doing our research, none of these organizations contact us; once we come to the field and we want to produce the real product, they show off and put a lot of various obstacles in our path.* (E20)

Finally, the role that the government should play in connecting businesses to the international business world emerged as one of the critical responsibilities of the government during times of severe crises. For instance, E16 described how the government should facilitate the access of small businesses to the international markets to explore the specific demands of the customers:

> *We are fighting with different problems because we do not have specific and fixed regulations to connect the business in the world . . . it is very important that the government makes access to the international markets easy and fast . . . if not how can we understand the needs and wants of the customers in the crises conditions?* (E16)

Government Roles During Crises

In addition to the functions that the founders/CEOs expected from the government prior to crises, our analysis also revealed the role of the government during the crises. More specifically, the founders/CEOs explained the government's responsibility in developing crisis-specific guidelines and strategies. This was evident in the statements of several of the participants and specifically E11 commented on this:

> *In the first two weeks, no one knew what to do . . . we all were very confused . . . it is the responsibility of top people there to seat and prepare some pathways for us . . . but you can see that it took a long time for them to find out what to do . . . that means they should quickly prepare ways to respond to the circumstances.* (E11)

Furthermore, the founders/CEOs commented on "the insufficient and inadequate supportive strategies that the government developed and implemented during the crises" (E15) to direct businesses in crises. Further into the interview, E15 stated:

> *It doesn't work if they just give the supporting packages without targeting them to those businesses that urgently need these supports, and without regulating how to use the supports to prevent their business from failure. . . . I mean they should have regulating strategies and implement the strategies effectively.* (E15)

Several of the founders highlighted the need for developing new crisis-specific strategies "because each crisis is unique, and you cannot solve a new problem with the old solutions you may have developed long ago" (E6) specifically for businesses facing monetary problems. Further into the interview, E6 postulated:

> *In terms of the security of the online services we need huge corrections . . . the government should investigate why monetary infringements happen. . . .*

> *I think because those who are preparing the online trading infrastructures, look at the surface and do know it deeply at this particular time.* (E6)

E15 also described the role that the government played in developing new crisis-specific guidelines and strategies:

> *They are guiding small businesses so that they can find their way. They asked the very essential businesses to work under specific care. . . . These helped businesses such as our business to find their ways. We need to work with this number of employees and follow these protocols.* (E15)

One of the themes that emerged from this study was the role that the founders/CEOs considered for the government in supporting the small businesses that failed because of the multiple crises. Comparing the support that small businesses receive from their governments with the insufficient support offered to small businesses in Iran, E19 stated:

> *Look at other countries. You see they prepared so many things and doing business is very easy, why? Because the support is there, they do not leave you alone when you are bankrupted . . . they at least make your life easier by exempting your taxes or postponing your duties.* (E19)

Furthermore, several participants in this study highlighted the government's responsibility to adapt existing strategies to the new needs of businesses during severe crises. For example, E20 stated:

> *The second factor is the capability of the government to think and develop good ideas to change the strategies which are already there based on the new conditions. They cannot produce extraordinary results just by the strategies they have developed long years ago . . . people are in a new condition now, and they cannot solve our problems today by looking at the problems through the lens of hundred years ago. . . . the government needs new approaches and policies regarding new and knowledge-based businesses.* (E20)

Agility of the government in developing crisis-specific strategies was an emerging theme in this study because fast responses and strategy development to deal with the challenges are of critical importance in the crises that affect the entire country, as well as the international business environment, as postulated by several of the participants. Specifically, E2 stated:

> *I feel the huge gap now; we did not react to the virus properly and in time. Creating the capacity to reflect very fast on the challenges created by the environment is the responsibility of government organizations. They can react*

> *very fast to crises or seat and look at how our businesses are killed by the crises.* (E2)

Some of the participants explained the reasons why the government did not respond quickly to the crises. They pointed out that the governments' heavy bureaucracy (E7), its large and cumbersome structure (E12), its reluctance to adopt new technologies (13), and its lengthy processes and procedures (E19) were the main contributing factors to the lack of agility in the government's response to the crises (Table 14.3).

Additionally, the founders/CEOs highlighted the role of the government in providing precise and fast information about the crises and how businesses need to overcome the crises. For example, founder (E9) emphasized:

> *I prefer the government to give me some information than monetary aid, for example, I as a business owner do not have enough analytical and predictive capabilities . . . so, you should give me the information and guide the behaviour of all businesses, give me the information that enables me to predict new scenarios and select from the available methods to cope with the virus. . . . If I had a list of the suppliers or the companies producing the materials for my products and my business and whether they are active or not now, I could have better decide which one to choose among them.* (E9)

An emerging theme from this study was the role that the founders expected the government to play in linking businesses, creating networks, and "Instead of giving money or loans to business owners . . . the government creates some shared resources such as shared storages or logistics, from which all of the businesses can benefit" (E10). On the critical function of the government in creating networks for small high-technology businesses, E12 also commented:

> *We are working on modems with high technology, and we need support from others. We are like some island where we work alone. . . . Some of the small businesses in our market died during the recession time, and if we were linked, we could support by just sharing some of our like things. So, we need to be connected by a hub in the hard conditions, and if we fail, other organizations are there to support us.* (E12)

Post-Crises

Some of the participants looked at the role of the government beyond the crises and in the post-period. Several of the founders/CEOs in this study highlighted the need for the government to be proactive and develop plans for supporting small businesses to recover and renovate after the crises, as E21 postulated:

> *Look at our plans; they need to think about what we should do for our business after all these finished . . . they should develop strategies and plans for the days after this, and they should think ahead, I think after this terrible storm, our businesses need more support than before, and they can play important roles on this.* (E21)

In addition, the founders/CEOs highlighted the importance of integrating different policy-making organizations related to crises to effectively direct small businesses during crises. This was evident in the statements of several participants and particularly E8 postulated:

> *We need to change the rules and regulations . . . so, we need to review and revise our rules and regulations,. . . I think it is like putting railways for trains; if you put the rails correctly, people go along them properly; if not we waste resources and energy,. . . it is a very good time for policymakers to seat and revise and correct the rules and regulations and develop more effective rules . . . they should develop related circulations and regulations how businesses can face crisis in the future,. . . how they help the businesses to go through the potential crises.* (E8)

Finally, our participants expected the government to proactively develop qualified groups and structures that can build the capacity of small businesses to manage future potential crises and challenges. For example, E6 commented on this:

> *And a qualified group specifically in the technical aspects of online business should develop the rules . . . there should be an effective structure in the government related to online businesses and the group include each and every aspect of the businesses in their rules and regulations.* (E6)

Discussion

Our findings show that small businesses expect regulatory institutions to play a proactive role in supporting them during times of crisis. Our findings revealed that small businesses used either adaptive or transformative approaches to address uncertainties caused by crises, and their approach is partly influenced by the government's response to these crises (Figure 14.1).

Small businesses expect regulatory institutions to support a transformative approach to uncertainties caused by crises, so that they receive support from their institutional environment, make commitments with other stakeholders, and collaborate in co-creating a new future. Small businesses expect to have an entrepreneurial government that takes risks and encourages them to be entrepreneurial in dealing with uncertainties (Figure 14.2).

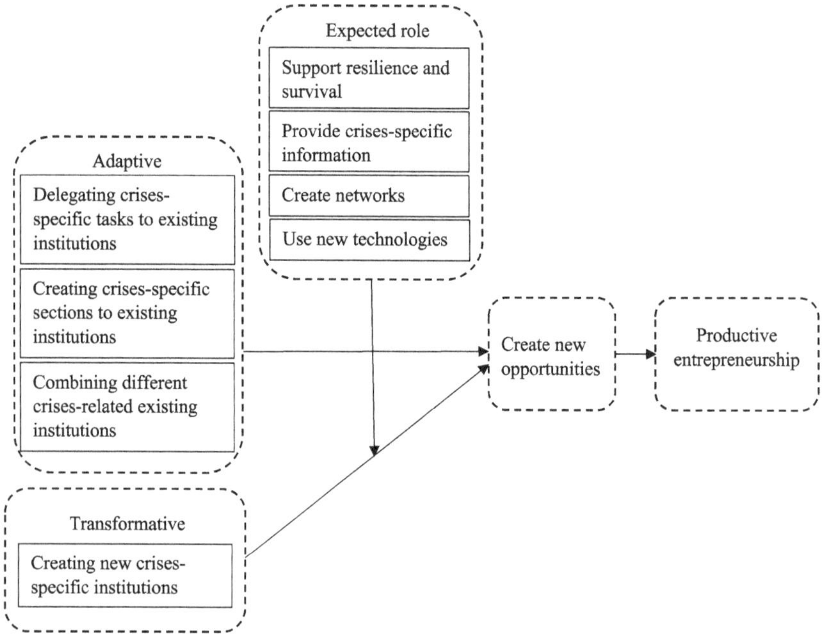

Figure 14.1 The expected roles of regulative institutions in empowering small businesses under multiple crises.

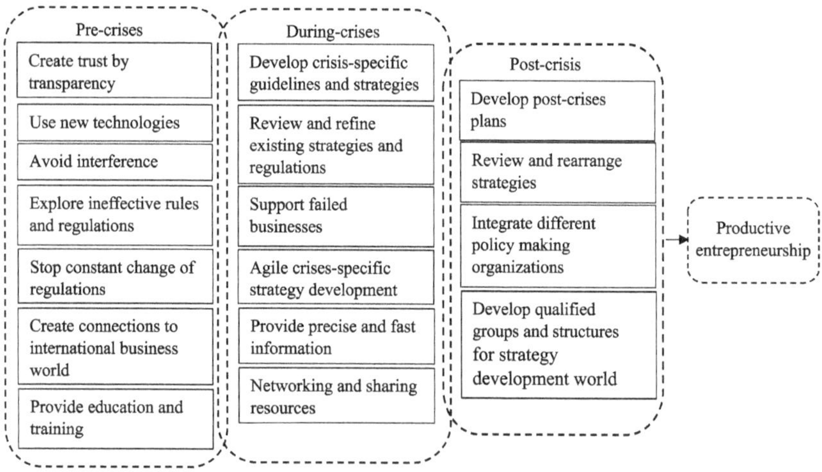

Figure 14.2 The expected roles of the government in empowering small businesses' productive entrepreneurship.

Additionally, small business founders in this study expected the government to take some steps and facilitate networking opportunities. They believe that the government can adopt a proactive approach by using its resources to create structural changes, thereby creating new opportunities for small businesses in the face of severe crises.

Our findings also break down the expectations into different periods of crises. The expectations for pre-crises are more related to the role of regulatory institutions in developing trust, stabilizing the environment and encouraging investment in new technologies. During crises, they expect a quick reaction and entrepreneurial approach from the government in support of entrepreneurship. And in the post-crises stage, they expect the government to develop long-term plans in support of entrepreneurship, have a strategic approach in supporting small businesses, and develop supportive infrastructure.

Implications of the findings for theory development and policy-making

The findings of this study have several implications for theory development and policy-making. First, this study sheds light on the specific strategies that government and regulatory institutions should develop to empower small businesses to persist and survive when dealing with multiple crises. The findings also provide a context-based understanding of the roles that government and regulatory institutions should play in directing small businesses towards productive entrepreneurship in an emerging market. Our findings underpin the link between strategy development and implementation in the whole process of dealing with crises including pre-, during, and post-crises. Our findings also enhance our knowledge of the importance of a proactive crises-specific strategy development by regulatory institutions in mitigating the effects of crises on small businesses. These findings may assist in theory development on the impact of government strategies and regulations during crises on small businesses and the effectiveness of these strategies in empowering small businesses to successfully navigate through crises in emerging markets. Specifically, our findings contribute to our understanding of the regulatory factors that drive productive entrepreneurship in emerging markets.

Our findings also contribute to policy development by highlighting the role of regulatory institutions in enabling small businesses to survive under multiple crises. Based on our findings, policymakers in emerging markets should develop supportive regulations for small businesses struggling with crises. They also need to enhance the flexibility and responsiveness of regulatory institutions during crises and encourage the adoption of new technologies to enable small businesses to overcome crises.

Implications of the findings for practice

Our findings have several implications for business founders/CEOs and entrepreneurs to recognize the importance of regulatory institutions and the government in supporting their survival during crises. The findings highlight the critical importance of responsive, effective, and agile regulatory institutions and governments in dealing with multiple crises. Focusing on the opportunities emerging from uncertainty allows entrepreneurs to consider regulatory institutions and changes in them as new resources that enable them to further develop emerging opportunities and create new sectors in the market, offer new products, and revise their existing business models.

Limitations and future research agendas

This study has some limitations that open the agendas for future research. First, we focused on the role of regulatory institutions in guiding small businesses during crises in general. Future studies should be conducted by focusing on specific regulatory institutions such as businesses and trade chambers to explore their impact on the persistence and survival of small businesses during severe challenges. This study only examined the role of regulatory institutions in supporting small businesses in dealing with crises and did not consider the processes and procedures that regulatory institutions and governments have established for policy and regulation development, which have a great potential for future investigations. This study employed a qualitative method of inquiry and involved 25 founders/CEOs. Although qualitative studies are not intended to be generalized (Eisenhart, 2009; Payne & Williams, 2005), future quantitative studies using larger sample sizes need to validate the models that emerged from this study. Our sample was also limited to the founders/CEOs of small businesses and only involved a small number of female founders/CEOs (n = 3). Future research including samples from regulatory institutions, government, and female founders/CEOs may provide deeper insights into the roles of regulatory institutions in guiding small businesses and female entrepreneurs towards productive entrepreneurship. Our study is limited to the perceptions founders/CEOs regarding the role of regulatory institutions in crises and did not investigate the actual practices of the institutions. The actual support provided by regulatory institutions to small firms during crises can be examined in future studies. Finally, our study enhances our understanding of the roles that regulatory organizations should play to direct productive entrepreneurship among small businesses in Iran. Future cross-cultural studies may provide a better understanding of the variations in how regulatory organizations address crises in different countries.

Conclusion

Based on the findings of this study, we can conclude that successful regulatory support for small businesses during crises serves to engender productive entrepreneurship. As such, governments need to establish a comprehensive framework to review, revise, and further develop regulatory institutions that support entrepreneurs. Specifically, regulatory institutions direct small businesses towards productive entrepreneurship by implementing effective approaches. This strategic approach not only is applicable during times of crises but also supports small businesses before the crises and continues after the crises. The findings of this study contribute to the development of effective strategies and approaches by regulatory institutions enabling small businesses to exploit opportunities and pursue productive entrepreneurship.

References

Aidis, R., Estrin, S. and Mickiewicz, T. (2008) "Institutions and entrepreneurship development in Russia: A comparative perspective", *Journal of Business Venturing*, 23(6), pp. 656–672.

Alvarez, S. A., Young, S. L. and Woolley, J. L. (2015) "Opportunities and institutions: A co-creation story of the king crab industry", *Journal of Business Venturing*, 30(1), pp. 95–112.

Berger, A. N., Hunter, W. C. and Timme, S. G. (1993) "The efficiency of financial institutions: A review and preview of research past, present and future", *Journal of Banking & Finance*, 17(2–3), pp. 221–249.

Bruton, G. D., Ahlstrom, D. and Li, H. L. (2010) "Institutional theory and entrepreneurship: Where are we now and where do we need to move in the future?", *Entrepreneurship Theory and Practice*, 34(3), pp. 421–440.

Bullough, A. and Renko, M. (2013) "Entrepreneurial resilience during challenging times", *Business Horizons*, 56(3), pp. 343–350.

Cao, Z. and Shi, X. (2021) "A systematic literature review of entrepreneurial ecosystems in advanced and emerging economies", *Small Business Economics*, 57, pp. 75–110.

Corner, P. D., Singh, S. and Pavlovich, K. (2017) "Entrepreneurial resilience and venture failure", *International Small Business Journal*, 35(6), pp. 687–708.

Davis, L. and North, D. (1970) "Institutional change and American economic growth: A first step towards a theory of institutional innovation", *The Journal of Economic History*, 30(1), pp. 131–149.

Denzau, A. T. and North, D. C. (1994) "Shared mental models: Ideologies and institutions", *Kyklos-Berne*, 47, pp. 3–31.

Djankov, S., La Porta, R., Lopez-de-Silanes, F. and Shleifer, A. (2002) "The regulation of entry", *Quarterly Journal of Economics*, 117(1), pp. 453–517.

Eisenhardt, K. M. (1989) "Building theories from case study research", *Academy of Management Review*, 14(4), pp. 532–550.

Eisenhart, M. (2009) "Generalization from qualitative inquiry", in *Generalizing from educational research* (pp. 61–76). Routledge.

Ericsson, K. A. and Simon, H. A. (1998) "How to study thinking in everyday life: Contrasting think-aloud protocols with descriptions and explanations of thinking", *Mind, Culture, and Activity*, 5(3), pp. 178–186.

Fabowale, L., Orser, B. and Riding, A. (1995) "Gender, structural factors, and credit terms between Canadian small businesses and financial institutions", *Entrepreneurship Theory and Practice*, 19(4), pp. 41–65.

Fredström, A., Peltonen, J. and Wincent, J. (2021) "A country-level institutional perspective on entrepreneurship productivity: The effects of informal economy and regulation", *Journal of Business Venturing*, 36(5), p. 106002.

Fu, K., Wennberg, K. and Falkenhall, B. (2020) "Productive entrepreneurship and the effectiveness of insolvency legislation: A cross-country study", *Small Business Economics*, 54, pp. 383–404.

Hassan, M. A. and Olaniran, S. O. (2011) "Developing small business entrepreneurs through assistance institutions: The role of Industrial Development Centre, Osogbo, Nigeria", *International Journal of Business and Management*, 6(2), pp. 213–226.

Honig, B. and Samuelsson, M. (2021) "Business planning by intrapreneurs and entrepreneurs under environmental uncertainty and institutional pressure", *Technovation*, 99, p. 102124.

Hwang, H. and Powell, W. W. (2005) "Institutions and entrepreneurship", in *Handbook of entrepreneurship research: Interdisciplinary perspectives* (pp. 201–232) Boston, MA: Springer US.

Jafari-Sadeghi, V., Mahdiraji, H. A., Bresciani, S. and Pellicelli, A. C. (2021) "Context-specific micro-foundations and successful SME internationalisation in emerging markets: A mixed-method analysis of managerial resources and dynamic capabilities", *Journal of Business Research*, 134, pp. 352–364.

Junaid, D., He, Z. and Afzal, F. (2022) "The impact of weak formal institutions on the different phases of the entrepreneurial process", *Journal of Business Research*, 144, pp. 236–249.

Karami, M. and Read, S. (2021) "Co-creative entrepreneurship", *Journal of Business Venturing*, 36(4), p. 106125.

Karami, H., Sayahnia, R., Mahmoudi, H., Azadi, H. and Salehi, S. (2023, February). Spatial analysis of resources and environmental carrying capacity in Iran. In *Natural Resources Forum* (Vol. 47, No. 1, pp. 60–86). Oxford, UK: Blackwell Publishing Ltd.

Kerr, J. and Coviello, N. (2020) "Weaving network theory into effectuation: A multi-level reconceptualization of effectual dynamics", *Journal of Business Venturing*, 35(2), p. 105937.

Kim, Y. (2011) "The pilot study in qualitative inquiry: Identifying issues and learning lessons for culturally competent research", *Qualitative Social Work*, 10(2), pp. 190–206.

Kirzner, I. M. (1999) "Creativity and/or alertness: A reconsideration of the Schumpeterian entrepreneur", *The Review of Austrian Economics*, 11(1–2), pp. 5–17.

Kshetri, N. and Dholakia, N. (2011) "Regulatory institutions supporting entrepreneurship in emerging economies: A comparison of China and India", *Journal of International Entrepreneurship*, 9, pp. 110–132.

Lee, C. K., Wiklund, J., Amezcua, A., Bae, T. J. and Palubinskas, A. (2022) "Business failure and institutions in entrepreneurship: A systematic review and research agenda", *Small Business Economics*, 58(4), p. 106002.

LiPuma, J. A., Newbert, S. L. and Doh, J. P. (2013) "The effect of institutional quality on firm export performance in emerging economies: A contingency model of firm age and size", *Small Business Economics*, 40, pp. 817–841.

Maguire, S., Hardy, C. and Lawrence, T. B. (2004) "Institutional entrepreneurship in emerging fields: HIV/AIDS treatment advocacy in Canada", *Academy of Management Journal*, 47(5), pp. 657–679.

Manolova, T. S., Eunni, R. V. and Gyoshev, B. S. (2008) "Institutional environments for entrepreneurship: Evidence from emerging economies in Eastern Europe", *Entrepreneurship Theory and Practice*, 32(1), pp. 203–218.

Miles, M. B. and Huberman, A. M. (1994) *Qualitative data analysis: An expanded sourcebook*. Thousand Oaks, CA: Sage Publications.

Montes, G. C. and Nogueira, F. D. S. L. (2022) "Effects of economic policy uncertainty and political uncertainty on business confidence and investment", *Journal of Economic Studies*, 49(4), pp. 577–602.

Naudé, W. (2010) "Entrepreneurship, developing countries, and development economics: New approaches and insights", *Small Business Economics*, 34, pp. 1–12.

North, D. C.. (1990) *Institutions, institutional change and economic performance*. Cambridge University Press.

North, D. C. (1994) "Economic performance through time", *The American Economic Review*, 84(3), pp. 359–368.

Nyarku, K. M. and Oduro, S. (2018) "Effect of legal and regulatory framework on SMEs growth in the Accra Metropolis of Ghana", *The International Journal of Entrepreneurship and Innovation*, 19(3), pp. 207–217.
Patton, M. Q. (2014) *Qualitative research & evaluation methods: Integrating theory and practice.* Sage Publications.
Payne, G. and Williams, M. (2005) "Generalization in qualitative research", *Sociology*, 39(2), pp. 295–314.
Pfeffer, J. and Salancik, G. R. (2003) "The external control of organizations: A resource dependence perspective", in *Series: Stanford business classics*. Stanford University Press.
Purnomo, B. R., Adiguna, R., Widodo, W., Suyatna, H. and Nusantoro, B. P. (2021) "Entrepreneurial resilience during the Covid-19 pandemic: Navigating survival, continuity and growth", *Journal of Entrepreneurship in Emerging Economies*, 13(4), pp. 497524.
Romanello, R., Karami, M., Gerschewski, S., Evers, N. and He, C. X. (2022) "International opportunity development of born global firms: The role of institutions", *Critical Perspectives on International Business*, 18(3), pp. 303–337.
Ryan, F., Coughlan, M. and Cronin, P. (2009) "Interviewing in qualitative research: The one-to-one interview", *International Journal of Therapy and Rehabilitation*, 16(6), pp. 309–314.
Sampson, H. (2004) "Navigating the waves: The usefulness of a pilot in qualitative research", *Qualitative Research*, 4(3), pp. 383–402.
Santos, S. C., Liguori, E. W. and Garvey, E. (2023) "How digitalization reinvented entrepreneurial resilience during COVID-19", *Technological Forecasting and Social Change*, 189, p. 122398.
Sarasvathy, S. D. (2001) "Causation and effectuation: Toward a theoretical shift from economic inevitability to entrepreneurial contingency", *Academy of Management Review*, 26(2), 243–263.
Saunders, M., Lewis, P. and Thornhill, A. (2009) *Research methods for business students* (5th ed.). Pearson Education, Prentice Hall, Financial Times.
Saunders, B., Kitzinger, J. and Kitzinger, C. (2015) "Anonymising interview data: Challenges and compromise in practice", *Qualitative Research*, 15(5), pp. 616–632.
Saunders, B., Sim, J., Kingstone, T., Baker, S., Waterfield, J., Bartlam, B., Burroughs, H. and Jinks, C. (2018) "Saturation in qualitative research: Exploring its conceptualization and operationalization", *Quality & Quantity*, 52, pp. 1893–1907.
Schumpeter, J. A. [1912] (1934) *The Theory of Economic Development*. Harvard University Press.
Scott, W. R. (1987) "The adolescence of institutional theory", *Administrative Science Quarterly*, pp. 493–511.
Scott, W. R. (2005) "Institutional theory: Contributing to a theoretical research program", *Great Minds in Management: The Process of Theory Development*, 37(2), pp. 460–484.
Spencer, J. W. and Gómez, C. (2004) "The relationship among national institutional structures, economic factors, and domestic entrepreneurial activity: A multicountry study", *Journal of Business Research*, 57(10), pp. 1098–1107.
Stake, R. E. (2005) *Qualitative case studies*.
Wiltbank, R., Dew, N., Read, S. and Sarasvathy, S. D. (2006) "What to do next? The case for non-predictive strategy", *Strategic Management Journal*, 27(10), pp. 981–998.
Yin, R. K. (2003) "Designing case studies", *Qualitative Research Methods*, 5(14), pp. 359–386.
Yin, R. K. (2009) *Case study research: Design and methods* (Vol. 5). Sage.
Yin, R. K. (2013) *Case study research: Design and methods* (5th ed.).Thousand Oaks, CA: SAGE Publications.
Zahra, S. A., Newey, L. R. and Li, Y. (2014) "On the frontiers: The implications of social entrepreneurship for international entrepreneurship", *Entrepreneurship Theory and Practice*, 38(1), pp. 137–158.

Index

Note: Page numbers in *italics* indicate a figure and page numbers in **bold** indicate a table on the corresponding page.

FSC
www.fsc.org
MIX
Papier | Fördert gute Waldnutzung
FSC® C083411

Kolibri 360 GmbH
Ferdinand-Jühlke-Straße 7
99095 Erfurt, Deutschland
produktsicherheit@kolibri360.de